Social Theory after the Holocaust

STUDIES IN SOCIAL AND POLITICAL THOUGHT
Editor: Gerard Delanty, *University of Liverpool*

This series publishes peer-reviewed scholarly books on all aspects of social and political thought. It will be of interest to scholars and advanced students working in the areas of social theory and sociology, the history of ideas, philosophy, political and legal theory, anthropological and cultural theory. Works of individual scholarship will have preference for inclusion in the series, but appropriate co- or multi-authored works and edited volumes of outstanding quality or exceptional merit will also be included. The series will also consider English translations of major works in other languages.

Challenging and intellectually innovative books are particularly welcome on the history of social and political theory; modernity and the social and human sciences; major historical or contemporary thinkers; the philosophy of the social sciences; theoretical issues on the transformation of contemporary society; social change and European societies.

It is not series policy to publish textbooks, research reports, empirical case studies, conference proceedings or books of an essayist or polemical nature.

Social Theory after the Holocaust

Edited by
ROBERT FINE and
CHARLES TURNER

LIVERPOOL UNIVERSITY PRESS

First published 2000 by
Liverpool University Press
4 Cambridge Street
Liverpool
L69 7ZU

British Library Cataloguing-in-Publication Data
A British Library CIP record is available

ISBN 0-85323-965-7 (hb) ✓
      0-85323-975-4 (pb)

Design and production: Janet Allan

Typeset in 10/13pt Monotype Plantin by
XL Publishing Services, Lurley, Tiverton, Devon
Printed by The Alden Press, Oxford

Contents

Introduction

ROBERT FINE and CHARLES TURNER

...while the individual is sensitive to even slight changes in his internal or external environment, only quite weighty events can succeed in changing the mental equilibrium of society.

Emile Durkheim[1]

Many of those who know little of Theodor Adorno's philosophy know his remark that to write poetry after Auschwitz is barbaric.[2] It is a puzzling remark in many respects, not least because of its (largely unstated) assumptions about the effects produced by poetic renderings of unspeakable events. Even if there are events legitimately describable as unspeakable, it is hard to see why poetry deserves more opprobrium than any other way of framing them. Social theory and sociology, for instance, appear prime candidates for the same charge. Indeed, perhaps the only reason that Adorno would not have mentioned them in the same breath was that sociology was already a lost cause. Unlike poetry or fiction, it would not attempt to speak of the event at all, but would rather do what sociology has always done: exhibit the barbarism of reason involved in transforming the event into processes, conditions, social systems, classificatory schemes or statistical tables.[3]

Anyone who has offered courses entitled 'Sociology of the Holocaust' knows of the difficulties this transformation causes. One begins in the hope of grasping the Holocaust, if not as a unique event then as a set of bounded events, only to find oneself talking about the conditions of possibility of totalitarianism, fascism, bureaucracy, or evil, and mobilising a series of familiar and trusted ideal types, in order to do so. Frequently enough, in order to grasp the 'event' itself one resorts to literature or survivor testimony in an effort to generate the kind of shocking immediacy worthy of the subject. When sociologists do seek to isolate and then explain the event in its uniqueness, they frequently fall back on debates

1

between 'structuralist' and 'intentionalist' historians. Even there, the emphasis on both sides is largely on conditions, parameters, on what was already in place when the event *took* place. The philosopher Hans Blumenberg expressed this problem with incomparable force:

> The consolation we derive from giving precedence to conditions over events is based only on the hypothesis that conditions are the result of the actions of an indeterminate large number of people instead of just a few who we can name. But it is just as natural to suppose that history then becomes a process in nature, a sequence of waves, a glacial drift, a tectonic fault movement, a flood, or an alluvial deposit...The more subtle the theoretical knowledge, the more it nourishes the suspicion that history does not take place and is not made in its great moments, and that no causality attaches to those of its scenes that are ready for engraving, but rather the chains of their motivations have already run out when the hammer is raised to nail up the theses, when the breaking of windows takes place or the trumpet is blown for the day of reckoning.[4]

The challenge to all accounts of an event such as the Holocaust, which consisted of an unfolding sequence of events, has been, Blumenberg suggests, to include a sense of the manner in which new links were added to the chain of motivations as the sequence of events unfolded, thereby avoiding the temptation to reduce the event to its conditions. Curiously enough, this is actually one of the achievements of a work often thought to have reduced the Holocaust to the most extreme manifestation of the set of conditions known as modernity. Bauman's *Modernity and the Holocaust* is innovative precisely in the sections where it analyses bureaucratic rationality less as mindless rule-following than as a search by individuals for innovative solutions to problems. In the more direct mode of address characteristic of the historian, Christopher Browning describes the progressive demoralisation of the ordinary men of Reserve Police Battalion 101 and the emergence of the characteristic *Einsatzgruppe* mentality. In neither of these respected studies has the chain of motivations been exhausted when the fatal papers are signed or processed, or when the gun barrel is placed against the victim's neck. At the same time, both have attracted criticism for their accounts of the broader social forces which give rise to the extreme situations they address. Bauman stands accused of implying that enlightenment culminated in the final solution and that the final solution's necessary conditions remain in place in contemporary society. Browning, with his appeals to the social psychology of Milgram and Zimbardo, implies that the necessary conditions for such behaviour are already in place in each of us as 'ordinary men'.

Much of the commentary which followed Bauman's book concentrated on the explanatory adequacy or otherwise of his causal account of the Holocaust, and in particular on the question of whether the terms in which he had construed it were not impossibly broad. What was less noticed or remarked upon was that by attacking modernity head on Bauman was calling into question the faith which most institutionalised sociology had placed in modernity, and by implication challenging it not only to treat the Holocaust seriously as an object of enquiry but to allow the Holocaust to affect its core categories and concepts. In other words, while Bauman's sociology of the Holocaust appears vulnerable to the charge that it sociologises the Holocaust out of existence by its neglect of its purported object, part of his point is to call into question the status of a sociology which would do such a thing.

The expression 'social theory after the Holocaust' points to the fact that the Holocaust, whatever the limits it imposes on the sociological explanation of it, may be construed as an epoch-making event which casts its shadow over all subsequent theorising of power, rationality, order and ideology. For all the problems it brings with it, the interdisciplinary vagaries of 'social theory', as opposed to sociology, allow for the projection into the past of a variety of epoch-inaugurating events. While sociology has allowed itself to be affected by events which produced changes in forms of order or the rearrangement of the furniture of social experience – most notably social revolutions or religious reformations – social theory's licence to speak of sequences and epochs and inaugurating events is perhaps broader. The events which social theory might then allow itself to be affected by include not only the framing of constitutions or social revolutions, but events which are held to alter an entire mode of collective perception or awareness: the discovery of America, the moon landings, or the Lisbon earthquake of 1755, which led the six-year-old Goethe to ask his father how such an event could be justified. The idea of a post-Holocaust or post-Auschwitz universe expresses a similar sensibility: it is not necessary that the Holocaust inaugurate a new order of stratification or generate a new form of polity in order for it to be an epoch-making event.

Yet ten years after Bauman claimed that sociology has not only not addressed the Holocaust but also not allowed it to affect its self-understanding, little has been done to take him at his word. The *Festschrift* marking Bauman's seventieth birthday, as well as a special issue of *Theory, Culture and Society* devoted to his work, discussed his contribution to Holocaust explanation but did not mention his conclusions regarding sociology's basic procedures and categories.[5] This volume does not seek to dismiss the increased scholarly and popular interest in the Holocaust as a topic, an interest which has generated many fine studies, but it does see that interest as an opportunity to treat the Holocaust as a resource, as an event which challenges existing categories of social and political analysis.

3

Introduction

The contributions to this volume address aspects of social theorising which, however indirectly, have been, or have allowed themselves to be, influenced in some way by that event. While they share a concern with the ways in which social theory might address the Holocaust as an object, they ask how some of social theory's key claims might be or have been affected through confrontation with the Holocaust. This is not to say that all of the contributions here draw the conclusions which Bauman does. While those of Turner and Stone use the Holocaust as an occasion to call into question conventionally accepted notions of history, those of Adler, Salter and Gorman conclude that established pre-Holocaust categories are still able to do an effective job in making sense of the dilemmas of the present.[6] Nor is it the case that there was *no* post-Holocaust social theory before Bauman stated that there needed to be one. As Robert Fine makes clear, the work of Hannah Arendt is a series of theoretical responses to the Holocaust. The 'late Marxism' of Adorno is the clearest example of an attempt to guard against philosophy's complicity in the justification of a crime against humanity, his negative dialectics the working out of a grammar of eternal vigilance. The extension of that grammar into a more robust conception of ethics is the challenge which Jay Bernstein has identified in the work of Jean-François Lyotard, and which is taken up by Andrew Benjamin with respect to the theorisation of friendship, popular once again.

To this one should add that in the 1950s newly published material from the camps was a challenge to the theorisation of such matters as super- and subordination. Studies such as Kogon's were referred to by Erving Goffman in *Asylums*, devoted to the study of the mental hospital as a total institution, emphasising props, clothing, front and back regions, and artefacts as resources for the maintenance of selfhood; the implied vulnerability of the social self; and the precariousness of the human sense of reality. In the context of post-war American complacency, this was a notable achievement, and with interpretative licence might be read as a veiled response to the stripping away of such artefacts in the camps. More prosaically, the centrality attributed by Giddens to 'ontological security' as a basic problem of modernity might be described as a piece of post-Holocaust social theorising. In a more direct reference to the Holocaust, Lawrence Langer's great study of testimony ended with the claim that once one takes witnesses' accounts seriously, much of the narrative conception of selfhood which proved so popular in the seventies and eighties, and which sustains an influential body of moral and political theory, falls apart.[7]

Finally, the theorisation of the grounds of human solidarity has been given fresh impetus by responses to the Holocaust. Jürgen Habermas has suggested on more than one occasion that both his ethical theory and his vision of a German/European future are unavoidably rooted in the events of the Holocaust and the core of universal human solidarity which confrontation with it is capable of promoting.[8] Norman Geras's critique of Richard Rorty owes much to the same impulse.[9]

In a theoretical world dominated by rational choice theory, neo-functionalism and cultural studies these are perhaps slim pickings. They deserve mention because, as Bauman's piece in this volume makes clear, if the Holocaust is to remain an unforgotten episode in the history of the West, the health of its continued existence depends upon its living on as a problem pressure and not as a ghost. The Holocaust's life as a ghost points to more troubling and difficult aspects of the Holocaust legacy than its becoming a topic for interdisciplinary studies. Today the Holocaust is readily appropriated as a metaphor for the sufferings of any group under threat of grave assault. The more hysterical aspects of the abortion and AIDS discussion in the United States are an obvious example of this process. The ambivalence generated by such appropriations is palpable. That the scholarly thematisation of the Holocaust and an increased popular awareness of it should have coincided with its being turned into metaphor places social theory before dilemmas which it has hardly begun to think through.

Notes

1 *The Elementary Forms of Religious Life*, New York: Free Press, 1995, pp.435–36.

2 T.W. Adorno, 'Kulturkritik und Gesellschaft', in *Soziologische Forschungen in unserer Zeit. Ein Sammelwerk. Leopold von Wiese zum 75. Geburtstag*, ed. Karl-Gustav Specht, Cologne: Westdeutscher Verlag, 1950.

3 For a classic statement see Adorno, 'The Sociology of Knowledge and its Consciousness', in *Prisms* (London: Neville Spearman, 1967). For evidence of the classification-and-exclusion of the Holocaust in postwar German sociology, see now Y. Michal Bodemann, 'Eclipse of Memory: German Representations of Auschwitz in the Early Postwar Period', *New German Critique*, No.75, Fall 1998, 57–89.

4 H. Blumenberg, *Work on Myth*, Cambridge, Mass.: MIT Press, 1985, p.102.

5 See R. Kilminster and I. Varcoe (eds) *Culture, Modernity and Revolution*, London: Routledge, 1996; *Theory, Culture and Society*, Vol.15, No.1, 1998.

6 Compare Leo Strauss's remark that in order to retain a sense of the drama of modernity one requires pre-modern categories. See *Thoughts on Machiavelli*, Seattle: Washington University Press, 1958, p.14.

7 See Langer, *Holocaust Testimonies: The Ruins of Memory*, New Haven: Yale University Press, 1991, Ch.5. The explicit target of Langer's attack is Charles Taylor, but figures such as MacIntyre and Ricoeur are guilty by association here. For a defence of Taylor, see Peter Barham, 'The Next Village', *History of the Human Sciences*, Vol.6, No.2, 1993.

8 See J. Habermas, 'On the Public Uses of History', in *The New Conservatism*, Cambridge: Polity, 1994.

9 See his *Solidarity in the Conversation of Mankind*, London: Verso, Ch.1.

CHAPTER 1

The Holocaust's Life as a Ghost

ZYGMUNT BAUMAN

Half a century has passed since the victory of the Allied troops put an abrupt end to Hitler's 'final solution of the Jewish question' – but the memory of the Holocaust goes on polluting the world of the living, and the inventory of its insidious poisons seems anything but complete. We are all to some degree possessed by that memory, though the Jews among us, the prime targets of the Holocaust, are perhaps more than most.[1]

Among the Jews in the first place, living in a world contaminated with the possibility of a holocaust rebounds repeatedly in fear and horror. To many, the world appears suspect to the core; no worldly event is truly neutral – each event is burdened with sinister undertones, each contains an ominous message to the Jews, a message that can be overlooked or played down only at the Jews' own peril. As E.M. Cioran, incisive and bitter French philosopher, put it:

> ...to be afraid is to think of yourself continually, to be unable to imagine an objective course of events. The sensation of the terrible, the sensation that it is all happening against you, supposes a world conceived without dangers. The frightened man – victim *of* an exaggerated subjectivity – believes himself to be, much more than the rest of his kind, the target of hostile events ... [He has attained] the extremity of a self-infatuated consciousness; everything conspires against the one...[2]

Self-defence calls the victim to learn the lesson of history, though in order to learn it, the victim needs to decide first what the lesson is. The precept of staying alive as the sole thing that counts, as the supreme value that dwarfs all other values, is among the most tempting, and the most common, interpretations of the lesson. As the direct experience of the victims recedes and fades the memory

7

of the Holocaust tapers and congeals into a precept of survival: life is about surviving, to succeed in life is to outlive the others. Who survives wins.

This reading of the Holocaust's lesson has been displayed – to world-wide acclaim and huge box-office success – in Spielberg's now well-nigh canonical image of the Holocaust. According to the *Schindler's List* version of the Holocaust experience, the sole stake of that most inhuman among human tragedies was to remain alive – while the humanity of life, and particularly its dignity and ethical value, was at best of secondary importance and above all of no consequence and was never allowed to interfere with the principal goal. The goal of staying alive took care of moral concerns. What counted in the last resort was to outlive the others – even if the escape from death required being put on a separate, unique and exclusive list of the privileged.

Offered by the Commandant of Birkenau a replacement for 'his Jewesses', Schindler refuses; it was not saving of lives that counted, but saving of specific, chosen lives. By definition, survival is selective; it is coveted because of its selectiveness. In that film, the value of staying alive was not diminished, but made more salient yet by the fact that others, less fortunate, travelled to extermination camps; the viewers of *Schindler's List* are invited to rejoice in the sight of Schindler's master of works pulled out in the nick of time – he alone – from the train destined for Treblinka. Through a wilful travesty of the Talmud's precepts Spielberg's film translates the issue of the salvation of humanity into the decision concerning who is to live and who is to die. ('The Talmud', pointed out the late Gillian Rose, sublime philosopher and Judaic scholar, in her last public lecture, 'is ironic – the most ironic holy commentary in world literature: for no human being can save the world'. [3] Rose spoke of the 'ruthlessness of saving one or one thousand' and comments that while the original Keneally book, *Schindler's Arc*, 'makes clear the pitiless immorality of this in this context', Spielberg's film *Schindler's List* 'depends on it as congratulation'.)

That elevation of survival to the rank of the supreme, perhaps the only value, is not Spielberg's invention and not at all a phenomenon confined to the artistic representations of the Holocaust's experience. Soon after the end of the war psychiatrists coined the concept of 'the survivor's guilt' – a complex psychical ailment which they ascribed to the survivors' asking themselves why they stayed alive when so many of their loved ones perished. According to that interpretation, among the survivors the joy of escaping death was permanently poisoned by the acute moral uncertainty about the propriety of sailing safe out of the sea of perdition, with disastrous consequences for the survivors' will to live and succeed in life after their rescue. Many practising psychiatrists acquired fame and fortune treating 'survivor's syndrome'. Whether the syndrome was rightly spotted and the psychiatric treatment well aimed remains an open question;

what is rather obvious, though, is that in the course of time the 'guilt' aspect, looming prominently in the beginning, has been progressively exorcised from the model of the 'survivor complex', leaving the pure and unalloyed, unambiguous and no more contested approval of self-preservation for self-preservation's sake. It was just the haunting pain left by those sufferings that staying alive required which has been blamed for the persistence of the 'syndrome'.

Such a shift brings us dangerously close to the spine-chilling image of the survivor as painted by Elias Canetti – as the man for whom 'the most elementary and obvious form of success is to remain alive'. For Canetti's survivor, the survival – unlike mere self-preservation – is targeted on the other, not on the self: 'they want to survive their contemporaries. They know that many die early and they want a different fate for themselves.' At the far end of the survivalist obsession, Canetti's survivor 'wants to kill so that he can survive others; he wants to stay alive so as not to have others surviving him'; 'the survivor's most fantastic triumphs have taken place in our own time, among people who set a great store about the idea of humanity... The survivor is mankind's worst evil, its curse and perhaps its doom.'[4]

The wider repercussions of that cult of survival contain dangers of potentially formidable proportions. Time and again the lessons of the Holocaust are reduced for popular consumption to a simple formula: 'who strikes first, survives'; or to an even simpler one: 'the stronger lives'. The awesome two-pronged legacy of the Holocaust is, on one hand, the tendency to treat survival as the sole, or at any rate the primary value and purpose of life, and on the other the positing of the issue of survival as that of the competition for a scarce resource, and so of the survival itself as a site of conflict between incompatible interests in which the success of some depends on the non-survival of others.

Sinister, pernicious and morally destructive as it is in its own right, this is not the only avatar of the Holocaust's ghost and not its only misdeed. Another is the phenomenon dubbed by Alain Finkielkraut *le juif imaginaire*[5] – a Jew manifesting his Jewishness, so to speak, in living on the account and at the expense of a 'categorical martyrdom', basking in the fame of his ancestral martyrs without paying the price for the glory. Such 'imaginary Jews', in Finkielkraut's caustic description, are the 'habitués of unreality', who 'have taken up residence in fiction', 'live in borrowed identities', 'have chosen to pass their time in a novelistic space full of sound and fury' – and as a result have become 'armchair Jews, since, after the Catastrophe, Judaism cannot offer them any content but suffering, and they themselves do not suffer'. For this generation Finkielkraut, prolific and refined French writer and one of its most illustrious and famous members, is full of contempt: they are, he says, 'cowards in life, martyred in dream' – 'they mask their inborn softness with the outcast's courage'.[6]

There is admittedly a specifically French flavour to Finkielkraut's analysis. When he writes of 'desperate striving... to plug into the great revolt of the day', this may sound outlandish and exotic to the members of the generation scattered in other, particularly the Anglo-Saxon, parts of the Jewish Diaspora. And yet the acid remarks about the 'pastiche' that 'was the governing principle of deeds', about the 'frantic masquerade sought to appease bad conscience', about 'exorcising the vapidity of lives... through acts of fictive intensity', and altogether looking 'at current events the way Emma Bovary read popular fiction: enraptured by escapism', may find an echo in many memories and cause the beating of many breasts. Living on a borrowed identity – as martyrs by appointment, martyrs who *never suffered* – '*we* could only bear to face ourselves unrecognisably disguised'; this spiritual predicament was the fate which the whole generation shared, even if the disguises were locally diversified.

Anne Karpf has recently reported, in a penetrating and sharply ironic survey of the thriving 'Holocaust syndrome' literature,[7] her own feelings of relief and spiritual comfort when first hearing of the inherited trauma of the survivors' children, and so finding out that she 'belonged to a group which might warrant being helped, rather than being purely privileged and morally obliged to help others'; she 'was relieved and even elated that [her] years of problems weren't necessarily the result of personal pathology but might have shared an external source'.[8]

Karpf put her finger on an open wound, gaping in many a soul. In this hectic, chameleon-like, deregulated and unpredictable world of privatised loners one has many problems finding and guarding one's place in life; one is indeed greatly relieved if at least the blame for one's trouble could be shifted onto something other than one's own shoulders.

Over seventy years ago, in his seminal study *Civilisation and its Discontents* Freud suggested that 'civilisation' is a trade-off; one cherished value is sacrificed for another, equally close to heart. He proposed that in the civilised society of his time a lot of personal freedom of expression had been sacrificed in exchange for a good deal of collectively guaranteed security. In my *Postmodernity and its Discontents*[9] I have suggested that were Freud writing his book seventy years later, he would probably need to reverse his diagnosis: the present-day most common troubles and discontents are, like their predecessors, products of a trade-off, but this time the security is sacrificed day by day on the altar of the ever-expanding individual freedom. On the way to whatever passes for greater individual liberty of choice and self-expression we have lost a good deal of that security which modern civilisation supplied, and even more of the security it promised to supply; worse still, we have stopped hearing promises that the supplying will be resumed, and instead hear more and more often that security is contrary to human dignity, much too treacherous to be sought and much too likely to breed dependency to be desired.

So there are good enough reasons to be nervous, anxious and angry. It is not clear, though, whence the ambient fear derives, what one is truly afraid of, where the danger lies and what one can do to mitigate it. Anxiety seeks a peg and may easily be hung on a wrong one and so prompt actions glaringly irrelevant to the genuine cause of trouble. When genuine reasons for agitation are difficult to locate and even less easy to control if discovered, there is a powerful temptation to construe and name putative, yet credible culprits against whom one can wage a sensible defensive (or better still offensive) action. One would bark up a wrong tree, but at least one would be barking.

Throughout the United States, 'self-help' groups were formed by the 'children of the Holocaust'; the self-invigorating group discussions added the extra dimension of a collectively sustained interpretation (and thus the authority of numbers) to the zealous search for the collectively hidden, yet exceptionless, Holocaust trauma, which would put the missing sense into the present personal troubles. This search was also given authority by the psychiatric profession; all over the country, psychoanalysts told their patients in no uncertain terms of the Holocaust roots of what in the psychiatrists' vocabulary they described as their 'maladjustments'. Some therapeutic experts, like Harvey and Carol Barocas (quoted by Karpf and prestigious enough to contribute to the *International Review of Psychoanalysis*[10]) went so far as to suggest that 'the children of survivors show symptoms that would be expected if they [had] actually lived through the Holocaust'. And so the ghost has been issued with the official permission of domicile, recognised as the lawful plenipotentiary of the 'real thing', and so (in tune with the spirit of our time) the troublesome and worrying distinction between the 'real' and 'virtual' reality has been declared null and void.

For those involved, the message hammered home by the psychiatrists, and sunk ever deeper in the course of the self-help sessions, could not but be richly rewarding. In Anne Karpf's words, 'there's undoubtedly something satisfying in joining the ranks of the unequivocally wronged, those with an irrefutably legitimate claim on our sympathy'.[11] To acquire the right to sympathy and benevolence before one earns them through personal exertions is an opportunity few people would willingly forfeit. The side effect of all this is, however, a sort of 'competition for victimhood', a 'pecking order of pain', reminiscent of the rivalry among the tuberculous residents of Thomas Mann's *Magic Mountain,* who quickly established their own eerie hierarchy of prestige and influence measured by the size of their pulmonary caverns.

There is something else, though, to the status of a 'victim by proxy' – one of belonging to a *sui generis* 'aristocracy of victimhood' (that is, having a *hereditary* claim to sympathy and ethical indulgence owed to those who suffer). That status can be, and often is, brandished as a signed-in-advance and *in blanco* certificate of moral righteousness; whatever the offspring of the victims do must be morally proper (or at least *ethically correct*) as long as it can be shown that it was done in order to stave off the repetition of the lot visited on their ancestors; or as long as it can be shown to be psychologically understandable, nay 'normal', in view of the super-susceptibility of the hereditary bearers of victimhood to the threat of a new victimisation. The ancestors are pitied, but also blamed for allowing themselves to be led, like sheep, to the slaughter; how can one blame their descendants for sniffing out a future slaughterhouse in every suspicious-looking street or building or – more importantly still – for taking preventative measures to disempower the potential slaughterers? Those who need to be disempowered may be not be kith and kin of the perpetrators of the Holocaust, neither bodily nor spiritually, and may in no juridical or ethically sensible way be charged with responsibility for the ancestors' perdition; it is, after all, the heredity of the 'hereditary victims', and *not* the continuity of their assumed victimisers, which makes the 'connection'. Yet in a world haunted by the ghost of the Holocaust such assumed would-be persecutors are guilty in advance, guilty of *being seen* as inclined or able to engage in another genocide. They need commit no crime; standing accused or just *being suspect,* true to the message of Kafka's *The Trial,* is already their crime, the only crime needed to cast them as criminals and to justify harsh preventative/punitive measures. The ethics of hereditary victimhood reverse the logic of the law: the accused remain criminals until they have proven their innocence – and since it is their prosecutors who conduct the hearings and decide the validity of the argument, they have only a slim chance of having their arguments accepted in court and every chance of staying guilty for a long time to come – whatever they do.

Thus the status of hereditary victim may take the moral reprobation off the new victimisation – this time perpetrated in the name of erasing the hereditary stigma. We often say that violence breeds more violence; we remind ourselves much too rarely, though, that victimisation breeds more victimisation. Victims are not guaranteed to be morally superior to their victimisers, and seldom emerge from the victimisation morally ennobled. Martyrdom – whether lived in a real or a virtual reality – is not a warrant for saintliness.

Memory of suffering does not assure the life-long dedication to the fight against inhumanity, cruelty and pain as such, wherever they happen and whoever are the sufferers. An equally probable outcome of martyrdom is the tendency to draw an opposite lesson: that humankind is divided into victims and victimisers, and so if you are (or expect to be) a victim, your task is to reverse the tables ('the stronger lives'). It is this lesson that the spectre of the Holocaust whispers into many ears. And for this reason we cannot be sure whether the lasting legacy of the Holocaust was not the very opposite of that hoped for by many, and anticipated by some: the moral re-awakening or ethical purification of the world as a whole or any of its parts.

The pernicious legacy of the Holocaust is that today's persecutors may inflict new pains and create new generations of victims eagerly awaiting their chance to do the same, while acting in the belief that they avenge yesterday's pain and ward off the pains of tomorrow; while being convinced, in other words, that ethics is on their side. This is perhaps the most awesome among the Holocaust's curses and the greatest of Hitler's posthumous victories. The crowds which applauded Goldstein's massacre of the Muslim worshippers in Hebron, which flocked to his funeral and go on writing his name on their political and religious banners, are the most terminally afflicted, but not the only bearers of that curse.

The phenomenon of hereditary victimhood ought not to be confused with genetic kinship, or with the family tradition preserved through the parental influence over the educational setting. Heredity in this case is mainly imagined, acting through the collective production of memory and through individual acts of self-enlisting and self-identification. Thus the status of the 'Holocaust children', that is of hereditary victim, is open to every Jew, whatever his or her parents might have been 'doing in the war' (in fact, embracing this status has turned for many into a main vehicle of Jewish self-definition). Psychiatrists conducted ample studies of the biological descendants (and/or educational objects) of the inmates of concentration camps and the inhabitants of ghettos; but the swelling numbers of the 'sons and daughters of the Holocaust', who are *not children of either*, still await a comprehensive study. There are many clues, though, to what such study may reveal. It may well transpire that the complexes of such 'imagined children', 'children pretenders', 'self-appointed children' (and for the same reason 'children *manqués*' – flawed, if not fraudulent, children) are more severe and vicious, and burdened with more sinister consequences, than those which the psychiatrists have described thus far.

One may say: this stands to reason. For the 'children *manqués*', the site they occupy in the world, from which they view the world and in which they want to be viewed by the world, is that of martyrdom; but it so happens that they are not, nor have been, personally, the butt of anybody's wrath and wrongdoing. They do not suffer, or do not suffer enough for the victims-by-birth that they are. The world seems reluctant to harm them and make them suffer, and under the circumstances such a world is too good to be acceptable – since the reality of a harmless world means irreality of life which derives its sense from the harm done to it and the harm yet to be done.

Living in a not-hostile and harmless world means the betrayal of the sense-giving parentage. To reach completeness, to fulfil their destiny, to get rid of their *present deficiency* and face their vexing (and in the end humiliating) impairment, to turn from children *manqués* into children pure and simple, they would need to reforge their own imagined continuity of victimhood into the real continuity of victimisation. That can be done only through acting as if their present site in the world was truly a site of the victims; through abiding by a strategy which may gain rationality only in a victimising world. Children *manqués* cannot be fulfilled unless the world they live in reveals its hostility, conspires against them – and, indeed, contains the possibility of another Holocaust.

The awesome truth is that contrary to what they say and think they wish, children *manqués* – the 'flawed children' – are unfit to live in, and feel out of place in a world free of that possibility. They would feel more comfortable living in a world more like that other world, populated by the Jew-hating murderers who would not stop short of including them among its victims if given a chance and not having their blood-soaked hands tied. They draw a sense-giving reassurance from every sign of hostility towards them; and they are eager to interpret every move of those around them as the overt or latent expression of such hostility. In their lives, the ghost of the Holocaust may feel safe; in their deeds, it has found a magic counterspell against other people's exorcisms.

The flawed children of the martyrs do not live in homes; they live in fortresses. And to make their homes into fortresses, they need them to be besieged and under fire. Where else can one come closer to their dreams than among the famished and destitute, despaired and desperate, cursing and stone-throwing Palestinians? Here, the comfortable and commodious, all-mod-con houses are unlike the houses the children *manqués* have abandoned – those comfortable and commodious, all-mod-con houses over there, in the stale and dull, too-safe-for-comfort American suburbs, where children would be bound to stay as they are, *manqués*. Here, one can tightly wrap the houses with barbed wire, one can build watchtowers in every corner and one can walk from one house to another proudly caressing the gun hanging from one's shoulder. The Jew-baiting world once forced the Jews into ghettos. By making a home in the likeness of the ghetto, one can make the world once more hostile and Jew-baiting. In that fully and truly flawed world, the children, at long last, would be no longer flawed. The chance of martyrdom missed by a generation would have been repossessed by its chosen representatives, who want to be seen as its spokesmen as well.

Whichever way you look at it, the ghost of the Holocaust appears self-perpetuating and self-producing. It made itself indispensable to too many to be easily exorcised. Haunted houses have an added value, and being possessed has turned for many into a valued, meaning-bestowing life formula. In this effect, one can spy out the greatest posthumous triumph of the *Endlösung* designers.

What the latter failed to accomplish when alive, they may yet hope to achieve from the grave. They did not manage to turn the world against the Jews, but in their graves they can still dream of turning the Jews against the world, and thus – one way or another – to make the Jewish reconciliation with the world, their peaceful cohabitation with the world, all the more difficult, if not downright impossible. The prophecies of the Holocaust are not quite self-fulfilling, but they do fulfil – render plausible – the prospect of a world in which the Holocaust may never stop being prophesied, with all the deleterious and disastrous psychic, cultural and political consequences which such prophecy is bound to bring forth and propagate.

Can one exorcise the ghost of the Holocaust? A big question and a daunting task no doubt. *And a different one from making the world Holocaust-proof,* although the state of being possessed makes that other task yet more daunting. It is not easy to write out a foolproof recipe for exorcism, and even if a medicine were available, there would be no guarantee that the patient would swallow the prescribed pills. Being possessed means seeing the world as one-dimensional. The only dimension which the ghost of the Holocaust renders visible to the eyes of the possessed (while effacing or removing from sight all other dimensions) is that measured by the degree of Jew-resentment. The world, though, is multi-dimensional.

Jean-Paul Sartre proposed that the Jew is a person whom others define as a Jew. What Sartre must have meant was that the act of such defining is also the act of reductive selectiveness: one of the manifold traits of the irretrievably multi-faceted person is hereby given prominence, rendering all other traits irrelevant. In the practice of the possessed, the Sartrean procedure is conducted once more, though in the opposite direction. The others, the non-Jews, emerge as one-dimensional just as the Jews appear in the vision of their haters. For the possessed, the others are not benign or cruel *patri familiae,* caring or selfish husbands, benevolent or malicious bosses, good or bad citizens, peaceful or pugnacious neighbours, oppressors or oppressed, pained or pain-inflicting, privileged or dispossessed, threatening or threatened. More precisely, they may be any or all of that, but the fact that they are all that and more is but of secondary and minor importance and does not count for much. What truly counts – perhaps the only thing that counts – is their attitude towards the Jews (and let us recall that the stance taken towards every person who happens to be also a Jew is read by the possessed as but a manifestation of the attitude taken towards *the Jews as such*).

This is why it is so tremendously important to accept and remember that many declared anti-semites stoutly refused to co-operate with the perpetrators of the Holocaust, while the ranks of the executors were full of law-abiding citizens and disciplined functionaries who happened to be free of any peculiar grudge against the Jews. To accept and remember that 'deportation of the Jews' (as the annihilation of European Jewry was officially defined) derived its meaning in the Nazi thinking from the overall, audacious plan of wholesale *Übersiedlung*, the vision of a European continent in which well-nigh everyone would be transported from their present, contingent site to the place where reason ordered them to be.[12] To accept and remember that the extermination of the Jews was conceived in the framework of a total 'cleansing of the world' (which included also the mentally deficient, physically handicapped, ideologically deviant and sexually unorthodox) by a state powerful enough and sufficiently immune to all opposition to afford such total plans and to execute them without fear of effective dissent; and to accept and to remember that the Nazis behind the Holocaust were also *'Bürgers'* who like all *Bürgers* now as much as then, here as much as there, had their 'problems' which they dearly wished to 'resolve'.[13]

The acclaim accorded to Daniel Goldhagen's version of the Holocaust, as primarily the story of the voluntary and Jew-hating helpers of Hitler, is itself a fruit cultivated in the haunted house. That some of the participants in mass murder did enjoy their part in crime, either because of their sadistic inclinations or because of their hatred of the Jews or for both reasons simultaneously, is not, of course, Goldhagen's fantasy (though it is not his discovery either). Taking that fact, however, as the explanation of the Holocaust, as its central point or the deepest meaning, says a lot about the ghosts haunting the house, while turning the attention away from what is the most sinister truth of that genocide and what is still the most salutary lesson which our haunted world could learn from the recent history which contains the Holocaust as its major event. The point is that for every villain of Goldhagen's book, for every German who killed his victims with pleasure and enthusiasm, there were dozens and hundreds of Germans and non-Germans who contributed to the mass murder no less effectively without feeling anything about their victims and about the nature of actions involved. And the point is also that while we know quite well that prejudice threatens humanity and we even know how to fight and constrain the ill intentions of people poisoned with prejudice, we know little about how to stave off the threat of a murder which masquerades as the routine and unemotional functioning of orderly society. As Enzo Traverso put it recently in reference to France, the causes of the Holocaust in general, and that 'wall of indifference' which surrounded the mass slaughter of the French Jews, need to be sought not in the 'Jewish question', not even in the circumstances of the genocide itself, but in pre-Vichy French society.[14] It is not in any society that a genocide of the unwanted strangers can take place, and the presence of a quantity of Jew-haters is not the only, not even the necessary, condition of such a genocide. Hannah Arendt pointed out long ago that in the phenomenon of the Holocaust anti-semitism may explain at most the choice of the victims, but not the nature of the crime. Nothing has happened since then to invalidate Arendt's verdict, while the monumental memoirs of Primo Levi, monumental historical research of Raul Hilberg and the monumental documentary of Claude Lanzman, to mention but a few landmarks, did a lot to confirm and reinforce it.

This is not to say that the world we live in differs from the world of the Holocaust to an extent which makes it Holocaust-proof and that the Holocaust fears are therefore illusory. Nevertheless, it does mean that the threat of such Holocausts as may yet come is all too often sought today in the wrong places and our sight diverted from the grounds in which genuine threats are rooted. These are the grave risks of living in a haunted house.

Notes

1 Though on no account the only ones. For instance, it has been pointed out by many authors that the curious phenomenon of 'anti-semitism without Jews', so widespread today in Eastern Europe, once teeming with Jewish communities and culture and now relatively emptied of both, can be explained at least in part by the *soi-disant* redistribution of wealth, accomplished by the Holocaust and being a lasting legacy of the gas chambers. A wholly new native middle class has emerged through the appropriation of Jewish businesses and real estate, and its heirs now live in fear of Jewish retribution or, purely and simply, of the Jews reclaiming their property. This is no doubt the case, yet another aspect of the Holocaust's lasting legacy, embracing a much wider population than those who benefited personally from the perdition of Jews, needs to be considered: forced to witness the murder of their neighbours, and threatened with capital punishment for any attempt to rescue the condemned, the native population as a whole was cast into an excruciating ethical choice without good options – a challenge transcending ordinary moral capacity, and one that most other people seldom face. I wonder whether, for instance, the Poles (the case I know best) will ever forgive the Jews the fact that the Jewish extermination they were forced to watch imbued their conscience with guilt for which – to a moral person – there is no atonement and no absolution. Forgiving would not come before forgetting – and for the time being there is little prospect of either.

2 E.M. Cioran, *A Short History of Decay*, trans. Richard Howard, London: Quartet Books, 1990, p.71.

3 In Brian Cheyette and Laura Marcus (eds), *Modernity, Culture and the Jew*, Cambridge: Polity, 1998.

4 Elias Canetti, *Crowds and Power*, trans. Carol Stewart, Harmondsworth: Penguin, 1973, pp.290–93, 544.

5 Alain Finkielkraut, *The Imaginary Jew*, trans. Kevin O'Neill and David Suchoff, University of Nebraska Press, 1994.

6 *Ibid.*, p.

7 Anne Karpf, 'The War After: The Psychology of the Second Generation', *Jewish Quarterly*, Summer 1996.

8 *Ibid.*, p.5.

9 Zygmunt Bauman, *Postmodernity and its Discontents*, Cambridge: Polity, 1997.

10 Harvey A. Barocas and Carol B. Barocas, 'Wounds of the Fathers: The Next

Generation of Holocaust Victims', *International Review of Psychoanalysis* Vol.6, 1979.

11 Karpf, 'The War After', p.6.

12 See the penetrating, thoroughly researched study by Götz Aly and Susanne Heim, *Vordenker der Vernichtung: Auschwitz und die deutsche Pläne für eine neue europäische Ordnung*, Hamburg: Hoffman und Campe Verlag, 1991.

13 As Klaus Dörner convincingly argues in his *Tödliches Mitleid: Zur Frage der Unverträglichkeit des Lebens, oder: Die soziale Frage: Enstehung, Medizinierung, NS Endlösung, heute, morgen*, Gütersloh:Verlag Jakob van Hoddis, 1988, pp.12ff.

14 Enzo Traverso, *L'histoire déchirée*, Paris: Cerf, 1996.

CHAPTER 2

Hannah Arendt: Politics and Understanding after the Holocaust

ROBERT FINE

Making Sense of the Senseless

Hannah Arendt described the Holocaust as a 'rupture with civilisation' that shattered all existing ideas of progress, all feelings of optimism, all previously engraved images of Europe as a civilised community, all notions of the innocence of modern political thought. In 'Mankind and Terror', for example, she writes: 'Not only are all our political concepts and definitions insufficient for an understanding of totalitarian phenomena but also all our categories of thought and standards of judgement seem to explode in our hands the instant we try to apply them.'[1] Arendt was one of the first to argue that the attempted extermination of Jews – only later to be called the Holocaust or the Shoah – was an event that marked, or should mark, a caesura in modern social and political thought.

The concern of this paper is with this notion of a 'gap' between past and future – of a 'fracture' in the continuity of political thought and moral judgement – which is provoked by the thought of the Holocaust. From the point of view of social theory, this question may be seen as a particular case study of the impact of historical events on social theorising and presupposes that social theory does not develop in isolation from the political world of which it is part. The focus on the writings of Hannah Arendt is chosen not only because she took seriously this question, the question of social theory after the Holocaust, soon after she learnt about the Holocaust itself,[2] and not only because she was an extraordinarily gifted and radical political thinker; it is chosen also because she offered a 'worldly' perspective on this rupture with civilisation which was rather lost in the later reflections on the Holocaust which stressed the uniqueness, singularity, non-representability and ineffability of the Holocaust and which treated 'Auschwitz' as an emblem for the breakdown of human history and the limits of human understanding. I am thinking here of a diverse tradition of thought, which Gillian Rose dubs 'Holocaust piety' because of its insistence on 'silence, prayer, the banishment equally of poetry and knowledge, in short, the witness of ineffability' at the expense of both understanding and politics.[3] In relation to this tradition of thought, Rose writes of its tendency to 'mystify something we dare not understand, because we fear that it may be all too understandable, all too continuous with what we are – human, all too human'. She asks of it: 'what is it that we do not want to understand? What is it that holocaust piety... protects us from understanding?'[4]

As the title of an essay she wrote in 1954 indicates – 'Understanding and Politics' – Arendt was one who at an early date foresaw the dangers of 'Holocaust piety' and resisted them.[5] The difference between Arendt's way of thinking and this later Holocaust discourse might be illustrated by a passage from the author-survivor, Elie Wiesel, in which he criticises the television drama called *Holocaust*:

> The series treats the Holocaust as if it were just another event... Whether culmination or aberration of history, the Holocaust transcends history... The dead are in possession of a secret that we, the living, are neither worthy of nor capable of recovering... The Holocaust? The ultimate event, the ultimate mystery, never to be comprehended or transmitted.[6]

Equally, it may be illustrated by the thought-experiment conducted by the French philosopher, Jean-François Lyotard, where he draws an analogy between the Holocaust and the image of an earthquake so catastrophic as to 'destroy not only lives, buildings, and objects but also the instruments used to measure earthquakes directly and indirectly'.[7] In Lyotard's thought-experiment, it is not only Jews who are exterminated in the Holocaust, but also the means to prove that Jews were exterminated. The point Lyotard seems to make is that Auschwitz cannot be grasped in thought simply as a *historical event* subject to the normal procedures of historical investigation and understanding. Imagine that there are no indicators of its existence that survive, all documents are destroyed, there is nothing to preserve memory from oblivion, the victims are condemned to silence, and the authority of the tribunal supposed to establish the crime and its quantity is itself discredited on the ground that the judge is 'merely a criminal more fortunate than the defendant in war'. Lyotard offers this thought-experiment to demonstrate that 'the name of Auschwitz marks the confines wherein historical knowledge sees its competence impugned', and on this basis he advances an ethical relation to 'Auschwitz' different from one based on understanding and politics: 'the impossibility of quantitatively measuring it, does not prohibit but rather inspires in the minds of the survivors the idea of a very great seismic force'.[8]

Now, Arendt also speaks of the 'explosion' of our categories of thought and standards of judgement when confronted by the Holocaust, but the conclusion she draws is not the same. Consider one key example of this 'rupture' which she offers: that of the impossibility of applying a 'means–ends' calculus to the phenomena of totalitarian terror. In the conventional use of terror, she argues in 'Understanding and Politics', violence is exercised as a means either to retain power, or to intimidate enemies, or to force people to work. But in circumstances where opposition has already become impossible, where it does not make a jot of difference what I do for my fate is already sealed, and where the exploitation of labour is at most only a secondary benefit subordinate to the main goal of extermination, such rationales make little sense. In the totalitarian use of terror, violence ceases to be a means to an end; it is deprived of that element of rational calculation which governs its exercise even in the worst of states; it becomes instead the very essence of rule and ends up, as it did in the Holocaust, in a 'frenzy of destruction' without political, economic or military utility.[9]

If this characterisation of totalitarian terror is correct, then Arendt's point is that categories of thought and standards of judgement which presuppose an element of rational choice on the part of social actors are stretched beyond their limit in the attempt to understand such phenomena. In an earlier essay on 'Social Science Techniques and the Study of Concentration Camps' (1950) Arendt explores this issue from its other side – that of the appearance of the impossibility of human understanding – when she writes as follows:

> If we assume that most of our actions are of a utilitarian nature and that our evil deeds spring from some 'exaggeration' of self-interest, then we are forced to conclude that this particular institution of totalitarianism is *beyond human understanding*... it is not only the non-utilitarian character of the camps themselves – the senselessness of 'punishing' completely innocent people, the failure to keep them in a condition so that profitable work might be extorted from them, the superfluousness of frightening a completely subdued population – which gives them their distinctive and disturbing qualities, but their anti-utilitarian function, the fact that not even the supreme emergencies of military activities were allowed to interfere with these 'demographic policies'. It was as though the Nazis were convinced that it was of greater importance to run extermination factories than to win the war.[10]

Arendt did not share the view that the death camps were 'beyond human understanding'. Rather, her argument is that it is only because we have a restrictively rationalistic model of human action that the death camps *appear* to

21

be beyond human understanding. The path which Arendt herself took was not to revert to the conventional view (characteristic of liberalism and Marxism alike) that there must be some rational explanation for the Holocaust in terms of economics, politics or military strategy, but neither was it to conclude that the Holocaust is beyond human understanding. The path she took is indicated by the subtitle of the essay on 'Understanding and Politics': it is 'The difficulties of understanding'. Neither *ease* of understanding nor *impossibility* of understanding but *difficulty* of understanding.

The conventional view and the radicalism which declares that the Holocaust is beyond human understanding are two sides of the same coin. The former cannot come to terms with what is unprecedented about the Holocaust. Most modern forms of organised violence are comprehensible inasmuch as they have a 'definite purpose' and 'benefit the ruler in the same way as an ordinary burglary benefits the burglar'.[11] Arendt mentions in this context aggressive wars, massacres of enemy populations, extermination of 'natives' in the process of colonisation, enslavement of subject peoples, etc. These modern forms of organised violence doubtless paved the way for totalitarian terror but they were different in kind. In totalitarian terror itself, she saw the absence of any such utilitarian criteria. Thus in respect of the Holocaust Arendt writes:

> The gas chambers did not benefit anybody. The deportations themselves, during a period of acute shortage of rolling stock, the establishment of costly factories, the manpower employed and badly needed for the war effort, the general demoralising effect on the German military forces as well as on the population in the occupied territories – all this interfered disastrously with the war in the East, as the military authorities as well as Nazi officials…pointed out repeatedly… And the office of Himmler issued one order after another, warning the military commanders…that no economic or military considerations were to interfere with the extermination programme.[12]

It is this absence of instrumental or utilitarian rationality which not only gives to totalitarian terror in general, and to the Holocaust in particular, its 'horrible originality' but makes it incomprehensible to a social science fixed within rationalistic ways of thinking. The counter-proposition, that the Holocaust is 'beyond human understanding', has the definite merit of recognising that rational choice models of social science cannot begin to explain the Holocaust nor other phenomena of totalitarian terror, but it refuses to extend human understanding beyond these rationalistic limits. *Contra* both ways of thinking, Arendt's basic message is that in the face of the Holocaust we do not encounter the limits of understanding as such, but rather the limits of a particular understanding which presupposes the rationality of human action.

Arendt defends the activity of understanding as such. It is, in and of itself, a mark of our humanity and a resistance to the conditions which made the Holocaust possible. It is an activity which totalitarianism suppresses and which conversely is one mark of our resistance to totalitarianism. It is an activity which 'begins where violence ends', which is 'profoundly and fundamentally human'; it is a way in which 'we come to terms with and reconcile ourselves to reality' and try to be 'at home in the world'; it is 'the specifically human way of being alive; for every single person needs to be reconciled to a world into which he was born a stranger and in which, to the extent of his distinct uniqueness, he always remains a stranger'.[13] To abandon the quest for understanding is to surrender to the totalitarian elements which survive within our own society. On the one hand, there is a moral argument: if people in the camps who were defencelessly exposed to a seemingly inexplicable power sometimes find the resources to make sense of it (let us think especially of Primo Levi or Paul Celan or Tadeusz Borowski),[14] then there is all the more reason for those of us who are not so exposed to ensure that this 'absolute betrayal of human values' does not rule supreme. In this context, the human activity of understanding is itself a re-affirmation of human values.

On the other hand, there is an intellectual argument. The perception that our existing categories of thought and standards of judgement are lacking when it comes to the Holocaust does not invalidate *all* our categories and standards and does not mean that they must *all* be abandoned. The notion that Auschwitz represents a *novum* in the exercise of evil implies that we still have the categories and standards which make it possible to recognise how unprecedented and original the Holocaust was in human history. The activity of understanding is not the *imperium* of the modern philosophical subject who represents the Holocaust like a voyeur removed from the terrible events which she observes. It is not about imposing abstract concepts onto lived experience and reiterating the false promise of a universal politics. It is not a sign of disrespect for the silence which the suffering of the victims demands nor an appropriation of their experience by the theoretician. It is certainly not about forgiving the perpetrators in the sense that *tout comprendre, c'est tout pardonner*, nor is it about using the Holocaust to indoctrinate people with 'final results' that can serve as weapons in ideological warfare. It does not mean engaging in some kind of 'dialectical acrobatics' based on the 'superstition that something good might come from evil' – a view which can only be justified as long as 'the worst that man could inflict upon man was murder'.[15] If such traits are confirmed in this or that representation of the Holocaust, it does not invalidate representation *as such* but demands reflection on the difficulties of representation. Making sense of the senseless remains the essential element in recovering the idea of humanity after the Holocaust.

The activity of understanding will not be able to confront the 'burden of events' which weigh down upon the twentieth century if, as Nietzsche put it in *The Will to Power*, it determines to 'reduce the unknown to something which is known',[16] or, as Arendt reformulates it, to 'submerge what is unfamiliar in a welter of familiarities'.[17] We resist the presumption that nothing can happen which our categories are not equipped to understand and which cannot be deduced from its precedents. In the case of the Holocaust and of other forms of totalitarian terror, 'all parallels create confusion and distract attention from what is essential'.[18] If the Holocaust has deprived us of our traditional tools of understanding, still we must confront the difficulty of constructing new tools: not of dissolving the unknown into the known but rather the opposite, of dissolving the known in the unknown. Every fixed idea dissolves in the face of the Holocaust.

In her *Origins of Totalitarianism* Arendt acknowledges the 'great temptation to explain away the intrinsically incredible by means of liberal rationalisations' – in each one of us, she writes, 'there lurks such a liberal wheedling us with the voice of common sense'.[19] The failure of liberalism to live up to its own ideals or effectively to oppose those who devalue them seemed to Arendt to be a clear and distinct lesson to be drawn from the origins of totalitarianism. Liberalism, she wrote in 'The Eggs Speak Up' (1951), has 'demonstrated its inability to resist totalitarianism so often that its failure may already be counted among the historical facts of our century'.[20] To former Communists who wanted to return after the war to the 'democratic way of life', she declares with apparent scorn that it is 'the same world against whose complacency, injustice and hypocrisy these same men once raised a radical protest... where the elements which eventually crystallised...into totalitarianism are still to be found'.[21] We might look back on the heyday of the liberal tradition with a certain nostalgic affection but not pretend that 'the past is alive in the sense that it is in our power to return to it'. The liberal way of thinking allows us only to 'take that which was good in the past and simply call it our heritage' and to 'discard the bad and simply think of it as a dead load which by itself time will bury in oblivion'.[22] Liberalism promises only 'an eventual restoration of the old world order', but if we are to confront the 'eventness' of the Holocaust, then we cannot remain content with this thin gruel.

If the catastrophe were so consuming as to destroy all our categories of thought and all our standards of judgement, then the task of understanding would indeed be hopeless: 'how can we measure length if we do not have a yardstick, how could we count things without the notion of numbers?' The conclusion, however, which Arendt draws from this thought-experiment is not that drawn by Lyotard. It is a representation of *what might have been* if the voice of resistance had been silenced, if the attempt to exterminate Jews – and the successors of the Jews – had been successfully carried to its conclusion, if the yardsticks which make possible human understanding, including the idea of humanity itself, were destroyed. This thought-experiment highlights the fact that 'total domination' was fully actualised – in the sense that it succeeded in destroying not only human beings but also the idea of humanity – *only* within the confines of the concentration and death camps. If it had been extended to the social body as a whole, then the activity of understanding may well have been killed along with the victims, but this hypothetical possibility reveals 'the necessary limitations to an experiment which requires global control in order to show conclusive results'.[23]

These sealed-off camps were to totalitarianism in power what the 'pan-opticon' was to normal disciplinary power or the factory was to capitalist production: they were the 'central institution' of totalitarian power because it was in these camps alone that the experiment of total domination, impossible to accomplish under normal circumstances, could be actualised. They were the laboratories in which the nihilistic credo that 'everything is possible' was translated into the totalitarian persuasion that 'everything can be destroyed', including the idea of humanity itself.[24] They were the site on which the project of stripping human beings of all that makes them human – human solidarity, a functioning body, a name, a space to make moral choices, the possibility of understanding – was tried and tested prior to the mass disposal of the bodies themselves. In the camps destruction was not a by-product of production, in the sense that one cannot make a wooden table without destroying a tree, nor in the sense that one cannot build a canal without killing workers. Destruction was rather the aim of production – an end in itself which was deprived of any 'element of utilitarian calculation'. The achievement of the camps lay neither in the making of the 'new man' nor in the making of a 'new order of things'. It did not lie in *making* anything but in 'robbing man of his nature… under the *pretext* of changing it'. The camps were the visible proof that human beings can be turned into inanimate things and that murder can be made as impersonal as 'the squashing of a gnat'.[25]

It was this 'peculiar unreality and lack of credibility' of life in the camps which generated the mystery of 'Auschwitz' as the emblem of that which is beyond human understanding. The extreme difficulty that faces victims or eyewitnesses or anyone else is to make sense of what happened, and for the victims it is even harder to find ways of communicating what happened to 'normal people' in the outside world. Commenting on the reports of survivors that were available at the time of writing *Origins* (first published in 1951), as well as on their reception, Arendt describes the difficulties with great insight:

There are numerous reports by survivors. The more authentic they are, the less they attempt to communicate things that evade human understanding and human experience – sufferings, that is, that transform men into 'uncomplaining animals'. None of these reports inspires those passions of outrage and sympathy through which men have always been mobilised for justice. On the contrary, anyone speaking or writing about concentration camps is still regarded as suspect; and if the speaker has resolutely returned to the world of the living, he himself is often assailed by doubts with regard to his own truthfulness, as though he had mistaken a nightmare for reality... What common sense and 'normal people' refuse to believe is that everything is possible. We attempt to understand elements in present or recollected experience that simply surpass our powers of understanding. We attempt to classify as criminal a thing which, as we all feel, no such category was ever intended to cover. What meaning has the concept of murder when we are confronted with the mass production of corpses... If it is true that the concentration camps are the most consequential institutions of totalitarian rule, 'dwelling on horrors' would seem to be indispensable for the under-standing of totalitarianism. But recollection can no more do this than can the uncommunicative eyewitness report. In both these genres there is an inherent tendency to run away from the experience; instinctively or rationally, both types of writer are so much aware of the terrible abyss that separates the world of the living from that of the living dead that they cannot supply anything more than a series of remembered occurrences that must seem just as incredible to those who relate them as to their audience... Only the fearful imagination of those who have been aroused by such reports but have not actually been smitten in their own flesh, of those who are consequently free from the bestial desperate terror which, when confronted by real, present horror, inexorably paralyses everything that is not mere reaction, can afford to keep thinking about horrors. Such thoughts are useful only for the perception of political contexts and the mobilisation of political passions. [26]

In passages such as these, Arendt expresses the difficulty confronted by survivors of distinguishing nightmare from reality; our own difficulty of understanding when confronted by the lunacy of a process based on the mass production of corpses; the difficulty faced by the human imagination in dwelling upon horrors; the difficult relation between survivors and people like herself, who are aroused by their reports and have the capacity to draw political conclusions precisely because they are not themselves traumatised by the actuality of 'real, present horror'. Difficulty compounded upon difficulty. Why should people construct this micro-world of senselessness in which 'punishment is meted out without connection with crime... exploitation is practised without profit, and ... work is performed without product';[27] why on earth should they make this representation of Hell in which 'the whole of life was thoroughly and systematically organised with a view to the greatest possible torment'?[28] The only categories which seem to make sense of this world are those of senselessness, madness, unreality, insanity. It has the *appearance*, as Arendt put it in a term drawn from Kant, of 'some radical evil previously unknown to us'.[29]

The sheer insanity of the camps is the overriding reason why they seem incomprehensible according to the normal rules of historical knowledge. But what was still to be explained, as far as Arendt was concerned writing in the 1950s, was 'the disturbing fact that our great tradition has remained so peculiarly silent, so obviously wanting in productive replies, when challenged by the "moral" and political questions of our time'.[30] The general silence with which the questions posed by the camps were met, at the time when Arendt was writing, was not because of any shortage of documents and testimonies, nor because the perpetrators succeeded in their attempt to abolish all trace of the camps and the killing fields – there survived an abundance of documents, signs, traces and testimonies precisely because the perpetrators in the end failed to eliminate Jews from the face of the earth. It was, according to Arendt, because the sources from which such answers should have sprung had themselves dried up. These sources were precisely 'the quest for meaning and need for understanding' which are the mark of our humanity. It was the drying up of these sources which Arendt discovered behind the idea of the 'ineffability' of the Holocaust.[31] To yield to the impossibility of understanding is an abdication that would grant totalitarian terror, as it were, the last word. But why do we lose the quest for meaning and the need for understanding? What is it that we do not want to understand?

The Juridical Point of View

The 'difficulties of understanding' were evident in the juridical categories that were applied to some perpetrators of the Holocaust after the war and institutionalised at Nuremberg. Both in legal prosecutions and in everyday speech the terms 'crime' and 'criminal' were regularly used to refer to the acts and agents of the Holocaust. Arendt certainly did not wish to invalidate the use of these categories, but she did problematise their application to the perpetrators and their deeds, and she observed in relation to the violence perpetrated by the Nazis against Jews and other victims of the Holocaust that the category of 'crime' and 'criminal' is hopelessly inadequate. First, she emphasised the difference

27

between mere criminality and the facts of mass extermination – between 'a man who sets out to murder his old aunt' and 'people who without considering the economic usefulness of their actions at all…built factories to produce corpses'.[32] What is distinctive about the latter is that they 'explode the limits of the law' and their guilt, in contrast to all criminal guilt, 'oversteps and shatters any and all legal systems'.[33] Second, Arendt emphasised the disproportion between the few Nazis who were tried and punished at Nuremberg and the mass of perpetrators who committed the deeds in question. When the machinery of mass murder forces practically everyone in a society to participate in one way or another, 'the human need for justice can find no satisfactory reply to the total mobilisation of a people to that purpose. Where all are guilty, nobody in the last analysis can be judged.'[34] The effacement of visible signs of distinction between the guilty and the innocent – through a policy of making each individual dependent upon committing crimes or being complicit in them or at least appearing to be complicit in then – marks the limit of criminal law.

Third, the inadequacy of legal categories was apparent in the language of 'personal responsibility' which criminal law presupposes. The perpetrators, as they appeared to Arendt, typically saw themselves as 'cogs in the mass murder machine' who did the job of killing 'only in a professional capacity, without passion or ill will', and no longer recognised any contradiction between being good fathers, husbands and dog-owners at home and killing Jews if that was their public duty and legal obligation. Between this 'modern type of man' and conventional notions of responsibility, a new kind of gap opens up: 'if we tell a member of this new occupational class which our time has produced that he is being held to account for what he did, he will feel nothing except that he has been betrayed'.[35] According to Arendt, this might explain why the Nuremberg trials met with so much sullen resentment on the part of Germans who would not recognise their own responsibility in the execution of the Holocaust, or on the part of a few Germans with an anguished guilt which in political terms was of little use. This new type of 'bourgeois' is no longer the *citoyen* who combines the public virtue of civic patriotism with the private virtue of personal responsibility, but the 'man of the masses' who does his duty, even at the expense of his own inclinations, and cannot think otherwise.

Such perpetrators are human beings, not cogs in a machine, yet they conceive of themselves *as if* they were cogs in a machine. It is this 'as if…' quality that is so difficult to comprehend. On the one hand, those positivistic social sciences which declare that the perpetrators were *in fact* merely cogs in a killing machine incapable of moral decision and which claim that modern bureaucratic rationality has *in fact* deprived them of all moral awareness merely mirror the illusions of the world they purport to explain. Against this Arendt saw it as a definite achievement of the trials that 'all the cogs in the machinery, no matter how insignificant, are *in court* forthwith transformed back into perpetrators, that is to say, into human beings'.[36] However, the juridical conception of personal responsibility would be a mere legal fiction if it were imposed upon a recalcitrant social reality in which responsibility had no factual existence (like holding peasants dispossessed of their land responsible for becoming vagrants).[37] The difficulty concerns the relation between the concept and its existence – between the representation of responsibility in court and the social reality thus represented.

If the question of responsibility cannot be adequately handled either by a positivism which denies its existence or by a juridical consciousness which turns it into an ontological absolute, Arendt's own writings initiate an approach which foregoes all *a priori*, metaphysical conceptions of responsibility in order to explore the actuality of moral responsibility within the killing machines. The subtext of her argument was that, if totalitarianism indicated the collapse of all *existing* moral standards, it was accompanied by a restructured moral point of view in which personal responsibility was not simply annulled but reconfigured as a matter of political organisation and consciousness. This is a complicated matter and beyond the terrain of this paper, but Arendt seeks to demonstrate that the totalitarian form of organisation is based on 'authority' rather than naked force and as such depends on 'the unquestioning recognition of orders' by those who are asked to obey, so that neither coercion nor persuasion is needed.[38] The fact of the matter is that the perpetrators of the Holocaust did not generally question orders, let alone disobey them, membership of murder-squads was not on the whole compulsory and individuals were not generally forced to kill under pain of death themselves.[39] It was not a case, as Dwight Macdonald mistakenly thought, of 'kill or be killed', and if it had been, this would have been a legitimate defence or at least plea of mitigation at Nuremberg.[40] As Adolf Eichmann put it in his trial, he acted according to his conscience and his conscience would have troubled him only if he had questioned orders – a thought which seems never to have occurred to him.

Max Weber long ago demonstrated that in a rational bureaucracy officials are not simply cogs in a machine, for the very act of 'following a rule' requires for its fulfilment all manner of interpretative endeavour and moral evaluation.[41] In the organisation of the Holocaust some use was made of some elements of rational bureaucracy, but these elements were subordinated to the Nazi movement and its secret police forces, and radically reconfigured according to the so-called *Führerprinzip* or Leader Principle. In place of hierarchical order, the Leader Principle demanded that every member of the killing machine think and act in accordance with the will of the Leader and owe allegiance to the

Leader himself. As Hans Frank formulated it, in mockery of Kant, the categorical imperative of the Third Reich was: 'Act in such a way as the Führer, if he knew your action would approve it'.[42] Wide latitude was given to officials in the execution of general policies and every position-holder was responsible not only for their own actions but also for the actions of their subordinates – even when they disobeyed or failed to fulfil orders. To grasp the 'will of the Führer' in this context demanded zeal and creativity far in excess of the old-fashioned plodding bureaucrat.

If this, or something like this, was the actuality of 'personal responsibility' in the Nazi killing machines – a responsibility which goes beyond the bureaucratic role of the perpetrator – the question raised by Arendt (drawn from Karl Jaspers and referring to Kierkegaard)[43] was how to create a new sense of 'universal responsibility' in which

> human beings...assume responsibility for all crimes committed by human beings, in which no one people are assigned a monopoly of guilt and none considers itself superior, in which good citizens would not shrink back in horror at German crimes and declare 'Thank God, I am not like that', but rather recognise in fear and trembling the incalculable evil which humanity is capable of and fight fearlessly, uncompromisingly, everywhere against it.[44]

One way was through the establishment of what Kant called 'cosmopolitan law' which would hold to account the perpetrators of such atrocities as were committed in the Holocaust. In spite of her reservations, Arendt saw the glimmer of a new dawn of cosmopolitan order in the Nuremberg Charter and the prosecution of leading Nazis that followed. It was an event that announced that individuals, rather than states, can be held responsible for crimes under international law; that individuals acting within the legality of their own state can be tried as criminals; that service to the state does not (as Alain Finkielkraut put it) exonerate any official in any bureaucracy or any scientist in any laboratory from his or her responsibilities as a thinking individual; that no one can hide behind the excuse of 'only obeying orders' and that those who sit behind desks planning atrocities are as guilty as those who participate directly in their execution. Not least, it announced that atrocities committed against one set of people, be it Jews or Poles or Roma, are an affront not only to these particular people but also to humanity as a whole and that humanity would find means of bringing the perpetrators to justice.[45]

To be sure, the promise of a new cosmopolitan order was precarious and almost stillborn. At Nuremberg it excluded in principle crimes committed by the Allied powers (including the terror committed under Stalin), and in respect of the Germans it focused mainly on traditional 'war crimes' and 'crimes against peace' rather than on the 'crimes against humanity' committed in the camps and killing fields. After Nuremberg, the cosmopolitan precedent set by the Charter and these trials quickly went into abeyance as consensus collapsed and the rival interests of cold war prevailed. Even in the few cases that were held for crimes against humanity (exclusively, as far as I know, in relation to the wartime activities of Nazis and none in relation to atrocities committed by colonial powers or anti-colonial movements after the war) Arendt saw the promise of a new cosmopolitan order distorted by nationalist aims.

This was the nub of Arendt's criticisms of the Eichmann trial. On the one hand, she upheld the legitimacy of the trial: the fact that Eichmann had been illegally kidnapped from Argentina was justifiable given that he had been indicted at Nuremberg, charged with crimes against humanity and was hiding in a country with such a bad record of extradition as Argentina. The use of an Israeli national court was justifiable in the absence of an international court or a successor court to Nuremberg and in light of the fact that Eichmann's job was to organise the killing only of Jews. The contention that there were more important issues at stake than the trial of a single individual – e.g., the political character of modern anti-semitism, the origins of totalitarianism, the nature of evil, the question of why the Germans?, etc. – was no reason not to seek justice in this particular case.[46] For Arendt, the trial of Eichmann was one of the means by which the abstract conception of universal responsibility, which was drawn from the experience of the Holocaust, could be made concrete and actual.

On the other hand, Arendt criticised the Eichmann trial for its misuse in the service of Israeli nationalist aims: the contention that only in Israel could a Jew be safe, the attempt to camouflage the existence of ethnic distinctions in Israeli society, the concealment of the co-operation of certain Jewish leaders in the administration of the Holocaust, etc.[47] What Arendt expressed was a growing sense of lost opportunity: that the precedent set by Nuremberg was being ignored in the era of cold war, that the universalistic import of crimes against humanity was being corralled back into a nationalist frame of reference, that the ethical significance of the Holocaust was being lost to a moral division of the world between them and us, good and evil, which served only as an index of a world purged of all political profundity. To those who thought that the institution of 'crimes against humanity' could achieve some sort of release from the elements of totalitarian thought which inhere within the modern world, the fear that Arendt expressed was that it was being used to reinforce the very situation it had sought to correct – the breaking up of the human race into a multitude of competing states and nations.[48]

In spite of all such difficulties, Arendt argued that the category of 'crimes against humanity' was particularly well chosen since in the most literal sense such crimes as the perpetrators of the Holocaust committed were 'against humanity'. In the Holocaust, as Arendt perceived it, 'individual human beings did not kill other individual human beings for human reasons'; rather an organised attempt was made to 'eradicate the concept of the human being'.[49] If the camps were an attempt to eradicate not only human beings but the idea of humanity, the institution of the legal category of 'crimes against humanity' was a re-affirmation of the idea of humanity. It expressed the realisation that:

> Something seems to be involved in modern politics that actually should never be involved in politics as we used to understand it, namely all or nothing – all, and that is an undetermined infinity of forms of human living together, or nothing, for a victory of the concentration camp system would mean the same inexorable doom for human beings as the use of the hydrogen bomb would mean the doom of the human race.[50]

It was a politics which strove for 'total domination' by 'eliminating under scientifically controlled conditions spontaneity itself as an expression of human behaviour and [by] transforming the human personality into a mere thing'; a politics whose aim was the destruction of all human spontaneity, plurality and differentiation; a politics based on the notion that 'all men have become equally superfluous'.[51] The international lawyers were more right than they probably knew when they said that the Holocaust was directed literally 'against humanity' and that the institution of 'crimes against humanity' was visible proof that the Holocaust did not and would not succeed. For Arendt, the point was not to declare prematurely the 'death of man', but to try to understand why the idea of humanity appeared as something so offensive that it had to be destroyed and how the idea of humanity could be restored as something more than an empty slogan or deception of power.

Totalitarianism and the Question of Evil

When Arendt wrote of the '*appearance* of some radical evil', it was doubtless to distinguish her use of the concept from any ontological conception of radical evil. This appearance was due to the ambition of the Holocaust project: to get rid not just of Jews and other 'undesirables' but of the idea of humanity. If the idea of humanity is the achievement of the modern age, the Holocaust may be understood as the ultimately failed attempt to undo this achievement. To declare the idea of humanity dead is to grant the Nazis a posthumous victory.

Implicit in the use of the term 'radical evil' is an opposition to any relativising of the evil of the Holocaust. The collapse of moral standards that was encountered in totalitarian terror, and the equally rapid adaptation of former

Nazis to the 'democratic way of life' after the war, gives the impression that what we call morality consists merely of 'our habits' and is no more than 'a set of *mores*, customs and manners which could be exchanged for another set with hardly more trouble than it would take to change the table manners of an individual or a people'.[52] If 'society' is the sole condition of moral life, as is sometimes held within sociology, and if the submission of individuals to 'society' is the condition of their liberation from their passions, then there can be no grounds for complaint against perpetrators who conform to the normative order of their society, internalise its values and act according to its conception of social duty – sometimes at great personal cost. The concept of 'radical evil' may be read as opposing any tendency in social theory to relativise morals in relation to contingent and transitory social norms. The Holocaust was visible proof, if any were needed, that the reduction of what is right to mere opinions about what is right is the mark of a subjectivism which leaves wide open the question of substance.

Karl Jaspers highlighted the risks, however, involved in the use of this term 'radical evil' in his correspondence with Arendt after the war. Jaspers argued that it might endow the perpetrators with what he called a 'streak of satanic greatness' and mystify them and their deeds in 'myth and legend'. It was against this danger that Jaspers emphasised the 'prosaic triviality' of the perpetrators and coined the phrase 'the banality of evil' to bring this to the surface. He argued, for instance, that the great advantage of treating the perpetrators as 'mere criminals' was to present them 'in their total banality'.[53] Arendt immediately expressed her agreement in principle and acknowledged that in her own use of the term she was coming too close to 'mythologising the horrible'.[54] No longer mindful of its original source she only introduced the term 'banality of evil' in her writings at the time of the Eichmann trial, to face up to the fact that the perpetrators were 'men like ourselves' who demonstrated what terrible deeds 'ordinary men' are capable of. It was a rejoinder to conventional images of the 'Nazi monster' that had nothing to do with 'men like ourselves' and which painted the world in terms of a dichotomy between our own absolute innocence and the unspeakable Nazi beast. What she took from the Eichmann case was that the perpetrators of the most radical evil could be rather pedestrian, bourgeois individuals, rooted in an everydayness that made them incapable of critical reflection or serious moral judgement, marked more by 'thoughtlessness' and 'remoteness from reality' than by any streak of satanic greatness. She thought that nothing was further from Eichmann's mind than 'to prove a villain' nor was he even a convinced anti-semite; in fact, he had few motives beyond his diligence in looking out for his own career advancement. The mark of his character was sheer 'thoughtlessness' and it was this which predisposed him to become one of the greatest criminals of the modern age. The lesson Arendt took from Jerusalem was that 'such remoteness from reality and such thoughtlessness can wreak more havoc than all the evil instincts taken together',[55] and that we have to come to terms with the fact that the man responsible for the execution of the Holocaust was terrifyingly normal: 'the deeds were monstrous but the doer...was quite ordinary, commonplace, and neither demonic nor monstrous'.[56]

The change in Arendt's work from the terminology of 'radical evil' to that of 'banality of evil' is a question I do not wish to pursue here, save to say that, as Richard Bernstein has demonstrated, between the 'monstrous deed' (the appearance of radical evil) and the 'commonplace doer' (the banality of evil) there is no contradiction.[57] What I do wish to raise, however, is the subtext of this terminological turn as a situated response to new ways of 'mythologising the horrible' and endowing perpetrators with 'a streak of satanic greatness' that were emerging in the 1960s in the shape of what I earlier referred to as 'Holocaust piety'. The experience of watching and hearing Eichmann was the trigger for Arendt's re-affirmation of a humanist tradition according to which only good is radical and evil is merely the deprivation of good with no independent reality of its own. Evil is never radical, she argued, 'it is only extreme, and...it possesses neither depths nor any demonic dimension... Only the good has depths and can be radical'.[58] With the Eichmann trial, the wall of silence which so often surrounded victims of the Holocaust during the 1950s was increasingly broken. Arendt, of course, welcomed this development, but what was at issue was the form in which the silence was broken.

The new discourse made use of old theological terms like 'Holocaust' and 'Shoah' to name the unnameable Event. It insisted upon its uniqueness and singularity. It took Auschwitz as the synecdoche for the Holocaust as a whole – giving rise to all manner of illusions about the 'industrial' and 'technological' character of the mass killing of Jews. On the one hand, the Jewish catastrophe was isolated from the wider catastrophe embodied in the rise of totalitarianism. On the other hand, Auschwitz was treated as irrefutable proof that, as Adorno put it, 'culture had failed':

All post-Auschwitz culture, including its urgent critique, is garbage... Whoever pleads for the maintenance of this radically culpable and shabby culture becomes its accomplice, while the man who says no to culture is directly furthering the barbarism which our culture showed itself to be... Not even silence gets us out of the circle. In silence we simply use the state of objective truth to rationalise our subjective incapacity, once more degrading truth into a lie.[59]

Drawing on the ontology of Martin Heidegger, philosophy even imputed the murderous tendencies evinced in the Holocaust to the metaphysics of the subject and to the hubris of Western humanism.[60] From Arendt's point of view, the concept of 'radical evil' was implicated in a discourse which went against the grain of the essentially political and humanistic response to the attempted extermination of Jews which informed her own work.

The idea of 'the banality of evil' was challenged by Jewish critics on the ground that it diminished the significance of the Holocaust. Gershom Scholem was by no means alone in reading the phrase as trivialising the Holocaust and diminishing the *novum* of this event.[61] In fact, for both Scholem and Arendt the Holocaust was the pivotal event in the definition of political modernity. The *real* difference between them concerned Arendt's refusal to singularise the Holocaust, to extract it from the wider phenomena of totalitarian terror, to accept its ineffability, or to rule out an essentially political response. For Arendt, too, the Holocaust was not just another event; it was a sign that new categories, new ways of thinking, new standards of judgement were needed. In this sense, it was a *novum*: not as a sign of something beyond human understanding but as the birth of an unprecedented violence. In this context, the use of the term 'banality of evil' was, I think, her way of saying that the Holocaust was 'human, all too human'.

In his memoir *At the Mind's Limits: Contemplations by a Survivor on Auschwitz and its Realities* (1966) Jean Améry argued that Arendt was unable to come face to face with the Event because she saw only 'codified abstractions'. Her use of the concept of totalitarianism was the case in point. Améry writes with unconcealed impatience:

> I hear indignant objection being raised, hear it said that not Hitler embodied torture but rather something unclear, 'totalitarianism'. I hear especially the example of Communism being shouted at me. And didn't I myself just say that in the Soviet Union torture was practised for 34 years? And did not already Arthur Koestler...? Oh yes, I know, I know.[62]

Améry wrote that Stalin and Hitler were different in principle: the one 'still symbolises an idea of man', the other 'hated the word "humanity" like the pious man hates sin'.[63] Yet this contrast, between one who symbolised the idea of man and the one who hated the word 'humanity', takes Stalin at his word and lets him off the hook on which Arendt hung him. Be that as it may, the crucial point for Améry takes off from a discussion of Proust:

> Proust writes somewhere: Nothing really happens as we hope it will, nor as we fear it will. But not because the occurrence, as one says, perhaps 'goes

beyond the imagination'...but because it is reality and not fantasy. ... What one tends to call 'normal life' may coincide with anticipatory imagination and trivial statement. I buy a newspaper and am 'a man who buys a newspaper'. The act does not differ from the image through which I anticipated it, and I hardly differentiate myself personally from the millions who performed it before me. Because my imagination did not suffice to entirely capture such an event? No, rather because even in direct experience everyday life is nothing but codified abstraction. Only in rare moments of life do we truly stand face to face with the event and, with it, reality.[64]

One such rare moment of life for Améry was when he faced torture by the Gestapo.

Gestapo men in leather coats, pistol pointed at their victim – that is correct, all right. But, then, almost amazingly it dawns on one that the fellows not only have leather coats and pistols, but also faces...like anyone else's. Plain, ordinary faces. And the enormous perception at a later stage, one that destroys all abstractive imagination, makes clear to us how the plain, ordinary faces finally become Gestapo faces after all, and how evil overlays and exceeds banality. For there is no 'banality of evil' and Hannah Arendt...knew the enemy of mankind only from hearsay, saw him only through the glass cage.[65]

The 'codified abstraction' of totalitarianism offended Améry because it draws the reader away from the sheer corporeality and sadism of that reality:

National Socialism in its totality was stamped less with the seal of a hardly definable 'totalitarianism' than with that of sadism. Sadism as radical negation of the other, as the denial of the social principle as well as the reality principle. The sadist wants to nullify this world, and by negating his fellow man, who also in an entirely specific sense is 'hell' for him, he wants to realise his own total sovereignty. [66]

'I have experienced the ineffable', Améry writes, 'I am filled with it entirely'.[67] In this context 'thinking is almost nothing else but a great astonishment'.

According to Améry, Arendt dissolves the experience of the Holocaust into an abstract codification, 'totalitarianism', spuriously identifies Hitler and Stalin as one and same thing, views the perpetrators only through a glass cage and diminishes the sheer sadism of their practices. And yet we must distinguish between the memoir of the survivor, Améry, and the analysis of one who is moved by the survivor's account. This is not the place to defend in detail Arendt's specific use of the term 'totalitarianism', except to say that a new word was needed to capture a new phenomenon. The term 'totalitarianism' had been coined by the Italian fascist, Giovanni Gentile, in the 1920s to express the actuality of 'total freedom' when the self-realisation of the individual is absolutely identified with the universality of the state and when the state itself is 'comprehensive, all embracing, pervasive... total'. Arendt's extraction of the concept from the megalomaniac ambitions of fascist ideology may be accused of turning the *fantasy* of the 'total' state into the *actuality* of a political formation and of neglecting the fact that megalomaniac ambitions encounter the obstacle of other people.[68] But this was precisely Arendt's point: the totalitarian consciousness dreamt of total domination but it was less the realisation of this dream than its collapse that led to escalating orgies of destruction. The concept of totalitarianism helps us to make sense of the senseless – not by offering an analysis of a social formation but by revealing the dynamics of destructiveness that lay at its core.

In this usage, totalitarianism was not, as for example Dana Villa has argued, the 'terrible revelation' of the essence of the West to itself: 'The presencing of everything as orderable and controllable is the *conditio sine qua non* for everything appearing to be possible – for the totalitarian project as such.'[69] Totalitarianism was not the 'result' or 'product' or 'final culmination' of any underlying tendency in modern political life. It was rather a 'crystallisation' or 'reconfiguration' of elements of political modernity.

The Will to Destroy

Why did the idea of humanity cause such offence and why did movements arise which tried so hard to destroy it? Arendt's answer draws on Nietzsche's *Will to Power* where he defines nihilism thus: 'what does nihilism mean? That the highest values devaluate themselves. The aim is lacking; "why?" finds no answer.'[70] Nietzsche prefigured the *fin-de-siècle* mood of irredeemable decline when the values and beliefs that were taken as the highest manifestation of the spirit of the West lost their validity. He believed that this loss of values bred a destructive and spiritless radicalism, full of hostility to culture and images of destruction,[71] and the spectre of barbarism which he anticipated turned out to be a pale image of the barbarism of later totalitarian movements.

Following Nietzsche, Arendt viewed European nihilism not so much as a pathological state of mind but as a valid expression of a disenchanted world. Nihilism was the spectre haunting Europe because it was well grounded and because all thinking beings shared the sense of revulsion felt by those who confronted the gulf between established values and the experience of extreme violence in the Great War:

Simply to brand as outbursts of nihilism this violent dissatisfaction with the pre-war age...is to overlook how justified disgust can be in a society wholly permeated with the ideological outlook and moral standards of the bourgeoisie.[72]

Disillusionment fed the 'anti-humanist, anti-liberal, anti-individualist and anti-cultural instincts' of a front generation which elevated violence, power and cruelty as the 'supreme capacities of humankind' and became 'completely absorbed by their desire to see the ruin of this whole world of fake security, fake culture and fake life'. What emerged in the place of conventional values was disgust with all existing standards and with all the powers that be; the hope that the whole culture and texture of life might go down in 'storms of steel' (Jünger); 'destruction without mitigation, chaos and ruin as such assumed the dignity of supreme values'. For the front generation, war was not just the offspring of the old world but the progenitor of the new: a means of 'chastisement' and 'purification' in a corrupt age (Thomas Mann), the 'great equaliser' in class-ridden societies (Lenin), the arena where 'selflessness' obliterates bourgeois egoism (Bakunin), the site of the 'doomed man' with 'no personal interest, no affairs, no sentiments, attachments, property, not even a name of his own' (Nechaev), the ruined ground on which philosophies of action dream of escape from society into the world of doing something, heroic or criminal, that is undetermined. The double standards of bourgeois civil society incited a politics of unmasking:

Since the bourgeoisie claimed to be the guardian of Western traditions and confounded all moral issues by parading publicly virtues which it not only did not possess in private and business life, but actually held in contempt, it seemed revolutionary to admit cruelty, disregard of human values, and general amorality, because this at least destroyed the duplicity upon which the existing society seemed to rest.[73]

In the twilight of double moral standards, it seemed radical to flaunt extreme attitudes: 'to wear publicly the mask of cruelty if everybody...pretended to be gentle'. But the desire for blunt admission and the blunt admission of desire were often welcome to a bourgeoisie tired of managing the tension between words and deeds and ready to take off their masks and reveal a more naked brutality. Arendt cited the case of Celine's *Bagatelles pour un Massacre* in which he proposed the massacre of all Jews, and the welcome which André Gide gave to it, 'not of course because he wanted to kill the Jews... but because he rejoiced in the blunt admission of such a desire and in the fascinating contradiction between Celine's bluntness and the hypocritical politeness which surrounded the Jewish question in all respectable quarters'.[74] Such 'spiritless radicalism' exposed the double standards endemic in the separation of *citoyen* and *bourgeois* only to attack the very separation of public and private life in the name of the wholeness of man. It revealed the false trust on which representative institutions were based, only to promote a philosophy of universal distrust. It turned the untruths of the bourgeois system of rule into a repudiation of the very distinction between truth and falsehood. Its contempt for facts preceded the determinate lies of totalitarian movements. Its contempt for political parties was channelled into a doctrine of 'movements' that suppressed all forms of representation except the totalitarian movement itself. The devaluation of the idea of humanity impelled many thinking beings into totalitarian movements, even if they later discovered that these movements were basically anti-intellectual and either devoured or expelled their intellectuals.

Drawing on Marx as well as Nietzsche, Arendt argued that it was under imperialism, when the political rule of the bourgeoisie was finally consolidated, that power was freed from all restraint and expansion for expansion's sake became the credo of the age:

> Expansion as a permanent and supreme aim of politics is the central political idea of imperialism... it is an entirely new concept in the long history of political thought and action...this concept is not really political at all, but has its origin in the realm of business speculation.[75]

The bourgeois principle of power came to mirror that of economics: unlimited accumulation of power accompanying unlimited accumulation of capital. What was new was not, of course, violence as such but the fact that violence now became the aim of the body politic and would not rest until there was 'nothing left to violate'.[76] In the age of imperialism the 'will to power' was increasingly emancipated from moral constraints and the ground laid for a power which 'left to itself can achieve nothing but more power'. Nihilism in this sense became the spirit of the age. If the practical nihilism of bourgeois society came up against political limitations – imposed by the proletariat and the nation-state at home and by the growth of national consciousness among conquered peoples abroad – the idea of a common humanity was further imperilled to the extent that proletariats, nation-states and national movements were themselves invested with the standards of violence and racism which they most opposed. It is in this context that the attempt to destroy the idea of humanity begins to become understandable as a political and philosophical end.

The Idea of Humanity

If totalitarianism shows that traditional moral values are no longer sufficient to prevent evil, because society reduces morals to the relativity of this or that normative order and can change them at the drop of a hat, we may want to believe that there is something about the human condition – some capacity for 'beginning', some individual particularity, some voice of conscience, some sense of judgement – that cannot be transformed according to plan: some relation that resists all reworking. The text of *Origins* is punctuated by Arendt's attempts to find this 'something' that resists all transformation. In a world where lives are 'superfluous' and the notion 'I want you not to be' prevails, she looked primarily among the victims, pariah peoples, stateless refugees to find those who affirm what she called that 'grace of love, which says with Augustine... "I want you to be" without being able to give any particular reason for such supreme and unsurpassable affirmation'.[77] In a world which suppresses uniqueness and portrays difference as alien, she looked to those who recognise 'the fact of difference as such and the disturbing miracle contained in the fact that each of us is made as he is – single, unique, unchangeable'.[78] In a world of the camps, where all spontaneity is denied, she looked to the capacity of human beings for creative action: '"That a beginning be made man was created", said Augustine'.[79] In a world in which friendship was subordinated to party loyalty and the duty to denounce disloyalty, she looked to a conception of friendship which is not only personal but makes its own political demands.[80] In a world where politics was equated with total domination, she looked to a conception of politics whose raison d'être is total freedom.

Arendt did not idealise the pariah as the cradle of a new universal class. When civilisation forces millions of people into 'conditions of savages', it may equally well produce new barbarians.[81] People who have lost the rights and protection that nationality once gave them may resort all the more desperately to nationalism; communal relationships built in the hope of preserving some 'minimum of humanity in a world grown inhuman' may generate a 'worldlessness' vulnerable to its own forms of barbarism.[82] The capacity to judge what is right and wrong and act according to conscience is not the exclusive property of the oppressed minorities – witness the case of the German sergeant, Anton Schmidt, executed for helping Jews – but what makes this planet 'a place fit for human habitation', as Arendt saw it, is simply that there are always *some* people who will not comply with power even under conditions of terror.[83]

Richard Bernstein points out that in *The Origins of Totalitarianism* Arendt did not hesitate to write about human nature and its transformation, later in *The Human Condition* she repudiated the notion of human nature:

The human condition is not the same as human nature and the sum total of human activities and capabilities which correspond to the human condition does not constitute anything like human nature... The problem of human nature...seems unanswerable... It is highly unlikely that we who can know, determine and define the natural essences of all things surrounding us... should ever be able to do the same for ourselves – this would be like jumping over our own shadows.... Nothing entitles us to assume that man has a nature or essence in the same sense as other things.[84]

Bernstein argues that behind these words we may see Arendt's abandonment of the consolation that there is 'something deep down in human beings that will resist the totalitarian impulse to prove that "everything is possible"'.[85] The spectre that the organised attempt to 'eradicate the concept of the human being' might succeed haunted Arendt, but her work also expresses the conviction that in the modern age the idea of humanity has a persistence and a power that was in this instance able to stand up to the supreme example of destructive will. The endless activity of understanding which her work both defends and exemplifies is one crucial aspect of this resistance.

Notes

1 Hannah Arendt, *Essays in Understanding 1930–1954*, New York: Harcourt Brace, 1994, p.302.

2 See also the important paper in this volume on the neglected works of H.G. Adler by Jeremy Adler.

3 Gillian Rose, 'Beginning of the Day: Fascism and Representation', in *Mourning Becomes the Law: Philosophy and Representation*, Cambridge: Cambridge University Press, 1996, p.43. She was thinking of Adorno's 'after Auschwitz', Holocaust theology, and Jean-François Lyotard's reading of 'Auschwitz' as the 'differend'.

4 *Ibid.*, p.43.

5 Arendt, *Essays...*, pp.307–27.

6 Quoted in J. Roth and M. Berenbaum, *Holocaust: Religious and Philosophical Implications*, New York: Paragon House, 1989, p.2.

7 Jean-François Lyotard, *The Differend: Phrases in Dispute*, Manchester: Manchester University Press, 1988, p.56.

8 See also Hayden White, 'The Politics of Interpretation: Discipline and De-Sublimation', *Critical Inquiry* Vol.9, No.1, Sept 1982.

9 Arendt, *Essays...*, p.316.

10 *Ibid.*, p.233.

11 *Ibid.*, p.234.

12 *Ibid.*, p.236.

13 *Ibid.*, p.308.

14 Primo Levi, *If this is a Man*, London: Abacus, 1995 and *The Drowned and the Saved*, London: Abacus, 1988; Tadeusz Borowski, *This Way for the Gas, Ladies and Gentlemen*, New York: Penguin, 1976.

15 Hannah Arendt, *The Origins of Totalitarianism*, New York: Harvest, 1976, p.442.

16 F. Nietzsche, *The Will to Power*, London: Weidenfeld and Nicolson, 1968, trans. Walter Kaufmann and R.J. Hollingdale, §608.

17 Arendt, *Essays...*, p.313.

18 Arendt, *Origins...*, p.444.

19 *Ibid.*, pp.439–40.

20 Arendt, *Essays...*, p.282.

21 *Ibid.*, p.281.

22 Arendt, *Origins...*, pp.viii–ix.

23 *Ibid.*, p.459.

24 *Ibid.*, p.459.

25 *Ibid.*, p.443.

26 *Ibid.*, pp.439–41.

27 *Ibid.*, p.443.

28 *Ibid.*, p.445.

29 *Ibid.*, p.443.

30 Arendt, *Essays...*, p.316.

31 *Ibid.*, p.317.

32 Hannah Arendt and Karl Jaspers, *Correspondence 1926–1969*, New York: Harcourt Brace, 1992, p.69.

33 *Ibid.*, p.54.

34 Arendt, *Essays...*, p.126.

35 *Ibid.*, p.130.

36 Hannah Arendt, *Eichmann in Jerusalem: A Report on the Banality of Evil*, New York: Penguin, 1994, p.289. Alain Finkielkraut picked up a similar theme when he argued in relation to the Barbie trial that though the Holocaust was 'from Eichmann to the engineers on the trains...a crime of employees...it was precisely to remove from crime the excuse of service and to restore the quality of killers to law-abiding citizens...that the category of "crimes against humanity" was formulated'. See Alain Finkielkraut, *Remembering in Vain*, New York: Columbia University Press, 1992, pp.3–4.

37 See Karl Marx, *Capital*, Vol.I, Harmondsworth: Penguin, p.896. Marx writes: 'at the end of the 15th and during the whole of the 16th centuries a bloody legislation against vagabondage was enforced throughout Western Europe. The fathers of the present working class were chastised for their enforced transformation into vagabonds and paupers. Legislators treated them as "voluntary" criminals and assumed it was entirely within their powers to go on working under the old conditions.'

38 Hannah Arendt, *On Violence*, New York: Harcourt Brace, 1970, p.45.

39 See, for example, Christopher Browning, *Ordinary Men*, New York: Harper Collins, 1993.

40 Dwight Macdonald, *Politics*, 1945.

41 Max Weber, *Selections in Translation*, ed. W.G. Runciman, Cambridge: Cambridge University Press, 1972.

42 Arendt, *Eichmann...*, p.11.

43 See Karl Jaspers, *The Question of German Guilt*, New York: Capricorn Books, 1961.

44 Arendt, *Essays...*, p.32.

45 According to Article Six, 'Leaders, organisers, instigators and accomplices participating in the formulation or execution of a common plan or conspiracy to commit any of the foregoing crimes are responsible for all acts performed by any persons in execution of such plan'. Article 7 added that 'The official position of defendants, whether as Heads of State or responsible officials in Government Departments, shall not be considered as freeing them from responsibility or mitigating punishment'. Article 8 added that 'The fact that the Defendant acted pursuant to order of his Government or of a superior shall not free him from responsibility, but may be considered in mitigation of

punishment if the Tribunal determines that justice so requires'. Articles 9, 10 and 11 authorised the Tribunal to declare that a particular organisation, like the Nazi party, is criminal and that individuals who join such an organisation are personally responsible both for their membership and for their participation in its criminal activities.

46 Arendt and Jaspers, *Correspondence*, pp.419ff.

47 It is for these comments that Arendt's account is most remembered by her critics, but she acknowledged the more positive effects of the trial: it encouraged the prosecution of leading Nazis in West Germany, it publicised the Holocaust to the world, it offered a forum for the testimony of victims, it accomplished a touch of justice (she had no compunction, for instance, about the imposition of the death penalty: 'no member of the human race can be expected to want to share the earth with a man who supported and carried out a policy of not wanting to share the earth with the Jewish people and the people of a number of other nations').

48 It was this sense of lost opportunity that was echoed some twenty-five years later by Alain Finkielkraut in his celebrated study of the Barbie trial, when he analysed contemporary trends toward the 'banalisation' of crimes against humanity, as it became part of the 'competition of memories' between different national movements and was extended to include all those forms of 'man's inhumanity to man' of which we might disapprove. Thus in the Barbie case Finkielkraut criticised the decision of the French court to muddy the distinction between the killing of Jews for what they *were*, and the killing of resistance fighters for what they *did*, and its decision to stretch the concept of crimes against humanity to include both. He also criticised the attempt on the part of Barbie's defence team to diminish the distinction between the extermination of the Jews and the violence of European colonialism. A certain 'emotional confusion' arises, he argued, when on the one hand the definition of crimes against humanity expands to include inhuman actions of every sort and on the other hand contracts to exclude those crimes that cannot be ascribed to Western imperialism. In its actual use, Finkielkraut argued along the same lines as Arendt, the concept was serving to reduce 'the unmasterable multitude of mankind to an exultant face to face confrontation between Innocence and the Unspeakable Beast', and to rewrite the Holocaust as a 'meaningless idiot's tale' which signifies nothing and leaves only a 'gaping black hole' (Finkielkraut, *Remembering in Vain*, pp.60–61).

49 Arendt and Jaspers, *Correspondence*, p.69.

50 Arendt, *Origins...*, p.443.

51 *Ibid.*, pp.438–39.

52 Hannah Arendt, *Life of the Mind*, New York: Harcourt Brace Jovanovich, 1978, p.5. See the excellent discussion of this in Richard Bernstein, *Hannah Arendt and the Jewish Question*, Cambridge: Polity, 1996, pp.146ff.

53 Arendt and Jaspers, *Correspondence*, p.62.

54 *Ibid.*, p.69.

55 Arendt, *Eichmann...*, p.288.

56 *Ibid.*, pp.3–4.

57 Bernstein, *Hannah Arendt...*, Ch.7 'From radical evil to the banality of evil'.

58 Hannah Arendt, *The Jew as Pariah*, ed. Ron Feldman, New York: Grove Press, 1978, pp.250–51.

59 Theodor Adorno, *Negative Dialectics*, trans. E.B. Ashton, New York: Continuum, 1987, p.366. Also cited and discussed in Jean-Luc Nancy, *The Experience of Freedom*, trans. Bridget McDonald, Stanford: Stanford University Press, 1993.

60 In his *Letter on Humanism* (1945) Heidegger argued that the consciousness that establishes 'humanity' as an absolute standard against which to measure the extreme violence of the age forgets that it is the principle of humanity that precipitates this violence by destroying everything and everyone deemed to be 'inhuman'. Humanism implies a

technological relation to the world based on the domination of things and people, and despite its anti-technological and anti-humanistic roots he argued that Nazism was a variant of the same technology and humanism. Humanism is an 'ism' which puts the human being at the centre of the world and elevates the human being as master of all things. Heidegger insisted that when he spoke against humanism, this did not mean that his argument was 'destructive' or that it implied 'a defence of the inhuman'. The vista he wished to open up was that humanistic interpretations of 'man' could not realise 'the proper dignity of man'. Humanism is opposed, as he put it, because 'it does not set the humanitas of man high enough'. The higher responsibility is to overcome the limits of humanism, to assume 'guardianship' and 'care' in the 'clearing of Being', to 'let beings be' or to 'will not to will'. Nazism was a catastrophe for humanitas only because it turned opposition to humanism into an advocacy of the inhuman. The higher goal remained 'to think the humanity of homo humanus...without humanism'. The story of the influence of this text, mediated via French Marxism, is recounted in Anson Rabinbach's excellent *In the Shadow of Catastrophe: German Intellectuals between Apocalypse and Enlightenment*, Berkeley: University of California Press, 1977, Ch.3 'Heidegger's "Letter on Humanism" as Text and Event', pp.97–128. See Martin Heidegger, 'Letter on Humanism', in David Krell (ed.), *Basic Writings*, San Francisco: Harper and Row, 1976, p.219.

61 Arendt and Jaspers, *Correspondence*, pp.240–45.

62 Extracts to be found in John Roth and Michael Berenbaum (eds), *Holocaust: Religious and Philosophical Implications*, New York: Paragon House, p.179.

63 *Ibid.*, p.180.

64 *Ibid.*, p.175.

65 *Ibid.*

66 *Ibid.*, p.184.

67 *Ibid.*, p.187.

68 We know, for instance, that social atomisation in Stalinist Russia was far less complete than the concept of totalitarianism might suggest.

69 Dana Villa, *Arendt and Heidegger: The Fate of the Political*, Princeton: Princeton University Press, 1996, p.257. See also Philippe Lacoue-Labarthe, *Heidegger, Art and Politics*, Cambridge: Blackwell, 1990.

70 Nietzsche, *The Will to Power*, p.9.

71 In a passage from *Untimely Meditations* Nietzsche captured the experience of 'devaluation' thus:

> Now how does the philosopher see the culture of our time? Naturally quite differently than those philosophy professors who are satisfied with their state. When he thinks of the universal haste and the increasing speed with which things are falling, of the cessation of all contemplativeness and simplicity, it almost seems to him as if he were seeing the symptoms of a total extermination and uprooting of culture. The waters of religion are ebbing and they are leaving behind swamps or ponds; the nations are again separating from one another in the most hostile manner and they are trying to rip each other to shreds. The sciences, without any measure and pursued in the blindest spirit of laisser-faire, are breaking apart and dissolving everything which is firmly believed; the edified classes and states are being swept along by a money economy which is enormously contemptible. Never was the world more a world, never was it poorer in love and good. The educated classes are no longer lighthouses or sanctuaries in the midst of all this turbulent secularisation; they themselves become more turbulent by the day, more thoughtless and loveless. Everything, contemporary art and science included, serves the coming barbarism. (Cambridge: Cambridge University Press, 1983, pp.148–49.)

72 Arendt, *Origins...*, p.328.

73 *Ibid.*, p.334.

44

74 *Ibid.*, p.335.

75 *Ibid.*, p.125.

76 *Ibid.*, p.137.

77 *Ibid.*, p.301.

78 *Ibid.*, p.300.

79 *Ibid.*, pp.478–79.

80 Hannah Arendt, *Men in Dark Times*, New York: Harcourt Brace Jovanovich, 1983, p.25.

81 Arendt, *Origins...*, p.302.

82 Arendt, *Men in Dark Times*, pp.13–17.

83 Arendt, *Eichmann...*, p.233.

84 Hannah Arendt, *The Human Condition*, Chicago: University of Chicago Press, 1958, pp.9–10.

85 Bernstein, *Hannah Arendt...*, p.146.

CHAPTER 3

Whither the Broken Middle?
Rose and Fackenheim on Mourning, Modernity and the Holocaust

ANTHONY GORMAN

Emil Fackenheim cites with approval Elie Wiesel's statement that the 'Holocaust destroyed not only human beings but also the idea of humanity'.[1] The evaluation of this claim, which raises the question of the very possibility of ethics after Auschwitz, rests upon a prior assessment of the relation of the Holocaust to modernity. In a nutshell, does the Holocaust represent an appalling 'hiatus' in the ongoing progress of modernity, or the disclosure of its essential nihilism? Do we still dwell in the shadow of Auschwitz or is it now possible to 'actively forget' and move on? My aim in this paper is to evaluate the contribution of Gillian Rose to this debate.[2] Rose's central claim is that we can *fully acknowledge the trauma of the Holocaust without continuing to be traumatised by it.* Moreover, Rose insists, we must not only remember the Holocaust; we must remember it *perfectly*.[3] For only on the basis of a total and fearless reconstruction of its antecedents and effects in their specificity – causal, conceptual, spiritual – along with a comprehensive understanding of its ramifications in the present, may we arrive at an uncompromising acknowledgement of the degree of our own implication in the nexus of factors that made the catastrophe both possible and actual. Only then will we be free to repeat the past differently. In short, for Rose, the work of comprehension is an act of mourning that can and must be completed, so that, educated by the experience, we may move forwards in life and history.

Although Rose's explicit reflections on the Holocaust are confined to her late works, their theoretical foundations are laid in her early writings on Adorno and Hegel. Accordingly, Rose's claim can only be adequately assessed in the context of the development of her authorship as a whole. From this point of view, I shall argue, the 'method' of her late authorship is quite different from that employed in her early works. Whereas *Hegel Contra Sociology* and *Dialectic of Nihilism* are phenomenological texts, the later works, *The Broken Middle*, *Judaism and Modernity* and *Mourning Becomes the Law*, are, on the whole, genealogical in form. Now, Rose herself rejects the idea that Hegelian phenomenology and Nietzschean genealogy can be sharply distinguished in this way, insisting to the contrary that the respective methods must be 'comprehended not dogmatically contrasted'.[4] The *tertium comparationis* of this comprehension is that both inquire into the 'legal language in which experience and discourse is ineluctably couched'.[5] However, in my view, this partial convergence is not sufficient of itself to offset the fact that the two forms of enquiry are orientated by divergent and incompatible concepts of truth and the good which ultimately renders them irreducible to one another. As Robert Pippin notes in regard to Hegel's *Phenomenology of Spirit*: 'There certainly is a common theme running through its turns and transitions, and a common goal Hegel thinks he must reach: a mutually recognising so mutually reassured social subjectivity'.[6] By contrast, the common theme and goal running through the turns and transitions of Nietzsche's *Genealogy of Morals* is the capacity of given forms of life, moral systems, religions, etc., either to inhibit and retard or promote and affirm 'life'.[7] My point, then, is that there is no necessary reason why the goal of a fully mutual social subjectivity should be considered life-enhancing in the Nietzschean sense – indeed Nietzsche himself evidently holds the opposite view. This lack of an inner connection between the regulative goals of the two methods is fatal to Rose's attempt to effect their speculative unity in her own work. Indeed, it is the impossible task of sustaining the two methods in speculative tension that results in the de facto usurpation of phenomenology by genealogy in her late authorship. This in turn renders her criticisms of the reception of the Holocaust in philosophy, social theory and theology perspectival rather than comprehensive, and lays her open to the charge of inconsistency. In summary, I aim to show that Rose's claim that the trauma of the Holocaust may be both acknowledged and overcome can be consistently defended, but only on the basis of a return to the Hegelian idea of phenomenology which comprehends history from the standpoint of the realisation of the goal of a fully mutual social subjectivity.

My argument proceeds in four stages. First, I shall situate Rose's critical interpretation of the reception of the Holocaust by outlining her reading of the work of Bauman and Fackenheim. Second, I will show the foundations of this criticism in Rose's early Hegelian-Marxist analysis of modernity; and third, I shall indirectly demonstrate – via an extended contrast between Rose's and Fackenheim's accounts of the 'broken middle' – that the 'genealogical turn' in Rose's late writings vitiates her claim that the Holocaust may be comprehended and successfully mourned. Finally, I argue briefly that a weak teleological philosophy of history may provide a more consistent basis on which to defend

Rose's call for a rational comprehension of the Holocaust than that found in her own account of the 'broken middle'.

Modernity and the Holocaust

Rose reads Fackenheim and Bauman together as forming two parts of a speculative chiasmus: Holocaust theology (Fackenheim) completes itself as unexamined sociology: Holocaust sociology (Bauman) completes itself as uncritical theology.[8] To help clarify the substance of Rose's criticism, I shall first say a few words on Fackenheim's and Bauman's respective projects.

Fackenheim contends that the Holocaust marks a unique, epoch-making event that has irretrievably changed forever our trust in human nature.[9] The event itself is beyond philosophical intelligibility.[10] After Auschwitz, the memory of the historical resistance of the victims provides the only remnant of human hope. This resistance, Fackenheim contends, can only be preserved through the continued survival of the Jewish people, and this in turn renders the state of Israel an ontological and moral necessity.[11] In this way, even though the Holocaust itself can never be overcome, the world may yet be 'mended'.[12] Conversely, Bauman argues that the Holocaust was not a *novum* in history but the outcome of the technological rationalism of modern society and the attendant normative socialisation of modern subjects; however, he agrees with Fackenheim's argument that ethical rationalism has been fatally compromised as a consequence of its complicity in the catastrophe. Bauman welcomes this development as he believes it clears the ground for the emergence of a new postmodern ethics, founded on Levinas' ethical phenomenology of the face-to-face rather than upon the unreliable socialised moral ego.[13]

Rose argues against Fackenheim that he inconsistently makes use of the very rationalism that is supposedly ruined in order to issue his call to history.[14] Furthermore, Fackenheim's historical eschatology is presented without reference to the political history of modernity and Zionism.[15] Hence, the claim that the world is 'mended' is both abstract and empty; as such it only serves to disguise and reinforce its brokenness. Similarly, Rose contends that Bauman's thesis depends on a non-dialectical technological determinism. Although she accepts Bauman's claim that sociology has tended uncritically to equate socialisation with civilisation, she argues that this does not disqualify sociological reason *tout court*.[16] Furthermore, she suggests that Bauman overlooks the extent to which the 'elimination of anti-social drives in the individual may also lead to the internalisation and specialisation of violence in the psychic economy of the social ego: morality'.[17] The implication here is that Bauman is unaware of the implicit violence of his own authorship, particularly in his appeal to Levinas in opposing the pre-social face-to-face to socialised ethics. For Rose, there can be no pre-social ethics; hence, the use of such a construct can only betoken an unacknowledged will to power.

Rose concludes that Fackenheim's and Bauman's premature pronouncement of, respectively, a mended world and a new ethics, betrays an anxiety over their own implication in the violence of civil society generally and the trauma of the Holocaust in particular. Rose counsels that rather than forsake rationality and construct ethical utopias, they should stay with the anxiety and seek to negotiate it. With respect to the Holocaust specifically, this involves entering into what she calls 'inaugurated' as opposed to 'aberrated' mourning.[18] The latter laments the Holocaust as a divine annihilation that shatters the world into unmendable fragments. Such mourning is 'aberrant' because it can never be complete; fixated on the catastrophe, it can only look backwards rather than develop forwards, and so it remains trapped in melancholia, unable to experience the world afresh. On the other hand, 'inaugurated mourning', as the term suggests, is able to confront and bear the agony of loss, work through and become educated by it, so that we may leave it behind; and this work of restitution may only be accomplished if we keep faith with the world.

Fascism as the Fate of Modernity

Rose's early work is firmly located in a Hegelian tradition which maintains that historically conditioned systems of thought are constitutive of concrete forms of social existence. In this vein, Rose follows Hegel in contending that since Kant's Critical Philosophy constitutes the categorical framework of modernity, contemporary critical theory must begin from within its unresolved dualisms and antinomies; for the latter re-present in conceptual form the unresolved contradictions of modernity itself. To this end, Rose counterposes Hegel's idea of phenomenology to Kant's transcendental method.[19] The idea of a phenomenology rests on the insight that the Kantian distinction between the transcendental and empirical consciousness falls within 'consciousness' itself, when the latter is reinterpreted as the sum of the historical presuppositions of modern subjectivity (*Geist* in Hegelian parlance). Phenomenological exposition, therefore, does not criticise the Critical Philosophy directly – for this would self-defeatingly reinstate a method external to its object when it is precisely the abstract separation of the knower from the known that is to be overcome. Rather, it presents an immanent reconstruction of the formation and genesis of the antinomies of modern philosophical consciousness, developed from the stand-point of their implied, but as yet unrealised, resolution ('the Absolute'), and then proceeds to return these antinomies to their social and political preconditions, so as to determine the possibilities (if any) for their future transformation.[20]

The phenomenological observer, therefore, begins from 'within' the dualistic categories of Kantian reason as they manifest themselves experientially. From this point of view, the Kantian paradox that the self can theoretically know itself only *qua* 'appearance' and not, as it were, 'in-itself', faithfully corresponds to the lived experience of modern subjects.[21] But it follows from this that the more the subject gives form to the world the more empty of form it becomes.[22] Moreover, this progressive disjunction between life and form also renders moral agency blind. The excessive formalism of Kant's categorical imperative condemns it to fail in its appointed task of bridging the gulf between practical reason and moral agency. The result is the modern triumph of ethical subjectivism in its several forms.

It is these antinomies within self and modern society that render the modern subject prey to the realm of dialectical illusion (*Schein*). Ignorant of the basis of its own self-formation and lacking grounds for its own moral judgements, it is predisposed to embrace phantasmagoric projections of a utopian nature in a self-deluded attempt to establish a unified experience of the whole. However, the dominance of illusory forms of being within modernity is not the effect of irrationality but rather its structural precondition; for the irrational is socially rooted in the commodity-form rather than in aberrant forms of individual psychology. Rose shows this by emphasising an important aspect of Marx's analysis of commodity fetishism that has been consistently overlooked. Whereas Marx places the major stress upon the way in which, within bourgeois society, social relations increasingly assume the form of a relation between things, Rose points up the 'logic of illusion' underlying this process, whereby 'value as a property of the object is re-presented as a "natural" property of the commodity'.[23] Thus she corrects Marx's one-sided emphasis on the reification of labour by highlighting the obverse process though which the commodification of labour also results in the *personification* of the worker – and not just of the worker but of every member of bourgeois society.[24] By this means, the status of 'personhood' is internalised by the subject as a 'natural' determination. Rose therefore maintains that the re-presentation of reflected categories under the guise of immediacy extends beyond economic relations to embrace the totality of social forms, including, most significantly, formal-legal rationality. Civil society is therefore subject to a logic of double illusion: the misrecognition of subjects and the fantasised projections to which this misrecognition gives rise. The relation between personification and (irrational) projection developed here is not derived from the orthodox Marxist base-superstructure model but conforms instead to Hegel's speculative exposition of the dialectic of essence and appearance. From this point of view, the emergence of Fascism is not contingent on the breakdown of the capitalist economic order but is always already immanent within the necessary fiction of the bourgeois legal form of the 'person'. Fascist ideology is the extension of this fiction into a myth of pure form: the projection of a natural self integrated into a harmonious, organic, social whole. The Fascist ideal purports to transcend the antinomies of self and society but in reality leaves them utterly unresolved. Therefore, it may only be sustained through the violent suppression of all that threatens to expose the contradiction between its image of society and the recalcitrant social reality upon which it is imposed. Fascism is, in short, the phantasmagoric idea of a pure, bourgeois culture carried to its ultimate (nihilist) political conclusion. In arguing this, Rose is not committed to the absurd 'social-fascist' thesis that capitalism *is* Fascism. On the contrary, she is careful to specify the different legal, political and ethical relations pertaining to their respective state formations.[25] Her point is, rather, that the legal commodification of persons creates inherently unstable forms of subjectivity which, in turn, produces an overall tendency towards the aestheticisation of modern politics. Fascist ideology is the most extreme manifestation of this process; but it is by no means its only form of expression.

It might be objected at his point that Rose's emphasis on commodification as a dual process of personification and reification is, if anything, even more totalising and deterministic than the total reification thesis putatively found in early Frankfurt School Marxism.[26] Indeed, is this not a *total commodification thesis*? Furthermore, Rose's argument that Fascism is immanent within and an extension of modern forms of legal-rationality seems indistinguishable in its overall approach from that taken by Bauman in *Modernity and the Holocaust*. However, Rose may be defended against this line of reductive criticism on account of the fact that her analysis of the process of commodification retains an implicit commitment to the irreducibility of human spontaneity. The dominance of form within bourgeois society can certainly occlude but never negate, at least not *in toto*, the reflective capacity of modern subjects. Therefore, Rose can quite consistently concur with the main thrust of Bauman's thesis on the social origins of the Holocaust while entirely dissenting from Bauman's conclusion that the normalisation of moral indifference can be so successful as not to give rise to its own dialectical counterpart. Of course, Fackenheim will object that the Holocaust is an epochal event precisely because, there and then, the negation of the 'idea of freedom' became a historically accomplished fact.[27] However, Fackenheim's own call to history is founded on the resistance of the victims.[28] Even under conditions of extreme terror, resistance was possible. What was the condition of the possibility of such resistance? Fackenheim believes that it is unethical even to pose this question; Rose contends that it is unethical *not* to: for the condition of the possibility of resisting evil – freedom – is the same as that of its perpetration.

Rose equates the idea of freedom with the concrete realisation of 'absolute ethical life',[29] which she defines as a society based upon fully mutual, real (as opposed to merely formal) recognition. However, in so far as the concept of real recognition arises in a society where it is not yet actual, then, on pain of being re-formed into the very kind of abstract *Sollen* it is designed to circumvent, no determinate statement of it can be given in advance of its real development; it can only be indirectly pointed to or 'insinuated' in and through the reconstruction of the bourgeois antinomies that imply its immanent realisation. In *Hegel Contra Sociology*, Rose appears undecided between two divergent conceptions of 'absolute ethical life'. On the one hand, it appears to have a merely heuristic, negative function. In a society where genuine revolutionary change is not an immanent possibility, philosophers must withdraw from the world and 'form a sanctuary apart'; 'an isolated order of priests', who do *not* act like priests by seeking to impose new law tables in advance of their time.[30] Under these conditions, the notion of 'absolute ethical life' is intended ironically to convey critically the disjunction between the idea of freedom and the experience of unfreedom. On the other hand, Rose elsewhere in the text suggests that she understands the work of philosophical criticism to be a praxis with transformative potential. The recovery of the law that determines the fate of modern subjectivity makes possible a renegotiation of the limits and boundaries that divide the self from itself and from the world.[31]

Retrieving the 'Middle'

In her 1987 essay on Adorno,[32] Rose counterposes her own speculative reading of Hegel to Adorno's 'negative dialectics'. Her complaint against Adorno is that 'negative dialectics' is too static; it retains the antinomies of thought in a frozen antithesis, thereby precluding their potential reconfiguration. Speculative thinking, on the other hand, does not 'use' the dialectic but, rather, participates in its immanent self-movement. In sum, it is the *praxis* of comprehending and suffering: 'the relation of universality and particularity as it is actually and potentially negotiated by the singular'.[33]

Ostensibly, *The Broken Middle* is structured in accordance with the method that informs the design of *Hegel Contra Sociology*, only here it is political theology rather than social theory that is at stake. That is to say, Rose begins by exploring the antinomies of modern theology and then attempts to return them to their source in the central contradiction of civil society, namely, the institutional separation of morality and legality. Rose locates the theological flight from anxiety in terms of two contemporary debates within philosophy: first, in the postmodern pitting of Kierkegaard's concept of 'repetition' against Hegel's System; and, second, in the 'return to Judaism' as a possible source of a new, postmodern ethics. Rose adopts a twofold strategy to counter what she considers to be the abuse of Judaic thought at the hands of postmodernist theology and philosophy. On the one hand, she sets out to correct the misrepresentation of Judaism as a non-worldly, ahistorical, ethical community. As a modern religion, Judaism is a culture, and like all cultures in modernity, it is fated to reproduce the central antagonisms and conflicts of civil society within its own internal life. On the other hand, she defends Judaism against Christian and Judaic misrepresentations of its particularity.

Rose's 'turn' to Judaism is conceptually rather than psychologically motivated. Her argument requires her to begin with the antinomies of theological reason as she finds them – and the philosophical interpretation of Judaism just happens to be at the crux of a critical debate within contemporary theology and philosophy. Rose, therefore, places Judaism and modernity in a dialectical relation to one another, through showing how the antinomy of modern law – which is itself the historical result of the repeated collisions between revealed and positive law – is revisited in modern philosophy and modern Judaism. Thus, the particular crisis of modern Judaism is understood to re-present the universal predicament of modernity. Rose, then, stakes her own self and her own authorship in the midst of this fraught and broken relation from out of which she articulates the difficulty of her own singularity.[34]

However, notwithstanding undeniable continuities, *The Broken Middle* represents a fundamental departure from the form of speculative exposition presented in *Hegel Contra Sociology*. The difference is this: in *Hegel Contra Sociology*, the antinomies of sociological reason are comprehended and criticised from the standpoint of the universal ('the Absolute') which, though not 'posited' or 'pre-judged', is nonetheless understood to be latent or implicit within the antinomies themselves. In *The Broken Middle*, on the other hand, the antinomies of theological reason are comprehended from the standpoint of a particular culture which is taken to *stand for or point towards* the universal. In her late authorship Rose speaks entirely from within the crisis of modern subjectivity. She contends that the diremption between the universal and the particular must be comprehended, lived and transformed by the single individual, who is willing to stake and risk her identity and to make it possible for others to risk theirs, while at the same time eschewing all dogmatic and illusory certainties. Therefore, she consistently stakes her own identity, as a philosopher, a woman and a Jew, living, comprehending and re-living the contradictions of civil society, and urging us to do the same from the standpoint of our own singularity.[35] This new emphasis on singularity is evident in the consistent autobiographical motif that emerges in her late compositions; in the movement from a 'severe' towards a facetious-humorous style; and in the development of an existential rather than a purely structural account of love and faith; all of which stands in sharp contrast to the rigorous impersonal austerity of her early texts. This reorientation, however, represents, in my view, a retreat from the idea of phenomenology set out in *Hegel Contra Sociology*. In particular, Rose moves away from the claim that we may 'think the Absolute', towards the idea that we must simply 'risk' acting in the universal interest, without really knowing whether we actually are or not.[36] By relativising the relation to the universal to the fate of a particular culture and of a single individual within that culture, she is unable to prevent her own position from being assimilated to the perspectivist, relativist and agonal politics of postmodernism against which she herself so relentlessly and vociferously protests. For those other singularities who are enjoined to take up the task of negotiating their own difficult passage through universality and particularity will inevitably construct heterogeneous narratives of how they got to be where they are. In forsaking the implied 'Absolute', Rose leaves herself with no criteria by which to justify rationally her particular version of the determination of modernity from those of other claimants. In short, the problem is that the desideratum of holding to the 'broken middle' is one that can be satisfied by a large number of incompatible philosophical and political positions. To escape this objection, Rose would have to be able to show that the Jewish question remains paradigmatic for the crisis of modernity in a way that must be universally acknowledged. However, even if this could be shown conclusively, which I doubt, we would still need further criteria to decide between rival versions of what this entails. For example, on the loose criteria that Rose presents, a quite convincing case could be made that it is Fackenheim rather than Rose who succeeds in witnessing the 'broken middle'.

Playing devil's advocate, I shall now attempt just such a demonstration. The purpose of this comparison is not to vindicate Fackenheim over and against Rose but to perform a *reductio ad absurdum* on the conditions that Rose sets out for holding to the 'broken middle'.

The term 'broken middle' was originally coined by Fackenheim.[37] It is strange that Rose never acknowledges Fackenheim's prior claim to the denomination. This is perhaps because she felt that the respective meanings they each attach to the term are so far apart as to betoken a merely nominal similarity. In fact, as we shall now see, Rose's and Fackenheim's understanding and application of the term are strongly convergent in both method and substance.

For Rose, the 'broken middle' is at once object and subject, *explicandum* and *explicans*, a condition and the means of investigating that condition. *Qua* object, *explicandum* and condition, the term refers to the broken logic of modernity: the 'breaks between universal, particular, singular, in individuals and institutions';[38] *qua* subject, *explicans* and mode of investigation, it denotes the form of speculative inquiry into these 'breaks' as they emerge and fail towards the 'third' implicit in the 'inversions of experience which phenomenology exposits'.[39] For the reasons adumbrated above, Rose insists that the terms of this enquiry must be indirect, ironic and facetious: pitting 'story against story, crisis against crisis'[40] as 'each configured concept is mismatched to its object and corrected by a newly configured concept and mismatched to its object, again – and then again'.[41] However, for Fackenheim, too, the 'broken middle' possesses an intrinsically dialectical character. On the one hand, it refers to the objective breakdown of the terms of the 'Hegelian synthesis' – 'a modern world composed of an unconquerable Christian faith and a boundless secular self-confidence'[42] – and the subsequent polarisation of its constitutive terms ('the flight to extremes'); on the other hand, it denotes the form of systematic but open-ended reflection on this broken actuality. Furthermore, Fackenheim's method, though neither facetious nor ironic, is similar to Rose's in another respect: it too studies the changing configurations of concept and reality from the point of view of their *indirect* manifestation in defining works of the philosophical canon. Fackenheim defines his own hermeneutics as adopting a 'historical-dialectical approach, i.e., to seek out relevant thinkers of the first rank, and to confront their thought with the events to which self-exposure is necessary'.[43]

It will be objected that Rose's *speculative* exposition of the 'broken middle' is nonetheless fundamentally distinct from Fackenheim's *dialectical* presentation of the concept. Whereas Fackenheim develops his exposition in a linear fashion, reading Kierkegaard and Marx as representing the polar extremes of the broken 'Hegelian synthesis', Rose denies that Hegel is in any respect a philosopher of the 'middle' at all; rather she reads Hegel and Kierkegaard together as thinkers of diremption and aporiae. Rose contends that, in contrast to dialectics, phenomenological presentation is unrestricted by considerations of chronology; therefore, it ranges freely across different historical periods and epochs, tracing the genesis and development of concepts in temporally unrelated forms of life in order to reconstruct their meaning and import in terms of their impact on the present.[44] Consistent with this tenet, her own phenomenological authorship employs a transgressive hermeneutic that pays scant respect to the boundaries of intertextual and intratextual context, as exemplified by her treatment of Hegel and Kierkegaard in *The Broken Middle*, which sets out to explore 'the diremption between law and ethics not between but *within* the conceptuality of Hegel *and* Kierkegaard'.[45]

Rose uses the occasion of her re-reading of Hegel and Kierkegaard to develop her own original speculative lexicon, based around four key interconnected terms: 'the equivocation of the ethical'; 'the anxiety of beginning'; 'the agon of authorship' and 'the suspension of the political'. I shall briefly explain the meaning of these terms in turn.

The 'equivocation of the ethical' involves the self-conscious recognition that the well-intentioned acts of moral agents are always liable to be inverted in their effect and this for two reasons: first because of what Benhabib has defined elsewhere as the 'interpretative indeterminacy of action'[46] – since all our actions are open to the interpretation of others they are equally open to misinterpretation and misrecognition such that agents often end up being understood as saying the opposite of what they meant to say; and second, because the imposition of the moral law is always bound up with the exercise of violence, and this renders even 'just' violence deeply equivocal. The 'anxiety of beginning' refers to the fact that we are always already situated within the 'equivocation of the ethical', i.e., in relation to moral and positive law. It is the very equivocality of the ethical that gives rise to anxiety and the desire to cancel this anxiety through the positing of imaginary beginnings and utopian ends. On this account, philosophy must be doubly aware of the danger of establishing itself as the source of a new utopia ungrounded in actuality. The 'agon of authorship', therefore, describes the Socratic predicament of the phenomenological consciousness or author whose task it is to induce her reader ('natural consciousness') to overcome their dependence on heteronomous forms of authority while at the same time avoiding setting herself up as a new authority to be followed or as an icon to be worshipped. The phenomenological author may only avoid this pitfall of 'arrogated' authority through perfecting the art of systematic illusion: withdrawing behind the veil of impersonation, disguise, mask, irony and facetious humour, so as to educe the continual re-education of her reader. Finally, the 'suspension of the political' defines a critical vantage point that allows the phenomenologist fictively to step outside of time for an 'instant' while remaining engaged with time and history. To 'suspend' the political is therefore neither to abolish the political nor to endorse it uncritically. It is rather to create a temporal hiatus which allows for a reconstruction of the political history of the present so as to keep open the possibility that the present may be repeated differently, not backwards in a spirit of loss and resignation, but forwards as something new and transformative.

The originality of Rose's approach, therefore, appears decisively to separate her notion of the 'broken middle' from that of Fackenheim. However, once again, on closer examination things are not so clear cut. For example, Fackenheim draws attention to precisely those passages in Hegel's *Lectures on the Philosophy of Religion* that Rose highlights, where Hegel speaks of the need for philosophers to form a 'separate sanctuary' and 'an isolated order of priests' until such time as the world finds its way out of its 'present state of disruption'.[47] In other words, Fackenheim recognises, no less than Rose, that there is or indeed was no 'Hegelian synthesis': rather the term performs a similar heuristic and counterfactual function to that played by the idea of the 'Absolute' in *Hegel Contra Sociology*. Therefore, although Fackenheim does not use the word, the concept of aporia is at the heart of his reflection on the 'broken middle'. In Fackenheim's own words: 'there can be no compromising the integrity of the extremes in a flat un-Hegelian syncretism';[48] rather philosophical thought must 'locate itself *between* the extremes, and if it can dwell in this precarious location and is not torn asunder, it is because the extremes show a new willingness to be vulnerable'.[49] The conditional nature of these statements belies Rose's charge that Fackenheim glibly believes philosophy has the power to 'mend' the world. On the contrary, Fackenheim maintains that the contemporary world 'is characterised by a fragmentation which is all-pervasive and inescapable'.[50] In the face of this fragmentation, philosophy must situate itself between the 'extremes' of revelation and reason, as personified by the religious thought of Kierkegaard and the philosophy of Hegel and Marx. There can be no question of cancelling one extreme by the other nor of seeking their *Aufhebung*. Fackenheim speaks instead of the need for an 'open-ended dialogue where the outcome is not fixed in advance'.[51] But is this not precisely what Rose herself undertakes in staging a dialogue between Hegel and Kierkegaard so as to 'bring Revelation into philosophy aesthetically, as the incursion of the incomprehensible; philosophically, as triune or aporetic reason – universal, particular, singular'?[52]

The convergence between Rose and Fackenheim becomes even more pronounced with respect to the special place awarded to Judaism within their respective authorships. This is no accident, but represents a necessary development within their mutual Hegelian understanding of the nature of modernity. For Rose and Fackenheim agree, albeit for different reasons, that modern Judaism represents a synecdoche of Hegelian comprehension in a world where the presuppositions of such a universal comprehension no longer obtain.[53] That is to say, both authors understand Judaism to be, as it were, the holy remnant of the Hegelian mediation. Rose expresses her agreement with Fackenheim thus:

> The *modus* of sublimity in which absolute meaning can only be pointed to or referred to, but never adequately expressed in a representation is the point of ultimate affinity between fear and trembling, Hegel's System and Judaism. In Hegel, Judaism is expounded as the religion of the sublime (and it is this – not the Kantian ethical universality attributed to the System – which is

relevant) in which god is said to be utterly remote from the natural world. If, as Fackenheim has commented, this remoteness is balanced by covanental mutuality, which does not 'mediate' but secularises everyday life in minute detail, then that for which de silentio has 'no strength' is already and fully comprehensible – regardless of whether it has been or can be achieved.[54]

That for which *de silentio*[55] has 'no strength' is to go beyond infinite resignation – swimming for or against the tide of infinite pain – to attain self-transcendence through faith – a 'mysterious floating' or remoteness, that far from involving the renunciation of the world, requires total immersion within it, to the point of invisibility. Faith thus defined expresses itself as the manifestation of the 'sublime in the pedestrian absolutely'.[56] Fackenheim draws on Hegel's discussion of Job to convey the same insight: 'One cannot exaggerate the importance of holding to Hegel's view that Judaism contains not only "renunciation" – the surrender of the human servant to the divine lord – but also a "renunciation of renunciation" whereby the finite human is restored in his finitude. (Hegel's Job thus is not unlike Kierkegaard's Abraham.)'[57] Fackenheim speaks of the 'double move of renouncing renunciation even while being *self*-renouncing'.[58] Rose makes the identical point when she states that 'The willingness to sacrifice Isaac brings Abraham to a crisis which does not return him to him*self*[59] but rather leads him to dissolve the fixity of his ego in a new self-relation. It is through this willingness to suffer the violence of risking oneself and others dearest to oneself while retaining absolute trust and confidence in the outcome, thereby eschewing stoic resignation and Christian self-sacrifice in equal measure, that one comes to acknowledge and experience 'the violence in love and the love in violence because the law is in both'.[60]

What Rose refers to as the 'exceptional qualification of the Jews in the stakes of faith'[61] is grounded in the fact that within Judaism the absolute paradox is always already balanced by what Fackenheim calls 'covenantal mutuality'. Revelation in Judaism is both the 'incursion of the incomprehensible' and the transmission of the Law. For Rose and Fackenheim, it is the indissociability of Revelation as event and Revelation as Law that allows for Hegel's speculative comprehension of the dynamic of the divine–human encounter to be detached from its dependence on the Christian dogma of the identity of the human and divine, and carried over into a Judaic conceptual framework that emphasises the *non*-union of the divine and the human. For Hegel, the essence of religion is the *descent* of the divine into the human (a divine self-othering) and the *ascent* of the human to the divine. Fackenheim acknowledges that for Judaism this '"double activity" is not one but two'.[62] However, he immediately adds that within the Judaic tradition the divine–human relation may be understood in a Hegelian sense, to be 'doubly representational', i.e., a 'descent of the one and the ascent of the other, even as both remain other to the other'.[63] Rose is in essential agreement with Fackenheim's Hegelian description of the religious dynamic.

Rose insists that without a boundary there can be no 'middle'; and without a 'middle' no movement, experience or faith. This is why law, far from being opposed to love and grace, is the means of its deliverance: 'Redemption would mean not only that the other, the neighbour is covered by love, is beloved, but that the bounded singularity of both one and the other fails towards the recognition of the sinful self-relation that denies the self-relation of the other in relation to the self – this is the configuration of atonement and forgiveness'.[64] This captures the core meaning of the Judaic idea of *Teshuva*, which Fackenheim defines as: 'a divine-human turning-toward-each-other, despite and indeed because of their persistent and unmitigated incommensurability'.[65]

It is the Law in Judaism that offers an experience of atonement unmediated by the Christian category of sin:

> Always already within the law, the commandment in Judaism is known both in its existence and its content which is negotiable and negotiated. There is therefore no anxiety of beginning or beginning of anxiety: the 'guilt' of being able is not an anxiety of possibility but always the actuality of the individual, because the law is 'actual' – collective, inclusive, contentful; on the one hand, 613 commandments, on the other, perpetual negotiation of their meaning.[66]

Rose goes on to contrast the Jewish and Christian experience of the law: 'The Jew is inside the law, the Christian outside: for the Jew, within the command, atonement is actual and annually renewable; for the Christian, within the anxiety of uncomprehended prohibition, the law is eternal, salvation only posited with sin'.[67] The Jew's primary relation to the law is therefore a non-anxious one – it only *becomes* anxious 'when the law he is always within meets the law without – the law of pagan Roman or Christian state and civil society'.[68] Thus exilic Judaism as a whole and *a fortiori* modern Judaism, whether orthodox or reform, is *made* anxious through its exposure to the prevailing tensions within the general political culture surrounding it.

Fackenheim's account of the genesis of modern Judaism aptly illustrates Rose's thesis. Once again Fackenheim takes his lead from Hegel. For Hegel, just as surely as the founding of the faith of Biblical Hebraism on the fear of the (transcendent) lord inaugurates ancient wisdom, Spinoza's 'oriental' acosmism marks the beginning of modern thought. Citing Gebhard, Fackenheim notes that in the Amsterdam Jewish community, from which Spinoza was famously excommunicated, 'there is for the first time a group of people without pre-determined categories of their own, a people with a ruptured consciousness.

From this ruptured consciousness emerged modern consciousness.'[69] This is perhaps the precise historical point where the 'Jew within the law meets the law without', the point where modern Judaism first became 'anxious'.

The significance of Spinoza for Hegel – and hence for Fackenheim – is that he was the first to affirm the principles of the free modern man: faith in an immanent god knowable through autonomous reason, the virtues of rational self-mastery, high-mindedness, tolerance, courage and self-preservation. Spinoza accuses the Jewish religion of emasculating the Jewish people. He declared that the Jews may only overcome their political impotence either by assimilating into the universal culture of mankind or by restoring their ancient state. Spinoza therefore unwittingly planted the seeds of modern Zionism. However, he himself determined to forsake the world by retreating into a life of pure contemplative reason. If, for Fackenheim, Spinoza embodies the pole of secular self-confidence that constitutes the one 'extreme' of modernity, Franz Rosenzweig represents the other. Rosenzweig's 'new thinking' is of epochal significance for modern Judaism because it brings about an irreversible 'shift from the centrality of the *Torah itself*, to the centrality of Israel *witnessing* the Torah'.[70] The law is no longer given on the basis of authority alone but is in addition attested through an individual commitment to the survival of the Jews as a people. Thus the 'return to revelation' initiated by Rosenzweig and Buber in the 1920s went hand in hand with a reaffirmation of the religious significance of the fact of Jewish existence itself, which, they held, 'not only precedes the commitment to Judaism but also in some way determines it'.[71]

Rose follows Rosenzweig and Fackenheim in holding that the Jew is always within the law, whether her relation to it is affirmative, equivocal, indifferent or negative.[72] Nonetheless, they both sharply repudiate Rosenzweig's representation of Judaism as the 'eternal star' withdrawn from the vicissitudes of history. Fackenheim objects that 'to make Judaism *absolutely* immune to all events except messianic ones is to a priori dismiss the challenge of contemporary events, rather than risk self-exposure'.[73] In similar vein, Rose avers that 'the most existential moment of ethical suspension is the most consistent witnessing of the history of ethical and political actuality'.[74] Rosenzweig's opposition of the eternal star (Judaism) and the eternal way (Christianity), each exposed to its own specific temptations, is unsustainable; for they 'court the same dangers, live in the same world, share the same paradoxes of sacred history because they have mutually related political histories'.[75] Fackenheim fully concurs with this: 'The problematics of modern Jewish thought are intertwined with the problematics of modernity as a whole'.[76] Furthermore, both Rose and Fackenheim agree that these political histories are structured and reconstructable from the standpoint of the present. As Fackenheim put it: 'All genuine dialogical thought begins not in a vacuum but "where one is". Its post-Hegelian setting makes the "where one is" more than an arbitrary personal given but, at the same time, also a given in the Western secular situation.'[77] Likewise, Rose states that 'Repetition, although it "makes something new" is not the embrace of sheer infinite possibility: "for that which is repeated has been"'.[78] In other words, for both thinkers, real possibilities are necessarily determinate.

We see therefore that contrary to first appearances, Rose and Fackenheim share an overlapping concept of the 'broken middle', in terms of both object and method. Nonetheless, they produce strongly opposed political responses to the Holocaust and its aftermath. Rose's disagreement with Fackenheim rests upon four specific objections, some of which I have already touched on above. First, Fackenheim is inconsistent in calling for the renunciation of the whole Western philosophical tradition while being dependent on this tradition to formulate his own argument.[79] Second, Fackenheim opens the 'broken middle' but then proceeds immediately and 'uninhibitedly' to mend it.[80] Third, the form of this 'mending' is 'soteriological and antinomian' and wholly 'unspecified' in terms of 'Its history, its polity, its anthropology, its sociology'.[81] Fourth, Fackenheim's 'call to history', his proclamation of a new imperative to remember the dead (*Zukor*) (the 614th commandment) by returning to Judaism and Zionism, issued without 'irony or embarrassment', represents an arrogation of authority and an unacknowledged violence.[82]

The first objection is exaggerated. As even the brief exposition above shows, Fackenheim does not renounce the intellectual tradition *tout court*, but only its capacity to comprehend the unique evil of the Holocaust. With respect to Rose's second point, Fackenheim nowhere speaks of a 'mended' world. Rather, post-Auschwitz, the task is *to* mend the world. It is not an achieved end but a work to be accomplished. Why, it may be asked, cannot this affirmative stance be taken to exemplify 'repetition forwards', a beginning from 'out of the middle' from within which, post-Auschwitz, modern Jewry finds itself? Fackenheim perhaps more than any other author is a witness of the anguish and anxiety of modern Jewish existence. The call to support the state of Israel is entirely compatible with the continuation of the diaspora and therefore does not represent a flight from the world, but quite the reverse. Apropos this point, Rose's third criticism is also clearly unjust. *To Mend the World* is not intended as a work of political theory; rather, its stated aim is to lay the basis of a 'post-Holocaust Jewish thought'. Fackenheim's supposed failure to specify the political institutions this entails cannot count against his argument any more than the absence of such detail in *The Broken Middle* invalidates the argument of Rose's text. Moreover, Fackenheim makes it clear throughout *To Mend the World* that the existence of the state of Israel is the necessary *presupposition* of his reflection on the 'broken middle' and the means through which it may be overcome. Thus Rose's remarks about antinomianism and soteriology are somewhat one-sided.

We may see, therefore, that Fackenheim's 'call to history' meets the main conditions for bearing the 'equivocation of the ethical', the 'anxiety of beginning' and even the 'suspension of the political' laid down by Rose herself. Fackenheim is evidently risking himself and calls on others to risk themselves, in a spirit of absolute confidence and trust in the future. Moreover, he is doing so not in the abstract but on the basis of a reconstruction of the fate of modern Judaism in the contemporary world. That is to say, he is staking himself from within the 'middle', 'where he is', that defines the possibilities of action open to him and others. And he is doing so in the full awareness that the defence of the Israeli state is necessarily implicated in violence. Is this not a prime instance of the experience of the 'violence in love and the love in violence, and the law in both'?[83] Finally, in the wake of the Holocaust, his decision actively to support and sustain the state of Israel is arguably the clearest possible example of inaugurated over aberrated mourning?[84]

Rose would of course reject this attempt to assimilate her categories to the terms of Fackenheim's argument. For Rose, the absence of irony in Fackenheim's account is no mere stylistic lapse but the ultimate source of their political differences, as she considers it to be indicative of his refusal to 'suspend the political'. Rose contends that the 'suspension of the political' allows one to suspend judgement and act – or 'stake oneself' – without freezing one's action into a position; for, under suspension, one's action does not *posit* anything that would immobilise the ongoing dialectic of individual and historical experience. Rose insists: 'It is this witness *alone* – this always-already knowing yet being willing to stake oneself again – that prevents one from becoming an arbitrary perpetrator or an arbitrary victim; that prevents one, actively or passively, acting with arbitrary violence'.[85] Therefore, the point of Rose's final criticism is that it is Fackenheim's willingness to take a position, without an accompanying ironic and humorous self-reflection on the possible unintended consequences of his own politically conscientious action, which blinds him to the violence implicit in the 'arrogated' authority of his own authorship.

But, as we have seen, Fackenheim is not blind to the actual and potential violence that his stance implies. Moreover, he is enough of a Hegelian to appreciate that the meanings of our actions routinely exceed our intentions. Indeed, and here is the rub, it may be argued that it is precisely because of his awareness of the process of dialectical inversion that he eschews an ironic style in favour of a rhetoric of outrage and indignation.[86] In the face of an epoch-making event, the ironic comprehension of the ironic reversals of history may well demand, irony of ironies, a suspension of irony and facetiousness; for a historical crisis serves to eliminate the space from which irony lives. Is this not perhaps the 'agon' of Fackenheim's authorship? At a critical juncture, to stake oneself and *not* take an ethical position involves a contradiction of the will that cannot be 'suspended'. In periods of heightened historical consciousness, the aesthetic distance granted to the artist at all times is denied to the ethical and political agent. In such times, 'the truth of the intention is just the deed itself',[87] or non-deed, as the case may be. It is difficult to see how, in the face of pressing events, exponents of that admixture of ironic distance and political commitment commended by Rose could in practice avoid adopting courses of action that would not perforce crystallise into determinate (and, indeed, opposing) political positions. In saying this, my aim is not to endorse a Sartrean criterion of political commitment but to point up the subjective nature of Rose's greater claim to mastery over irony.

As we have seen above, Rose repudiates Fackenheim's claim that the Holocaust is a *novum* in history that obliges the world to support the state of Israel as a collective act of expiation for the genocide of European Jewry. In short, she denies that the Holocaust is an 'epoch-making event' in the sense that Fackenheim ascribes to the term. Unfortunately, the application of the terms of Rose's speculative lexicon does not provide the necessary grounds for this, in my view, wholly legitimate judgement. On the contrary, as I have sought to show, they may equally be taken to refute it. In saying this, I am not denying that this is the judgement that Rose in fact makes; only her *entitlement* to make it on the basis of the speculative terms that she presents. Rose's incapacity to ground her judgement reflects the elevation in her late work of the genealogical criterion of life-enhancement – repetition forwards or backwards – over the phenomenological standard of progression towards full mutual self-recognition. Although Rose asserts that the one is inseparable from the other, there is in fact no necessary connection between them. Indeed they fall apart in the course of her own exposition as a result of her attempt to determine the broken relation between the universal and the particular from the side of the particular and the singular, rather than comprehend the particular and the singular from the standpoint of the broken universal.

I do not doubt Rose's commitment to a critical universalism and a pluralist politics. It is this commitment that is the source of her suspicion of an uncritical universalism that claims to have reconciled all particularisms to itself and of all particularisms that seek to isolate themselves from or supplant the universal. The problem, however, is of knowing where to situate oneself as a political agent in the 'middle' that this implies. How can we be sure that in acting even while at the same time 'suspending the political', we are not unwittingly falling back into the 'double dangers' of uncritical universalism and self-interested particularism? Rose, of course, does not see this as a problem.[88] She argues that it is a common mistake of Marxists to believe that they must endlessly defer action until such time as the programme that will 'necessarily' determine the universal interest has been deduced with absolute theoretical precision.[89] This belies the fact that in the meantime they are already, like everybody else, politically involved in a run of 'quotidian practices and cultural rituals'.[90] Political action, on this account, is not limited to membership of parties or political institutions, but extends to include an active, though largely inconspicuous, engagement with the manifold questions of representation that constitute everyday life. Politics, thus defined, is a preparedness to intervene, *without guarantees,* for the good of all – this is to take *the risk* of the *universal* interest'.[91]

However, to my mind, this does not represent a satisfactory response to the problem posed. If we act 'without guarantees', i.e., rational criteria by which to orient our judgement and action, then we have no way of knowing that the universal good we seek to further is not in fact merely a disguised particular interest. The absence of an implied extensional concept of the good in Rose's account renders her concept of the political deeply equivocal in the pejorative sense. Rose hovers between holding that there is a universal interest but one which we are unable to determine with any exactitude, and implying that there is no universal interest but only the play of interested parties and colliding wills. In the latter case, action that 'risks' the universal interest is identified exclusively with the politics of cultural criticism. It is this latter view that predominates in Rose's later writings. The 'middle' that we are to 'fail' towards is not an identification with the balance of social forces that will advance the universal interest of full mutual recognition, but with our own singular relation to politics, aesthetics, law and faith, that will further our individual self-actualization. The accent is placed firmly on the 'how' rather than the 'what'. We may see this in Rose's reading of Rosa Luxemburg,[92] whom she presents as holding to the 'middle' between the standpoint of 'judgement' (reformism) represented by Bernstein and that of 'culture' (centralism) embodied by Lenin. The question is: was the 'middle' to which Luxemburg held *the* middle? In retrospect, it is perhaps more reasonable to suggest that it was Bernstein not Luxemburg who succeeded in holding the 'middle'; for it was he who grasped that the 'third' – the historically determinate progressive possibility immanent within the present – did not lie in the choice of a non-authoritarian form of revolutionary socialism over reformism or Leninism, but between reformism, on the one hand, and the extremes of reactionary authoritarianism and revolutionary socialism (in either of its variants), on the other. What this example illustrates is that, for Rose, holding to the 'middle' in a singular sense need not actually promote the goal of a fully mutual social subjectivity; it is enough that it intends to do so. But if we are not to sacrifice substance to subjectivity, it is clearly not enough. The point of the above comparison between Rose and Fackenheim has been to show that we cannot identify what is to count as 'holding' to the 'broken middle' unless we have a reliable philosophical account of its historical preformation; and that the possibility of such an account is precisely what Rose's 'genealogical turn' places in jeopardy. As a result, her own philosophical reconstruction of the fate of both modernity and Judaism becomes simply one tale of many that may be told.

Conclusion

I recognise that my criticism of Rose relies heavily on the not unchallengeable assumption that there is currently available to us a universal philosophy of history. Sceptics will no doubt object that, alas, such a 'grand narrative' is nowadays not to be had. My response to this objection is that it is indeed the case that a fully-blown metaphysical philosophy of history, claiming knowledge of the efficient and final cause of world history, is both philosophically indefensible and morally dubious. However, in recent years an alternative, non-metaphysical philosophy of history has emerged, proposing a 'weak' teleological interpretation of the modern paradigm, which is both philosophically coherent and ethically permissible and, moreover, necessary.[93]

The 'weak' form of teleology I am appealing to here is not prospective but purely retrospective; it does not involve proffering causal explanations of the past (that task is left to the historians) or indulging in predictive hypotheses about the future; it is rather, the practice of reconstructing the dialectical inter-twinement of justificatory conceptual systems and the forms of life they legitimise, by tracing the pattern of their emergence, development, breakdown and reconfiguration in history.[94] Thus the object of philosophical history is the retrospective significance events come to acquire in the present for the way that we justify our contemporary social practices. It is important to maintain this distinction in order to avoid the anachronism of arguing that forms of life emerge *in order to* conform to the interpretative frameworks of philosophical historians. Rose makes a related point when she rightly insists that the 'search for a decent response to those brutally destroyed' must not be conflated with the 'quite different response called for in the case of the "inhuman" capacity for such destruction'.[95]

Events in history do not have an immanent telos, they happen as a result of the convergence of an infinite number of factors; they become historical only when they enter into narratives, and they become 'world-historical' when they are retrospectively adjudged by the philosophical historian to have completed one decisive historical phase of conceptual development and/or originated another. Pinkard concisely expresses the point when he states that a contingent historical event attains 'world-historical' importance if it can be shown that in retrospect it 'produced a form of self-understanding that is better able to account for itself than its predecessors'.[96]

In proposing a teleology of the Holocaust, therefore, we are not reproducing that 'dismal metaphysic'[97] which holds that the catastrophe occurred in order that we might learn from it. Rather, we are responding to the question: 'Is the Holocaust a "world-historical event"?' That is to say, has it brought about a decisive revision of our conceptual and ethical self-understanding that represents an improvement on that of our predecessors? The answer to this question must be no; but by the same token, neither has it succeeded in completely ruining our ethical capacity. Posing the question in this way also allows for an assessment of Rose's notion of 'inaugurated mourning'. Although the latter is a necessary corrective to cultural pessimism, the idea errs in the opposite direction of appearing too affirmative, too voluntarist and too premature in the light of the traumatic impact that the Holocaust continues to exert upon the modern world. The fact that we can neither perfectly remember nor actively forget the Holocaust ultimately reflects the broken modernity we inhabit. The vocation of philosophical reason therefore is to *make* the Holocaust into a 'world-historical event'. Only then shall we finally be able to emerge from under its terrible shadow. But for this, as Rose has shown, we need more comprehension, not less.

Notes

1 Emil Fackenheim, *To Mend the World*, Bloomington: Indiana University Press, 1984, Introduction, p.xxxiv.

2 Gillian Rose (1947–95) was Professor of Social and Political Thought in the Department of Sociology, University of Warwick. The author of seven books, her collective work constitutes an ambitious, unified philosophical project that seeks to redefine the nature and scope of Critical Theory. Her writings have made important contributions to postmodern legal and political philosophy, social and cultural theory, political theology and the study of the Holocaust. A full assessment of her legacy is now overdue. This essay is intended as a small contribution towards this wider desideratum.

3 Gillian Rose, *The Broken Middle*, Oxford: Blackwell, 1992, pp.101–10. Rose assimilates Freud's notion of perfect memory to Kierkegaard's concept of forward repetition.

4 Gillian Rose, 'From Speculative to Dialectical Thinking – Hegel and Adorno', in *Judaism and Modernity*, Oxford: Blackwell, 1993, p.53.

5 'From Speculative to Dialectical Thinking...', p.53.

6 Robert Pippin, 'You Can't Get There from Here', in *The Cambridge Companion to Hegel*, ed. Frederick C. Beiser, Cambridge: Cambridge University Press, 1993, p.78.

7 For a masterly treatment of Nietzsche's concept of genealogy, see Raymond Geuss, 'Nietzsche and Genealogy', in *Morality, Culture, History*, Cambridge: Cambridge University Press, 1999, pp.1–28.

8 'Is There a Jewish Philosophy?', in *Judaism...*, pp.22–25. See also the discussion in Rose, *Broken...*, pp.288–96.

9 Fackenheim, *To Mend...*, pp.15–19.

10 *Ibid.*, p.238.

11 *Ibid.*, p.14.

12 Preface to the Second Edition, p.xxv.

13 Zygmunt Bauman, *Postmodern Ethics*, Oxford: Blackwell, 1993.

14 Rose, *Broken...*, pp.293–96.

15 *Ibid.*, p.291.

16 *Ibid.*, p.295.

17 *Ibid.*, p.295.

18 Rose develops the distinction between these two terms in her essay 'Walter Benjamin – Out of the Sources of Judaism', in *Judaism...*, pp.175–210.

19 Gillian Rose, *Hegel Contra Sociology*, London: Athlone, 1981, p.45.

20 *Ibid.*, pp.46–47.

21 Immanuel Kant, *Critique of Pure Reason*, trans. Norman Kemp-Smith, London: MacMillan, 1985, B158.

22 Jay Bernstein (*The Philosophy of the Novel: Lukacs, Marxism and the Dialectic of Form*, Brighton: Harvester, 1982, p.85) successfully captures this point when he notes with respect to modern artistic creativity: 'the project of objectifying meaning in a work is then a metaphysical adventure which succeeds on the basis of the defeat of the project as a life'. Increasingly, this observation may be extended beyond aesthetic production to embrace all form-giving acts in modernity.

23 Gillian Rose, *The Melancholy Science: An Introduction to the Thought of Theodor W. Adorno*, London: Macmillan, 1979, p.47.

24 Gillian Rose, *Dialectic of Nihilism*, Oxford: Blackwell,1984, p.3.

25 Gillian Rose, 'Beginnings of the Day – Fascism and Representation', in *Mourning Becomes the Law*, Cambridge: Cambridge University Press, 1996, p.60.

26 In particular, a 'total commodification thesis' is often mistakenly attributed to Adorno on the basis of an overly literal interpretation of certain of his ironically intended passages. For a discussion of Adorno's view on commodification/reification that places his remarks in their proper context, see Simon Jarvis, *Adorno: A Critical Introduction*, Cambridge: Polity, 1998, pp.72–77.

27 Fackenheim, *To Mend...*, p.238: 'The Holocaust is inexplicable – we can only accept it to be possible because it was actual'.

28 *Ibid.*, p.25: 'To hear and obey the commanding Voice of Auschwitz is an ontological possibility, here and now, because the hearing and obeying was already an ontic reality, there and then'.

29 Rose, *Hegel...*, p.69.

30 *Ibid.*, p.119.

31 *Ibid.*, p.187.

32 Rose, 'From Speculative to Dialectical Thinking...'.

33 *Ibid.*, p.59.

34 Rose, *Judaism...*, Preface.

35 'Athens and Jerusalem: A Tale of Three Cities', in *Mourning...*, p.3.

36 Rose, 'Beginnings of the Day...', p.61.

37 Emil Fackenheim (*The Religious Dimension in Hegel's Thought*, Bloomington: Indiana University Press, 1967, Ch.7, 'The Crisis of the Hegelian Middle', pp.223–45) provides an extensive discussion of the 'broken middle', although the actual term is not

used. However, the designation is employed throughout *To Mend the World*.

38 Rose, *Broken...*, Introduction, p.xii.

39 *Ibid.*, p.175.

40 *Ibid.*, p.14.

41 *Ibid.*, p.10.

42 Fackenheim, *To Mend...*, p.119.

43 *Ibid.*, p.20.

44 Rose, *Hegel...*, p.50.

45 Rose, *Broken...*, Introduction (p.xiv).

46 Seyla Benhabib, *Critique, Norm and Utopia*, New York: Columbia University Press,1986, p.136: 'By the interpretative indeterminacy of action I mean that the actions and the intentions embedded in them can only be identified by a process of social interpretation and communication in the shared world. This identification of the "whatness" of an action and the "whoness" of the actor is a social and communicative process intrinsically liable of disputes of interpretation, misconstrual and misident- ification.'

47 Fackenheim, *To Mend...*, p.119. See also the discussion in *The Religious Dimension in Hegel's Thought,* pp.233–35.

48 Fackenheim, *To Mend...*, p.127.

49 *Ibid.*

50 Fackenheim, *The Religious Dimension in Hegel's Thought*, p.235.

51 Fackenheim, *To Mend...*, p.129. See Rose's correlative statement in *The Broken Middle*, 18: 'Revelation leaves the ethical open and unresolved'.

52 Rose, *Broken...*, p.18.

53 Fackenheim, *To Mend...*, p.145: 'the secular religious conflict that elsewhere in the modern world exists *between* the extremes, so far as modern Jewish existence is concerned, exists *within* it'.

54 Rose, *Broken...*, pp.16–17.

55 The pseudonymous author of *Fear and Trembling*.

56 The phrase is *de silentio*'s, cited in Rose, *Broken...*, p.16.

57 Fackenheim, *To Mend...*, p.109, fn.

58 *Ibid.*

59 Rose, *Broken...*, p.16.

60 *Ibid.*, p.148.

61 *Ibid.*, p.111.

62 Fackenheim, *To Mend...*, p.138.

63 *Ibid.*

64 Rose, *Broken...*, p.152.

65 Fackenheim, *To Mend...*, p.141.

66 Rose, *Broken...*, p.100.

67 *Ibid.*, p.101.

68 *Ibid.*

69 Fackenheim, *To Mend...*, p.41.

70 *Ibid.*, p.81.

71 *Ibid.*, pp.83–84.

72 See Rose's discussion of Kafka in *Broken...*, 72–81.

73 Fackenheim, *To Mend...*, p.16.

74 Rose, *Broken...*, p.152.

75 'Franz Rosenzweig – From Hegel to Yom Kippur', in *Judaism...*, p.151.

76 Fackenheim, *To Mend...*, p.101

77 *Ibid.*, p.129 fn.

78 Rose, *Broken...*, p.22.

79 See above.

80 Rose, *Broken...*, p.290.

81 *Ibid.*, p.291.

82 *Ibid.*

83 See note 60 above.

84 Fackenheim's 'Epilogue' to Chapter IV of *To Mend...*, p.313, relates the following story:

> Simha Holzberg is an orthodox Jew and a Hasid. He fought in the Warsaw Ghetto Uprising. He survived, made his way to Israel and prospered. Holzberg, in short, was fortunate. But he was also haunted and without peace, rushing from school to school, kibbutz to kibbutz, synagogue to synagogue, always urging Jews to do more, to mourn more deeply, to remember more profoundly. It was not enough. It could not have been enough. Then came the Six-Day War, and with it its widows and orphans, and Simha Holzberg made the deepest commitment of his life: he became the adoptive father of orphans, vowing to care for them until they were married. Holzberg has remained a man of anguish. The great wound is not healed nor can it be healed. The unprecedented rupture is not 'overcome' or reduced to a 'problem' about to be 'solved' or already solved. But this Israeli Jew has ceased to be haunted. He has even found a measure of peace. When last heard of by this writer, he was already the adoptive grandfather of more than a hundred grandchildren.

85 Rose, *Broken...*, p.148.

86 For Fackenheim's self-reflection on the appropriate language, style and tone for a work dealing with the Holocaust see *To Mend...*, pp.26–28.

87 The quotation is taken from *Hegel's Phenomenology of Spirit*, trans. A.V. Miller, Oxford: Oxford University Press, 1977, § 159.

88 'Beginnings of the Day...', p.61, 'The question "What ought I to do?" is valid within the mesh of theory and practice. Some of my students still pose it: whatever the particular class position of the individual, they yearn to find the mode of effective political action which will *necessarily* further the universal interest.' Some of her students pose it still, albeit not precisely in this way.

89 *Ibid.*, p.61.

90 *Ibid.*

91 *Ibid.*, p.62.

92 Rose, *Broken...*, pp.198–216.

93 See Robert Pippin, *Modernism as a Philosophical Problem: On the Dissatisfactions of European High Culture*, Oxford: Blackwell, 1991 and Terry Pinkard, *Hegel's Phenomenology: The Sociality of Reason*, Cambridge: Cambridge University Press, 1996.

94 The following remarks are indebted to Pinkard's discussion of Hegel's historical teleology in *Hegel's Phenomenology*, pp.333–43.

95 Rose, 'Beginnings of the Day...', p.43.

96 Hegel, *Phenomenology*, p.336.

97 The phrase is Theodor W. Adorno's, taken from his essay 'Commitment', in *The Essential Frankfurt School Reader*, ed. Andrew Arato and Eike Gebhardt, Oxford: Blackwell, 1978, p.313.

CHAPTER 4

Good against Evil?
H.G. Adler, T.W. Adorno and the
Representation of the Holocaust

JEREMY ADLER

There are several worthwhile reasons for considering H.G. Adler in terms of the current debate about the Nazi genocide.[1] Not only did he begin to reflect on the problem of representing these events at an early date when, in 1942, he was deported, but his views, even when not cited, have been deeply implicated in the current discussion, whether because of their role in confrontation with Adorno's philosophy, or because they are, albeit unwittingly, echoed almost word for word by Zygmunt Bauman in *Modernity and the Holocaust*.[2] There is, so to speak, a public side to H.G. Adler's role in the study of the extermination of the Jews, marked by the innumerable books, essays, articles, and reviews which he published, and also an unknown aspect, which it is time to examine.

H.G. Adler is frequently cited as a source in the German-speaking world. Thus, for example, in an open letter to Hannah Arendt published in the *Neue Zürcher Zeitung* in 1963,[3] Gershom Scholem invokes him as a standard reference; but it is also as a witness that he is invoked, as when Hermann Levin Goldschmidt refers to him in *Das Vermächtnis des deutschen Judentums* (The Heritage of the German Jews) where Adler's *Theresienstadt* monograph serves him as the sole example of a Jewish testimony from the camps.[4] Goldschmidt calls his book 'invaluable, not only as a voice of Jewish self-definition, but even more important as a voice of Jewish self-reflection and self-examination'. Thirty years later, when the voices of other survivors had become widely known, Peter Demetz wrote: 'I see Adler in the Shoah as a companion to Primo Levi and Elie Wiesel'.[5] This evaluation led Demetz to conclude his chapter on Adler in his book *After the Fires* with the words: 'It is one of the great intellectual scandals of our time that his most important books, both the personal ones and those in search of historical truth, have yet to be translated into English.'[6]

71

Good against Evil?

Adler's literary and scholarly work passes unnoticed in English and American texts like Langer's – admittedly selective – *The Holocaust and Literary Imagination*[7] and Friedländer's *Probing the Limits of Representation*,[8] which both take Adorno's dictum that there should be no art after Auschwitz as their starting point. They may, as in Langer's case, refute it with respect to art,[9] but even Langer's refutation to some extent affirms Adorno's pessimism in upholding the view that 'men were driven to choose survival at the expense of their humanity, creating a kind of solipsistic animality as the supreme value',[10] as if this were a necessary truth. This has been powerfully contradicted by Hermann Langbein, the Auschwitz resistance fighter, historian of Auschwitz, and chronicler of the Frankfurt Auschwitz trial. As Langbein maintains, people in Auschwitz who were 'defencelessly exposed to a seemingly invincible power, found the resources to resist it'; the most absolute betrayal of human values 'did not rule supreme', and this provides ground for 'hope'.[11] However, a widespread pessimism that overlooks this possibility ensures that Adorno's perspective dominates the current debate. As Gillian Rose forcefully argues, Adorno's writing is celebrated as 'the gospel of aporetics, of non-identity'. For many thinkers, even his opponents, his argument defines the parameters of modernity and the debate about how the 'Final Solution' can be represented. Consequently, contrary voices which cannot be located in terms of this definition, such as Adler's or Langbein's, have been excluded from the current discussion. In Adler's case, the reason lies specifically both in his aesthetics and in his ethics as well as in his method.

The aesthetic point can clearly be seen by comparing the treatment of other voices in the books by Friedländer and Langer. In both works, Paul Celan receives due attention; oddly, however, neither mentions a truly great poetic voice who actually experienced the camps, the Yiddish poet Itzhak Katzenelson. Katzenelson wrote his harrowing threnody, *The Song of the Exterminated Jewish People*, in the French concentration camp Vittel, and successfully hid it there before being transported to his death in Auschwitz in 1944.[12] Similarly, Langer and Friedlander also refer to Sylvia Plath, but not to the Jewish poet, Gertrud Kolmar, who died in Auschwitz.[13] There is something uncomfortable about documentary utterances which are also great art, like the poems of Katzenelson and Kolmar, that prevents their assimilation into a debate broadly based on the belief that there can be no art after Auschwitz, let alone art during Auschwitz. Katzenelson, in adopting the voice of a psalmist, writes with an aesthetic profoundly antithetical to that of the 'no art after Auschwitz' school, which virtually precludes him from being cited in contemporary discussions. Kolmar's late poems, written in Berlin before her deportation, adhere to a similar aesthetic of lament. Friedlander's preface details some of the parameters which, perhaps unintentionally, exclude writers like Katzenelson, Kolmar, Langbein and Adler from the current debate. For example, he approvingly quotes David Carroll's claim that 'we do not have the system of belief, the historical certainty or the philosophical or political concepts necessary to derive or determine judgement ...when it comes to the Shoah'.[14] There is a profound contradiction in this widespread view. Did we not possess precisely these categories, we would have no means of judging that a crime had taken place, let alone a crime of such enormity. The fact that the crime defies our normal system of belief, our senses, our empathy, our judgement and all our categories, does not invalidate that system as such. On the contrary, the existence of the abnormal can only be recognised by categories like these, and anyone who claims that a monstrous event occurred implicitly relies on them, however inadequate they may be. The fact that, as Gillian Rose argues (in Adornoesque terms) 'Reason, the critical criterion, is forever without ground',[15] does not invalidate reason. Rose precisely pinpoints the issue in *Judaism and Modernity*:

> Rome haunts the *agon* between Athens and Jerusalem, but only the imperial Roman eagle has been admitted, while the Rome which invented private property law, the law of persons, and separated it from citizenship is forgotten because so familiar. In the eagerness to eschew the metaphysics of subjectivity, recent philosophy and Jewish philosophy lose the means to discern the structuring of our anxiety, the modern mix of freedom and unfreedom in civil society...[16]

Against what I would call the fallacy of negativism, H.G. Adler's work seeks to argue the opposite position, ultimately grounded in his Jewish faith, that a system of beliefs, ethical values and the basic political concepts of human rights and democracy do make sense. Their abuse, however terrible, did not destroy them. If they failed us, they require re-examination, historically and conceptually, not condemnation, whether naïve, reflected or dialectical. I will return to this problem shortly, by treating the ultimate failure of communication between Adorno and H.G. Adler, who shared several points of contact, as exemplary of this wider dilemma. For it is time to reflect upon those taboos tacitly erected in discussions about representing the 'Final Solution', which have enabled works of the kind commended by Adorno to gain widespread currency – broadly speaking, those which can be accommodated to a wider cultural negativism – whilst ignoring others that contradict these categories and assert the ultimate sovereignty of the good.

Hans Günther Adler did not appear singled out for the fate which was to shape his life and work. Born in Prague in 1910 into the same German-speaking community that had produced Rilke and Kafka, he seemed destined to lead the life of a poet, a career for which his pre-war literary friendships with Franz Baermann Steiner, Hermann Grab and Elias Canetti boded well. Professionally, he planned to be an academic, specialising in literature, although he studied musicology. Nothing more clearly shows his place in the German tradition than the fact that he was in Berlin collecting material for his dissertation on 'Klopstock and Music'[17] when he became a witness to Hitler's *Machtergreifung* in 1933. The rise of the Nazis put paid to his career, yet his plans to emigrate fell through. In August 1939, he managed to obtain a train ticket to Paris, but no visa for France, let alone an entry permit into Great Britain, and was trapped in Prague at the outbreak of the war. He endured a period of forced labour building a railway in 1941, as recorded in chapter eight of the novel *Panorama*. Back in Prague later that year, he married his first wife, Gertrud Klepetar. They were deported to Theresienstadt together with Gertrud's parents on 8 February 1942, where they were imprisoned for two-and-a-half years. As we now know occurred with others destined to survive, Adler derived strength from the need to bear witness, and specifically from the desire to represent his experiences. In an interview for German television in 1986, he recalled:

> When it came to the deportations, I told myself: I won't survive this. But if I do survive, I want to represent it, and in two different ways: I want to explore it in a scholarly manner and so separate it from myself completely, and I want to portray it in a literary manner. I have done both, and the fact that I have done so is no great achievement, but it does provide a small justification for having survived...[18]

Transforming his experiences into literature was a survival strategy: 'It was an act of self-liberation. I always said to myself: if I have to go under, I want to go under with decency... I wanted to preserve my dignity.'

He acted on this belief with a perilous equanimity, which several times led almost beyond the brink of the very disaster from which it finally extricated him. He told the following anecdote:

> An SS-man wanted to beat me because I had done something awkward. I said to him: 'Could you wait a moment, please. I just want to take off my glasses.' The chap really waited. Of course he beat me, but not as badly as he would have done, and that was that. Those were my personal reactions. I knew that it could destroy me, but I just behaved like that and it gave me a lot of strength.[19]

On 12 October 1944, he was transported to Auschwitz with his wife and her mother. On the ramp, Gertrud's mother was sent to the 'bad side'. Gertrud joined her, so that she might accompany her mother into death. H.G. Adler was placed in the so-called 'Gypsy Camp'. After a fortnight he was dispatched to outlying camps of Buchenwald, where he was liberated on 13 April 1945.

The first literary transposition of these experiences occurred in over 130 poems, only a selection of which have been published.[20] About 100 were written in Theresienstadt, and the rest followed immediately after Auschwitz. Initially, in a sequence entitled *Theresienstädter Bilderbogen* (Theresienstadt Picturebook) written in spring 1942, Adler attempted to capture the physical details of the cruelties he witnessed; to do so, he used language with an expressionistically heightened precision: he describes the emaciated bodies of the living, the '*Herde*' (human cattle)[21] with their '*gegerbte Gerippe*' (tanned ribs) and '*mit hängender Lippe*' (hanging lips),[22] or the 'rotting corpse of an old woman' ('*Ein greises Weib fault auf dem Leichenkarren*').[23] The poems convey a set of physical images of the kind that, after the liberation of Belsen in 1945, imprinted themselves on the collective imagination as the emblems of the 'Final Solution'. They show the bodily torment of human beings condemned to extermination. Besides physical details the poems evoke an all-pervasive sense of fear and a tangible, suffocating feeling of anguish. The heavy stress in the lines literally chokes the reader's breath in verses like '*Die Angst verschwimmt in dicker Glut*' (Fear dissolves in a fat glow) and '*In engen Gassen haust der Tod*' (Death dwells in cramped lanes)[24] The diction approaches reality with nauseous vividness:[25]

> *Durch Klumpen Dreck gespült, mit qualmenden Gesichtern*
> *In Käfige gehetzt, sich Leiber quetschen,*
> *Ein Brei zerkochter Not mit stieren Augenlichtern*
> *Und schlaffen Schnauzen, die irr fletschen.*
> *Es züngeln Schreie, gierig aufgespalten,*
> *Zur Nacht mit gleißendem Erkalten.*

> Swilled through clods of filth, with smoking faces,
> Driven into cages, bodies squash,
> A pulp of suffering boiled to rags with staring eyes
> And torpid snouts that crazily gnash their teeth.
> Screams dart from the tongue, greedily split,
> At night with the glistening cold.

The clotted, suffocating diction, which evokes the victims in terms of dirt and animal imagery ('snouts'), stresses the physicality of their suffering. The speaker of these poems displays abundant pity for the victims, but as the poems unroll their catalogue of torment, they reach the limits of representation. The impossibility of representing the unimaginable in terms of physical detail and the ferocity of emotion produced by the events seem to have led H.G. Adler to a reorientation in his writing; in a remarkable change, his aesthetic underwent a reversal and his poetry entered a new, major phase. He now wrote with a technical virtuosity that would have been noteworthy even if he had not been incarcerated, as if refusing to allow the involuntary experiences that decided his fate to affect his spirit. Outwardly, he returned to the quasi-antiquated mode of the German Baroque, and thereby reclaimed his right as a Jew and as a native speaker to one of the most potent moments in the German poetic tradition from which his captors were attempting to excise him. Despite the historical distance, the style was appropriate insofar as it belonged to that other epoch of devastation in Germany, the Thirty Years War, and echoed earlier poets of suffering, Andreas Gryphius and Johann Christian Günther. To overcome the material depredation of his surroundings, Adler turned now to the most difficult of all stanza-forms, such as *terza rima*, but handled them with innovative freedom: the fixed form correlates to his physical imprisonment; the virtuosity – recalling Rilke's liberation of the sonnet – celebrates the speaker's spiritual freedom. This can be seen in lines like the following, where the poet's voice vows to escape his captors, and, in so doing, leaps across the normal poetic structures:[26]

> *...hämisch schleichen*
> *Die Büttel um dich, böses Pack,*
> *Sie schwuren dir den Tod. Jedoch entweichen*
>
> *Wirst du der Meute...*

> ...maliciously,
> The stooges creep around you, wicked pack,
> They swore to kill you. Yet you will
>
> Escape their treachery...

The lines re-enact both the cunning cruelty of the stooges and the triumphantly anticipated escape from their clutches. Yet if the artificial form of such poems recalls the Baroque, the voice depends on a newer concept of subjectivity (which entered German poetry with Adler's admired namesake, Johann Christian Günther) and reached its apogee at the height of the Enlightenment in Goethe's *Erlebnislyrik*: it is this subjective sense of self which gives the expression of pain in these poems their keen, if unbearable, edge of authenticity. Moreover, reconstructing a subjective human self – of the kind Adorno was to question – enables Adler to oppose his fate with the moral categories of good and evil.

The significance of the turn from the outer to the inner perspective in Adler's poetry cannot be exaggerated, not least since it enables him to rescue a sphere of goodness within the subject. The turn marks an aesthetic shift which distinguishes his writing from much other poetry of the camps. His gesture implies that to focus on observable details remains external, and in effect adopts the perspective of the perpetrators by treating the sufferers as physical victims. The reader, correlatively, becomes a voyeur: our outrage rails against the materiality of the crime without regard to the spiritual identity of the victim. Similarly, concentrating on the sheer number of victims – as we do when contemplating photographs of inmates or corpses, or reflecting on the numbers of the dead – defines the enormity of the crime, without regard to the uniqueness of the individual sufferers. Such a viewpoint, given the scale of the sufferings, needs no defence. However, its disadvantage is that it metaphysically reasserts the position of the perpetrators and perpetuates their own master-slave ideology: the perspective of the prisoners as victims becomes absolute at the expense of their humanity. Memory condemns the victims to everlasting subjugation – a central, but, I think, largely unreflected aporia of our collective remembrance. If the victims are to be understood as people, this can only be achieved by imagining their inner selves: the gesture may retrospectively reinstate their humanity, and remove them, at least in memory, from the clutches of their murderers. The reversal of perspective in Adler's camp poetry signifies such a freeing of the victims from their chains, metaphysically if not actually, and their reinstatement no longer as objects of the actions of others but as spiritually free agents, i.e., human subjects. Both aesthetically and ethically, therefore, this is a poetry of protest and affirmation: a protest against inhumanity and the collapse of values that brought it about; an affirmation of human worth, even in Hell.

It was in the camps, too, that H.G. Adler – like Eugen Kogon, the author of the first full study of the Nazi machinery – began to collect material for a scholarly representation of the genocide, which he then wrote in 1945–48 and eventually published in 1955 as *Theresienstadt 1941–1945*.[27] The monograph is one of the earliest attempts to create a sociology 'after the Holocaust', as indicated by its subtitle 'History – Sociology – Psychology'. Constructed like a classic ethnographic field-study in the manner of Malinowski's monographs on the Trobriand Islands, *Theresienstadt 1941–1945* attempts a detailed, empirical reconstruction of the camp, its history, its functioning, and its institutions, and concludes with a general analysis of Nazi ideology, interpreted as a perfidious, highly specific yet in some ways also typical manifestation of modernity and what Adler calls its 'mechanical materialism'. A foundational work in Holocaust studies, the book does not, against the author's intentions, appear to have fed into mainstream post-war sociology.

Around this central book, a host of other publications clustered, which together, in Jürgen Serke's phrase, add up to a single *Gesamtkunstwerk*:[28] the popular study *Die Juden in Deutschland* (The Jews in Germany)[29] describes the long path into catastrophe; the *magnum opus* of 1974, *Der verwaltete Mensch* (The Administration of Man)[30] takes up the story, and treats the entire process of deportation; the intractible dilemma of Auschwitz is illuminated in a volume of eye-witness accounts;[31] one study deals with Hitler;[32] another portrays the resistance to the 'Final Solution';[33] and a host of major essays examine related issues of political philosophy, like the baneful influence of Nietzsche.[34] Here Adler attempts a critique of the modern ideology of the 'masses'[35] and seeks to buttress human rights, centring them on a reassessment of individual freedom. Methodologically, these works encompass a similarly huge span, from first-person accounts and documentation to statistical, medical, sociological, cultural, and metaphysical analyses. Simultaneously, Adler's literary works focus on and move beyond these lamentable events. The novel *Panorama*,[36] first written in 1948 and published in 1968, treats his life from childhood through the labour camp and Auschwitz, and on to England. The unpublished *Die Ansiedlung* (The Colony) examines Theresienstadt, which is omitted from *Panorama. Eine Reise* (A Journey),[37] written in 1950 and published in 1962, shows the deportation to Theresienstadt, the transport to Auschwitz, Gertrud's death in the gas chamber, and his own liberation. The novel *Die unsichtbare Wand* of 1954, which was published posthumously, then looks back on the events from the viewpoint of a survivor, desperate to communicate his experiences to an uncomprehending world in his 'sociology of the oppressed'. As a meditation on the possibilities of a sociology of the Holocaust, *Die unsichtbare Wand* – inter alia – reviews the cataclysm in terms of values:

> The dignity of man is guaranteed by the assignation of material and non-material values, bestowed on the individual by society. The complete attainment of this dignity corresponds to the optimum of freedom from oppression which society permits. Any person is oppressed, who is denied or deprived of inner or outer values. The more powerful this deprivation of values, the less free the individual. Deprivation of rights and exploitation, servitude and slavery are defined by a specific deprivation of values.[38]

The discussion here connects with the treatment of values in the final chapter of *Theresienstadt 1941–1945*, which analyses in detail the Nazi system of values, or rather 'non-values' (*Unwerte*), according to which Jews and others were initially assigned a purely negative value as a prelude to their physical extinction (pp.634ff.).

As such parallels indicate, the fiction and the scholarship are closely linked. Indeed, Rüdiger Görner stresses,[39] and Peter Stern tellingly observes, how the different modes of representation reciprocally illuminate one another.[40] The fiction sometimes exhibits the character of historical documentation (notably the Auschwitz chapter of *Panorama*, which has been cited as a historical source)[41] and the scholarship is throughout composed in a literary manner (thus *Theresienstadt*, though written as a documentation, has the structure of a novel). The monumentality which is so striking a feature of Adler's books (*Der verwaltete Mensch* is a thousand pages long) turns them into what *Theresienstadt* was the first to state explicitly: that is, memorials to the dead. The dedication of *Theresienstadt* to the memory of Gertrud and of *Der verwaltete Mensch* to that of Adler's parents are, however, almost the only personal details in these scholarly works, which are written with almost unbearable objectivity, whereas the novels are correlatively subjective in their almost excessive focus on the perspective of the central figure: in *Panorama* it is Josef who provides an unusually rigorous organising consciousness for the narrator, and in *Die unsichtbare Wand* it is Landau's self-centredness which dominates the point of view in his attempt to publish his 'sociology of the oppressed'. The complementary handling of subjective and objective perspective in the scholarly and literary modes has as its counterpoint the technique of balancing massive sections of divergent material within a single book – perhaps inspired by the work of Adler's Jewish sculptor friend, Bernard Reder – and this same device also serves to connect the various texts into a coherent oeuvre. If, as Heinrich Böll observed, *Der verwaltete Mensch* is 'an encyclopaedia of the deportations',[42] it would be fair to call Adler's complete works, amounting to thirty volumes in all, 'an encyclopaedia of the pogroms' (though, as will shortly be seen, this term is somewhat limiting). The whole enterprise is bounded by a theological study which Adler first began to write in a series of letters to England under the threat of impending disaster in 1938, and which fifty years later became in its final form his last publication, *Vorschule für eine Experimentaltheologie* (Introduction to an Experimental Theology).[43] The book came out in the year before Adler's death. Its ideas, tested and developed under extreme circumstances, served as the spiritual foundation of his work.

After liberation, Adler returned to Prague, where he first worked as a tutor for children from the camps and subsequently at the Prague Jewish Museum. In 1947 he fled to England in the face of a likely Communist take-over and settled in London. A few friends assisted Adler as he sought to bear witness, yet it seems inconceivable today how difficult a task it was, how little moral support he received – there was no question of financial aid! – and how much opposition he encountered. Alfred Wiener provided practical assistance at the Wiener Library; Leo Baeck, who had befriended him in Theresienstadt, offered moral support; and Hermann Broch joined the search for a publisher, approaching Hannah Arendt for assistance, but without success. With a handful of notable exceptions, the scholarly establishment proved at best indifferent, and at worst hostile. The noted Jewish historian, Cecil Roth, poured scorn on the plan to write a lengthy monograph on Theresienstadt, given its 'minuscule' significance in the history of the Jews. However, the seven-year quest for publication was followed by immediate success and the book established itself as the best single study of any Nazi camp.[44] It attracted the interest both of noted Germans, such as President Heuss, and Jews, such as Martin Buber. Indeed, its historical impartiality was held in such regard that in Germany it was treated as legal evidence of the 'Final Solution' and was used as the documentary basis for passing the compensation laws.[45] In Israel, at the instigation of the authorities, it was read before his trial by Adolf Eichmann to remind him of his role in the genocide.

The hallmark of Adler's method lies in combining scholarly documentation in an objective style with intellectual analysis and an ethical viewpoint. This entails not only a critique of the Nazis but also, in the manner of the prophets, a condemnation of Jewish failures. Two additional features similarly stand out. The first is the effective demonstration that the 'Final Solution' arose directly out of the character of modernity, and specifically from bureaucracy, administration, and technology, as well as from political ideology and materialism;[46] in this analysis, he shares much ground with Adorno, as he signalled by the echoing of Adorno's concept of 'die verwaltete Welt' (the administered world) in the title of *Der verwaltete Mensch*. Secondly, Adler attached to this critical analysis proposals to prevent the disastrous consequences of modernity from becoming its paradigm. For example, in recognising the failure of the Enlightenment, he did not dismiss it out of hand but tried to disentangle the precise intellectual and historical causes of particular effects, whether in the French Revolution or in Montesquieu's theory of the state, and then to propose clearly defined remedies.[47] This method, then, is one which I would call *practical memory*: the writer re-members the fractured past in the light of history, in order to safeguard the future. In distinguishing specific errors in Enlightenment thought, he remained free – as Demetz has recognised – to ally himself with the radical Enlightenment, as represented by Moses Mendelsohn, and therefore to develop, not reject, the tradition of German-Jewish humanism. However, no less radically than Scholem denied that there had ever been a German-Jewish 'dialogue',[48] Adler opposed any attempt to create a new national symbiosis, whilst aiming to achieve a new and fruitful dialogue.

Ethic and method probably combined to prevent the book's absorption by English and American sociology. A character in *Die unsichtbare Wand* pinpoints some of the obstacles that Adler's sociology faced in the British academic context:

My interest in your sociological ideas is undiminished, even if I myself have entered a completely different stream in the British and American schools. To tell you the truth, I doubt whether you and your methods, as one says here, are up-to-date. Over here, people usually laugh about continental sociology, and not without reason.[49]

Both the method and the fact that the sociology, like the fiction, attempts a restatement of values in the face of the Shoah, will have made it highly unfashionable in terms of British social sciences in the 1940s and 1950s. This may explain why this early attempt to engage sociology with the Shoah could remain unattended by the discipline, leaving Zygmunt Bauman to draw his own, well-known conclusions.

As John and Ann White were the first to recognise, Adler's novels are similarly unusual in embedding the literary portrayal of the camps into a wider frame, whereas most representations treat *l'univers concentrainnaire* as a negative *telos*. In *Panorama*,[50] *Die unsichtbare Wand*, and to some extent even in *Eine Reise*, Adler treats it at a greater distance, in the wider context of European history and in relation to the post-war years. This does not amount to a relativisation of the kind advocated by Ernst Nolte at the beginning of the *Historikerstreit*. On the contrary, Adler remains painfully conscious of the uniqueness of the disaster he narrates. Indeed, his narratives are shot through with an awareness, which is not present in Primo Levi's earliest writings, of both the historical and the metaphysical dimension of events.

Jean-François Lyotard, in a famous passage, has compared the Jewish cataclysm to an earthquake:[51]

Suppose that an earthquake destroys not only lives, buildings, and objects but also the instruments used to measure earthquakes, directly and indirectly. The impossibility of quantitatively measuring it does not prohibit, but rather inspires in the minds of the survivors the idea of a very great seismic force. With Auschwitz something new has happened in history...

The idea of a catastrophe which destroys both human life and the very possibility of measurement recalls Adler's earlier image of the cataclysm in terms of a natural disaster which obliterates human life, its paths, and the very signposts which should signify them; in *Die unsichtbare Wand*, in a passage first noted by Serke,[52] Adler writes of his main character:

A surviving person at a signpost, scorned by disaster in a deadly snowstorm; when the storm had moved on, all his companions had been frozen to death, the signpost is shattered, no destinations can be deciphered on its fragments, and the paths themselves have ceased to exist...[53]

Like Lyotard's 'earthquake', Adler's 'snowstorm' entails a total, almost wholly inescapable disaster, which destroys both the underlying reality (paths), its signs (names), and the very possibility of signification (signposts): the shattered signpost, standing for spatial orientation, indicates that all direction is destroyed. The physical disaster embeds an equal, metaphysical loss. The novel, *Eine Reise*, similarly presents life after Auschwitz in terms of a devastation in which semiotic images interlock with the tortured horrors of narrative, to reflect dislocation. Ghastly emblems of the body impugn the emptiness of the soul:

> ... what the hacked-off hands say, has no meaning. They do not signify, they lack thought, empty direction does not signify any goal. So everything is meaningless.

> The eye searches once again, and then it discovers names by the hands. Once, paths were meant. But there are no paths. The paths don't say anything, they have faded, the colour has drained from the names, they have been severed from the hands, just dust-covered stumps. And when the gaze wishes to reconnect hands and names, it cannot recognise how they belong together, they are so damaged, they aren't right any more. But there are no owners, either ...[54]

The narrative, heavily reliant on the tradition of visual art, introduces a new form of image with which to capture the historical fissure: the self-cancelling emblem. The grotesque interlocking of semiotic and physical reality symbolically laments a world bereft of meaning; but the text at this point painfully avoids the obvious imagery of the age – stacked bodies, smoking chimneys, human ashes, barbed wire, watch-towers – reverting instead to the vivid details of the kind depicted by Callot and Goya in their sequences on the horrors of war, in order to interpose a reflective distance between the reader and the present day, without sacrificing anything of its visceral terror. Moreover, the categorical interlocking of the horrific detail (the severed hands and the bleeding stumps) with spatial and semiotically orientated ideas (pointing and naming) imbues the burden of pain with a sophisticated theoretical import. Besides Callot and Goya, one senses in this passage the presence of Picasso's *Guernica*, with its physical horrors and semiology of pointing and looking (there denoted by arms, hands, eyes, and mouths). However, in *Eine Reise*, the entire aftermath of war is captured in the single synecdoche of the hacked-off hand, which provides the central emblem for this passage. The Jewish calamity, from the survivor's perspective – represented by the similarly synecdochal 'eye' – merges with the universal catastrophe in which both parties are maimed, both are perpetrators, and both ultimately are victims (though, as will become clear shortly, this certainly does not entail an equation of suffering between the two sides). The use of an allusively visual technique, moreover, embeds the almost medieval image of torture into the aesthetic scenery of modernity: at issue is not some single, framed act of barbarity, but more widely a culture of barbarism.

Besides the visual echoes, the semiotic imagery locates the barbarity in a culture typified by a clearly definable mode of reflectivity, a concern with 'naming' which turns the metaphor of the 'hand' into an emblem. The severed hand evokes cruelty, impotence, waste, and rupture; and it is the paradoxical failure to 'signify' that translates the image into a self-cancelling emblem which represents the collapse of all meaning, the impossibility of signification, and the reduction of life to a moment of inexpressible suffering. What Lyotard will call 'the dismantling of the bastion of signification' is fully anticipated here, though not with Lyotard's bloodless negativism.[55] Accordingly, Adler's representation encompasses both a vividly real survivor-account and a highly intellectual reflective account.

The novels approach the catastrophe in related but differing ways. Like the poems they assert their artistic independence in formal terms, refusing to use the obvious first-person narrative of the survivor-account; instead, they are grounded in the modernist tradition of Kafka, Joyce, and Broch. They de-familiarise events by avoiding references to any national stereotypes, whether 'Jewish' or 'German', and by employing a host of techniques – documentation, montage, stream-of-consciousness, irony, lyricism – in order to mediate the unimaginable. The disaster experienced by others thereby becomes onto-logically problematic for the reader.

As Langer observes, writers on the 'Final Solution' evolve very different techniques for representing the changed world: 'an implacable past encroaches on all attempts to restore imaginative...tranquillity', and 'assaulted the very notion of temporal sequence'. [56] This also applies to *Panorama, Eine Reise* and *Die unsichtbare Wand* which, especially in the latter novels, challenge traditional notions of time and narrative. They evolve complementary methods of depicting the unspeakable, as can be seen in the three very different ways that they represent Auschwitz. Different styles capture the same events, which leads to different representations: the first may be called 'spiritual witnessing'; the second, to use Adler's own term, involves 'lyrical irony'; and the third entails 'reflective distancing'. The categories are not entirely separate, as the modes alternate and overlap; nonetheless each one produces a very different type of image.

Panorama offers the most direct portrayal, but even here the novel employs Adler's characteristic distancing device by abstaining from the standard categories such as 'Jew', 'German', 'Prisoner', 'Guard', 'SS' and so on. Isolated references like '*Juden*' (p.485) or '*Sonderkommando*' (p.482) would suffice to contextualise the novel, were that necessary. Here, the reader is confronted with the 'Lost Ones' and their oppressors, the 'Conspirators':

> Among the Lost Ones, all forms have become invalid, for decay is formless, and the lost ones have been condemned to decay, their hair was clipped off, it was scraped from their bodies with blunt instruments, the Lost Ones were undressed in Birkenau, their shoes and clothes lie on the cold concrete floor like fat dung; it is a large hall, the Lost Ones are standing there naked and freezing, two heavily armed Conspirators are trotting around on the clothes, they rummage around in the pockets looking for money ...[57]

In the place of the usual ideological stereotypes, the novel's categories impose a moral framework on the events which operates independently of nationality and religion. The breathless 'panoramatic' style which runs throughout the novel reflects the perceptions of the hero, Josef Kramer, whose surname echoes Adler's own, whilst his first recalls his biblical namesake who similarly found himself dispatched into slavery. Correlatively, Josef Kramer takes a moral, religious attitude to his fate. His factual witnessing is shot through with two contradictory tendencies: satire, directed against the perpetrators; and ennoblement, directed towards their victims. Thus, the 'Conspirators' are trapped by an accuracy of terminology at odds with their own perverted diction, and the 'Lost Ones' are elevated by the dignity of truthfulness. These opposing tendencies merge in the depiction of the gas chambers. The satire on the perpetrators, which voices the victim's ethical superiority, merges with praise for the dead on whom the narrative bestows retrospective dignity. The 'Lost Ones' become sacrificial victims and are referred to as 'Consecrated' ('*Geweihte*'), while the gas chambers in a cruelly sublime neologism become a '*Mordtempel*' (Temple of Murder). Whilst maintaining the horror of the events, the narrative voice rescues the victims from the meaninglessness imposed on them by the 'Conspirators' and elevates them into the religious sphere ('*Tempel*') of their fathers:

> Undressed and hardly covered, the Consecrated Ones are transported by lorry, the Conspirators don't let their tired feet walk much further, carefully they count the Consecrated Ones off on their lists, order is always met, now the Consecrated Ones are driven on a final journey through the camp of the Lost Ones up to the Temple of Murder made of concrete, they are unloaded between the flower-beds of the front garden, they are driven or carried down a number of steps...[58]

The affectionate tenderness towards the victims grants them in death the solicitude they actually deserved in life, reinterpreting the Conspirators' cattle-trucks as a gesture of kindness that both satirises their evil, mocks them by the attribution of good intentions, and imbues their victims with love. Similarly, the oxymoron 'Temple of Death' reinvests the disinherited dead with the sanctity of their own religion. The authorial witness wrests back the nobility of his faith from the very instrument of destruction. Yet notwithstanding the elevated tone, the text does not spare the reader the most gruesome details:

> then the Sonderkommando comes ..., they fetch the mortal remains from the shrine; the bodies cover the floors with bleeding noses and mouths, and are filthily pressed together in thick clumps, so close together, that often they cannot fall over... (pp.482f.)

The vivid facticity of such passages provides a potent reminder that sublimity, in this novel as elsewhere, is not achieved at the cost of truthfulness or at the expense of witnessing horror. The result is a moving, subtle, and shocking representation of Auschwitz. A spectrum of sometimes conflicting devices, modes, and attitudes ensures that the unspeakable becomes art: objective, sharply observed details; language that appeals to all the senses, visual, even tactile, olfactorily and acoustically evocative imagery; Swiftian irony and satire; affectionate tenderness; and a vision that ranges from the sordid horror of the camp to religious transcendence. This variety reflects the difficulty of the task and produces a representation of Auschwitz that can both shock and console. One is dealing not just with a representation but with a theological response to the brutalities of the camp, which is only fully articulated in the novel's final chapter. As with Adler's poetry from the camps, this response entails (retrospectively) rescuing the victims from their tormentors and answering the unfathomable crimes with an essentially Jewish affirmation of humanity. As the narrator says, his 'weapon is the power of goodness in the jaws of evil' ('*und so ist die Waffe die Macht des Guten im Rachen des Bösen*').

'Lyrical irony' (*lyrische Ironie*) was the mode that H.G. Adler invented to capture the story of his anabasis through the camps in *Eine Reise,* though today its defining feature would more likely be located in its magic realism.[59] Heimito von Doderer, in his review of the novel, captured this magical lyricism thus:

> ... the novel always almost imperceptibly departs from the factual level, and perhaps this is one of the most basic methods, by which the book masters its unbearable subject and makes it soar.[60]

Adler himself called the text a *Ballade* because of its lyrical narrative, and only adopted the epithet *Erzählung* (story) for the title-page at the publisher's request for a more commercial term, but von Doderer, whilst recognising it as a ballad, unequivocally defines the text as a novel. Largely anchored in Paul, the central character, the narrative voice flits between the perspectives of his aged parents and his sister, Zerlina, through whose consciousness the reader witnesses the death machinery in Auschwitz, though the stream-of-consciousness technique also leads us disconcertingly into the satirised viewpoint of the perpetrators. This mixing of eye-witness perspectives, the traumatised consciousness of the victims, and satire on the unnamed Germans, leads to a highly idiosyncratic narrative in which the story shifts continuously between fact and fantasy, and literal and metaphorical truth, in order to capture the events both as a physical and as a psychological event. The physical torment of a ruptured reality merges with its traumata, such that the unfeeling psychosis of the perpetrators and the consequent disorientation and even hysteria among their victims influence the very texture of the novel. For example, the delayed narration of Zerlina's 'selection' on the ramp is witnessed retrospectively by Paul on his way to freedom in his attempt to grasp what has just occurred; in effect, he frees himself from this repressed event but stops short of recalling her actual death. In a dialogue with himself, he reports:

> ...when we arrived and stepped down from the train, it was as dark as it is now. It was infinitely dark, darker than it can ever be. The darkness was so dark that no one saw it. It was like that, even if cruel arc lights hung on high posts and illuminated the resilient darkness.
>
> So it was not dark. It was simply night, but one could see. – No, it was dark. No one could see, we certainly could not see, we were blinded, but in the darkness... and then there was a man... he stood in his magnificence and had a hand...[61]

At this painful moment, the realistic narrative breaks off, reverting to a different strand of the story. Unlike *Panorama*, the novel does not literally record the victims' fate in the gas-chambers at all but introduces further narrative dimensions, both to reflect the impossibility of representation and the deeper inability of the mind to grapple with the material truth. Like Ilse Aichinger's *Die grüßere Hoffnung* (Herod's Children, 1948), *Eine Reise* returns to the technique of fairy-tale. Paul's sister, whose name 'Zerlina' evokes the transfigured reality of Mozart's *Zauberflöte*, takes on the unexpected guise of a 'rabbit' ('Kaninchen') – an epithet whose apparent harmlessness is contradicted by the fact that the victims of the Nazis' criminal experiments in Auschwitz were locally referred to as (*Versuchs-*)*kaninchen* (experimental rabbits, i.e., guinea-pigs).[62] The quasi-harmlessness of her story proves to be a literal metaphor which signifies how the guards treat human beings, i.e., like animals:

> Zerlina folds her front paws and hangs down her ears. How peaceful it is in

the narrow box. She can make herself comfortable there, just like at home, she is given some cabbage leaves, which would otherwise rot unused in the garbage, and a bowl with water. Zerlina does not mind that the box is almost too small to turn around in... (p.207)

Into the painful idyll, the panic-stricken reaction of the victim to her imminent murder irrupts with brutal horror: the anti-semitic stereotype of the Jewish nose reappears in the guard's reaction to the rabbit's nose, and the process of *Selektion* and slaughter is evoked in a bitter pun on *Vivisektion*:

> ...the poor rabbit trembles all over its body, since what it had forgotten is suddenly here again and appears with a thousand terrors.
>
> 'I am not here. I have gone out. ...I have committed suicide. You will find me on the dissection table, because they want to find out what poison I used to kill myself with. And I only fell out of the train...'
>
> 'Everyone can recognise you by your long nose...'
>
> 'I don't have a wolf-skin. How can you insult a rabbit so!'
>
> 'No-one believes your story with the rabbit... have you heard? A body search, not vivisection. They don't do that with people, only with rabbits and guinea pigs...' (p.209f.)

The linguistic jumble of puns, proverbial details, fairy-tale, anti-semitic stereotypes and nightmare records the panicking consciousness of the victim in a representation twinned with factual details (the train), ironic reversals (suicide by poison) and the callous prejudice of the murderer. Far more extreme than the traditional topos of the 'topsy-turvy world', the categorical confusion that reigns in episodes such as this represents a chaos so total as to defy ultimate analysis. Not the least distinguishing feature, however, is the naïvety, even tenderness that imbues the vision, as if ultimately the victims lay beyond the executioners' grasp and the reality of the victims transcends the grasp of their destroyers. The tone switches yet again to describe the moment of murder and the crematoria. Whereas *Panorama* presents the gas-chambers, *Eine Reise*'s complementary account represents the original form of slaughter used by the Nazis, a pistol-shot in the back of the head (gas was only introduced later, as much to ease the traumatic burden on the SS as to expedite the murders):

> Our executions are all expedited with the utmost speed right in the crematorium. After undressing, the patients are shot on marble tiles in the back of the neck, everything is clean and conducted with the necessary mercy to avoid disagreeable incidents. The corpse is conveyed to the grate of the oven immediately by means of a swing-mechanism, without the lifeless body coming into immediate contact with human hands. (p.212)

The perspective is that of the modern technician, comparable to that of the officer describing his torture-machine in Kafka's *In der Strafkolonie* (In the Penal Colony). Indeed, Adler's place of execution possibly echoes the mechanism which ejects the corpse in Kafka's tale. As *In der Strafkolonie* evokes the mechanical slaughter of the First World War and thereby condemns modern technology, so Adler's Swiftian crematorium indicts not just the Nazis but modernity's technology of efficiency:

> The crematorium is practical and hygienic. It is one of the most beautiful and useful inventions of the modern age, which was dreamt up not just by the mind, but by the educated heart, to do quickly what has to be done, and to save the gravediggers work... The period for the burning of a grown rabbit, which, as is well known, reaches the size of a well built man, has been reduced to ten minutes and even less thanks to constant improvements. This period does not only apply to the more effective but uneconomical burning of a single corpse, but can be attained by simultaneous use for twenty to thirty clients. (p.210)

The terminology here satirises the entire paraphernalia of modernity, from medical exigency to economic rationality (right down to consumerism in describing the victims as 'clients'). Even the German tradition of *Bildung*, whose role in preparing for Nazism has been studied by W.H. Bruford, is here implicated in the disaster by the term reminiscent of Weimar Classicism, '*das gebildete Herz*' (the educated heart).[63] The multiplicity of viewpoints in *Eine Reise* transforms the representation of Auschwitz into a communal narrative, wherein perpetrators and victims, beliefs and prejudices, hopes and ideologies are equally incorporated into a single stream of consciousness, resulting in a composite portrait of historical cause, contemporary attitude, and dire effect.

Whilst inviting empathy, the novels reject the normal literary consolation, the illusion of identification. Whereas literature otherwise shows what a specific event 'was like', these novels painfully assert that the reality of the camps cannot be known. As the hero of *Die unsichtbare Wand*, Arthur Landau, tries to explain:

> 'I don't know if I really was there. I didn't die, after all, and then you can't know.'
> 'I don't quite understand that.'
> 'There's not much to understand. Only the dead were there...'[64]

Landau adopts a radical position: the 'final solution' could only be 'understood' by those who fully suffered it; hence, even for himself, as a survivor he rules out 'knowing', let alone mediating, the disaster. This excludes the possibility of intellectual or emotional representation; and this places severe demands on the reader, too, who normally turns to imaginative literature precisely in order to represent and comprehend an alien experience. This novel, however, refuses to represent the unimaginable.

As they reflect back on the unknowable, it has been seen how the novels simultaneously encompass both the causes and the consequences of the cataclysm, even to the extent of anticipating the most recent turn in memory, the Museum of the Holocaust. Landau in *Die unsichtbare Wand* works in a museum and in *Eine Reise*, the deportees entering Auschwitz imagine themselves becoming objects in a museum. The narrative further ennobles the victims by granting them that which their murder prevented, knowledge of the future:

> What will happen to the treasures of the travellers? Everything will be placed in showcases; after it has been cleaned and conserved, and there will be clean inscriptions... The teacher will come with the school-children and explain everything to them exactly.[65]

The motif recurs when the narrative recounts the arrival at the ramp:

> It was murder. Ida was driven out of the train. Then everyone stood there, the people to the left, the luggage to the right. The people were done away with, the luggage was sent into the museum. Technical progress couldn't be impeded. That was why the people were destroyed, but they didn't want to waive collecting their ashes.

The corollary is inescapable: gas chamber and museum stem from the same voyeuristic culture, driven by the simultaneous desire to see and ultimately to destroy all. Technology, voyeurism, and consumerism are equally implicated in the catastrophe. The view implied here exhibits close correlations to that elaborated in the chapter on '*Kulturindustrie*' in *Dialektik der Aufklärung*.[66] Interestingly, both Adorno and Adler were developing impulses from Karl Kraus on these questions at approximately the same time, Adorno in California and Adler in Theresienstadt and Auschwitz. Scholarship itself does not escape guilt in *Eine Reise*, where a parallel emerges between the museum of the future and the crimes of the Egyptologists: 'People broke open the Egyptian tombs and robbed them, but the thieves were proud of their theft, wrote books, and were praised in the newspapers for their crime.' (p.172) The culture that removes mummies from their tombs and places them on public display proves to be ultimately the same as one which will destroy human beings and place their remains in a museum of memory.

Such radicalism in the representation of Auschwitz entails a wholesale critique of modernity. Technology, the economy, consumerism, education, scholarship, medicine and – a constant Krausian theme in *Eine Reise* – the press, all participate in the crimes as here represented. Indeed, the texts implicate the reader, too, not as cause nor agent nor participant in some undefined collective guilt, but as retrospective, if unwitting, accomplice. The continuity of culture and the very act of observing the past sucks the reader into a crime which lies, paradoxically, beyond comprehension The reader therefore falls victim to a double-bind: to experience the guilt of ignorance, or that of knowledge. Hence the imperative for the reader to engage in active memory and respond to the texts not just aesthetically, but ethically. But can this offer a way out from the aporia of guilt?

To grasp Adler's views on representing the genocide, it is instructive to examine his relations with Adorno, whose cultural critique his views on occasion closely resemble and with whom he enjoyed a complex relationship. It was in 1949 that Adorno formulated the now famous dictum printed in 1951 in his essay *Kulturkritik und Gesellschaft* (Cultural Criticism and Society), that to write a poem after Auschwitz was 'barbaric'.[67] The essay actually has nothing to do with Auschwitz as such, but invokes the name for a symbolic and effective conclusion to his analysis of contemporary culture. Not until later, and partly to deal with responses to his thesis, did Adorno develop his position.

It is precisely into this period that the beginnings of Adler's relationship with Adorno fall. He approached Adorno both as a fellow musicologist and as a survivor of Auschwitz. In his first letter of 4 April 1950, Adler begins by introducing himself apropos of a review that he had written of Adorno's *Philosophy of Modern Music* for the BBC Third Programme.[68] He offers a highly detailed appreciation of Adorno's musical aesthetics, which he also extends to literature, then turns to Adorno's contribution to *The Authoritarian Personality*, and finally comes to his own as yet unpublished Theresienstadt book. As a survivor of Auschwitz and fellow sociologist, Adler hoped for Adorno's understanding and – as he would again later – hinted that he would appreciate the opportunity to lecture in Germany. Adorno's reaction is interesting. He did not reply. When prompted by a mutual acquaintance, the publisher of Adorno's book and the later publisher of Adler's *Theresienstadt*, he wrote back two-and-a-half months later, pleading overwork, an urgent business trip to Paris and above all, the labours involved in reconstructing the Institute for Social Research in Frankfurt. Of the two topics in Adler's letter, aesthetics and the camps, it is only the former that Adorno addresses. Not a word about Auschwitz. Nothing on Theresienstadt or on the *Authoritarian Personality*. The major part of the letter attempts to clarify what he meant by 'negativity' in modern music. In his reply of 22 July, Adler tried again. After regretting the poor response to his review of Adorno's book, he devotes a lengthy paragraph to the question of 'ugliness' in new music, and then returns more briefly to his own studies of the causes of the persecutions. In Adorno's reply of 26 July, it is once again aesthetics which come first, though Adorno does now voice an interest in the lecture on *The Sociology of the Concentration Camp*. On aesthetics, Adorno writes: 'I would be very happy if we soon had the opportunity of continuing our discussion concerning the aesthetic concept of harmony and its peculiar dialectics.'[69] Two months later Adler responded with an irony that was probably lost on Adorno. Echoing the latter's formulation almost word-for-word, he writes: 'I, too, would be particularly happy if we could one day continue our discussion of the aesthetic concept of harmony.'[70] At least one of the correspondents seems to have been aware of the absurdity inherent in debating aesthetics with an Auschwitz survivor, but it does not seem to have been Adorno.

The contact continued over several years, during which Adorno reacted very favourably to Adler's work on Theresienstadt and enthusiastically supported his research.[71] Years later, when disagreements between the two men had emerged, this book remained exemplary in Adorno's eyes. In a posthumously published aphorism, 'On H.G. Adler', he recorded the following testimony:

> What I admire most about H.G. Adler is the strength with which he wrung his book on Theresienstadt from conditions which seemed to make such a work impossible. It lies beyond the bounds of the imagination that a gentle and sensitive person could maintain his self-awareness spiritually and remain capable of objective thought in the organised Hell, the open purpose of which was the destruction of the self [...]. [His was a] sensorium that found brutality and injustice so unbearable, that even *in extremis*, when nothing could be changed, it felt the duty to express the unutterable, and so remain true to the victims. [...] A combination of sensitivity and resistance became the moral motor for a Kantian 'necessity' in Adler, and for this he deserves not only the thanks of those on whose behalf he wrote, but the undiminished admiration of all the rest of us who believe that they could never equal him.[72]

This generous praise, dated 1965, indicates the centrality of the *Theresienstadt* book in Adorno's reflection on the Shoah. After the publication of *Theresienstadt*, at the invitation of Adorno and Horkheimer, Adler delivered the prestigious Loeb Lecture in Frankfurt in 1956, speaking on *Theresienstadt – Die Lehren einer Zwangsgemeinschaft* (Theresienstadt – The Lessons of an Enslaved Society). The lecture seems to have gone extremely well, and the 'agreement and recognition' (*'Zustimmung und Anerkennung'*) Adler received from Adorno and Horkheimer[73] held out prospects for future collaborative ventures. Accordingly, the lecture was soon followed by a more specialised talk to members of the Institute early in 1957. There was some discussion about the topic, which indicates the gulf that actually separated the correspondents. Adorno reformulated Adler's offer of a paper on *Film Theresienstadt – Menschliche Verblendung in einer Zwangslage*

Good against Evil?

(The Theresienstadt Film: Human Blindness under Slavery)[74] into a topic more to his own taste: *Film Theresienstadt – Ideologien in der Zwangsituation* (The Theresienstadt Film: Ideologies under Slavery).[75] Presumably Adler wished to discuss the psychological phenomenon of the inmates' self-deception in contributing to a propaganda film in the camp, whilst Adorno wanted to couple this with a specific critique of ideology. The different concept of ideology inherent in Adler's work did not allow this, whereupon he settled for *Ideologien in Zwangssituationen* (Ideologies under Slavery),[76] a topic which, I suspect, would automatically have forced the differences between Adler and Adorno into the open. The talk does not seem to have gone well. In his letter of thanks after his visit, Adler writes:

> I am aware that this time I did not fulfil your expectations and much less those of your students, which I greatly regret. The lesson I draw from this is that in a scholarly circle, which has thoroughly developed its own scholarly terminology, one should not introduce another terminology, or, if one does so, one should only do it with well-founded circumspection.[77]

One can imagine the carnage and the humiliation which lay in store for the guest in Frankfurt, who presumably gave as well as he got, since the concept of 'ideology' would have provided them with the ground for a battle royal. Despite some considerable convergences in their standpoint, which attracted Adler to Adorno on music and Adorno to Adler on Theresienstadt, they occupied opposite positions on many key issues, including questions of language, method and ethics. Adler's sociological approach was largely based on that of Simmel, whose revival had to wait almost another fifty years and who was treated with derision by Adorno.[78] While Adorno was grounded in Kant and then followed a line through Hegel, Marx and Freud, Adler too was grounded in Kant but followed a line set by Schelling and interpreted Hegel, Marx and Freud as symptomatic of the very problem – a falsely constructed ideology – which he attempted to resolve. From Adler's perspective, Adorno would have been the victim of ideological self-deception, while Adorno would no less vehemently have regarded Adler as an exponent of bourgeois ideology. In ethical matters, Adorno problematised the kind of naïve decency that Adler stood for. Neither of them adopted a public stance on their relationship, and although there was no break between them, and they continued to see each other from time to time, the friendship did not develop. They avoided public debate but, I suspect, continued to debate through their writing. I have noticed several references in their works which suggest that the debate continued and which emphasise the unbridgeable gulf that separated the viewpoint of the survivor of Auschwitz from the philosopher whose life was *beschädigt* (damaged) by emigration. In both cases, it is the question of 'ideology' that resurfaces.

It seems likely that Adorno contributed to the satirical portrait of Professor Kratzenstein in Adler's *Die unsichtbare Wand*. The mixture of Marxism and psychoanalysis that Kratzenstein spouts reads like a parody of Adorno's views, though this character – conceived as working in England – is perhaps a composite of various figures. Kratzenstein's greeting is, I suspect, more representative of the problems Adler had in putting across his views than of Adorno himself, who would hardly have been quite as insensitive as this: 'You have such experiences, my word, the things you have survived! You're not bitter at all and have kept your love of scholarship, congratulations! Wonderful, I say, wonderful!'[79]

Adler's attempts by letter to prompt Adorno to invite him to lecture may here be transposed into a visit with the same objective, but it is Kratzenstein who delivers the lecture. It is at this point that one most senses a parody of the Frankfurt Professor:

> The Professor held me a lecture...in which he could not sufficiently emphasise that all suffering, insofar as it was not based in human nature, derived from economic factors. Concentration camps, for example, evolved from a specific form of exploitation, and everything else which made them so disgusting must be explained by socio-psychological means.[80]

Kratzenstein's mixture of vulgar-Marxism and psychology cannot be mistaken for Adorno's own views, but parodistically shrinks them into stereotypical details. In the eyes of the speaker, Kratzenstein is guilty of applying ideological constructs to the events, in ignorance of the historical facts, and thereby loses sight of the human dimension to the catastrophe. Kratzenstein is blinded by a personal mix of ideologies.

Just as Adler may be ironising Adorno in a composite portrait, Adorno more unequivocally pours scorn on Adler. In the now famous section of his *Negative Dialektik* entitled '*Nach Auschwitz*' (After Auschwitz), he offers a satirical portrait of his old antagonist, which – to anyone who knew Adler well – is unmistakable in its reference:

> A man who survived Auschwitz and other camps, with a strength that is truly admirable, once opposed Beckett with considerable feeling: he said that if Beckett had gone to Auschwitz, he would have written differently, namely with the front-line religion of the one who got away, that is to say, positively.[81]

The whole episode has the ring of truth: this was Adler's habitual response to Beckett, with whose work he had been familiar since the early 1950s. The only uncharacteristic element in Adorno's account (even the 'considerable feeling' rings true) is Adorno's use of the term *Schützengrabenreligion*. But then, Adorno's whole turn of phrase warrants scrutiny. His term for H.G. Adler is not the normal, acceptable 'survivor' (which would be *der Überlebende*), but *der Entronnene*, i.e., 'the one who escaped': it is a term which takes death's party against the victim, by implying the superiority of the cataclysm over the individual. The word *Schützengrabenreligion* – literally 'trench-religion', a term which has distinct overtones of the First World War – gives the belief imputed to this survivor a half-baked, home-made, last-ditch quality. Normally, however, this religion goes by quite another name: Judaism. In his haste to denigrate the survivor, Adorno has engulfed him in an unwitting but all the more sophisticated form of anti-semitic abuse. For Adorno, Auschwitz provides material evidence of Nietzsche's belief in the death of God, but retrospectively this denies the victims, as Jews, the very ground of their existence. And yet, in dialectically divesting the victims of their own identity, Adorno inadvertently concedes the falsity of his own premises. He continues:

> The one who got away was right, but not in the way that he meant it: Beckett, and whoever remained in control of himself, would have been broken in Auschwitz, and would probably have been forced to confess to that front-line religion which the one who got away cloaked in the words, he wanted to give people hope...[82]

Here, as elsewhere, too, Adorno becomes the victim of his own dialectic: in plain language, by agreeing that Beckett too would have adopted a more positive attitude in Auschwitz, he concedes the very point that he attempts to deny: the superior power of hope over nihilism. This is another variation on the 'circularity' in which, as Gillian Rose argues, Adorno entraps himself in *Negative Dialektik*,[83] which has serious implications for his argument when he takes Beckett's view as the only valid response to life after the camps:

> Beckett reacted to the concentration camps...in the only way proper. What exists, is like a concentration camp. The only hope is that nothing exists. ... the image of nothingness steps forth, which his writing describes.[84]

This passage is fraught with difficulties. On one reading, against Adorno, it could be argued that the aesthetic nihilism he propagates metaphysically sides with the evil it purports to unmask, by re-empowering the very forces that attempted to destroy the Jews. Rose argues that Adorno is 'caught in an illusion' in *Negative Dialektik* because he has no concept of 'law',[85] and it is possible that at this juncture his argument again becomes highly problematic: the failure to provide a viable concept of 'law' would then be symptomatic of a wider dilemma. Because, to quote Rose again, his work is celebrated as 'the gospel of aporetics, of non-identity',[86] it may lead into the very maelstrom that apparently he would have us resist. This fashionable negation of humanity, derived from or at least strengthened by his wrestling with the past, leaves a moral vacuum that has no place for humanity. On a more positive reading, based on Adorno's avowed method in his preface, it is not in the 'content' of thought but in 'consciousness' that thought attains its true goal. Moreover, we are then led, as Werner Brändle argues, to a theological reading[87] in which due weight must be given to Adorno's 'recuperation of hopelessness':

> Nothing untransmuted can be rescued, nothing which has not gone through the gate of its own death. If rescue is the innermost impulse of the spirit, there is no hope beyond unconditional surrender: of that which is to be rescued as of the spirit, of the one who hopes. The gesture of hope is to think nothing of that upon which the spirit wishes to support itself...[88]

There is a theological core at the heart of this thinking which, on a dialectical reading, leads to a restoration of negative hope.

This is the same dilemma of negativity with which Adler wrestles and it is this which gives his representation of mass murder its ethical coherence. But whereas Adorno would transfer discourse into consciousness, Adler clings to positive good. Thus Adorno took Schoenberg's *Survivor of Warsaw* to task for 'aestheticising' the Jewish fate 'as if it had any sense'.[89] Adler, siding with Schoenberg, sought ways which, whilst not denying what had occurred, would go beyond it, and this included maintaining faith in the continuity of human ethics, the potential for ethics to regenerate, and the positive representation of hope.[90] Hence the alternation of viewpoint in a novel like *Eine Reise*, which seeks to represent both nothingness and its opposite, and from nothingness brings forth a new dialectic of transcendence. Adler here focuses directly on the issue raised by Adorno. The narrative follows Paul through the machinery of extermination to the point of nothingness:

> ...this is the nothingness, that hides from nothing, the dismantled wall, the unseen face which cannot see, the fairy-tale of nothingness, the fairy-tale without magic, the betrayal, which cannot betray...everything flees...the graves are torn open... nothingness is left to its own devices... Severed hands lie round about... But suddenly there is a thought, the first moment of creation ... even if it is only the being of nothingness, it is a being... the thought grows stronger... it is a human being...[91]

Adler insists on restoring the very subjectivity that Adorno problematises and with that restores enlightenment and hope in an affected but unfractured form. Like the rebirth of life after the Flood, wrought by God, rebirth becomes possible after the cataclysm enacted by Man. The text reaches but relativises nothingness, and confronts it with the superior principle of life. In moral terms, this represents the victory of the victims over the perpetrators. Ultimately, therefore, Adler's representation of the genocide, like Adorno's analysis, reaches a theological ground, but it reinstates the validity of the very religion on account of which the Jews were persecuted and thereby answers nihilism with the religion of life.

The clashing parallel between 'The Fairytale of Nothingness' and Adorno's paean to Negativity, with its attack on Adler, in 'After Auschwitz' is, I suspect, no coincidence. Adorno's last letter to Adler, written in 1962, four years before the publication of *Negative Dialectics*, was a letter of thanks for a copy of *Eine Reise*. Adorno had not yet had time to read the novel but was 'very affected' ('*sehr berührt*') by its dedication to Canetti, with whom he had recently begun a friendship.[92] One can only surmise Adorno's reaction to the novel, but one can imagine that he would take the 'Fairytale of Nothingness' as a personal attack – and an attack on Adorno's position it certainly is. I suspect that Adorno's reaction may well have contributed to those critical pages in the *Negative Dialectics*. He cannot but have grasped what the book was doing, as can be gauged from Canetti's response to the novel, when he praised it for the very 'hope' that Adorno questioned. In a letter to H.G. Adler, Canetti writes:

> The most terrible things that can happen to people are here described, as if they were ethereal and tender and could be overcome, as if they could not affect the core of a human being. I would say that you have introduced *hope* into modern literature once again.[93]

Canetti's view of *Eine Reise* was shared by Heinrich Böll, who used the novel as a key example in his *Frankfurter Vorlesungen*, his lectures on poetics delivered at the University of Frankfurt in the winter semester of 1963–64. After attacking Adorno's by now famous dictum in his opening lecture,[94] Böll discussed *Eine Reise* at length in his second and third lectures as a key example of how literature could be written after Auschwitz. Böll's assault, delivered in Adorno's own university, cannot but have reinforced the perception of *Eine Reise* as a work inimical to Adorno's aesthetics, and may again have contributed to Adorno's silent attack on H.G. Adler in 'After Auschwitz'. Be that as it may, the time is clearly ripe for a reassessment of H.G. Adler's work, not just because it contributed significantly to the most central debate in post-war aesthetics, but more importantly because of its uniquely hard-won humanity.

Notes

1 For bio-bibliographical details of H.G. Adler, see *Archiv Bibliographia Judaica. Lexikon deutsch-jüdischer Autoren,* ed. Renate Heuer, Munich: Saur, 1992–, Vol.I, pp.47–58; Peter Staengle, 'H.G. Adler', *Kritisches Lexikon der deutschsprachigen*

Gegenwartsliteratur, Supplement 44, Munich: Edition Text und Kritik, 1978–; and Heinrich Hubmann and A.O. Lanz (eds), *Zu Hause im Exil. Zu Person und Werk H.G. Adlers*, Stuttgart: Steiner Verlag 1987; here, the invaluable article, A.O. Lanz, 'Zu Hause im Exil. Biographische Skizze über H.G. Adler', pp.139–46. For a richly illustrated portrait, see Jürgen Serke, 'H.G. Adler', in *Böhmische Dörfer. Wanderungen durch eine verlassene literarische Landschaft*, Vienna: Zsolnay, 1987, pp.326–43. Now also Marcel Atze, 'Ortlose Botschaft', *Der Freundeskreis H.G. Adler, Elias Canetti und Franz Baermann Steiner im englischen Exil: Marbacher Magazin* 84, Marbach, 1998. A complete bibliography has recently appeared: Franz Hocheneder (ed.), 'Special Bibliography: The Writings of H.G. Adler (1910–1988)', *Comparative Criticism* 21, 1999, pp.293–310.

2 Zygmunt Bauman, *Modernity and the Holocaust*, Cambridge: Polity, 1989. Bauman's apparently innovative wish '*to open up the findings of the specialists to the general use of social science, to interpret them in a way that shows their relevance to the main themes of sociological inquiry, to feed them back into the mainstream of our discipline*' (p.xiii) (Bauman's emphasis) was central to Adler's project almost from its inception, as is apparent from his only English paper, 'Ideas Toward a Sociology of the Concentration Camp', *The American Journal of Sociology*, Vol.LXIII, No.5, 1958, pp.513–22; Bauman's thesis is also anticipated in the title of Adler's first collection of essays in sociology, *Die Erfahrung der Ohnmacht. Beiträge zur Soziologie unserer Zeit (*The Experience of Powerlessness. Essays on the Sociology of our Age), Frankfurt am Main, 1964. Bauman's central argument that '*the very idea of the Endlösung was an outcome of the bureaucratic culture*' (p.15) and was '*generated by bureaucracy*' (p.17) (Bauman's italics) echoes both Adorno's ideas of the 'verwaltete Welt' (administered world) and the thesis of Adler's magnum opus, *Der verwaltete Mensch* (Administered Man), Tübingen: Mohr, 1974, which, however, demonstrates why in discussing the 'Final Solution' the Weberian category of 'bureaucracy' needs to be replaced by a new concept of 'administration'. The refusal of modern sociologists to listen to the views of a Holocaust survivor provides a major theme in H.G. Adler's novel, *Die unsichtbare Wand* (The Invisible Wall), Vienna: Zsolnay, 1989.

3 *Neue Zürcher Zeitung*, No.4247, 20 October 1963, Literatur und Kunst, p.5. Reprinted in Gershom Scholem, *Briefe*, 2 vols., Munich: Beck, 1994–95, II, pp.95–100.

4 Hermann Levin Goldschmidt, *Das Vermächtnis des deutschen Judentums* second edition, Frankfurt am Main, 1957: Europaische Verlagsanstalt, p.137.

5 Peter Demetz, Afterword to H.G. Adler, *Panorama* [1968] second edition, Munich: Piper, 1988, p.582–92; see p.582.

6 Peter Demetz, *After the Fires. Recent Writing in the Germanies, Austria and Switzerland*, San Diego and London: Harcourt Brace Jovanovich, 1986.

7 Lawrence L. Langer, *The Holocaust and the Literary Imagination*, New Haven and London: Yale University Press, 1975.

8 Saul Friedländer (ed.), *Probing the Limits of Representation. Nazism and the 'Final Solution'*, Cambridge, Mass. and London: Harvard University Press, 1992.

9 Friedländer, *Probing...*, p.2; Langer, *The Holocaust...*, pp.1ff.

10 Langer, *The Holocaust...*, p.6.

11 Hermann Langbein, *...nicht wie die Schafe zur Schlachtbank. Widerstand in den nationalsozialistischen Konzentrationslagern*, Vienna: Fischer Taschenbuch Verlag, 1980.

12 Itzhak Katzenelson, *Dos lid funem ojsgeharetn jidischn folk*, New York, n.d. German translation, Hermann Adler, *Das Lied vom letzten Juden*, Zurich and New York: Edition Hentrich, 1951.

13 See Gertrud Kolmar, *Das lyrische Werk*, Heidelberg: Schneider, 1955; *Gertrud Kolmar. Leben und Werk in Texten und Bildern*, ed. Beatrice Eichman-Leutenegger, Frankfurt am Main: Jüdischer Verlag, 1993; *Gertrud Kolmar 1894–1943*, ed. Johanna Woltmann, *Marbacher Magazin* 63, 1993.

14 David Carroll, Foreword to Jean-François Lyotard, *Heidegger and 'the jews'*,

Minneapolis: University of Minnesota Press, 1990, p.11; Friedländer, *Probing...*, p.6.

15 Gillian Rose, *Love's Work*, London: Chatto and Windus, 1995, p.119.

16 Gillian Rose, *Judaism and Modernity*, Oxford: Blackwell, 1993, p.x.

17 H.G. Adler, 'Klopstock und die Musik', unpublished dissertation, German University, Prague, 1935. A single copy, without the relevant musical examples, survives in the Estate of H.G. Adler, Schiller Nationalmuseum, Deutsches Literaturarchiv, Marbach (hereafter DLA).

18 *Zeugen des Jahrhunderts. Jüdische Lebenswege: Nahum Goldmann, Simon Wiesenthal, H.G. Adler. Nach der Sendereihe des ZDF 'Zeugen des Jahrhunderts'*, ed. Karl B. Schnelting, Frankfurt am Main, 1987, p.170.

19 *Ibid.*, p.169f.

20 On these poems from the camps, see Josef Strelka, 'H.G. Adlers KZ-Gedichte', in Hubmann and Lanz (eds), *Zu Hause im Exil*, pp.3–9. For published poems, see H.G. Adler, *Der Wahrheit verpflichtet. Interviews, Gedichte, Essays*, Gerlingen: Bleicher, 1998, pp.63–107. Jeremy Adler (ed.), *Der Wahrheit verpflichtet*, Gerlingen, 1998, pp.63–107.

21 Texts cited after *Der Wahrheit verpflichtet*. Here, Poem 3, 'Einzug' (Arrival), p.65.

22 *Ibid.*, Poem 11, 'Enge Stuben' (Cramped Rooms), p.73.

23 *Ibid.*, Poem 9, 'Übersiedlung' (Moving House), p.71.

24 *Ibid.*, Poem 23, 'Nachtlied' (Night Song), p.85.

25 *Ibid.*, Poem 26, 'Totentanz' (Dance of Death), p.87.

26 'Hingang' (Decease), Poem 2 in the cycle 'Einsam in Banden' (Solitary in Chains), p.89.

27 *Theresienstadt 1941–1945. Das Antlitz einer Zwangsgemeinschaft* (Theresienstadt 1941–1945. The Portrait of a Concentration Camp) (1955), second, revised edition, Tübingen: Mohr, 1960.

28 Serke, 'H.G. Adler', p.327.

29 *Die Juden in Deutschland. Von der Aufklärung bis zum Nationalsozialismus* (The Jews in Germany. From the Enlightenment to National Socialism) (1960), fourth edition, Munich: Kösel, 1988.

30 *Der verwaltete Mensch. Studien zur Deportation der Juden aus Deutschland* (The Administration of Man. Studies in the Deportation of the Jews from Germany), Tübingen: Mohr, 1974.

31 H.G. Adler, Hermann Langbein and Ella Lingens-Reiner (eds), *Auschwitz. Zeugnisse und Berichte* (1962), fifth edition, Hamburg, 1994.

32 Hans Buchheim, Edith Eucken-Erdsieck, Gert Buchheit and H.G. Adler, *Der Führer ins Nichts. Eine Diagnose Adolf Hitlers*, Rastatt/Baden: Grote, 1960.

33 *Der Kampf gegen die 'Endlösung der Judenfrage'*, second edition, Dusseldorf, 1960.

34 'Der Umwerter aller Werte. Nietzsche und die Folgen', in *Die Erfahrung der Ohnmacht*, pp.42–82; also in *Die Freiheit des Menschen. Aufsätze zur Soziologie unserer Zeit*, Tübingen: Mohr, 1976, pp.116–55.

35 H.G. Adler, 'Mensch oder Masse?', in *Die Erfahrung der Ohnmacht*, pp.5–41; revised version in *Die Freiheit des Menschen*, pp.1–85.

36 H.G. Adler, *Panorama. Roman in Zehn Bildern*, Olten and Freiburg im Breisgau, 1968. See A.O. Lanz, 'Panorama von H.G. Adler – ein moderner Roman', *Europäische Hochschulschriften*, series 1, Vol.808, Bern, Frankfurt am Main, New York, 1984; Ingeborg Drewitz, 'Zu H.G. Adlers Roman *Panorama*', in Hubmann and Lanz (eds), *Zu Hause in Exil*, pp.28–31; John and Ann White, '"Die Vermächtnisse von Schloß Launceston". Darstellung und Überwindung des Bösen in H.G. Adlers Roman "Panorama"', in Hubmann and Lanz (eds), *Zu Hause in Exil*, pp.32–43; Irene Lanz-Hubmann, 'Zeit und Zeitstruktur in H.G. Adlers Roman "Panorama"', in Hubmann and Lanz (eds), *Zu Hause in Exil*, pp.44–68.

37 H.G. Adler, *Eine Reise. Erzählung*, Bonn, 1962; second edition, Vienna, 1999.

38 *Die unsichtbare Wand*, p.307.

39 Rüdiger Görner, 'Überleben – Überwinden? Eine Betrachtung zum Werk H.G. Adlers', *Salzburger Jahrbuch für Philosophie*, 35, 1990, pp.75–88; here p.76.

40 J.P. Stern, 'Zum 75. Geburtstag von H.G. Adler', in Hubmann and Lanz (eds), *Zu Hause in Exil*, pp.147–50; see p.148.

41 Hermann Langbein, *Menschen in Auschwitz*, Vienna: Europaverlag, 1972.

42 Heinrich Böll, 'Die R32,80 des Jakob Strauss. Zu H.G. Adlers Buch "Der verwaltete Mensch"', *Der Spiegel*, 22 April 1974. Reprinted in W.P. Eckert and W. Unger (eds), *H.G. Adler, Buch der Freunde: Stimmen über den Dichter und Gelehrten mit unveröffentlicher Lyrik. Zum 65. Geburtstag am 2 Juli 1975*, Cologne: Wienand, 1975, pp.66–72; see p.67.

43 H.G. Adler, *Vorschule für eine Experimentaltheologie. Betrachtungen über Wirklichkeit und Sein*, Stuttgart, 1987.

44 *Die Zeit*, 18 October 1974.

45 Personal communication of a *Bundesverfassungsrichter* to H.G. Adler. See *Bundesentschädigungsgesetz. Bundesgesetz zur Entschädigung für Opfer der national-sozialistischen Verfolgung vom 29. Juni 1956* (Frankfurt am Main, 1957).

46 See for example *Theresienstadt 1941–1945*, second edition, pp.627ff.

47 See the analysis of administration in *Der verwaltete Mensch*, pp.867–1038.

48 Gershom Scholem, 'Wider dem Mythos vom deutsch-jüdischen "Gespräch"', in Scholem, *Judaica 2*, Frankfurt am Main: Suhrkamp, 1970, pp.7–11; see p.11.

49 Adler, *Die unsichtbare Wand*, p.225.

50 '"Die Vermächtnisse..."', p.32.

51 Jean-François Lyotard, *The Differend: Phrases in Dispute*, Minneapolis: University of Minnesota Press, 1988 [1983], p.55.

52 Jürgen Serke, 'Nachwort: "Die Toten, die uns hinterlassen hatten...". H.G. Adler und das Gedenken als Pflicht zum Beginn', in *Die unsichtbare Wand*, pp.645–56; see p.647.

53 Adler, *Die unsichtbare Wand*, p.647.

54 *Ibid.*, p.217.

55 Sande Cohen, 'Between Image and Phrase: Progressive History and the "Final Solution" as Dispossession', in Friedländer, *Probing...*, pp.171–84; here, p.181.

56 Langer, *The Holocaust...*, pp.250f.

57 Adler, *Panorama*, p.470.

58 *Ibid.*, pp.481–82.

59 On *Eine Reise*, see Benno Reifenberg, 'Eine radikale Gewissensforschung' (1959), in Eckert and Unger (eds), *H.G. Adler*, p.74, Roland Wiegenstein, 'Eine sanfte Stimme beschwört den Massenmord', in Eckert and Unger (eds), *H.G. Adler*, pp.75–78 (taken from 'Drei KZ-Romane', *Neue Rundschau*, 74 [1963]), and Heinrich Böll, *Frankfurter Vorlesungen*, Cologne and Berlin: Kiepenheuer und Witsch, 1966, pp.42–46, 54–56, 59–74.

60 Heimito von Doderer, 'Die Schule des Lesers', in Eckert and Unger (eds), *H.G. Adler*, p.82 (originally in *Forum*, 121, 1964).

61 Adler, *Eine Reise*, p.229.

62 Langbein, *Menschen in Auschwitz*, p.107 passim.

63 W.H. Bruford, *Society and Culture in Classical Weimar*, Cambridge: Cambridge University Press, 1962.

64 Adler, *Die unsichtbare Wand*, p.196.

65 Adler, *Eine Reise*, p.172.

66 Max Horkheimer and Theodor W. Adorno, *Dialektik der Aufklärung* (1944), Frankfurt am Main: Fischer, 1969, pp.128–76.

67 For an anthology of Adorno's statements on 'poetry after Auschwitz', see Petra Kiedasch (ed.), *Lyrik nach Auschwitz? Adorno und die Dichter*, Stuttgart: Reclam, 1995; for a study of his views, Klaus Laermann, '"Nach Auschwitz ein Gedicht zu schreiben ist barbarisch." Überlegungen zu einem Darstellungsverbot', in Manuel Köppen (ed.), *Kunst und Literatur nach Auschwitz*, Berlin: Erich Schmidt, 1993, pp.11–14.

68 Theodor W. Adorno, *Philosophie der neuen Musik*, Tübingen: Mohr, 1949.

69 Unpublished letter from T.W. Adorno to H.G. Adler, 21 June 1950. DLA.

70 Carbon copy of an unpublished letter from H.G. Adler to T.W. Adorno, 28 September 1950. DLA.

71 Carbon copy of an unpublished letter from H.G. Adler to T.W. Adorno, 21 April 1955 and Adorno's reply of 25 April. DLA.

72 Theodore W. Adorno, *Gesamelte Schriften*, ed. Rolf Tiedemann, Vol 20.2, *Vermischte Schriften* II, Frankfurt: Suhrkamp, 1986, p.495.

73 Carbon copy of an unpublished letter from H.G. Adler to T.W. Adorno, 2 August 1956, DLA.

74 Carbon copy of an unpublished letter from H.G. Adler to T.W. Adorno, 29 October 1956. DLA.

75 Unpublished letter from T.W. Adorno to H.G. Adler, 31 October 1956. DLA.

76 Carbon copy of an unpublished letter from H.G. Adler to T.W. Adorno, 2 November 1956 and letter from Adorno's secretary to H.G. Adler, 8 November 1956. DLA.

77 Carbon copy of an unpublished letter from H.G. Adler to T.W. Adorno, 4 April 1957. DLA.

78 T.W. Adorno, *Minima Moralia*, Frankfurt am Main: Suhrkamp, 1973, p.100.

79 Adler, *Die unsichtbare Wand*, p.348.

80 *Ibid.*, p.351.

81 Theodor W. Adorno, *Negative Dialektik* (1966), Frankfurt am Main: Suhrkamp, 1970, pp.358f.

82 *Ibid.*, p.358.

83 Rose, *Judaism and Modernity*, p.62.

84 Adorno, *Negative Dialektik*, p.371.

85 Rose, *Judaism and Modernity*, p.62.

86 *Ibid.*, p.63.

87 Werner Brändle, *Rettung des Hoffnungslosen. Die theologischen Implikationen der Philosophie Theodor W. Adornos*, Göttingen: Vandenhoeck and Ruprecht, 1984; here, p.223. I wish here to record my thanks to Dr Christopher Thornhill for reading this paper and particularly for adjusting my views on Adorno, not least by stressing the theological dimension of his work.

88 Adorno, *Negative Dialektik*, p.222.

89 T.W. Adorno, 'Engagement', in Kiedaisch (ed.), *Lyrik nach Auschwitz?*, p.54.

90 H.G. Adler, 'Arnold Schoenberg. Eine Botschaft an die Nachwelt', *Literatur und Kritik* 103 (1976), pp.129–39.

91 Adler, *Eine Reise*, pp.215–16.

92 T.W. Adorno, unpublished letter to H.G. Adler, 13 December 1962. DLA.

93 Elias Canetti, letter to H.G. Adler, printed in Eckert and Unger (eds), *H.G. Adler*, p.72f.

98 Böll, *Frankfurter Vorlesungen*, p.26ff.

CHAPTER 5

'After Auschwitz':
Trauma and the Grammar of Ethics

J.M. BERNSTEIN

The name 'Auschwitz' stands for what was without question one of the most traumatic events of the century. Equally, it names an event which emphatically dissolves moral scepticism; we feel morally certain that there evil of an unspeakable kind occurred. Perhaps, then, it is the utter proximity of these two thoughts, the *traumatic insistence* of the event of the Holocaust and our moral *certainty* about its evil character, that lies behind and is the genealogical origin of recent attempts to identify trauma with ethicality as such. For example, in Emmanuel Levinas' *Otherwise than Being* we read:

> A passivity of which the active source is not thematisable. Passivity of traumatism, but of the traumatism that prevents its own representation, the deafening trauma, breaking the thread of consciousness which should have welcomed it in its present: the passivity of persecution. But a passivity that only merits the epithet of complete or absolute if the persecuted is liable to respond to the persecutor.[1]

This passage is exemplary since its shows how trauma is being used in order to think an irrevocable passivity which will thus serve as the ethical binding of one to another. The insistence of traumatic experience, its unavoidability and its laceration of subjectivity, and the way that non-representable experience creates an ethical bond to the other, offers a model or paradigm of ethical experience. Arguably, it is the traumatic modelling of ethicality, as a reinscription of the Holocaust, that is the source of the continuing claim of Levinas' thought. Jean-François Lyotard takes up the thesis explicitly in *Heidegger and 'the jews'*. After arguing for there being a traumatic origin of the self or subject, a moment which accounts for 'the constitutive infirmity of the soul, its infancy and its misery',[2] he goes on to interpret Judaism as a collective embodiment of this traumatic formation. The relation between 'the Jews' and their God is best understood on the model of a traumatic relation; and when it is so understood, Western anti-semitism, including the Holocaust, can then be interpreted as the attempt of the West to free itself from this torturous ethical burden.

What has philosophically motivated these attempts to construe the ethical through an unrepresentable traumatic insistence? The answer I want to track involves a formal thesis and a substantive one. Formally, the structure of trauma parallels the structure or grammar of moral insight; so, formally, there is an overlap or convergence between the nature of traumatic experience and the arguably characteristic features of ethical experience. Substantively, *either* the traumatic insistence of the event of the Holocaust can be regarded as itself providing an empirically verifiable and unavoidable actualisation of that structure; *or* the fate of 'the Jews' in the Holocaust reveals a traumatic dimension of subjectivity substantiated by psychoanalytic theory. In order to make the exploration of these claims manageable, I will focus on their emergence in the thought of Lyotard.

Lyotard's various analyses of ethics can seen as moving from an attempt simply to isolate the autonomy of the grammar of moral insight through a discrete but critical engagement with Levinas' thought, to a reflective anxiety about the status of that grammar – why should we believe there is such an irreducible grammar? What secures the grammar of ethicality against theoretical incursions which seek to displace it? – to his attempts to implicate the fate of ethics, grammatically understood, in the historical exigency denominated by the names: Auschwitz, the Holocaust, the Nazi genocide, the Shoah. My argument will have three parts: (i) an account of the grammar of moral insight, including an account of Lyotard's first engagement with the thought of Emmanuel Levinas; (ii) an examination of Lyotard's generalisation of the grammar of ethicality in *The Differend*; (iii) a critical reading of his re-casting of his previous elaborations and generalisation in *Heidegger and 'the jews'* in which he returns, via psychoanalysis, to an austerely Levinasian position. Simplifying greatly, my contention is that either these arguments depend on a philosophical optical illusion in which legitimate grammatical insights are mistaken for substantive ones, or, when real traumas (or their like) are at issue then the relation is not, through that very fact, foundational for the ethical. There may be structural homologies between the traumatic and the ethical, and traumatic insistence may provide a metaphorical image of what ethical demands are like, but there are no grounds for identifying the one with other.

The Grammatical Reduction

While the attempt to elucidate a logic or grammar or formal structure of moral insight into the good is very much the point of Lyotard's essay 'Levinas's Logic', it will prove useful to have access to an analysis of this grammar independently of Lyotard's reconstruction. In his now classic essay 'The Concept of Moral Insight and Kant's Doctrine of the Fact of Reason' Dieter Henrich offers a four-part analysis of the concept of moral insight.[3] Throughout his analysis, Henrich is guided by the belief that there is a categorical distinction to be drawn between theoretical and moral insight. Consider: a deductive or reflective demonstration of the good would necessarily fail because without individual acceptance and approval moral claims lose their capacity to be action guiding. Part of the meaning of any statement of the form 'X is (morally) good' is the claim that I accept and approve of X as governing (or as the ultimate goal) of my action. To say 'X is morally good' and 'I am wholly uninterested in X and have no intention of pursuing it or putting my desires and actions into relation with it' is tantamount to saying that X is not good (for me). The morally good can determine action only if it demands and receives approval; hence insight into the morally good includes moments of demand and approval.[4] Without demand moral life could not be about claims *on* the self to act in an appropriate manner; all normativity would be lost. Without approval the demand could not be action guiding. The demand/approval structure is the first element in the grammar of moral insight.

'The concept of the good,' Henrich states, 'cannot be defined without the inclusion of an element of meaning that indicates *the passivity of moral consciousness* in understanding the good.'[5] Such passivity is taken as incommensurable with the theoretical affirmation of what is true since here one must 'always already' have accepted the demand in order to perceive what the good is; without acceptance there is no good to be seen. Conversely, and this is the second feature of moral insight, despite the moment of passivity, what is approved of is necessarily available for discursive articulation, where this articulation itself makes a claim to cognition, to knowledge. If it were not so available then the good would not be 'this' good – the Moral Law, the sacredness of human life, the ideal of human flourishing – to which one was responding. Hence, secondly, moral consciousness must be a form of insight and knowledge.

The third element of the grammar of moral insight according to Henrich, and the one which shows its distinctly modern aspect, concerns the relation between the approval given to the demand of the good and the self which does the approving. We have already begun to broach this claim in noting how the demand of the good is indexed to an agent via the passivity through which it can come to be recognised. But let me quote Henrich at length:

Approval, without which the good is nothing, is the expression of the good's obligatory character for the existence of the self. When I know in moral insight what is good, I also know that I understand myself in relation to it, or that I must understand myself in relation to it in order to become a self. The first is the case in substantial moral relations, the second in moral conflicts... Accordingly, this approval is a spontaneous achievement of the self. We can say that by means of this approval, the self first constitutes itself as a self.[6]

Approval is a 'spontaneous achievement of the self' in that the self that does the approving is in part a product of its act of approval. It is this modern conception of human identity and agency that Henrich is referring to when he claims that only through approval does the self first constitute itself as a self. Whoever the self is, it is constituted through its self-conception of what being a self involves. Hence, for any self it is true that it performatively realises (or fails) some conception of the good, that it has always already given its approval to some good: 'The self of concrete existence can become itself not by abstractly knowing some idea (the good), but by making a factual choice.'[7] Choice presupposes that the demand of the good has been felt (thus providing motive for choice) and approved. While the feeling does not cause the approval (moral knowledge too is involved), feeling must be a component if the demand is going to be sufficient for choice and action. Because the factual choice of the self presupposes what is thereby chosen, no self can emerge without always already having chosen itself, and hence being in permanent cognitive deficit to its conditions of possibility. None the less, the very idea of a human self and human agency operates within the matrix of a normative self-understanding presupposed by or with the act through which the self comes into being: 'Moral insight founds the self.'[8]

Finally, then, the concatenation of these three features of moral insight leads to a characterisation of its ontological significance. If moral insight founds the self, then vice withers self *and* good. To act otherwise than for the sake of the good is thereby to act under the belief that the good has no place in the world. Conversely, approval 'is identical with the affirmation *that* the good exists. The practical contradiction with the demand denies its existence. Therefore moral insight places all being under the condition that the good is possible in it.'[9] The appearing of the good, which is coextensive with both realising and showing how the world includes the good, is conditional upon the performance of activities being explicitly enacted within the horizon it makes possible. Moral insight into the good, the choice of the good and the performance of acts it licenses, and the revealing of the world as a place in which the good is possible *überhaupt* imply one another.

Now I have elaborated Henrich's account of the grammar of moral insight at length because I want to give a sense of how seductive this grammar is. Although nothing of any content is being urged, it is almost as if simply by announcing this grammar, and the way in which it fixes the demand of the good in relation to passivity and feeling, on the one hand, and then identifying what is demanded and felt as what founds the self, on the other hand, the morally good, the ethical, is somehow legitimated and salvaged. Lyotard is initially seduced by the grammar of the good. But when he comes to see through the seduction, the role of horror and trauma emerge. They emerge, quite simply, because traumatic episodes are ones that 'found' the self, or at least bind it, to moments of passivity that can never be turned into mere objects of theoretical knowing. Hence, the most problematic feature of ethical experience, the structure of demand and acceptance, is apparently bolted into place in traumatic episodes. First, however, there is the matter of the grammatical seduction.

Following the leads provided by Kant and Levinas, the basic elements of Lyotard's ethics compellingly work the fundamental elements belonging to the concept of moral insight. Lyotard attempts to unearth this grammar by considering the logic of prescriptives. Lyotardian prescriptives are context-bound, non-demonstrable, possessing their own authority, immediate, and addressed to a particular subject who must passively receive them. Lyotard's primary objection to the belief that prescriptives can be discursively demonstrated turns on two claims: (i) the imperative force of a prescriptive is only intelligible if the prescription can be executed. This is what makes prescriptives situation- and context-bound. Their force evaporates, and their meaning as prescriptions lapses, as soon as the action is executed or the presently non-existing state of affairs projected by the prescriptive comes into being. (ii) Any commentary on a prescriptive that would attempt to justify it would inevitably come from another form of discourse, and thereby displace the message's own genre. In that displacement, however nuanced, there occurs a neutralisation of the executive force of the order. Neutralisation occurs because in providing a commentary the original addressee of an order becomes its addressor. The asymmetry of persons, addressee and addressor, you and I, is constitutive of prescriptives; the you addressed is fallen upon, demanded, commanded by the prescription. There is no *must* without asymmetry. But since all commentary will be in the mode of discursive understanding, all commentary falsifies the force of prescriptives.

The distinctly philosophical attempt to justify ethics is just such a commentary, and therefore will inevitably fail. Lyotard contends that while Levinas, in *Totality and Infinity*, forcefully distinguishes the logic of the ethical from the representational, he does so in a philosophical mode. If I say 'it must be the case that X', then my saying organises the discourse, relegating the 'must' to my pronouncing of it. Lyotard's way of pressing this thought is to say that philosophical commentary on an imperative takes it as an object, substituting itself for the imperative on the model of reported speech: 'He said: close the door.' Evidently a report of a prescriptive is not prescriptive; it brackets the force of the order and objectifies it. This is what philosophy does to ethics: puts itself in the place of the demand of the good, thus losing the good as a demand.[10]

What holds for commentaries that seek to justify prescriptives, equally holds for claims concerning general criteria for their correctness, i.e., the meta-principles of moral theory.

> Injustice cannot be detected by any constant signs; on the contrary, to have recourse to the constancy of would-be clear signs, to the articles of the code, to established institutions, recourse to the *letter* as that which allows the just to be separated from the unjust – that is unjust. The criterion 'exists' but cannot be the object of omnitemporal descriptive statements. If it is grasped [reflectively], it is not understood [prescriptively]; it is grasped in the command received 'before' it is understood, before it is repeated by the addressee of the order, before it can give rise to commentary. It is grasped as beyond the appearance, as trace.[11]

The ethical *frisson* in passages like this lies in the attempt to show that the grammatical distinction between the ethical and the theoretical is *itself* ethical: it is *unjust* to have recourse to the letter (commentary or descriptive statement) as that which allows the just to be separated from the unjust. This is the most emphatic element of the seduction of the grammar of moral insight: to infer from the grammatical autonomy of the ethical an ethics of the relation between ethics and representation. As I will argue directly, the most Lyotard can claim is that it would be unjust to displace the claim of justice with an abstract (propositional) criterion of justice *if* there was justice. But this second-order ethicality, the reflexive normativity of ethical commands, is dependent on there being some ethical demand. The grammatical point by itself cannot generate this second-order ethicality and turn it into a ground for empirical ethical demands. Although Lyotard does not quite see it, his defence of Levinas' logic turns on making the second-order reflexive normativity of moral demands into their ground even though he assumes that first-order, context-bound prescriptives are logically prior to any norms which might be thought of as grounding them.

The singular effort of the essay on 'Levinas' Logic' is to demonstrate that Levinas' thought attempts to articulate or express (rather than providing a commentary on) the metaprinciple of asymmetry: *That/Thou/shalt never be/I/!* – which is nothing but a version of the first and third elements of Henrich's grammar (demand and approval, and selfhood founded on moral insight).

Hence, in commenting upon a passage of Levinas' that begins 'The incomparable character of an event like the giving of the Torah [is that] it is accepted before it is known...' Lyotard turns to an analysis of the classical paradoxes implied by the command 'Disobey!' The analysis of these paradoxes is meant to reveal that Levinas' elaborate discourse around the same and the other, with its puzzling insistence upon the otherness of the other and the irreducibility of the other to the same, finally comes down to grasping the command 'Obey!', which in its turn is exhausted by the metaprinciple of asymmetry.

> ['Obey!'] is an absolutely 'empty' proposition, since it is not provided with an instruction to make it executable... It is not executable, but it is that which renders executory... So it is not understood in the sense of being comprehended, but only in the sense of being received. However, it is never in fact received in its own right but merely hidden in the form of complete or 'full' prescriptive statements... [The ethical] begins with the obligation by which the *Thou* is seized. Not with the power to *announce* [which corresponds to the power of freedom]..., but with the other power, which in the West is regarded as a powerlessness – that of being *bound to*...[12]

Bar a few closing remarks, this is where Lyotard's essay on Levinas concludes. And this is puzzling, for however illuminating Lyotard's remarks are they remain grammatical; in being transformed into a grammar, Levinasian existential phenomenology, above all the face-to-face, loses its seductively ethical character.

Lyotard could attempt to defend himself against this charge by claiming that Levinas' most noteworthy formulations about alterity do no more than institute the autonomy of the grammar of prescriptives; their meta-ethical character is just the announcement of the metaprinciple of alterity. This appears a pointed way of expressing the elusiveness of Levinas' fundamental thought, the constant sense that his exorbitant claims for the ethical outrun their phenomenological setting while none the less, somehow, prising open a space between the ethical and the cognitive at the expense of the latter. The move into a conception of discrete and autonomous genres of language returns to prescriptives their irreducible force while protecting them against usurpation, above all by philosophy. That much can and should be said in defence of grammatical analysis.

Even if this does answer the Levinasian, it does nothing for ethics. Even if it is true that every concrete ethical demand, every moral prescription, has embedded *within* it the metaprinciple of alterity, even if, that is, valid prescriptives reiteratively imply the *ethical* necessity of their autonomy from theoretical recuperation, *this would only matter if there were valid prescriptives.*

Lyotard is deceived because he infers from the valid thesis that the executory character of moral demands is intimately bound up with their grammatical form that the 'shalt never be' of the metaprinciple is autonomously ethical. Grammatical insight is not, self-sufficiently, moral insight, even if it is derivatively true that if there are moral demands then the grammatical necessity separating the ethical from the representational given by the metaprinciple *becomes* ethical necessity. If no moral demand is valid, then how could grammatical impropriety be unjust, a moral wrong?[13]

Among the other transformations that take place in the construction of the moral theory of *The Differend* is the recognition that the force of grammatical insight must finally be parasitic upon ethical experience itself. But if ethical experience is to bear philosophical weight, then it must be of an experience whose validity is somehow, in the context of the theory, beyond doubt. And if one were searching through the ruins of the twentieth century for a non-circumventable instance of moral wrong, then almost certainly one's first port of call would be the Nazi genocide of the Jews; it might even be thought to form the exemplary case of moral wrong, that in virtue of which we come to comprehend the very idea of wrong and of injustice.

The Linguistic Displacement

Lyotard's *The Differend* can be read as a rewriting of *Negative Dialectics* under the aegis of the linguistic turn;[14] and like Adorno's work, it construes the Holocaust as putting an end to the ambitions of totalising philosophy. 'After Auschwitz' there are only phrase regimes and the necessity of linking one phrase to another because a totalising philosophical theory, on the model of Hegelian speculative discourse, is no longer possible. The idea of phrase regimes and the necessity of making linkages is strictly formal in character: phrases present addressors, addressees, events, instances, objects, situations.

> The phrase universe is not presented to something or someone as if to a subject. The presentation is that there is a universe. There are as many universes as there are phrases, as many situations of instances as there are phrase universes, that is, as many as there are forms of phrases. Space and time are situations of instances in phrase universes... Man is not what is; what is, is what is presented, an existent, situated at a given instance.[15]

In presenting universes phrases stipulate 'places' for addressor, addressee, and referent. Outside phrases nothing can be made of what is identified through those terms. Lyotard's anti-humanism, his eschewal of reliance on any knowledge of or empathy with human subjects, as in the experience of a human face, is co-extensive with this insistence on phrases, regimes of phrases, genres which supply general rules for the linking phrases, etc.

By making phrases and their linkages the focus of his concern, Lyotard desires once more to replace the substantive claims of philosophy with grammatical insight. However, from a grammatical perspective, prescriptives now appear to Lyotard as hopelessly fragile. The very fact that one experiences oneself as already obligated before one can judge the worth of the demand opens the space of ethicality to blindness and arbitrariness: 'Is the order Abraham receives to sacrifice his son any more intelligible than a memorandum directing round-ups, convoys, concentration camps, and either slow or quick death?'[16] Within the phrase regime of prescriptives this question is unanswerable since when insight into the legitimacy of a prescriptive arrives it arrives too late and in a form that is no longer prescriptive. The point is not just that finding oneself obligated is a scandal for the addressee of a prescriptive, but that scandalousness and powerlessness necessarily include so extensive a cognitive deficit that there is little to choose between sceptical anxiety and dogmatic acceptance. One might suppose this to be the grammatical lesson of the Abraham story.

The grammatical lesson of the Abraham story secretes the nihilistic problematic: if one stays within the space of ethicality, then formally each idiolect is as good as any other idiolect; while if one seeks objectivity, that is, some way of measuring the legitimacy of the authority of an ethical demand, then this will involve making the addressee of the original prescriptive its addressor, thus permanently displacing obligation from the centre of ethics. At one level, Lyotard clearly accepts this displacement. Without attempting to flesh out all the details, Lyotard appears to adopt a familiar modern strategy, namely, to make the legitimacy of a prescriptive depend on the authority of a norm, and then to make the authority of norms a matter of collective autonomy: 'We declare as a norm that "it is obligatory for us to accomplish action *a*."' In place of an original passivity in which an obligation is suddenly thrust upon me, norms involve us giving the law to ourselves so that every event of being addressed is, if legitimate, the counterpart of an event of self-addressing. Notice how formal the principle of autonomy is in this setting: if the problem and scandal of obligation is the asymmetry of addressor and addressee, then placing the original addressee in the position of addressor is the *only* solution that can remove the source of the problem. This would make of the principle of autonomy a piece of grammatical engineering.[17]

Lyotard does not seek to deny the principle of autonomy, and he affirms the emergence of politics as a forum for argumentation over norms. None the less, if the principle of autonomy and the politics that arises from it are, finally, grammatical devices, then the suspicion must arise that something fundamental about ethical experience has been lost in the transition from the regime of prescriptives to the regime of norms. Vindication of that suspicion is underlined once we notice that even within the collective authorisation of norms there must remain a split between the 'we' who authorise the norm and the 'us' who must carry out its requirements. It is not just a matter here of the familiar question 'Who is We?' but of the significance of the split within 'we' between its role as addressor and addressee. If I have understood him correctly, Lyotard's belief is that the difference of grammatical position, addressor and addressee, is more than grammatical; it is the locus of what gets passed over and remains unresolved in the transition from the discourse of ethical obligation to the discourse of collective authorisation of norms; and it is with Auschwitz that the fracturing of the autonomous 'we' and the emergence of an ur-ethicality that belongs to neither prescriptives nor norms occurs.

> 'Auschwitz' would have no speculative name because it would be the proper name of a para-experience or even of a destruction of experience. What determination would Auschwitz be lacking so as to turn it into an experience with a *Resultat* [a Hegelian determinate content]? Would it be that of the impossibility of a *we*? In the concentration camps, there would have been no subject in the first person plural. In the absence of such a subject, there would remain 'after Auschwitz' no subject, no *Selbst* which could prevail upon itself to name itself in naming 'Auschwitz.' No phrase inflected in this person would be possible: we did this, we felt that, they made us suffer this humiliation, we got along in this way, we hope that, we didn't think about..., and even: each of us was reduced to solitude and silence. There would be no collective witness. From many deportees, there is only silence.[18]

For Lyotard it is this silence that disperses the 'we', a fully self-conscious and self-assured collective subject that would transparently know itself, name itself, and in naming itself authorise itself as the giver of norms.

Lyotard's way of prosecuting this argument is deeply unpersuasive. He appears to want to claim that from the radical incommensurability between the SS as addressee and addressor of a command to kill the Jews – who thus remain only a *referent* of the norm without voice, wholly external to Nazi self-legislation – it immediately follows that any 'we' is dispersed.[19] What is unpersuasive here is not the shakiness of the inference, but its specificity: what distinguishes the SS norm from all the other norms where one 'we' takes the death of others only as a referent? Will not any 'we' which is particular and which constitutes itself through reference to some particular ethnic identity regress to a pre-modern conception of the grounds for collective autonomy? Perhaps what Lyotard is claiming is that what Auschwitz shows is that no 'we' can authorise itself without remainder because the remainder will never appear 'in' it, but only for it as a referent. The silence of the Jews, their inability to partake in the norm authorising their slaughter, is the historical marker of the silence that disturbs any claim to autonomous authorisation, which is to say that their silence is not merely grammatical, a formal difficulty in tracking the transition from prescription to norm, and from the addressee to the addressor within the principle of autonomy; their silence is the ur-ethical contestation of those transitions. Showing how any such transition must entail a remainder would provide a powerful critique of the ethical limits of collective will-formation as a legitimate route to the authorisation of norms. But it is unclear how Lyotard's account of the SS does provide such a demonstration.

Having delimited the ethical by identifying it as merely a grammar of a certain sort – prescriptives – it might be thought that Lyotard is here seeking through the instance of the Holocaust to reintroduce some ethical substance into his account that bypasses his restrictedly grammatical accounting. But is the silence of the Jews a matter of ethical substance or merely another grammatical device, a trans-genre grammatical operator? In *The Differend* Lyotard complains against Levinas that expressing obligation 'as a scandal for the one who is obligated: deprived of the "free" use of oneself', one remains within phenomenological or psychoanalytic descriptions which are 'far too human and humanist'.[20] By this Lyotard presumably means that an appropriately anti-humanist phrasing of obligation must be austerely grammatical. However, Lyotard can only sustain the force of his anti-humanism by a shift which is also a sleight of hand: the question of the ethical, or at least the force that was traditionally associated with the ethical, is not to be located in prescriptives or the phenomenon of obligation, but rather in what eludes or falls between different grammars, discourses, genres, in what grammar or genre has not yet phrased or found a sentence for. Lyotard's general term for this moment of the yet-to-be-phrased, of what must be put into sentences but cannot be, is 'the differend'.

> In the differend, something 'asks' to be put into phrases, suffers from the wrong of not being able to be put into phrases right away. This is when the human beings who thought they could [freely] use language as an instrument of communication learn through the feeling of pain which accompanies silence... they are summoned by language, not to augment to their profit the quantity of information communicable through existing idioms, but to recognise that what remains to be phrased exceeds what they can presently phrase.[21]

The notion of the differend is complex and conceptually slippery because in it the logic of prescriptives, especially the metaprinciple of alterity, is retained albeit without the force of obligation – the differend imposes a 'necessity' (to link phrases) not an 'obligation' to perform a particular action[22] – while none the less relying upon the same type of experiential material that Lyotard had dismissed as all too human in Levinas: through feeling or sentiment, in a moment of pain and passivity, we are alerted to a here-and-now demand to make good a wrong, a damage that occurs simply through something escaping all existing idioms. In virtue of this demand our freedom over language and language as a means of communication is eclipsed; acknowledging the differend requires the recognition of another axis of language which is 'responsible' to, beholden and in debt to 'the object', the other. At its most primitive level language is here being conceived of as having two fundamental and incommensurable axes: an axis oriented toward the exchange of information (communication), and an axis that is bound to the world, to what is not yet phrased or expressed and appears to be 'asking' to be phrased. For Lyotard, communicative interaction and instrumental rationality *both* belong to the communicative axis of language, to the dimension of language where control, freedom, full speech, and activity are manifest. The differend signals a mode or condition of language that marks what is said as a response to the world, as a response or the necessity of a response to a silence that is, in part at least, a consequence of communicative discourse. The differend reveals how language differs from itself, remains outside itself, always as such subject to a demand that as 'spoken' has always already been approved. Through the institution of the differend as forming the core of an axis of language opposed to communication the pluralism of genres, e.g., representational discourse and ethical discourse, implied in the account of Levinas is taken over by a conception of *language in general* in which a quasi-ethical moment, a moment that descriptively tokens the grammar of ethicality, has priority. All this, needless to say, is uncannily Adornoesque; in the passage just quoted one could substitute 'the nonidentical' for 'the differend' without adjustment.

The logic of the differend copes with the discovery of the fragility of ethical discourse proper – the regression to an idiolect that threatens prescriptives, and the inevitable indeterminacy of all norms – by removing ethicality as such from the narrow confines of prescriptive and normative grammar and into a transgrammatical condition of language. Recall the original flaw we discovered in Levinas' thought, namely, that the metaprinciple of alterity could not be assigned the role of the ground of the ethical since it only possesses its full force as a reiteration of some concrete ethical obligation. What is thus needed is an analysis of the meaning of the ethical that detaches it from the grammatical requirements of prescriptives and norms.

In Levinas' thought, the obligation in question does not result from an authority previously legitimated by me or us. If I am obligated by the other, it is not because the other has some right to obligate me which I would have directly or mediately granted him or her. My freedom is not the source of his or her authority; one is not obligated because one is free, and because your law is my law, but because your request is not my law, because we are liable for the other. Obligation through freedom or consent is secondary. It presupposes a liability, a fracture in the ego's fortress... *This liability is nonetheless not a condition for the possibility for ethics... It is already the entirety of ethics, it contains together its two faces, freedom and persecution.* The latter does not differ from the former as heteronomy differs from autonomy. Each requires the I's attachment to the other, its dependency, its being taken hostage. What gives rise to persecution is when the I is 'passively' attached against its will, and in its recurrent narcissism, which protests against this liability and does not accept exteriority.[23]

What is crucial in this passage is Lyotard's separation of liability for the other, which is 'already the entirety of ethics', from persecution which is the experience of liability as refused. If persecution is the phenomenological expression of obligation, then Lyotard's contention that logically obligation cannot be prevented from collapsing into a maddened idiolect does no more than take Levinas at his word. Equally, however, in isolating liability and dependence as the entirety of ethics Lyotard makes possible the detaching of ethicality from the grammar of obligation. The differend is liability without obligation, necessity without ought; the differend offers a pagan, translinguistic instantiation of the grammar of moral insight.

Finding sentences and idioms to articulate the wrong of the differend can occur in any number of genres: moral, scientific, historical, aesthetic. In each, in so far as they seek to give voice to the differend they are responding to wrong. However anti-Hegelian the impetus of Lyotard's thought, the ethical logic governing the differend is one of dependence and liability (the moment of silence, pain, suffering) and independence (the moment in which an idiom is found). While the silence or yet-to-be-phrased of the differend (which although a translinguistic phenomenon is, for that very reason, considered by Lyotard a part of language, language's difference from itself) inscribes the idea of there being an indeterminate condition for the punctual determinacy of particular sentences, thus implying the existence of a translinguistic indeterminacy, it is unclear why one would call this indeterminacy (or silence) *wrong*, or typify its existence in the language of pain and suffering. Must not the feeling of pain which accompanies silence latch onto something more than the indeterminacy of what has yet to find determinate linguistic expression? Why should we not consider the pain and suffering involved here as metaphorical, as co-opting the silence which real pains and sufferings result in to the more refined and abstract purpose of providing an account of language? And why consider the silence of the differend the *type* of all wrong? What of all the numerous wrongs we can determinately articulate: the cruel, the mean, the vicious, the self-righteous, the insensitive, the murderous, what betrays, slanders, dominates or maliciously injures?

Running through *The Differend* and implicitly responding to these questions is the example of Auschwitz. Awkwardly, Lyotard presents Auschwitz as the principal example of the differend, as if the thought of the differend is given with and through the event of the Holocaust. Yet this use of Auschwitz is ambiguous. Again, following Adorno, Auschwitz puts out of play the claims of Hegelian dialectic; with the dispatch of the dialectic goes the claim to omnicompetence of all theoretical discourse: 'Auschwitz is the most real of all realities... Its name marks the confines wherein historical knowledge sees its competence impugned.'[24] The ground for this claim is not, as one might anticipate, the extreme horror of the camps, but rather the destruction of what would render an account of what happened there determinate, namely, the voices of the victims. Because they cannot testify to and thus make determinate their murder, their genocide, then no historical account of their slaughter can saturate, completely and adequately account for, what happened. Hence, Lyotard's bizarre analogy of Auschwitz with an earthquake that destroys not only lives and buildings, but also the instruments used to measure earthquakes.[25] The weight of this strange analogy is that the indeterminacy of Auschwitz, its pleading for phrasing and its being forever beyond determinate phrasing, yields the differend and its status as the type of wrong; what, after all, could be more wrong than *that*? It is as if because Auschwitz can never be phrased, it becomes the exemplary differend, an absolute differend.[26]

Let us ignore the fact that it is not what happened at Auschwitz, the manner and the fact of the Nazi genocide, the cold brutality and the deaths, that Lyotard claims is at stake in the name 'Auschwitz' but the consequence – that the victims are forever barred from stating the wrong done to them – and that this altering of the stakes of Auschwitz is offered in the name of a displacement of all too human ethicality for the sake of pagan grammaticality. Even so there is an evident disproportion amongst the elements of Lyotard's argument. At its crudest, one might say that one does not require an absolute differend, one does not require Auschwitz, in order to underwrite the principle of indeterminacy; there are other ways – pragmatic, hermeneutic, Wittgensteinian – that could be employed to demonstrate the indeterminate conditions for all determinate meaning. Worse, because Auschwitz appears as an absolute differend, then its role of demonstrating indeterminacy as wrong, which is the idea of the differend, is undermined. Even if one agreed with the thesis that it is impossible to render Auschwitz fully determinate, and that this impossibility is tied to what was done to the victims, it would not follow that every case of indeterminacy, every case of the yet-to-be-phrased, is wrong. On the contrary, by making Auschwitz an *absolute* differend Lyotard removes it from the class of items of which it is meant to be exemplary. Finally, in pressing indeterminacy into the mould of wrong is not Lyotard, through the efficacy of the negative instance of Auschwitz, doing precisely what he stated in the Levinas essay could not be done, providing an omnitemporal criterion of wrong? So a formula might run: if yet to be phrased, then a wrong seeking redress.

The Traumatic Return

The evidence of *Heidegger and 'the jews'* is that Lyotard came to recognise that transcendental liability could not be secured directly through the historical event of Auschwitz; yet it is equally evident that his ethical project remains bound to the instance of Auschwitz and committed to the securing of transcendental liability. The path he will follow in *Heidegger and 'the jews'* is already adumbrated in *The Differend*. Following Adorno, Lyotard pursues the claim of transcendental liability through a critique of Hegelian speculative dialectic. In the *Phenomenology of Spirit* Hegel states that 'the wounds of the Spirit heal and leave no scars behind'.[27] To deploy Auschwitz against speculative dialectic is to urge that there is about it something that cannot be healed over, that its wounding is permanent. But for that wounding to have the role Lyotard wants to assign it, it would have to be a wounding of Spirit, a wounding of collective humanity; none of Lyotard's arguments in *The Differend* succeeds in showing how any one historical event could assume this role.

Still, Lyotard wants to aver, there is something about Auschwitz that connects with the idea of a permanent wound, a wound beyond healing. A wound to the mind or psyche that cannot be scarred over is called a trauma; in attempting to raise the instance of Auschwitz to universality, to make it an absolute differend, Lyotard meant it to be a concrete historical trauma for Western thought and language, thus historically putting an end to our will to truth, and inaugurating the epoch of the differend as transcendental liability, a liability that has always structured human experience but whose force is only realised in the secularising destruction that is Auschwitz. The inference that makes *Heidegger and 'the jews'* possible is simple: if the force of Auschwitz is its traumatising effect, and it is through this traumatising effect that it can be an absolute differend securing transcendental liability, then, in default of the idea of a uniquely historical trauma of humanity, transcendental liability is to be found ahistorically in the traumatic constitution of the subject. The traumatic event of the Holocaust reveals, in a way to be shown, the ahistorical trauma that is at the root of Western subjectivity. Trauma is the model of a wholly secular exteriority that cannot be made interior, of a demand that can never be fully understood or represented, of a law that forever wounds me. The path of *Heidegger and 'the jews'* is the transcription of the differend into the sublime unconscious.

The strategy of *Heidegger and 'the jews'* turns on demonstrating the constitutive split or fracturing *within* the subject that is necessary in order to satisfy the first moment of the grammar of the ethical, only here Lyotard will use psychoanalytic theory to substantiate his claim in place of his unconvincing construal of the prescriptive of the SS to kill all Jews. The fracturing of the subject must be internal in order that the *demand* of the good be always already *approved*. What keeps the good external to the subject is its posing of a normative demand; but, again, without approval, without the subject finding that it has somehow already given assent, the good would remain a sheer exteriority. Lyotard's difficulty here will be analogous to the problems he faced in *The Differend*: he must not only demonstrate that the subject is necessarily internally fractured or divided, haunted by an exteriority it cannot fully internalise, but show that this fracturing of the subject *is ethical* rather than being only a necessary condition for the possibility of ethics.

As in *The Differend*, the stakes here are posed in terms of the reach and competence of history since it is the task of the discipline of history to render human events cognisable, to remember what has been forgotten or what a community would prefer to forget. Lyotard contends that the meaning of history, and hence what makes a past significant, is necessarily betrayed by the practice of history. The referent of historical reflection is not 'reality' but 'the stakes of a question' which take place in an argument;[28] this referent is invoked in the course of historical writing, but the course of that writing is dictated not by those stakes but by the requirements of proof and demonstration: 'But this argued "proof"...gives rise to scientific argumentation whose stakes are cognitive: is it true that it was really like this? In this way, the value of the probe is submitted to probing, to renewed argumentation, and thus into infinity.'[29] There is betrayal here because the satisfaction which historical argument can achieve, the satisfaction of having established the true facts of the matter, is a way of forgetting the stakes of the question, the sense that knowing and remembering these facts matter. History as a scientific practice of remembering is always subtended by something that it cannot cognise, by something which its remembering is a way of forgetting.

Without much in the way of transition, Lyotard moves directly from the idea that what is 'at stake' in the past, what makes a certain past significant, is not something that can be remembered or cognised, to the idea that we are concerned with a 'past that is not past, that does not haunt the present, in the sense that its absence is felt... which is not an object of memory like something that might have been forgotten and must be remembered (with a view to a "good end", to correct knowledge)'.[30] The model or type of such a past is a traumatic episode. An event is traumatic if its 'shock' to the psyche is of such a kind that it cannot, at the time of occurrence, be taken in and assimilated, grasped, cognised, dealt with. Because the traumatic event is not taken in when it occurs, it is never present for consciousness as a discrete and temporally locatable happening. But if the event is never present for consciousness, then it is not something that could be forgotten, repressed, left behind. The unassimilability of the shocking event makes it a temporal past that is for consciousness never past, a heterogeneous scrap of history permanently haunting consciousness. When it occurs, the force of the shocking event is not registered (it is 'too much' for consciousness to take in); when its force does register, in the acting out and suffering of the subject, there is no event, no shock.

Now if we consider our standard understanding of human consciousness on the model of the operations of the historian, and I assume that this is what Lyotard is asking us to do, then consciousness *as such* must be constituted by *stakes* that it cannot make conscious and cognisable, by some immemorial past. Speculatively, following Freud, Lyotard identifies this immemorial past with sexual difference: 'One can, one must (one cannot not) give it a thousand names: the sexual, castration of the mother, incest taboo, killing of the father, the father as name, debt, law, paralyzing stupor, seduction, and, perhaps the most beautiful: exogamy...'[31] Lyotard can be cavalier about the name of this traumatic event because on analogy with the delimiting of history he is confident that there must be such formation of the psyche if anything like consciousness is to exist.[32]

Let us ignore the central ellipsis in Lyotard's argument, namely, the transition from the acceptable thesis that the referent for a historical question are stakes that cannot be determined historically, cognitively, to the claim that what makes a past significant is that it is not past, and thus traumatic and immemorial. Let us grant that consciousness is formed through an original repression on the model of a traumatic event. What does any of this have to do with the Jews and with the Nazi genocide, and hence with the ethical?

What distinguishes the Jews is that they, however mythically or fabulously, identify themselves collectively in terms of this traumatic wounding, or, we might say, in terms of a transcendental liability.[33] In the economy of Western history 'the jews' are the constant reminder of the originary terror that lies at the basis of every psyche since they make that terror the constitutive source of their collective identity. In the form of an unrepresentable god who holds them hostage, 'the jews' bear witness to a liability to the other that will never be satisfied. As a consequence, 'the Jews' lie outside the central developmental lines of the West: Greek science, Roman law and politics, Christian spirituality, and the Enlightenment.[34] Whatever positive sense each of these has, they are also defence mechanisms against the original terror, against 'the jews'. Western anti-semitism, of which these defence mechanisms are a part, is thus 'one of the means of the apparatus of its culture to bind and represent as much as possible – to protect against – the originary terror'.[35]

The Shoah can now be recognised as simply the most exorbitant form of Western anti-semitism. The Shoah cannot be represented not because of its horror, nor because it was a genocide, the project to exterminate an entire people, but because what the Nazis sought to exterminate was 'the jews', the unrepresentable itself. Auschwitz's never-ending silence, determinate language's inability ever to get on level terms with it, to make it a historic event simpliciter, is the sign of its being a traumatic instance: never to be forgotten because never present (determinately) in order to be later forgotten. Rather than seeking to avoid this identification of Auschwitz, trauma and the ethical, Lyotard attempts to forge the connections more firmly, to make 'the jews' into the historic embodiment of the traumatically formed unconscious and the Shoah into the most radical attempt by the occident to rid itself of the unforgettable. Thus, despite a long detour, Lyotard offers us a defence of Levinas: (ethically) testifying to 'the jews' is (ethically) testifying to the unrepresentable other at the core of each human psyche. A last extended quotation from Lyotard:

> 'the jews'...testify that this misery, this servitude to that which remains unfinished, is constitutive of the spirit. From them emanates only this anguish that 'nothing will do,' that this thought harbours a lack it does not even lack, and that if one can hope for some progress in freedom, it is of course against this feeling, yet thanks to it, steeped in it. Now, the final solution consists in exterminating this feeling and along with it the secret of thought, even of occidental thought. Its other side. It destroys the other side of thought. Another side that is nowhere.[36]

For Lyotard the Shoah is the effort to exterminate the emblem of the originary terror, the trauma, at the root of the psyche. The very otherness of the other, of alterity beyond sameness, of forgetting beyond and before presence, that Lyotard sought to tame in his grammatical analysis of Levinas, here returns. Despite himself, for Lyotard there is no ethics without 'the unknown law', an absolute differend.

Grammatical Problems, Again

While Lyotard's comprehension of 'the jews' is suggestive, it must be asked whether his deployment of psychoanalysis cannot be subject to the same sort of grammatical critique to which he submitted Levinas' thought. What is the status of the originary terror of sexual difference in relation to ethics? And in what sense are 'the jews' a witness to it?

Even if accepted, what does the account of the traumatic formation of the psyche show us? It might well show that the occidental project of seeking radical individual or collective self-possession, the project of the mastery of nature within and without, is bound to be self-defeating. If it is a condition of anything we might recognise as a human subject that this subject, in virtue of the social practices in which it participates and through which it is formed, must acknowledge, implicitly or explicitly, its radical dependence, then it would follow that failure to make this acknowledgement would lead to pathology. But the most that shows is that for a human being to be a non-pathological subject it must have the resources to acknowledge dependence. Psychoanalysis can demonstrate a necessity, a functional requirement, perhaps even a transcendental constraint on subject-formation, but what it does not show is liability, responsibility. It might justly be said that thus far the West has discovered very few mechanisms for acknowledging radical dependence, most notably religion and ethics, and that what the grammar of the ethical properly inscribes is the logical form for what, so far as we know, would count as the acknowledgement of dependence. But this still leaves a gap between psychoanalysis' discovery of the transcendental constraints on the formation of the subject, radical psychological dependence, and the mode or modes in which that constraint is satisfied. Ethical liability, transcendental or empirical, cannot be inferred from the traumatic formation of the subject.

This thesis parallels the objection lodged to the metaprinciple of the ethical: concrete ethical requirements cannot be rationally grounded in a general principle which preserves their formal autonomy. Recourse to sexual difference does not reveal or necessitate any form of transcendental liability; ethical demands, if there are any, promote the satisfaction of the functional requirements of sexual difference. The existence of the functional requirement does nothing by itself toward showing what would make any particular ethical demand rationally acceptable.

What of 'the jews'? In what sense do 'the jews' testify 'that this misery...is constitutive of the spirit', to the anguish that 'nothing will do'? There is an ambiguity in Lyotard's words: in austerely psychological terms, the claim that 'nothing will do' can only mean that nothing will heal the wound, and thus nothing can transform the condition of radical dependence into complete autonomous independence. But this is only to say that any quest for radical independence is bound to fail. Ethically, however, the thought that 'nothing will do' means that nothing will remove our liability. But for us to accept this latter thought, it would be necessary that we accepted some symbolic terms of reference, religious or ethical. Hence, for the Jews themselves this would mean nothing more than that they must continue to obey their unrepresentable god within the same symbolically elaborated terms as they have always done. And for us, we who witness their testimony? Here Lyotard's own terms of reference fall into the grammatical void. If we accept Lyotard's reading, then we must perforce accept the claim that there exist transcendental constraints on subject formation which the symbolic and cognitive regimes of the occident struggle against and tendentially rationally occlude. But at the symbolic or discursive level, the most that can be inferred from this is that these projects are rationally self-defeating. At his level of generality, the reflective comprehension of the misery of 'the jews' is not ethical but cognitive since it depends upon interpreting Jewish religion in the light of psychoanalytic thought, and thus, precisely, of seeing 'the jews' (in quotation marks) as an embodiment of the exigencies of sexual difference. If we were to remain at this reflective and cognitive level, then, as Lyotard himself submits,[37] the consequence would be a rational critique of Enlightenment rationalism in the name of what cannot be represented; which, of course, is but a statement of the process of 'negative dialectics'.

None of these reproaches to Lyotard appears to engage explicitly with the purported entwining of ethics and trauma. But what would an explicit engagement look like? Because in traumatic wounding there is an event which is formative for consciousness that it cannot cognitively assimilate, it structurally overlaps with, at least, the first element of the grammar of the ethical (demand and approval – or, as here, disapproval), and arguably overlaps with the other three elements as well.[38] And traumatic wounding requires acknowledgement, requires the subject to admit that what has never happened as a cognisable event has happened and remains formative. Finding an adequate form in order to make such an acknowledgement is the therapy appropriate to pathological trauma. But everyday life is not therapy, nor can we easily identify the kind of traumatic events that *disable* subjects with, however it is expressed, the traumatic instance constitutive of subjectivity. This thought is overdetermined. A traumatic event is that which disables a well-functioning psyche. How can the traumatism that is wounding and disabling be structurally the same as the traumatic occurrence which constitutes and makes the psyche possible? Is not the description of the founding event as traumatic a metaphorical extension (or deletion) of its use in reference to pathology-inducing events? What could legitimate this metaphorical extension? Certainly, as Lyotard asserts, both types of occurrence partake of the strange logic and temporality of *Nachträglichkeit*: shock without affect, affect without event. 'The essence of the event: that *there is* "comes before" *what* there is.'[39] But, as has been insisted upon throughout, this primacy of event over representation belongs to a wider range of phenomena than trauma, above all practical and aesthetic consciousness. No one has tracked this range of non-traumatic *Nachträglichkeit*-type episodes as persistently as Lyotard, including his continual deployment of the aesthetic sublime as the core element in delimiting representational thought. The presence of *Nachträglichkeit* itself, then, cannot be used to anchor the thesis that the psyche is formed through a traumatic moment.

Without detailing the diversity of accounts of originary repression, it can none the less be said that they all agree with some version of the thesis that the formation of the subject crucially involves the experience of loss and separation, and that this experience must be broadly understood as one of the intrusion into the subject-to-be of a radical exteriority (law and language for Lacan, the enigmatic message for Laplanche, enigmatic otherness for Kristeva) that must be negotiated and without the negotiation of which there is no possibility of subjects. Suffering separation (from the mother, say) and learning separateness are constitutive moments in the formation of a human subject; without the first moment, the second could not occur. Hence, while the originary moment of intrusion formally *appears* to recapitulate the kind of intrusion found in empirical traumatic events, its character as *simultaneously*, with the same movement, instituting loss and separation implies a significant difference. Loss and separateness are what are to be acknowledged; the temporal and genetic processes through which this acknowledgement occurs are the hurdles and conditions of being a subject.[40] As such these stages are the critical points of the negotiation, the points at which crises may occur and failure threatens. Now if the intrusive moment is emphasised at the expense of the institution of separation and loss, together with the processes of negotiation and acknowledgement required by that institution, then the formative event could not be formative. If the intrusive event is thematised apart from what it institutes, then it is being imaged melancholically. The melancholic, like the victim of trauma, is overwhelmed by the nonpresentable other – the dead other, the traumatic event. However, the melancholic sustains what appears as deeply akin to traumatic repetition and haunting by *failing* to acknowledge loss and separation. Both the melancholic and the pre-oedipal infant must acknowledge constitutive loss. The victim of empirical trauma must learn to live with the permanent wounding, which is not constitutive of anything, but disabling. Hence, while originary repression does possess a potentially trauma-inducing moment, an event which even if it is successfully negotiated at the time may become traumatic afterward, that event is not itself traumatic but constitutive. If it is theorised in terms of trauma rather than loss and separation, then all distinction between melancholy and mourning is dissolved. What constitutive intrusion requires of the spirit, of culture, is that it find symbolic resources to express the dependence of the subject on what cannot be represented. An ethic of infinite liability would indeed capture and satisfy this requirement; saying so, however, is only to pose the question of a post-Holocaust ethics, not to answer it.

The Holocaust was a traumatic event; but insofar as it was traumatic, disabling, does not that itself negatively signify the self so wounded as having been normatively constituted? And thus that insofar as the self can suffer traumatic dislocation, then that and that alone testifies to a normative constitution of the self beyond and before the field of trauma? In a sense, it is true that the trauma of the Holocaust opens or reopens the space of ethicality; but it is the fragile space of the vulnerable and injurable animal we are. Might it not be animal injurability that truly represents our 'constitutive infirmity'? Adorno thought that Auschwitz demanded of consciousness a return to a vulgar materialism of the injurable animal. That thought has yet to be properly heard.[41]

Notes

1 *Otherwise than Being or Beyond Essence*, trans. Alphonso Lingis, The Hague: Martinus Nijhoff, 1981, p.111. For a lucid and thoughtful exposition of this aspect of Levinas' thought in relation to Freud and Lacan see Simon Critchley's essays 'The Original Traumatism: Levinas and Psychoanalysis', and '*Das Ding*: Lacan and Levinas', both in his *Ethics-Politics-Subjectivity: Essays on Derrida, Levinas and Contemporary French Thought*, London: Verso, 1999, pp.183–216. This essay is part of a continuing conversation with Critchley on this topic.

2 Trans. Andreas Michel and Mark Roberts, Minneapolis: University of Minnesota Press, 1990, p.17.

3 Dieter Henrich, *The Unity of Reason: Essays on Kant's Philosophy*, London: Harvard University Press, 1994, pp.55–87. 'The Concept of Moral Insight' was translated by Manfred Kuehn. Henrich means his analysis, however much guided by the Kantian instance, to be a consequence of a historical induction.

4 Henrich, *Unity*, pp.61–62.

5 *Ibid.*, p.62; my emphasis.

6 *Ibid.*, p.63.

7 *Ibid.*, p.227, note 5.

8 *Ibid.*, p.64.

9 *Ibid.*, p.66; practically: ought implies can.

10 For Levinas' own recognition of the problem see E. Levinas, *Difficile liberté*, 2nd edn, Paris: Albin Michel, 1963, p.379. This passage from Levinas is quoted by Lyotard in 'Levinas' Logic', in Andrew Benjamin (ed.), *The Lyotard Reader*, Oxford: Basil Blackwell, 1989, p.281. This essay was translated by Ian McLeod.

11 'Levinas' Logic,' p.286.

12 *Ibid.*, pp.307–08.

13 For an acute awareness of this problem and a remarkably subtle attempt to respond to it on Levinas' behalf, see Robert Bernasconi, "'Only the Persecuted...'": Language of the Oppressor, Language of the Oppressed', in Adriaan T. Peperzak (ed.), *Ethics as First Philosophy: The Significance of Emmanuel Levinas for Philosophy, Literature and Religion,* London: Routledge, 1995, pp.77–86. Bernasconi rightly underlines how non-philosophical experience both gives rise to and contests philosophical thought, and indicates where acknowledgement of this can be located in Levinas. The centrality of Bernasconi's claim for the validity of Levinas' philosophy and the simultaneous confession of how marginal this moment is in Levinas leads me to doubt that the thesis can be reasonably sustained.

14 *The Differend: Phrases in Dispute,* trans. Georges Van Den Abbeele, Manchester: Manchester University Press, 1988, p.xiii.

15 'Discussions, or Phrasing "After Auschwitz"', in Benjamin (ed.), *The Lyotard Reader,* pp.372, 373. The essay was translated by Georges Van Den Abbeele.

16 *The Differend,* p.107.

17 Or better: the Lyotardian point is that Kant's Copernican turn in ethics and its Hegelian extension from 'I' to 'We' should be seen as formal and grammatical rather than substantive.

18 *The Differend,* pp.97–98.

19 Even Geoffrey Bennington, the most knowledgeable commentator on Lyotard, in his *Lyotard: Writing the Event,* Manchester: Manchester University Press, 1988, p.151, presents him as making an immediate inference of this kind.

20 *The Differend,* pp.109–10.

21 *Ibid.,* p.13.

22 *Ibid.,* p.116.

23 *Ibid.,* p.112, my emphasis.

24 *Ibid.,* p.58.

25 *Ibid.,* p.56.

26 *Ibid.,* p.57.

27 G.W.F. Hegel, *The Phenomenology of Spirit,* trans. A.V. Miller, Oxford: Clarendon Press, 1977, p.407.

28 *Heidegger and 'the jews',* p.9.

29 *Ibid.,* pp.9–10.

30 *Ibid.,* p.11.

31 *Ibid.,* p.19.

32 I do not mean to suggest that Lyotard is saying that sexual difference is necessary for sentience or even some primitive forms of cognition. By 'consciousness' I assume he means the consciousness of biologically under-determined agents. The idea of the 'stakes' of consciousness is meant to imply the practical horizon of conscious activity.

33 *Ibid.,* pp.21–22.

34 *Ibid.,* p.23.

35 *Ibid.*

36 *Ibid.,* p.27. For comparison, consider Levinas' conclusion to a long footnote in 'Substitution' concerning 'nonconsciousness' (Levinas' term for the unconscious): 'the nonconscious is understood as the nonvoluntariness of persecution, which, as persecution, interrupts every justification, every apology, and every logos. This reduction to silence is a passivity this side of all material passivity. This side of the neutrality of things, absolute passivity becomes incarnation, corporeality, that is to say, susceptibility to pain, outrage, and unhappiness. In its susceptibility, it bears the trace of this *hither side* of things as a responsibility for what the persecuted, in her or his ipseity, did not will, that is, a responsibility for the very persecution she or he undergoes.' *Emmanuel Levinas: Basic Philosophical Writings,* ed. Adriaan T. Peperzak, Simon Critchley and Robert Bernasconi,

Bloomington: Indiana University Press, 1996, p.183.

37 *Heidegger and 'the jews'*, p.29.

38 Because it must be 'this' event of wounding, it will have one of the names of sexual difference; the epistemic requirement is satisfied. Because the agent must take a stand on the wounding of sexual difference as a condition for selfhood, the requirement of grounding the self in 'the good' is satisfied. Finally, the very nature of traumatic wounding is, as Lyotard reiterates (*ibid.*, p.16), the acknowledgement *that* the unrepresentable exists apart from 'what it is' so satisfying the ontological requirement.

39 *Ibid.*, p.16.

40 In *'Das Ding*: Lacan and Levinas', *op. cit.*, Simon Critchley beautifully comments: 'In a Kleinian register, might one not wonder whether the radical *separation* of trauma that defines the ethical subject, requires *reparation* in a work of love? With this in mind, might one not imagine the rhythm of Levinas's discourse as a movement between separation and reparation, between the tear and repair, between the traumatic wound and the healing sublimation, between the subject and consciousness...?' (p.206). Critchley here seems to be admitting that the structural reality that appears under the title of 'originary trauma' is nothing other than 'separation', as if what is at stake here is the standard Hegelian dialectic of separateness and connectedness. If so, then 'traumatic wound' is metaphorical.

41 For a partial exception to this claim see Elaine Scarry's still luminous *The Body in Pain: The Making and Unmaking of the World*, New York: Oxford University Press, 1985. I offer a reading of Adorno's interpretation of Auschwitz in my *Adorno: Disenchantment and Ethics*, New York: Cambridge University Press, forthcoming, Chs 8–9.

CHAPTER 6

Lyotard: Emancipation, Anti-Semitism and 'the Jews'

DAVID SEYMOUR

The word of God must be infinite, or, to put it in a different way, the absolute word is as such meaningless, but it is pregnant with meaning. Under human eyes it enters into significant finite embodiments which mark the innumerable layers of meaning... The key itself may be lost, but an immense desire to look for it remains alive.[1]

In this essay I investigate Jean-François Lyotard's thinking on the related questions of anti-semitism and the Holocaust. However, as a way in it is useful to locate his thought within the context of social theory's reflections on these issues as a whole.

Background

Beginning with Marx's *On the Jewish Question*[2] and continuing to the present day, social theory has reflected upon the causes of modern anti-Jewish hostility. However, despite the many varied ways in which social theory has approached the issue of anti-semitism, one theme constantly re-appears. Drawing on the fact that the term 'anti-semitism' first gained popular acceptance in 1879,[3] social theory has recognised some connection between anti-semitism, political emancipation and the granting to Jews of political and civil rights. Yet this enduring thematic should not mask the fact that the way in which the relationship has been theorised has changed considerably over the past century and a half. Perhaps the most dramatic change has been brought about as a result of the events that occurred in the middle of the twentieth century and which have since come to be known as 'the Holocaust'. If we compare social theory's accounts of anti-semitism before the Holocaust with those that came after, we are struck but not surprised by a definite change in tone. It is as if the Holocaust has inflicted a trauma upon social theory which is most evident in its increasingly negative (even nihilistic) attitude adopted toward emancipation.

Reflections on anti-semitism can be delineated into three distinct periods. The first period covers the period of the struggle for Jewish emancipation and its immediate success. According to Marx and Nietzsche[4] the causes of anti-semitism are understood as connected with the shortcomings of emancipation. However, it is also the case that they stress the *potentiality* of emancipation in the sense that whilst anti-semitism *may* be *one* of the outcomes of the limits of emancipation, it is not necessarily the only possible outcome. Correspondingly, they also emphasise the positive or beneficial aspects of modern emancipation. Most noticeable is the idea that it brings with it the social and political forms of universal freedom and equality. To paraphrase Marx, whether freedom, equality and fraternity will reign, or barbarism, remains indeterminate.

In the accounts of anti-semitism written during and in the immediate aftermath of the Holocaust, the factors present in the earlier accounts undergo a change of emphasis. Most noticeable and significant amongst these modifications is the manner in which the relationship of modern emancipation to the emergence of anti-semitism is reformulated. The ambivalence and open-endedness of political emancipation is restricted and, as a consequence, its degeneration into anti-semitism is explained in a more deterministic and structural manner. This more stringent critique is exemplified by Hannah Arendt[5] and Adorno and Horkheimer[6] who understand the relationship between political emancipation and anti-semitism as an inversion of freedom into barbarity and equality into inequality. In accounting for this inversion they still rely upon a mediating factor: it was emancipation's imbrication with social forms of domination tied to capitalist development that resulted in the emergence of anti-semitism. For Arendt, it was emancipation's entanglement within the contradictions of nation and state.

This idea of a mediating 'space' between emancipation and anti-semitism is also reflected in the view that, whilst the seeds of anti-semitism are identified as existing within the structures of bourgeois society in the period immediately following political emancipation, anti-semitism only emerges in its absolute form as an element of a new social configuration: totalitarianism in the thought of Arendt and fascism and late capitalism for Adorno and Horkheimer. However, in seeking to establish the connection between these general conditions and anti-semitism, the latter appears as the lightning-conductor for more fundamental and complex problems. The idea that the Jewish Question is of central significance comes to the fore.

The third period, which can be characterised as 'postmodern', represents a further and radical abandonment of any trust or hope in the praxis of emancipation. In these accounts any space or distance between political emancipation and anti-semitism is occluded. In this period the critique of political emancipation is so harsh that anti-semitism comes to be read as inhering within its very substance and nature. Political emancipation becomes synonymous with the exclusion of the Jews and as a result, rights – as the medium through which emancipation was concretised – come to be represented as coercive instruments of dismissal and denial. Corresponding to this view of anti-semitism, the Holocaust is read as an event inscribed within the substance of political emancipation and the *ambivalence* of emancipation present in earlier accounts is replaced by an all-encompassing negativity.

Jean-François Lyotard's reflections on the question of anti-semitism can be located in this third period. In the account of his thought that follows, the consequences of his loss of faith in the praxis of emancipation will be pursued. In the most general terms, these consequences can be reduced to one troubling element. Put briefly, Lyotard's reflections on anti-semitism in general and its relationship to emancipation in particular fail to establish the critical distance that social theory requires between the object of its investigation and the nature of the theory. This loss of critical distance manifests itself in an unwitting 'mirroring' (in reverse) of many of the staples of the anti-semitic worldview: resistance to all forms of emancipation that are dependent upon notions of equality; the belief that there is 'something about' the Jews that will always belie the attempt at emancipation; the conviction that the 'Jewish Question' is not merely one aspect of the modern condition but the marker or index of modernity itself. I am, of course, in no way suggesting that Lyotard's thinking can be described as anti-semitic but rather that his species of philosemitism reflects the trauma that the Holocaust has inflicted upon social theory: its negative reading of emancipation which leaves nothing of the modern world that may be of use now or in the future.

Lyotard's Theory of Anti-Semitism

Lyotard's contribution to critical theories of anti-semitism is contained in a series of books and articles written from the early 1980s to the early 1990s. Although the historical context of any text is important to illuminate its meaning, for Lyotard's work it is in many ways decisive. The immediate spur for Lyotard's contemplation of anti-semitism was a series of scandalous issues in France that grabbed popular and academic attention. The first of these episodes was the publication of Faurisson's 'denial' of the existence of gas chambers at Auschwitz in 1981.[7] It was partly as an intervention in this controversy that Lyotard wrote and published *The Differend* in 1983.[8] This dispute was followed a couple of years later by the so-called 'Heidegger Affair' which followed the publication of Victor Farias' indictment of Heidegger's commitment to National Socialism.[9] It was as a contribution to this debate that Lyotard published *Heidegger and 'the jews'* in 1988.[10] Finally, two articles published in 1990, 'Europe, the Jews, and the Book' and 'The Grip (*Mainmise*)' comprise Lyotard's reflections on the desecration of the Jewish cemetery in Carpentras.[11] Yet, while these specific episodes may have served as the impetus for a series of publications focusing on anti-semitism and the Holocaust, in many ways these publications also became a critique of the entire tradition of 'Western' thought and in particular of its discourses of progress and emancipation.

The cumulative effect of these controversies upon the realm of public affairs in France was great. They broke the silence around the Holocaust that had reigned in France for almost forty years. Along with the trial of Klaus Barbie, these 'affairs' challenged the orthodox self-representation of France as the nation of resistance and brought to light awkward questions of collaboration and responsibility. Lyotard's writing in response to these 'affairs' bears witness to the national trauma experienced there in the 1980s and early 1990s.

Lyotard's treatment of the Holocaust and anti-semitism is constantly mediated by this historical context. He refuses all attempts to 'seek the truth' of these issues; indeed, he argues that such a goal is all but impossible. Rather, he is concerned to understand what it is about these phenomena that permitted them to be forgotten so quickly and apparently so easily. He implies that it is only by answering that question that we can even begin to think about the actual events under investigation and it is partly for this reason that he argues that the issues surrounding the Holocaust and anti-semitism require a thoroughly critical reading of the 'Western' tradition of political praxis.

This context may also shed light upon the distinct character of Lyotard's writing. His investigations not only lead him to a 'writing of ethics' but his writing is itself a praxis of ethics. It demands that readers *think about what they are thinking about*. Lyotard's argument in *The Differend* is that no event contains meaning in itself, rather that meanings are only ascribed once the event has been 'phrased', that is, put into language, and only when that phrase enters into a 'genre of discourse' or 'language game'. In this way, meanings are ascribed (and continue to be ascribed) only when the event/phrase is discursively represented. However, of all events the Holocaust and anti-semitism defy such 'phrasing'; they escape even the possibility of the ascription of meaning – they cannot be spoken about. Confronted with the question of *why* these 'events' cannot be phrased, the reader is led to think about the 'events' themselves. And it is this thinking about what is being thought about that breaks or disrupts the genre of discourse within which the reader is implicated. It is in the silence that follows from this lack of words that, without one word of description or representation, the reader is confronted with a presentation (and not the knowledge) of the unspeakable terror and horror that was the Holocaust. What Lyotard has to say about Claude Lanzmann's film, *Shoah*, may also be applicable to Lyotard's own writings:

> Claude Lanzmann's film *Shoah* is an exception, perhaps the only one. Not only because it scarcely offers a testimony where the unpresentable of the holocaust is not indicated, be it but for a moment, by the alteration in the tone of a voice, a knotted throat, sobbing, tears, a witness fleeing off-camera, a disturbance in the tone of the narrative, an uncontrolled gesture. So that one knows that the impassable witnesses, whoever they might be, are certainly not lying, 'play-acting', hiding something.[12]

It is this idea of the unrepresentability or ineffability of the Holocaust that informs Lyotard's account of this event. His writing resonates with the shock of having to be reminded of something forgotten which should not have been forgotten.

Lyotard's thesis about why the Holocaust and the anti-semitism it embodied cannot be represented or 'phrased' is provided in a nutshell in a small passage from his article 'Europe, the Jews, and the Book':

> My claim is that the Jews represent *something that Europe does not want to or cannot know anything about.* Even when they are dead, it abolishes their memory and refuses them burial in its land. All of this takes place in the unconscious and has no right to speak. When the deed is done in full daylight, Europe is seized for an instant by the horror and the terror of *confronting its own desire.*[13]

In this passage we see the seeds of Lyotard's contribution to the social theory of anti-semitism. Rather than understanding it politically he transforms it into a question of ethics. For Lyotard, politics is defined precisely as the attempt to silence and forget ethics. Conversely, ethics is defined through its incapacity to be phrased and even the possibility of phrasing. Lyotard expresses this point as the conflict between autonomy and heteronomy. It follows, therefore, that since Europe or the West believes it has successfully overcome any form of dependency, of heteronomy, no place or 'genre of discourse' is left accessible to ethics. It is this situation that makes ethics the 'Other' of politics.

Lyotard argues that despite all proclamations to the contrary, Europe's attempt to deny ethics is always doomed to failure. Ethics remains deep in its unconscious. The disconcerting feeling that something is not quite right is often present as an unlocatable anxiety which, every now and then, gives rise to an obsessive attempt to rid itself of those who appear to personify the limits of its own putative success. The Holocaust is one such episode, yet, since it was a further attempt to extinguish ethics, it is said to take place beyond politics. Lyotard explains this point as follows:

> The solution was to be final: the final answer to the 'Jewish' question. It was necessary to carry it right up to its conclusion, to 'terminate' the interminable. And thus to 'terminate' the term itself. It had to be a perfect crime, one would plead not guilty, certain of the lack of proofs. This is a 'politics' of absolute forgetting, forgotten. Absurd, since its zeal, its very desperation distinguishes it as extra-political. Obviously, a 'politics' of extermination exceeds politics. It is not negotiated on a scene. This obstinacy to exterminate to the very end, because it cannot be understood politically, already indicates that we are dealing with something else, with the Other.[14]

Emancipation and 'the Jews'

The essential point for Lyotard is that politics and ethics, autonomy and heteronomy cannot be understood as a *relationship*, since the concept of a relation implies that the 'phrase' of the one can be linked to the other. It is exactly this linking that Lyotard claims is not possible. It is in this way, therefore, that Lyotard's thought on these issues breaks free of any relational understanding between modernity and anti-semitism.

Lyotard argues that politics' aim of emancipation has always involved the attempt at autonomy, the attempt to be free of any dependence upon an Other; the attempt to free oneself from ethics.

> The Christian Churches had introduced the motif of fraternity. The French Revolution extended it, by turning it on its head. We are brothers, not as sons of God but as free and equal citizens. It is not an Other who gives us the law. It is our civic community that does, that obliges, prohibits, permits. That is called emancipation from the Other, and autonomy. Our law opens citizenship to every individual, conditional on respect for republican principles.[15]

Lyotard explains how the discourse of political praxis, premised upon emancipation and the related concepts of rights, equality and the rule of law, comes to be defined solely in terms of its (final) overcoming of heteronomy. Lyotard argues that the nature of politics (autonomy) and the nature of ethics (heteronomy) differ in one essential aspect, namely the inability for the addressee of an ethical command to name and recognise the Other and so to place themselves in position of the addressor. James Williams explains this point as follows:

Lyotard translates ethical obligation as a phrase that puts its addressee in the position of being obliged, that is, of being solely the addressee of the phrase and not the addressor of a reaction to the phrase. In obligation the addressee is solely a 'you' as in the phrase 'You must obey'; there is no corresponding phrase of the form 'I must obey', where the self becomes a subject again prior to obeying.[16]

The ethical obligation is in marked contrast to the nature of political obedience:

In speaking the law [the legislator] decrees that he or she must respect it. In respecting the law, [the obligated one] decrees it anew. Their names, x and y, are in principle perfectly commutable between at least the two instances of normative addressor and prescriptive addressee. They are thus united in a single we... The authorisation is then formulated thus: *We decree as a norm that it is an obligation for us to carry out act a.* This is the principle of autonomy.[17]

Lyotard argues that because Western political consciousness is premised upon recognition, any attempt at representing the Other thereby results in that Other becoming assimilated to the one seeking to represent it. It becomes no different from the consciousness that inaugurates the attempt. As it is a consciousness that recognises itself as autonomous and self-standing, it will represent the other in the same way and so the relationship of heteronomy will be occluded.

Yet this attempt at emancipation and autonomy – at citizens' becoming master of their own political fate – cannot but fail because what is forgotten, ethics, does not for the mere fact of being forgotten cease to exist. Buried and disturbed within the realm of the unconscious, it makes itself felt in the realm of consciousness when for no apparent reason it feels itself assailed from the outside. Lyotard explains this point in the following way:

This sudden feeling is as good as a testimony, through its unsettling strange-ness, which 'from the exterior' lies in reserve in the interior, hidden away and from where it can on occasion depart to return from the outside to assail the mind as if it were issued not from it but from the incidental situation.[18]

It is through this process that the autonomy which believes itself to be the victor will always remain alert to the stirrings of its own unconscious connection with heteronomy, i.e., ethics. Because it cannot be ordered through conscious-ness, the unconscious effect will appear suddenly as a bolt out of the blue. Believing it has emancipated itself consciousness will unexpectedly be seized by an anxiety which it cannot place. Yet this forgotten something, itself forgotten and buried within the unconscious, is continually present as a lack, or lapsus, within consciousness. And in turn consciousness will continually respond to an unconscious desire to be rid of that which it senses, but does not know and which disrupts its search for autonomy. It is in this way that Lyotard explains how it is that ethics – heteronomy – remains but remains in excess of politics and acts as its constant disturbance.

The question remains why this conflict, which Lyotard locates within the heart of the praxis of European modernity, should effect the Jews as *the* Jews and why it should have given rise to the Holocaust. In answering this question, Lyotard identifies something he believes is distinctive about the Jews that brings down upon them the obsessive wrath of the West. The Jews, Lyotard claims, are the representatives of an ethics that can never be extinguished and remain as the constant challenge and reminder of the limits of the European political praxis of emancipation. It is the Jews who in the face of claims of autonomy stand out as the intimation of what politics forgets: that one is always in debt to the Other, that heteronomy can never be overcome.

In formulating the thesis that the Jews are the embodiment of ethics, Lyotard focuses upon the Jews' constitution as Jews. He argues that the Jews were constituted as 'the Jews' through

> a promise and an alliance that are not the contract and the pact, a promise made to a people who did not want it and had no need of it, an alliance that has not been negotiated, that goes against the people's interests, of which it knows itself unworthy. And so this people, an old communal apparatus already well-to-do, hypothetically, with intact defence mechanisms and dynamic, economic, linguistic regulations without which it would not be a people, this simple people taken hostage by a voice that does not tell it anything, save that it (this voice) is, and that all representation and naming of it are forbidden, and that it, this people, only needs to listen to its tone, to be obedient to a timbre.[19]

Central to Lyotard's interpretation of this origin is that the Call was so traumatic an event that it could not be registered within consciousness. Forbidden to be represented, the Other (the Voice) remains beyond and unknown to consciousness. Never able to be recognised, known or named, it lingers as a feeling that exceeds all knowledge and language. Lyotard argues that the purpose of the Jews' 'Book' (in which this origin is recounted) is, therefore, *not* to represent (to recognise and name) the Other so that the debt and obligation to the Other is cancelled, but rather is constantly to remind the Jews that they have 'forgotten the Forgotten'. As a consequence, the Jews are eternally reminded of this debt to the Other: they are

> Forgetting souls, like all souls, but to whom the Forgotten never ceases to

return to claim its due. The Forgotten is not to be remembered for what it has been and what it is, because it has not been anything and is nothing, but must be remembered as something that never ceases to be forgotten. And this something is not a concept or a representation, but a 'fact', a factum (Kant, *Critique of Practical Reason*, A56): namely that one is obligated before the Law, in debt.[20]

Lyotard suggests that the Jews are unable to work through the trauma of their origins because of the prohibition of representing the Other that called them into existence. Consequently, the Jews are unable to free themselves from their obligation, their debt to the 'Voice', or to embark on the project of emancipation and autonomy. They are, therefore, the personification of ethics and as such are the Other of modern political praxis.

> Thus it is that the Jews cannot manage to find their place in the systems by which thought is represented in the politics and social practices of the European West. They cannot form a 'nation' in the medieval sense, nor a people in the modern sense. The Law forbids them to acquire the communitarian status of an ethnic group. Their relation to the Event of the Covenant and the Promise is a relation of dependence, not a relation to a land and a history but a relation to the letters of a book and to a paradoxical temporality.[21]

According to Lyotard, the Jews exist 'within' Europe in the same manner as ethics exists within consciousness. They exist as the 'absent-present' that exceeds politics but that remains deeply entrenched within the unconscious of Europe. As such, their 'presence' is registered within Europe's consciousness as a challenge and limit to its self-proclaimed autonomy.

> '[T]he jews' are within the 'spirit' of the Occident that is so preoccupied with foundational thinking, what resists this spirit; within its will, the will to want, what gets in the way of this will; within its accomplishments, projects and progress, what never ceases to reopen the wound of the unaccomplished. 'The jews' are the irremissible in the West's movement of remission and pardon. They are what cannot be domesticated in the obsession to dominate, in the compulsion to control domain, in the passion for empire, recurrent ever since Hellenistic Greece and Christian Rome. 'The jews', never at home wherever they are, cannot be integrated, converted, or expelled.[22]

It is in this way and for these reasons that the 'conflict' between politics and ethics, autonomy and heteronomy, turns into a conflict that cannot but involve the Jews and inevitably becomes anti-semitism. Indeed, Lyotard argues that anti-semitism is precisely this antagonistic encounter.

...anti-Semitism is one of the means of the apparatus of its culture to bind and represent as much as possible – to protect against – the originary terror, actively to forget it. It is the defensive side of its attack mechanisms – Greek science, Roman law and politics, Christian spirituality, and the Enlightenment, the underside of knowledge, of having, of wanting, of hope. One converts the Jews in the Middle Ages, they resist by mental restriction. One expels them during the classical age, they return. One integrates them in the modern era, they persist in their difference. One exterminates them in the twentieth century.[23]

At this point, Lyotard's thesis comes to resemble what Arendt has called that of eternal anti-semitism. Because Lyotard implies that all (European) post-Judaic religious and political movements have sought emancipation and autonomy (in the sense of closing the debt to the (originating) Other), it follows that those who are aware that the debt has not been cancelled will remain as a thorn in their side. Therefore, anti-semitism is detached from any specific relationship to modernity even while Lyotard remains aware that the Holocaust arose within the context of a specific historical period characterised by a modern form of political praxis.[24]

Lyotard's claim that anti-semitism – the desire to be rid of ethics – occurs in the unconscious of Europe, that is, in a realm that exceeds politics, means that anti-semitism need not be part of any political project. Indeed, this is precisely the situation within the modern political nation-state, where tolerance and assimilation appear to deny either the space for Jews as Jews or the possibility of anti-semitism. As Lyotard states, 'Our law opens citizenship to every individual, conditional on respect for republican principles. The Jews are allowed in like anyone else. This is called assimilation.'[25]

However, Lyotard echoes Hannah Arendt's observation that for the Jews, assimilation means assimilating anti-semitism.[26] For Lyotard, this is because political emancipation signifies the denial of ethics, the denial of the very premise that constitutes the Jews as the Jews. Perhaps more importantly, assimilation as understood in its political and legal sense takes place only at the level of appearances, at the level of consciousness. At the level of the unconscious, anti-semitism still abounds.

What then can a 'French or German citizen of Israelite profession' be – above all if he is an officer like Dreyfus or a head of government like Blum? In the European unconscious, it is recognised that his debt to the Other will prevail over his duties to the others, to the national community. And that he is bound to be a potential traitor. Unless he forgets himself as Jew. This is the great temptation for the 'assimilated' themselves. The 'final solution' will come as a monstrous reminder to them that they are always, *even despite themselves*, witnesses to something about which Europe wants to know nothing.[27]

Political assimilation, then, appears in some senses to be a purely cosmetic measure. Beneath its surfaces, the conflict with ethics will continue unabated and the superficiality of republican political universalism will collapse. And it is in this realm that Lyotard locates the mass murder of Jews conducted by the Nazi regime, a realm of which Europe is unaware but which reflects a silence that 'speaks'. For Lyotard, this silence is not the referent of a nothing, an absence, but rather that something *is* which is inexpressible but present as a feeling. It is a feeling which can only be intimated or pointed toward.[28]

In *The Differend* Lyotard argues that the impossibility of articulating the occurrence in its singularity through understanding does not mean that the event is forgotten, but rather that it leaves its trace as a 'feeling'. This feeling in turn is evidence of the fact that the crime of Auschwitz is a sign, meaning here the sudden appearance of something so absolute, so total that it can only be acknowledged (as opposed to recognised) when the faculties of the mind are thrown into complete disarray and confusion. Lyotard explains it as follows:

> Signs are not referents to which are attached significations validatable under the cognitive regimen, they indicate that something which should be able to be put into phrases cannot be phrased in the accepted idioms. That, in a phrase universe, the referent be situated as a sign has as a corollary that in the same universe the addressee is situated like someone who is affected, and that the sense is situated like an unresolved problem, an enigma perhaps, a mystery, or a paradox – This feeling does not arise from an experience felt by a subject.[29]

Thus, the effect of being confronted by the sign of 'Auschwitz' is to throw the addressees into a state of confusion, to disorient them to such an extent that they receive this sign only as a 'something' which they cannot grasp and which throws their sense of autonomy (that is, to use the language of *The Differend*, their role as addressor) into doubt.

Lyotard appears to make of the Holocaust something akin to the initial Call to the Jews. Both are outside the realm of consciousness, of thought, of knowledge and of politics. Both the Holocaust and the Jews become the forgotten and not forgotten. Moreover, Lyotard's writing itself is aimed to make us remember that we have forgotten this forgotten, in a manner similar to that which he says is the purpose of the Jewish 'book'. The paradox of Lyotard's account is that the Holocaust, which is claimed to be unknowable and to be beyond (political) meaning, is endowed with an excess of (ethical) meaning. It becomes the most significant ethical event in over five thousand years.

Lyotard is able to maintain his claim that both anti-semitism and the Holocaust can be explained without recourse to any notion of a dialectical relationship. Anti-semitism is neither the antithesis of modernity – of a system of social relations premised upon emancipation and manifested in the forms of equal rights – nor is it the logical conclusion or culmination of modernity. It is rather modernity's Other and presents itself in the social world in a manner unrelated to specific social and political developments.

Europe could, therefore, forget the Holocaust so quickly and so easily because it never knew about it in the first place. Europeans did not know what was happening, because what was happening exceeded the realm of politics. Concerned as 'Auschwitz' is with ethics, it is the Other of politics and so cannot be phrased within the discourses that relate to that realm – language games or discourses that have and know no place for what is outside themselves. Taking place in the realm of the unconscious, they remain unknown and unknowable to consciousness. They escape the realm of thought and knowledge and reach us only in the silence of a feeling. It is to this feeling that Lyotard's writing testifies.

Conclusion

In the introduction I made the claim that Lyotard's thinking on the question of anti-semitism 'mirrors in reverse' many of the mainstays of the anti-semitic worldview itself. I am now in a position to expand on the implications of this thesis.

I see the two central tenets of modern anti-semitic thought thus. On the one hand, the universal nature of political emancipation and its recognition of individuals as abstract citizens means that Jews must cease to exist as an empirical group within the modern body-politic. On the other hand, 'underneath' the emancipated (Jewish) citizens, there reside the 'real' and 'unchangeable', 'true Jews' who cannot but follow their own narrow, particularistic interests at the expense of the 'general good'. Thus from the perspective of the anti-semite, political emancipation represents an unwarranted and dangerous subversion of the 'natural order of things'.

In Lyotard's own account of anti-semitism we see a similar division established between on the one hand a polity defined in terms of abstract universalism, in which differences between individuals have been erased,[30] and on the other hand a society in which the specific quality of 'the Jews' remains intact. Moreover, this notion of 'the Jews' is dependent upon non-social criteria, those of ethics, which indicate that there is something eternal and unchanging about 'the Jews' that will make a mockery of all attempts at emancipation and equality.

Both views – both those of the anti-semite and those of Lyotard anti-anti-semitism – explicitly reject social and political conceptions of 'the Jews' which attribute their perpetuation as a unitary, definable and distinguishable group to the limits of political emancipation and to the conditions of modernity. There is nothing mysterious about the existence of a body of individuals collectively known as 'the Jews'. Throughout the modern era, the always dangerous question of 'who is a Jew?' has proved virtually impossible to answer. Several 'explanations' continue to co-exist, each one as theoretically suspect as the others. Thus, both within and without the Jewish community, one hears of 'the Jews' being defined in terms of religious belief (and this is the view that Lyotard comes closest to replicating), cultural identity, ethnicity, or even anti-Jewish hostility. The point is that the meaning of 'the Jews' at any one *particular moment* arises from a multifarious intermingling of social relations which, as Marx noted, 'become outmoded before they ossify'.[31]

Consequently, the notion of the division between the 'universal citizen' and the 'true Jew' is itself a fiction, inasmuch as any attempt to define the Jews once and for all serves the purpose of wrenching people out of their social context whilst simultaneously reifying one particular aspect of their identity at the expense of all others. To argue that 'the Jews' were butchered because they were in some way the 'embodiment of ethics', is to accede to the idea that the Yellow Star forced upon many millions of individuals speaks the truth about those wearing it. Such a view masks the fact that all attempts to speak of 'the Jews' as a reified category involve a dangerous measure of arbitrariness and violence.

Just as Lyotard can only represent Jews as 'the Jews' by abstracting individuals from the complexity and confusion of social relations in which they are immersed, and simultaneously by mystifying one aspect of their social identity, so too he wrenches the Holocaust from its social and historical context and presents it as an insulated event. This exercise of arbitrary isolation and boundary-marking is evidenced by Lyotard's emblematic use of the term 'Auschwitz' as representative of the Holocaust as a whole.[32] Indeed, in some points in *The Differend*, most notably in his confrontation with the revisionism of Robert Faurisson, Lyotard appears to come close to conflating the Holocaust only with the gas chambers sited at Auschwitz. This subsumption of the Holocaust under the name of 'Auschwitz' is not unique to the work of Lyotard. Such a conflation has been prevalent in the popular mind since the trial of Eichmann in 1961 and in academia since Adorno's *Negative Dialectics* in 1968.[33] The problem with representing the Holocaust by the emblem 'Auschwitz' is that, by substituting part for the whole – the gas chambers of Auschwitz for the

Holocaust in general – other equally important questions are taken out of the frame of enquiry, especially socio-theoretical questions concerning the causes and consequences of mass extermination. Not only is a focus on these issues lacking in Lyotard's work, but they are in a more fundamental way denied any explanatory validity. The alleged lack of legitimacy of these types of investigation stems from Lyotard's insistence that we understand the Holocaust as taking place outside or beyond the realm of social and political relations and in the realm of ethics. Not only does such exclusion of socio-theoretical investigation arbitrarily restrict our understanding of anti-semitism and the Holocaust, but it simultaneously does not allow the experience of the Holocaust to impact upon the categories of thought and standards and judgement that are present within the social sciences. In socio-theoretical investigations, not only would the insights of various disciplines be applied to anti-semitism and the Holocaust, but these phenomena themselves would correspondingly act as a critical yardstick of the ways of understanding of the social sciences.[34] As Nietzsche states in the *Genealogy of Morals*, 'the *more* affects we allow to speak about one thing, the *more* eyes, different eyes, we can use to observe one thing, the more complete will our "concept" of this thing, our "objectivity", be'.[35]

My final comment addresses the question of the place of emancipation within Lyotard's account of anti-semitism. I claimed at the start of this essay that Lyotard's work is representative of a loss of faith in the praxis of human emancipation and freedom. I argued that for him, emancipation and autonomy, especially in their modern form of rights and equality, exclude or occlude heteronomy and that this in turn is resented by the emancipated themselves. Lyotard's account sounds similar to the dialectic of rights and ressentiment which we find in Nietzsche's understanding of anti-semitism. Where Nietzsche and Lyotard differ, however, is that whereas Nietzsche's dialectic becomes a conflict played out on the political plane of equivocal emancipation, Lyotard's two combatants remain dissociated in separate spheres: the equivocality is suspended. Throughout his discussion of the Jews, anti-semitism and the Holocaust, Lyotard has sought a strict demarcation between politics and emancipation on the one side, and ethics on the other, coming to represent evil and good respectively.

It seems to me that within Lyotard's de-politicised notion of ethics we can detect a lack of equivocality that carries with it the risk of perpetrating the very terror that Lyotard wishes to avoid. Lyotard cannot guarantee in advance that the response to the Call of Auschwitz will in fact follow the pattern of ethics that he himself wishes. This point can be evidenced in Lyotard's own writings through the 'absent presence' of the Nazis. Apart from one small discussion of the Nazis in *The Differend*, Lyotard has little to say about them in any great detail.

All we are told in that brief discussion, which centres upon the location of both the Jews and the Nazis within the confines of Auschwitz, is that the Nazis (as do the Jews) stand out against the narrative of universal political emancipation and autonomy. But we are not told who the Nazis are or from where they originate.

Lyotard's claim that the (gentile) population of Europe has always responded to the trace of ethics that is represented by the Jews with acts of barbaric violence – conversion, expulsion, integration and extermination – offers no reason why similar terrifying strategies of response would not occur in the future when what has been forgotten again enters the realm of consciousness.[36] As a possible indication of such unethical response, one can only note in passing the resentment of certain sections of non-German populations when reminded of their own countries' implication in the mass murders. Lyotard's theory of anti-semitism aims to make people think about what they are thinking and to disrupt the flow of political and social relations through the image of the Jews as a sign of the ethical, but it is fraught with the lack of equivocality in its very notion of ethics.

Lyotard elevates both the Jews and the Jewish Question to a status of central significance in discussions of modernity. It is as if the Jews are the markers of the limits of modernity and the question of anti-semitism becomes the question of modernity itself. It is a question, moreover, that we can never answer if it is placed beyond the field of politics and human understanding. In this way, 'the Jews' come to represent the nemesis of the entirety of Western political and social praxis and the struggles for emancipation that have punctuated it. What I find politically troubling, if not dangerous, is the implied futility of any political praxis of emancipation. It is, of course, true that after the Holocaust, the praxis of emancipation is in need of questioning but not in a way that discounts what has been achieved. We should attend, as Lyotard has done, to the traumas that the Holocaust has inflicted upon our understanding of the world, but also to a determination not to turn a philosophy of trauma into a traumatised philosophy.

Notes

1 Gershom Scholem, *On the Kabbalah and its Symbolism*, New York: Schocken, 1969. Quoted in Zygmunt Bauman, *Modernity and Ambivalence*, Cambridge: Polity, 1991, p.173.

2 K. Marx, 'On the Jewish Question', in Lucio Colletti (ed.), *Early Writings*, London: Penguin, 1992.

3 'The term was first used in 1860 by a Jewish writer, M. Steinschneider in a polemic against Ernest Renan. It next appeared in 1879 with Wilhelm Marr's "Anti-Semites' League". The abstract term "anti-Semitism" came into use soon after', Paul Lawrence Rose, *German Question/Jewish Question: Revolutionary Anti-Semitism from Kant to Wagner*, New Jersey: Princeton University Press, 1990, p.288.

4 Friedrich Nietzsche, *On the Genealogy of Morals*, trans. and ed. W. Kaufmann, New York: Vintage, 1989.

5 Hannah Arendt, *Origins of Totalitarianism*, London: Harcourt, Brace, 1979.

6 Theodor Adorno and Max Horkheimer, *Dialectic of Enlightenment* (2nd ed.), London: Verso, 1989.

7 In 'A Paper Eichmann', in Pierre Vidal-Naquet, *The Jews*, New York: Columbia University Press, 1981.

8 Jean-François Lyotard, *The Differend: Phrases in Dispute*, Minneapolis: University of Minnesota Press, 1988.

9 Victor Farias (1987), *Heidegger and Nazism*, Philadelphia: Temple University Press, 1989.

10 Jean-François Lyotard, *Heidegger and 'the jews'*, trans. Andreas Michel and Mark Roberts, Minneapolis: University of Minnesota Press, 1990.

11 In Jean-François Lyotard, *Political Writings*, trans. Bill Readings and Kevin Paul Geiman, London: UCL Press, 1993.

12 Lyotard, *Heidegger and 'the jews'*, p.26.

13 Lyotard, *Political Writings*, p.159, emphasis in the original.

14 Lyotard, *Heidegger and 'the jews'*, p.25.

15 Lyotard, *Political Writings*, pp.161–62.

16 James Williams, *Lyotard: Towards a Postmodern Philosophy*, Cambridge: Polity, 1998, p.123.

For other discussions of Lyotard's thought see Geoffrey Bennington, *Lyotard: Writing the Event*, Manchester: Manchester University Press, 1988; Stuart Sim, *Jean-François Lyotard*, Hemel Hempstead: Prentice Hall/Harvester Wheatsheaf, 1996; Andrew Benjamin, *Judging Lyotard*, London: Routledge, 1992.

17 *The Differend*, p.98.

18 Lyotard, *Heidegger and 'the jews'*, pp.12–13.

19 *Ibid.*, p.21.

20 *Ibid.*, p.3.

21 Lyotard, *Political Writings*, p.143.

22 Lyotard, *Heidegger and 'the jews'*, p.22.

23 *Ibid.*, p.23.

24 The modern emancipated political nation-state premised upon the rule of law, equality and rights Lyotard terms 'republicanism'.

25 Lyotard, *Political Writings*, p.161.

26 Arendt, *Origins of Totalitarianism*, p.22.

27 Lyotard, *Political Writings*, p.161.

28 Lyotard, *The Differend*, p.57.

29 *Ibid.*

30 Such a view of society is presented most clearly in *The Postmodern Condition*, but it informs all of Lyotard's later works.

31 Karl Marx, 'The Manifesto of the Communist Party', in Terell Carver (ed.), *Marx: Later Political Writings*, Cambridge: Cambridge University Press, 1996, p.4

32 This use of the term 'Auschwitz' is particularly prevalent in *The Differend*.

33 Theodor Adorno, *Negative Dialectics*, trans. E.B. Ashton, London: Routledge, 1973.

34 For such an exercise, see Hannah Arendt's *Origin of Totalitarianism*, and *On Revolution*, London: Faber & Faber, 1964.

35 Nietzsche, *The Genealogy of Morals*, Part III, §12.

36 Lyotard, *Heidegger and 'the Jews'*, p.23.

CHAPTER 7

Eradicating Evil:
Levinas, Judaism and the Holocaust

VICTOR J. SEIDLER

Modernity and Jewishness

Within the modern West we have learnt to think of the Enlightenment as a secular project which claims to think of individuals as rational selves. Where faith was positioned within pre-modern societies which were organised around tradition, we learnt within an Enlightenment vision of modernity to find reason. People were no longer expected to accept beliefs as a matter of faith but could confidently expect to have to prove their beliefs according to reason. This helped radically to redefine the relationship between public and private spheres and religious belief became a matter of individual choice alone. So it was that social theories tended to be framed in the terms of a secular rationalism. This made it difficult, however, to recognise the extent to which modernity had been shaped as a secularised form of a dominant Christian tradition, so that the philosophical traditions of modernity encoded in their very categories secularised Christian notions.

The Kantian tradition in ethics has had enormous impact in shaping the traditions of social theory which have flowed from Durkheim and Weber. In their different ways they have learnt to accept an identification between morality and an independent faculty of reason. Reason was deemed to be radically separated from nature, as the intelligible realm was for Kant split from the empirical. It was through reason that we were to discern the dictates of the moral law and it was as rational selves that we were to be subject to its demands. This promised a universalism within moral theory which was to leave its marks on the dominant frameworks of social theory within modernity.[1] It made it as difficult to identify the disdain for nature which was encoded within the dualism between 'nature' and 'culture' as it was to illuminate the disdain for the body and sexuality which came to be identified with the 'sins of the flesh'. These concerns were to be radically excluded from the frameworks of classical social theory for they threatened a rationalism that was constructed around a fierce distinction between reason and nature.

As we learn to discern the dictates of the moral law with Kant, so we learn to 'rise above' our 'animal' natures.[2] It is through separating or splitting from the impulses of our 'animal' natures that we 'rise above' our empirical selves and recognise ourselves as rational moral agents. It is crucial to Kant that we have an inner relationship with reason which becomes the source of our freedom and autonomy. So it is that in the Kantian tradition people also have to learn to separate themselves from their class, race and ethnic backgrounds – deemed to be forms of unfreedom and determination – in order to exist for themselves as free and autonomous agents.[3]

Within the modern public sphere people do not exist as Christians, Jews or Moslems, but as 'free and equal' citizens, bearers of legal and political rights within a liberal democratic state. People have to learn to separate themselves from these identities which are no longer recognised as bearers of discrete moral and ethical traditions. If they want to take their place as citizens within a modern state, they have to be prepared to treat these 'particularistic' identities as a matter of individual and private concern. At some level it is assumed that these religious identities would fade away as religious beliefs, traditions and rituals give way under the challenges of rationalism. It seems that modernity, as a secular project, asks for equal sacrifice from these discrete spiritual traditions, but the particular ways in which modernity remains the project of a secularised form of Christianity are thus rendered largely invisible.

The various moral traditions within modernity have often felt uneasy thinking about evil, which seems to reflect a pre-modern sensibility within a dominant Christian symbolic in which people learn to imagine how the forces of evil challenge the forces of good. This language continues, if in a somewhat muted and rationalist form, within Kant's writings on radical evil. In Kantian ethics we learn to think in terms of a language of 'eradication' where emotions and desires need to be 'eradicated' if they threaten the moral will. We still have to struggle against the temptations of the flesh, even if they are now moderately framed as 'inclinations'. If Kant acknowledges that people will pursue their self-interested desires and that this will bring happiness, he wants to separate this from anything to do with morality. Kant insists that people have to be free to make their own moral choices and that they can choose between doing good and doing evil. As rational moral selves they can exercise their moral freedom.

Within modern societies it has been easy to think of anti-semitism as irrational, even as we learn to demarcate pre-modern and modern forms of anti-semitism.[4] But in the face of Nazi anti-semitism, and the Shoah which was to follow, it has proved necessary to rethink the relationship between the modern and the pre-modern. We have to recognise that Jews were not the only people who wanted to think of Nazism as a temporary aberration that was bound to give way in a relatively short period of time because it was 'irrational' and could not be sustained. As we learn to think of modernity in different terms, so we have to respond to Bauman's claim in *Modernity and the Holocaust* that the Shoah was the product of a secular and modern form of instrumental rationality.[5] To think about the persistence of evil within modernity, we need to think about the relationship of ethics to technology.

Levinas: 'Less Than Human'

In a piece that Levinas collected in *Difficult Freedom*, entitled 'Simone Weil against the Bible', he writes:

> There are two troubling theses in Simone Weil's doctrine. She imposes a reading of the Bible such that the origins of Good are always foreign to Judaism, while Evil is specifically Judaic. And she turns Good into an absolutely pure idea, excluding all contamination or violence. Because the second thesis seems evident to the intuition, if not the thinking, of today's European, the first thesis can be a crippling one. Its anti-Judaism is of the gnostic type...[6]

Although Simone Weil grew up in a Jewish family, she learnt to identify with French history and culture. She was ready to renounce her Jewishness which she felt very little relationship with. She requested a teacher's position and argued that any restrictions on Jews in Vichy France should not apply to her. She seemed ready to deny her Jewish roots and wanted others to accept her as 'French' since these were the traditions she identified with. As far as she was concerned she did not share in Jewish beliefs and practices and therefore should not be regarded as 'Jewish' by the authorities.[7] Weil's antagonism to her Jewishness was then reflected in her writings on and evaluations of the Hebrew Bible.

An array of questions flows from Levinas' comment. How is good to be set against evil? Are we to understand that today's European will willingly accept the notion that Good is an absolutely pure idea, excluding all contamination or violence? Is this acceptance of a radically dualistic conception of 'good' and 'evil' itself part of a secularised Christian inheritance which is structured to silence otherwise competing ethical traditions within modernity?[8] Is this radical dualism between 'good' and 'evil' itself a way of thinking that helped to prepare the conditions that made the Holocaust possible? Does the split between 'good' and 'evil' in some way link modernity with the pre-modern? Has it made it easier to figure the Other as evil within modernity? Does it also serve to undermine traditions of tolerance which we might otherwise associate with modernity?

When Levinas argues that for Weil 'the origins of Good are always foreign to Judaism, while Evil is specifically Judaic', he is touching a raw nerve in Western culture concerning the historical relationship of Christianity to Judaism. It voices a long tradition which would eradicate or deny the Jewish sources of Christianity and so the 'Jewishness' of Jesus. Judaism is identified with the body and the 'earthly', which are disdained, in contrast to the 'spiritual' which exists as a transcendent realm. The 'human' is set in radical contrast with the 'animal' as the 'spirit' is set against the 'body'. Weil was ready to argue within this mode of thinking that everything 'good' within the Christian tradition has somehow derived from Plato and that everything that needed to be 'eradicated' has come from Judaism. As Levinas put it, 'Simone Weil explains that the Passion took place in Palestine, since it was there that it was most needed.'[9]

In possibly his most autobiographical writing, a piece entitled 'Signature', a version of which appears in *Difficult Freedom*, Levinas says that part of the appeal which Husserl's phenomenology has for him is that:

> Ideas transcending consciousness do not separate themselves from their genesis in the fundamentally temporal consciousness. In spite of his intellectualism and his conviction about the excellence of the West, Husserl has thus brought into question the Platonic privilege, until then uncontested, of a continent which believes it has the right to colonise the world.[10]

At some level the Jewish world had also been colonised, learning to see itself within modernity through prevailing Christian eyes which, according to St Augustine, needed the Jews since it was the 'blindness' of the Jews that somehow affirmed the 'truth' of Christianity. Jews needed to be included so that they could then be excluded as the 'Other'.

Levinas acknowledges that his own biography and thinking 'is dominated by the presentiment and memory of the Nazi horror' and his work can in part be read as a questioning of those traditions which consciously and unconsciously prepared the ground for the Shoah.[11] This is as true of Levinas' philosophical writings, which he identified as 'Greek', as it is of his more Jewish writings. Although he retains a sharp divide between philosophy and Judaism and refuses to acknowledge that his reflections on Jewish sources can constitute philosophy, this separation is difficult to sustain. Levinas' relationship to Rosenzweig only highlights his more general attempt to take up Adorno's challenge: to think in ways which could not foster the evil of the Shoah.[12]

Levinas draws upon a revised phenomenology in his more explicitly philo-sophical work as a questioning of the reductive thought which has characterised modern secular rationalism. He recognises the difficulties this tradition has had in giving recognition to those made to suffer evil and injustice and he acknow-ledges, alongside Weil, the need to question a sharp split between the 'earthly' and the 'spiritual' which would refuse to recognise the moral harm we do in everyday relationships. Weil recognises the injustice we do, for instance, in rape as a form of 'violation' of a person. She recognises how violations of the body can do injuries to the soul and in this respect refuses to separate 'body' from 'soul'. She knows that the 'moral reality' of this violation cannot be illuminated in terms of a liberal discourse of the infringement of rights. She feels the necessity to draw upon a Christian spiritual tradition to understand the 'evil' that is done.[13]

Levinas too draws upon a phenomenological tradition to question the ease with which Others can be objectified within a secular rationalist tradition. He summarises his thinking in 'Signature' thus:

> an analysis which feigns the disappearance of every existent – and even of the cogito which thinks it – is overrun by the chaotic rumbling of an anonymous 'to exist', which is an existence without existents and which no negation manages to overcome. 'There is' – impersonally – like 'it is raining' or 'it is night'. None of the generosity which the German term 'es gibt' is said to contain revealed itself between 1933 and 1945. This must be said![14]

Levinas draws a direct relationship between the reductivism fostered by the Cartesian tradition and the terrible historical events after 1933 which were to prepare the way for the Holocaust. He questions 'this horrible neutrality of the "there is"'. For Levinas it is important to connect the question of consciousness and subjectivity to the realisation of a different vision of time. Here he is drawing upon his reading of Husserl implicitly to question a Platonic / Christian tradition which has been inscribed in the West.

> Time must not be seen as 'image' and approximation of an immobile eternity, as a deficient mode of ontological plenitude. It articulates a mode of existence in which everything is always revocable, in which nothing is definitive but everything is yet to come, in which even the present is not a simple coincidence with itself, but is always an imminence. This is the situation of consciousness. To have consciousness is to have time... From this comes the power to judge history, instead of awaiting its impersonal verdict... Time, language and subjectivity delineate a pluralism and consequently, in the strongest sense of this term, an experience: one being's reception of the absolutely other being.[15]

Explaining his difference with Heidegger he writes:

In the place of ontology – of the Heideggerian comprehension of the Being of being – is substituted as primordial the relation of a being to a being, which is none the less not equivalent to a rapport between a subject and an object, but rather to a proximity, to a relation with the other (Autrui)… The fundamental experience which objective experience itself presupposes is the experience of the Other. It is experience *par excellence*. As the idea of the Infinite goes beyond Cartesian thought, so is the Other out of proportion with the power and freedom of the I. The disproportion between the Other and the self is precisely moral consciousness. Moral consciousness is not an experience of values, but an access to external being: external being is, par excellence, the Other. Moral consciousness is thus not a modality of psychological consciousness, but its condition… The face of the Other puts into question the happy spontaneity of the self, this joyous 'force which moves'.[16]

The openness to others which Levinas looks for might not be a matter of moral values, but the objectivity he looks for can too easily be evaded. There might be situations where seeing the suffering in the face of the poor brings me into a different relationship with myself, but all too often I find myself looking away. I do not want to recognise my responsibilities to the other and what is striking within modernity is the ease with which we can regard others as 'less than human'. This is something of which Levinas is, of course, aware. But this also means that being reminded of our responsibilities for others is often not enough. We also need to understand the ease with which we can still within modernity treat others as 'less than human' and what this means about the ways we understand the relationship between 'modern' and 'pre-modern' forms of anti-semitism. At least it means that we have to rethink the relationship between the 'religious' and the 'secular' if we are to understand the nature of post-modern evil.

Levinas wants us to resist tendencies towards the reductiveness and impersonality which inform modern philosophical traditions. He wants to remind us of something different. As he explains it:

> in *Totality And Infinity*, an attempt was made to systematise these experiences by opposing them to a philosophical thought which reduces the Other (l'Autre) to the Same and the multiple to the totality, making of autonomy its supreme principle.[17]

But it might be that Levinas shares too much of this tradition himself, at least in relation to its rationalism. His relationship with Judaism might awaken different concerns but he has been educated into a particular Lithuanian rationalist tradition within Judaism. He can also be tempted into modes of interpretation which carry the marks of his philosophical training.

A Jewish tradition helps Levinas question a particular 'dualistic' way of thinking the relationship between good and evil. Judaism is not a religion of perfection, nor does it believe that the sources of evil can be 'eradicated'. It refuses to exclusively identify the body and sexuality with an 'animal nature' and with the 'sins of the flesh'. Rather than deny our sexuality as the source of evil and temptation, we have to learn to come to terms with it. Rather than set up a monastic ideal of celibacy on the assumption that sexuality is itself 'evil', so that people are constantly berating themselves for falling short of these 'ideals', we have to recognise, as Freud has it, that we are 'sexual' beings and that sexuality can be transformed. Rather than identify sexuality with the temptation of women's bodies and so with lust as essentially 'animal', it can just as well be an expression of our humanity. This is not to deny that in crucial respects Judaism developed as a patriarchal tradition, even though it also acknowledged women's sexual desire.[18]

Levinas has been crucially important in opening up ways to think a phenomenology of the body and embodied experience, but he remains partly trapped within a culture of denial in relation to sexuality, even though he does acknowledge some differences in Jewish and Christian traditions of the body, love and sexuality. His way of challenging conventional Christian notions relates to his questioning of Israel as 'a model people'. In his piece on 'Simone Weil against the Bible', he writes:

Israel is not a model people, but a free people. It is of course, like any people, filled with lust and tempted by carnal delights. The Bible tells us of this lust in order to denounce it, but also knows that it is not enough to deny. It seeks to elevate matters by introducing the notion of justice. It is in economic justice that man glimpses the face of man. Has Christianity itself found a horizon for its generosity other than in famine and drought?[19]

Levinas recognises how myths remain to play a crucial role within modernity. Modernity is cast within the terms of a secularised Christianity and so inherits its tendencies towards the 'idealisation' of everyday life. Despite crucial differences between Kant and post-Kantians, there is a shared conception of the relationship between culture and nature where freedom lies in the control and domination of nature. Even if they develop different conceptions of the conditions of self-legislation and moral autonomy, they share a secularised, Christian assumption about the radical separation between 'good' and 'evil'.[20]

In his piece entitled 'For a Jewish Humanism', also collected in *Difficult Freedom*, Levinas thinks of humanism – a much misused and ambiguous word – as a term which can 'none the less designate a system of principles and disciplines that free human life from the prestige of myths, the discord they introduce into ideas and the cruelty they perpetuate in social customs'.[21] For Levinas Judaism can also help to question a tendency towards abstraction which remains inherent with modernity. As he explains it:

> Mendelsohn put to the moderns a view that Spinoza had borrowed from Maimonides: the most ancient monotheism is not a revealed religion, but a revealed Law. Its truth is universal like reason; its rule and moral institutions, Judaism's particular support, preserve this truth from corruption.[22]

It seems that for Levinas Judaism can help question the rule of abstractions and so the metaphysical temptation alive in the eighteenth century which was 'in love with eternal truths to the point of believing them to be active and effective even in a state of pale abstractions'. Judaism can awaken us to the dangers of 'the inconsistency of truths when separated from conduct, ideas from culture'.[23] Too often within the terms of an Enlightenment vision of modernity:

> Reason, sovereign and subject to the truth, succumbs to the idolatry of myths that tempt, betray and shackle it. Truth according to Judaism finds a faithful symbolism that preserves it from the imagination only in practical attitudes, in a Law.[24]

For Levinas 'Monotheism is a humanism' and, as he explains, a most paradoxical notion, drawing an implicit contrast with Christianity:

> The monotheism that brings it to life, which is the most dangerous of abstractions since it is the highest, does not consist in preparing man, with all his weak imperfections, for a private meeting with a consoling God; but in bringing the divine presence to just and human effort, as one brings the light of day to the human eye, the only organ capable of seeing it. The vision of God is a moral act. This optics is an ethics.[25]

According to Levinas the Bible with its crucial commentaries 'leads us not towards the mystery of God, but towards the human tasks of man'.[26] The Hebrew language and texts are 'the vehicle[s] for a difficult wisdom concerned with truths that correlate to virtues'. In their own way they can contribute to a postmodern ethics through their ability to question 'the idolatry of myths' that show a sinister continuity between tradition and modernity we too often fail to recognise.

Anti-Semitism and Evil

For the true anti-semite, there can be no good Jew. As far as Hitler was concerned it was only Weininger who broke this rule. As Sartre observes in *Anti-Semite and Jew*, for the anti-semite: 'The Jew is free *to do evil*, not good; he has only as much free will as is necessary for him to take full responsibility for the crimes of which he is the author; he does not have enough to achieve a reformation.'[27] As the Jew is taken to be the source of all evil and so blamed for the ills of society, then the anti-semite does not have to explore the interrelation between good and evil. As Sartre has it, 'If all he [the anti-semite] has to do is to remove Evil that means that the Good is already given. He has no need to seek it in anguish, to invent it, to scrutinise it patiently when he has found it, to prove it in action, to verify it by its consequences, or, finally, to shoulder the moral choice he has made.'[28]

Since anti-semites fight evil, their goodness and the goodness of the society they are fighting for cannot be questioned. This makes it possible for anti-semites to use the most ignoble of methods. According to Thomas Szasz in *The Manufacture of Madness*, 'when the liberal defines certain individuals or groups as sick, he does not mean they have a right to be sick – any more than, in the eye of the anti-semite, the Jew has a right to be a Jew... In both cases, the oppressor is unwilling to recognise and accept human difference.'[29] According to Szasz:

> For the conscientious mental health worker there can be no mental illness useful to the patient in society, nor any mental patient capable of achieving his own self-transformation. This justifies the debasement of *all* persons labelled mentally ill, and the imposition of treatment on *any* of them by the authorities (whether such 'treatment' exists or not).[30]

The references to sickness and discourses of health are not accidental since they were a crucial part of the myth which the Nazis worked to perpetuate. As Szasz reminds us, psychiatrists in Nazi Germany played a leading role in developing the gas chambers whose first victims were mental patients. Even in occupied territories, where soldiers were used for the mass murder of civilian populations, the inmates of mental hospitals – in Kiev, for example – were killed by doctors.[31] In Poland alone, about 30,000 mental hospital patients were put to death. All this was done in the name of protecting the health of the sane members of the population.

Szasz reminds us in late the 1960s, in a period when many preferred to forget and before thinking about the Holocaust had become a central cultural concern, that:

> The Nazis had pioneered... not only in developing new techniques of mass murder, but also – and this apparently has largely been forgotten, if indeed its significance was ever appreciated – in perfecting a fresh rhetoric of hygiene to justify their programs. For example, Heinrich Himmler, chief of the Nazi SS explained that 'Antisemitism is exactly the same as delousing. Getting rid of lice is not a question of ideology. It is a matter of cleanliness.'[32]

Similarly, Paul Otto Schmidt, press chief of the Nazi Foreign Office, declared that 'The Jewish question is no question of humanity, and it is no question of religion; it is solely a question of political hygiene.' [33] According to Raul Hilberg in *The Destruction of the European Jews* the imagery of the Jews as vermin was the accompaniment to their extermination by gassing. 'The most dramatic application of this theory' (of the Jew as insect), writes Hilberg, was that:

> a German fumigation company, the *Deutsche Gesellschaft für Schädlings-bekämpfung* [was] drawn into the killing operations by furnishing one of its lethal products for the gassing of millions of Jews. Thus the destruction process was also turned into a 'cleansing operation'.[34]

More recently Robert N. Procter in the *The Nazi War on Cancer* shows how imbued with organicist metaphors was Nazi discourse on Jews, Marxists and other enemies portrayed as *cancers* on the German national body (*Volkskörper*). In turn, cancer cells appeared in public health propaganda as insidious, parasitic Jews.[35] Returning to themes to do with the relationship between science and politics, which he explored in his earlier *Racial Hygiene: Medicine under the Nazis*, a study of German eugenics and racial science, Procter again questions the assumption about the impossibility of doing 'good' science under repressive regimes. The earlier book attacked the premise that Nazi leaders imposed their murderous, racist pseudo-science on a reluctant medical profession, showing the widespread support for National Socialism in Germany's biomedical community. He establishes the complicity of respected doctors in designing and even carrying out the regime's unspeakable atrocities. At the same time, he acknowledges that there were also real scientific advances (e.g. those made in relation to the link between smoking and cancer) under a regime of unprecedented cruelty.

The invocation of a medical discourse of cleanliness goes some way to show how the Holocaust was part of a modern collective imaginary, as it also encourages us to rethink the relationship between modernity and pre-modern forms of anti-semitism. Sartre explores this theme in *Anti-Semite and Jew*:

> there may not be so much difference between the anti-semite and the democrat. The former wishes to destroy him as a man and leave nothing in him but the Jew, the pariah, the untouchable; the latter wishes to destroy him as a Jew and leave nothing in him but the man, the abstract and universal subject of the rights of man and the rights of the citizen.[36]

Within modernity fear of the Other is expressed through a discourse of 'eradication' in which the Other is feared, deemed to be a threat to the civilised order and so must be destroyed. But paradoxically, as Szasz also recognises, 'he needs the Other and, if need be, creates him, so that, by invalidating him as evil, he may confirm himself as good'.[37] In different periods people have endeavoured to simplify their tasks by drawing connections between health and virtue, illness and sin. As Szasz has it:

> It is as if men could not accept, and still cannot accept that good men may be sick and evil men healthy; or that healthy men may be evil, or sick men good. The same intolerance of moral complexity and of human differences has led men to reject the image of a just godhead, who loves all his creations equally: Jews and Christians, whites and blacks, men and women, healthy and sick.[38]

'Of all the religions,' observed Voltaire, 'Christianity should of course inspire the most toleration, but till now the Christians have been the most intolerant of all men.'[39]

Goodness and 'Eradication'

Drawing upon a radical distinction between good and evil, a dominant Christian tradition has unwittingly shaped otherwise secular traditions of classical social theory. An Enlightenment vision of modernity has been structured around a sharp distinction between nature and culture. Nature has been taken as a given and is often presented as a threat to culture and civilisation. As the 'human' has been defined in opposition to the 'animal' this fosters an ethics of self-denial and resentment, as Nietzsche has recognised. This unwittingly produces forms of self-rejection through a tacit rejection of an 'animal' nature, that in Kantian ethics we have to 'rise above' in order to realise a 'true' nature as rational moral selves within an intelligible realm. The 'earthly' is identified with the 'empirical' and at some level is being condemned as a site of sin and transgression. Set in radical contrast to the 'spiritual' it is only through the 'eradication' of emotions, feelings and desires which spring from their 'beastly' natures that people can aspire to goodness untainted by 'selfish' desires.[40]

Szasz attempts to explain some of these connections:

> The moral aim of Christianity is to foster identification with Jesus as a model; its effect is often to inspire hatred for those who fail... If man cannot be good by shouldering the blame for others, he can at least be good by blaming others. Through the evil attributed to the Other, the persecutor authenticates himself as virtuous.[41]

Within the Christian West the 'good' of the community is established through getting rid of evil and this includes eradicating signs of evil within oneself, as it does protecting the boundaries of the community. The good has to be introjected and the evil has to be expelled. Within the Christian symbolic which shaped the

Middle Ages, the struggle of (good) Christians against (bad) Jews became the essential dynamics of anti-semitism. As Joshua Trachtenberg has shown in *The Devil and the Jews*, in the Middle Ages the God of the Europeans was a Christian; his Devil was a Jew. Satan was an explicitly Jewish demon often depicted wearing a Jew's hat or yellow badge. Believing in the reality not only of Christ but also of Antichrist, the medieval mind, Trachtenberg notes, climaxed this parallel by making the latter 'the child of a union between the devil and a Jewish harlot – in deliberate contrast to that other son of God and a Jewish virgin'.[42]

Within a postmodern ethics we can think about a new humanism which validates human diversity and refuses to treat Others as 'less than human', but we cannot actualise such an ethic unless we come to terms with the continuing influence of religious traditions which have often tacitly lived on in secularised forms. Within the West there has been a long Christian tradition which has been given a secular form within modernity. As Trachtenberg expresses it, the refusal of the Jew to identify with Christendom in the face of apparently conclusive evidence only serves to prove that the Jew was *not* human – not in the sense that the Christian was.

> He was a creature of an altogether different nature, of whom normal human reactions could not be expected. 'Really, I doubt whether a Jew can be human for he will neither yield to human reasoning, nor find satisfaction in authoritative utterances, alike divine and Jewish,' protested Peter the Venerable of Cluny. What then? He was the devil's creature! Not a human being but a diabolic beast fighting the forces of truth and salvation with Satan's weapons. Such was the Jew as medieval Europe saw him. One might as soon expect the devil himself to submit of his own free will to Christ, as the Jew. And against such a foe no well of hatred was too deep, no war of extermination effective enough until the world was rid of his menace.[43]

As Levinas recognised, the devil was never very prominent in Jewish thought as a distinct personality – but to the medieval Christian he was very real as the world was conceived as involved in a struggle between the forces of good and the forces of evil. So it was that Satan was imagined as seeking to destroy the world as Jesus had come to save it. Though in the Synoptic Gospels the episode of Jesus' temptation is little more than a preliminary test, the tendency became increasingly strong for Jesus to become the god in Christian belief and to represent the principle of good in its eternal struggle with the forces of evil. Trachtenberg puts it thus:

> All the power of Christian propaganda was exerted to arouse fear and hatred of the Jews, for while Jesus fought the devil on his ground, his followers must

destroy the agents of the devil on theirs, lest Satan inherit the earth and truth and salvation be lost. Christendom was summoned to a holy war of extermination, of which the Jews were only incidentally the objects. It was Satan whom Christian Europe sought to crush.[44]

Other Voices

Lest we fall into simplifying a moral complexity, we have to recognise that there are other voices who speak within a Christian tradition, even if these voices have remained marginal. Nevertheless these voices have the potential for opening up a different kind of dialogue between good and evil. They also help to set in contrast the dualistic traditions of 'good' and 'evil' that have continued to influence classical forms of social theory. Beginning to recognise how secularised forms of Christianity have served to underpin traditions of social theory within modernity, we can open up a more complex discussion about the processes of secularisation and the relationship between the sacred and the profane.

As we have learnt to think about morality in terms of social rules, particularly within a Durkheimian tradition, it has been difficult to think about the existence of evil other than in individualistic terms. Where moral laws are imagined to present individuals with a higher, more altruistic vision of themselves which allows them to escape from their selfish egoism, it has been difficult to explain how an evil ethic of Nazism could take hold in the heart of Europe.

The Gospel of Philip, which is still considered a marginal text according to Elaine Pagels in *The Origin of Satan*, offers an alternative to the common Christian perception that shaped the secularised vision of modernity – of good and evil as cosmic opposites. Much as they disagree on context, both orthodox and radical Christians, according to Pagels,

> assume that morality requires prescribing one set of acts, and proscribing others. But the author of Philip wants to throw away all the lists of good things and bad things – lists that constitute the basis of traditional Christian morality. For, this author suggests, what we identify as opposites – 'light and dark, life and death, good and evil' – are in reality pairs of interdependent terms in which each implies the other.[45]

Intending to transpose Christian moral principles into a new key – possibly something Levinas could also appreciate – the author of Philip traces the story of the tree of knowledge of good and evil as a parable that shows the futility of the traditional approaches to morality, so opening a space for what we might conceive as a postmodern ethics. Philip doubts whether we can distinguish good from evil in such simple and categorical ways. He tells a parable of a householder responsible for an estate that includes children, slaves, dogs, pigs and cattle. Each has to be fed appropriately to its kind and this becomes an image of the disciple of God 'who "perceives the conditions of [each person's] soul, and speaks to each one" accordingly, recognising that each has different needs and stands at a different level of spiritual maturity'.[46]

As Pagels also points out, Philip refuses to argue over whether Christians should marry or remain celibate. Posed as opposites, these choices present a false dichotomy. For one person marriage might be appropriate but not for another.

> Do not fear the flesh, nor love it. If you fear it, it will gain mastery over you; if you love it, it will devour and paralyze you.[47]

This goes some way towards articulating an ethic of self-acceptance – at least of taking ethical questions seriously and recognising that the problem is not whether a certain act is 'good' or 'evil' but how to reconcile the freedom gnosis conveys with the responsibilities we have towards others. According to Pagels:

> The central theme of the Gospel of Philip is the transforming power of love: that what one becomes depends upon what one loves. Whoever matures in love takes care not to cause distress to others: 'Blessed is the one who has not caused grief to anyone.'... The gnostic Christian, then, must always temper the freedom gnosis conveys with love for others.

Sometimes Levinas seems to place an emphasis upon our responsibilities towards others but finds it difficult to reconcile this responsibility with an adequate vision of freedom. The centrality he gives to the responsibilities we have towards others is understandable knowing, in the way he does, how Jews were forsaken in continental Europe when the Nazis came to power. Even though they were 'free and equal' citizens, they were not protected by the liberal democratic state. People did not recognise the responsibilities they had for Others. Levinas is also aware of the complex relationship between freedom and law within a Jewish tradition. He would be able to identify the false analogy Pagels suggests when she says, following Philip, that:

> Instead of commanding one to 'eat this, do not eat that,' as did the...'tree' of the law, the true tree of gnosis will convey perfect freedom... In the place where I shall eat all things is the tree of knowledge... That garden is the place where they will say to me, 'Eat this, or do not eat that, just as you wish.' [48]

But this is not a harmony or blend between love, freedom and justice that can be willed into existence. These ideals are often in conflict within the liberal democratic state and, as ideals, they often remain unrealised. In a Jewish tradition it is law that can serve as a crucial reminder when people fall short of the ideals they aspire to live by. What matters is what people are ready to do for each other, their deeds rather than their thoughts. This expresses the priority which a Jewish tradition gives to ethics in relation to epistemology. It is through ethical relations that we can come to know ourselves. The law does not have to be coercive but it exists as a path that can also help people on the way. As people learn to think a different relationship between 'good' and 'evil', in which they are no longer tied into traditions of self-rejection but can more easily appreciate their own evil inclinations rather than feel they have to project them on to Others, so they can recognise the complex interrelation between 'evil' and 'good'. In this way they can come to terms with the dignity of diverse aspects of their experience and so also with an embodied spirituality that is concerned with issues of peace and social justice.

Recognition of the sources of dualistic ethical traditions, and of the ways they have been sustained within a secularised vision of modernity, opens a space for new thinking towards a postmodern ethics. It helps us appreciate some of the difficulties which classical traditions of social theory, set within the terms of a secular rationalism, have had in coming to terms with the Holocaust. As I learnt social theory in the late 1960s and early 1970s, it was often passed over in silence as some kind of aberration which traditional social theories seemed powerless to illuminate. Even in those years I was interested in questions of ethics but social theory seemed caught within a tradition which identified ethics with prevailing social and cultural values. Having moved beyond the concerns with the conditions for social order and social conflict, it still found it difficult to articulate social theory as a critical ethical discipline.

Even prevailing theories of race and ethnicity found it difficult to illuminate the workings of anti-semitism. Within the terms of a materialist analysis it seemed as if anti-semitism was also to be passed over in silence. It was only when the Holocaust began to figure in contemporary culture in the mid-1980s, with the Hollywood television series which had such an impact and years later with Steven Spielberg's *Schindler's List*, that social theorists turned their attention to the relationship between modernity and the holocaust. Bauman's contribution, *Modernity and the Holocaust*, proved to be seminal but again it proved difficult to bring together concerns over Christian anti-semitism and the figuring of the Jew as evil within the Western world with the idea that the Shoah was largely the product of a secular modern form of instrumental rationality. The difficulty seems partly to lie in the ways we conceive of relations between pre-modern and modern forms of anti-semitism, but it also connects to the ways we think about evil within a tradition of secular rationalism.

155

Notes

1 For a discussion which helps to relate Kantian ethics as a central tradition within modernity to diverse traditions of social theory see, for instance, Zygmunt Bauman, *Modernity And Ambivalence*, Cambridge: Polity, 1991; and Victor J. Seidler, *Recovering The Self: Morality and Social Theory*, London: Routledge, 1995.

2 I have argued in *Kant, Respect and Injustice: The Limits of Liberal Moral Theory*, London: Routledge, 1986, that Kant defines 'inclinations', emotions, feelings and desires as forms of unfreedom and determination which can only distract us from following a moral path. So too he also conceives of history and culture as forms of unfreedom which try to influence and determine behaviour externally.

3 In *Kant, Respect and Injustice* I try to show how culture and history are framed within a Kantian tradition as forms of unfreedom and determination. For Kant they operate in an analogous way to emotions, feelings and desires, which as 'inclinations' distract people from acting out a sense of pure will to do what the moral law requires. They become aspects of the 'empirical realm' that people have to 'rise above' and disavow if they are to be free as moral agents. This helps to shape a liberal conception of freedom in which individuals can think for themselves, when this means erasing their class, gender, 'race' and ethnic backgrounds.

4 For an interesting historical survey of different forms of antisemitism in pre-modern and modern times see, for instance, Shmuel Almog (ed.), *Anti-Semitism Through the Ages*, Oxford: Pergamon Press, 1988.

5 Zygmunt Bauman's *Modernity and the Holocaust*, Cambridge: Polity, 1989, has proved seminal in opening up central issues of the relationship of the Holocaust to modernity. He tends to focus upon the crucial role of technologies of death in ways which loosen connections with racism and antisemitism. It is in relation to modernity that modern forms of antisemitism are to be understood. As Bauman put it: 'Through most of modern history the Jews were the principal carriers of tensions and anxieties modernity declared out of existence, brought to an unprecedented intensity and supplied with formidable tools of expression' (p.46).

6 Emmanuel Levinas, *Difficult Freedom: Essays on Judaism*, trans. Sean Hand, Baltimore: Johns Hopkins University Press, 1990, p.134. For some helpful reading on Levinas' relationship to Jewish thought and tradition see Richard A. Cohen, *Elevations: The Height of the Good in Rosenzweig and Levinas*, Chicago: University of Chicago Press, 1994; Edith Wyschogrod, *Emmanuel Levinas: The Problem of Ethical Metaphysics*, The Hague: Martinus Nijhoff, 1974; and Tamara Wright, *The Twilight of Jewish Philosophy: Emmanuel Levinas' Ethical Hermeneutics*, London: Harwood Academic Publishers, 1999.

7 For a discussion of Simone Weil's difficult relationship with Judaism see the extensive discussion in Thomas R. Nevin, *Simone Weil: Portrait of a Self-Exiled Jew*, Chapel Hill and London: University of North Carolina Press, 1991. For a broader discussion which attempts to situate Simone Weil in a tradition of social theory see Lawrence Blum and Victor J. Seidler, *A Truer Liberty: Simone Weil and Marxism*, New York and London: Routledge, 1989. Bergson was to take quite a different position. He was to insist on registering as a Jew, so identifying himself with the fate of the Jewish people even though he had converted to Catholicism. He insisted on going himself to register as a Jew in Paris.

8 For discussions within an analytical tradition of the relation between good and evil, see for instance, Bernard Williams, *Ethics and the Limits of Philosophy*, London: Fontana, 1985; Elizabeth Anscombe, 'Modern Moral Philosophy', in *Collected Philosophical Papers*, Vol.3, Oxford: Blackwell, 1981; Stanley Cavell, *The Claims of Reason*, Oxford: Clarendon, 1979; and Raimond Gaita, *Good and Evil: An Absolute Conception*, London: Macmillan, 1991.

9 *Difficult Freedom*, p.134.

10 *Ibid.*, p.292.

11 *Ibid.*, p.291.

12 To reflect on Levinas' relationship and continuing debt to Franz Rosenzweig, see 'Between Two Worlds (The Way of Franz Rosenzweig)', in *Difficult Freedom*, pp.181–201.

13 These themes of justice and violation of the person are explored in Simone Weil's essay 'Human Personality' in G.A. Panichas (ed.), *The Simone Weil Reader*, Mt. Kisco, NY: Boyer Bell, 1977, pp.313–39.

14 *Difficult Freedom*, p.292.

15 *Ibid.*, p.293.

16 *Ibid.* Drawing upon different sources, Adorno opens the first section of his 'Meditations on Metaphysics' (part three of his *Negative Dialectics* entitled 'After Auschwitz') also wanting to question a Platonic/Christian tradition in the West, saying: 'We cannot say any more that the immutable is truth, and that the mobile, transitory is appearance. The mutual indifference of temporality and eternal ideas is no longer tenable even with the bold Hegelian explanation... After Auschwitz, our feelings resist any claim of the positivity of existence as sanctimonious, as wronging the victims; they balk at squeezing any kind of sense, however bleached, out of the victims' fate...'. Theodor W Adorno, *Negative Dialectics*, London: Routledge, 1973, p.361. He was working on what became Part 3 in the post-war lectures that he was giving in Frankfurt on metaphysics. We can contrast these lectures with the formulations which he decided on for the concluding part of *Negative Dialectics*.

17 *Difficult Freedom*, p.294.

18 For an interesting historical exploration of the relationship of Judaism to the body and sexuality see David Biale, *Eros and the Jews: From Biblical Israel to Contemporary America*, New York: Basic Books, 1992; Howard Eilberg-Schwartz (ed.), *People of the Body: Jews and Judaism from an Embodied Perspective*, New York: SUNY Albany, 1992.

19 *Difficult Freedom*, p.135.

20 For a discussion of ways in which Christian traditions have thought about a radical separation between 'good' and 'evil' see Elaine Pagels, *The Origins of Satan*, New York: Random House, 1997; and Wayne A. Meeks, *The Origins of Christian Morality: The First Two Centuries*, New Haven: Yale University Press, 1993.

21 *Difficult Freedom*, p.273.

22 *Ibid.*, p.274.

23 *Ibid.*

24 *Ibid.*

25 *Ibid.*, pp.274–75.

26 *Ibid.*, p.275.

27 Jean-Paul Sartre, *Anti-Semite and Jew*, New York: Schocken Books, 1967, p.39. Sartre's understanding of forms of anti-semitism remains implicated within a liberal moral culture. For a sense of how Sartre's thinking about anti-semitism developed over time, so that he no longer assumed that the Jew is defined negatively through the anti-semitism, see Judith Friedlander, *Vilna on the Seine*, New Haven: Yale University Press, 1990.

28 *Anti-Semite and Jew*, p.44.

29 Thomas Szasz, in *The Manufacture of Madness*, London: Routledge and Kegan Paul, 1971, p.272, asks some very provocative questions about the Inquisition as well as the Mental Health Movement. In doing so he throws traditional perspectives into question and helps to ask different questions. I was struck when I returned to this text after many years by the resonances it has for postmodern discussions.

30 *Ibid.*, p.270.

31 Anatoly Kuznetsov, *Babi Yar*, London: Sphere Books, 1970, p.236.

32 In a speech in 1937, quoted in Hannah Arendt, *The Burden of our Time*, London: Secker and Warburg, 1951, p.373.

33 Quoted in *ibid.*, p.214.

34 Quoted in Raul Hilberg, *The Destruction of the European Jews*, Chicago: Quadrangle Books, 1961, and in Bernard Rosenberg, Israel Gerver and F. Willian Howton (eds), *Mass Society in Crisis*, New York: Macmillan, 1971, p.295.

35 Robert Procter has written *Racial Hygiene: Medicine under the Nazis*, London: Harvard University Press, 1988, and more recently *The Nazi War on Cancer*, Princeton: Princeton University Press, 1999.

36 Sartre, *Anti-Semite and Jew*, p.57.

37 Szasz, *The Manufacture of Madness*, p.290.

38 *Ibid.*, p.275.

39 Voltaire, *Philosophical Dictionary*, Harmondsworth: Penguin, 1979, p.485.

40 I have explored diverse tensions in Christian conceptions of respect and equality through the writings of Kant, Kierkegaard and Weil in *The Moral Limits of Modernity: Love, Inequality and Oppression*, London: Macmillan, 1991.

41 *The Manufacture of Madness*, p.262.

42 Joshua Trachtenberg, *The Devil and the Jews: The Medieval Conception of the Jew and its Relation to Modern Anti-Semitism*, Philadelphia: The Jewish Publication Society, 1943, p.35.

43 *Ibid.*, p.18.

44 *Ibid.*, p.22.

45 *The Origins of Satan*, p.171.

46 *Ibid.*, p.172.

47 *Ibid.*, p.173.

48 *Ibid.*

CHAPTER 8

Silence – Voice – Representation

HEIDRUN FRIESE

Impossible donc de l'oublier, impossible de s'en souvenir. Impossible aussi, quand on en parle, d'en parler – et finalement comme il n'y rien à dire que cet événement incompréhensible, c'est la parole seule qui doit le porter sans le dire.   Maurice Blanchot, *L'entretien infini*, p.200

Et comme si cette parole ne pouvait s'ériger que sur les ruines de l'autre, avec et sans elle.

Poussière. Poussière.

Le silence, nul écrivain ne l'ignore, permet l'écoute du mot. A un moment donné, le silence est si fort que les mots n'expriment plus que lui.

Ce silence, capable de faire basculer la langue a-t-il sa propre langue à laquelle on ne peut attribuer ni origine ni nom?

Passage ininterrompu du silence au silence et du mot au silence.
                                    Edmond Jabès, *La mémoire des mots*, pp.13–14

'Only one thing remained close and reachable amid all losses: Language. Yes, language. In spite of everything it remained unlost. But it had to go through its own lack of answers, through terrifying silence [*Verstummen*], through the thousand darknesses of murderous speech. It went through and gave no words for what happened; but it went through this event. It went through and was allowed to resurface [*zutage treten*], enriched [*angereichert*] by it all.' So Paul Celan remarked upon receiving the literary prize of the city of Bremen in 1958.[1]

Celan's meditation on language, memory and history, his reflections of this time, a time of radical losses, opens with the commemoration of topographical dislocations,[2] a motion through the distant sites of a literary landscape which once seemed unreachable for him, the young poet: '...Bremen, brought closer

159

to me by books and the names of those who wrote books and published books, retained the sound of the unreachable. The reachable, though far enough, which was to be reached was named Vienna. You know, what even this reachableness meant over those years.'³ This construction of readings, books, names of authors and their imaginary places, this topographical history which defines what is close and reachable, is completely destroyed by what happened. This history Celan is commemorating has radically cancelled 'any thought of destination or of homecoming',⁴ but what has remained reachable and close, 'in spite of everything and amid the losses' is language: 'Only one thing remained close and reachable amid all losses: language.'

It is not the intimate and secret monologue of personal commemoration which is evoked by places, objects, their traces and resonances, that is, the infinite and unspeakable images of memory which suddenly appear and vanish or become entrenched in their horror and cannot be evaded – this is not what I want to address here. Instead I want to think about the possibilities of words and their silences to designate something, to recall, to recall *this* event, as language, voice and representation. Paul Celan has already indicated the different constellations whose elements are moved in speech and in its silence about what has happened, and whose poles will guide my annotations too. He speaks of a 'terrifying silence and the thousand darknesses of murderous speech'; he speaks of 'language that gave no words for what happened'. The reference here is to speech whose power enforces falling silent, brings nameless and unspeakable death and silence, the reference is to the silence of words and to the possibility or impossibility of re-presenting what happened in and through language and writing. There are other attempts to describe these relations between silence, voice and representation, and to emphasise the need to break the silence, to find words for something that cannot be expressed and re-presented in and through words, something that is marked by a very different silence. Let me just mention Theodor Adorno's dictum of the impossibility of poetry after Auschwitz,⁵ Jean Améry's insistence on the need for speech⁶ and Saul Friedländer's insights into the limits of representation;⁷ likewise Jean-François Lyotard's 'différend' to characterise a state in which something has to be said that cannot be said (yet), and his attempt to face the darknesses of speech without – again – falling victim to them;⁸ Sarah Kofman's 'suffocated words'; finally, a terrible falling silent.⁹

I want to read the relations and the different linkages, the internal affinities, partitions and communicating boundaries between silence, voice and representation, and do so from three perspectives which echo and invoke each other and form intersections – intersections where I find Paul Celan, Primo Levi, and Sarah Kofman. My primary aim is not to address these relations and intersections in general terms. I am not going to explore the frantic and febrile duplications of absences: the representation of absence in language and narration which, in writing as the language of the absent and the absent voice (Freud), repeats and duplicates this former absence. Nor do I want to engage in a theoretical discussion about some ontological status of silence as related to voice and representation. Instead I am much more interested in attempting to listen and to trace how these authors undertake this inscription and link phrases. Thus I will not propose a thesis, nor develop a model, nor search for a way out, but want to recall these authors and the different constellations to which these relations are submitted, and represent the transitions, densities, alliances and the shared fields created by them.

Paul Celan, Primo Levi, and Sarah Kofman: they share a unique date which marks their voice and their falling silent, a unique date which figures in their speech. To them and you I'm about to demonstrate my failure.

Paul Celan

1920: born in Czernowitz (Bukovina)
1942: deportation and death of his parents
1970: commits suicide

For Celan, nothing can remain unaffected by the events during the time of 'terrifying silence', 'the thousand darknesses of murderous speech', nothing can remain untouched by the losses, this death he addresses, this death for which language gave no words and no answers. All that could be known about death and dying is henceforth related to and endowed with the time of 'terrifying silence' and 'murderous speech', to a time thus when language failed humans. 'This death continues. Hence the obligation of never dying again only once, without the repetition being able to familiarize us with the always inevitably fatal end,' as Blanchot says.[10] Language gave no words to reach *this* event, all existing relations were shattered, none of the meanings that events had previously been endowed with could survive. Still, 'amid all losses' language itself remained close and reachable. And though its words have been condemned to silence, language nevertheless 'remained close' to itself and, if it cannot offer anything else, it persists as a possibility, as a virtual relation. Fallen silent, it is a mere possibility, not reaching to anything other than to itself in its very being.[11]

Writing, writing poems in a language that has no words for what has happened, after a world of signification has been destroyed. The possibility of language, of writing poems in this language, 'in which and through which death came to him and those close to him, to the millions of Jews and non-Jews, an event without an answer', as Blanchot says,[12] writing poems in a language 'of which nothing can any longer be read but the rift', as Jabès says,[13] this writing cannot re-present the relations which existed before this unspeakable rupture, this wordless death, this unique occurrence – I will return to the uniqueness of this date.

Yet language 'went through this event. Went through it and was allowed to surface "enriched" with it all', says Celan. Without words that hold in the face of what happened, language went through its 'lack of answers', it survived in the darknesses in the night of words and 'was allowed to come to light [*zutage treten*]'. When language resurfaces from the darknesses to speak again and to establish relations with what is, to 'design reality', then the relation it proposes is a temporal one, a question of 'the sense of the clock's hand [*Uhrzeigersinn*]'.[14] The effort required of writing in this language therefore, is not designation as closure, but opening, 'event, movement, being on the way', the 'attempt to gain direction'. As the poem, this language is not timeless, even though it is making a claim to infinity, for this language seeks 'to grasp through time, not above it'.[15]

This language which has gone through silence – the word 'earned by silence [*das erschwiegene Wort*]'[16] – has changed due to this passage, it was 'enriched' by time and in its very temporality now appears as a basis for potential relations. Language being 'enriched', it seems to be more, even richer, to Celan, after the event it went through. But 'enriched' refers to a difference, to the otherness of language (Blanchot), and it refers to a language being marked by time. Its capacity to relate to events cannot be restored, nor re-acquired, nor regenerated; it cannot master what happened, not even dialectically, it can never provide meanings to the losses through which it went. Language is marked by the event, it is itself in time, its own temporality has irrefutably appeared, it resurfaced in its historicity and 'as the ground of a relation that is radically finite'.[17] It can speak again, but it is not the names, nor the words, nor the designations through which it will speak, but through the marks time has imprinted on its words.

Accordingly, language offers the possibility of a poetic relation to an Other, conceived as a relation of dialogue or conversation. 'The poem, as it is a manifestation of language and thus dialogical in essence, can be a message-in-a-bottle... Poems, too, are on their way in this sense: they are drifting toward something... toward something open, ready to be occupied, a you that is approachable, a reality that can be approached.' Language needs an Other, it is only within the 'space of this dialogue that the addressed constitutes itself, gathers around the approaching and designating I', as Celan will say in the 'Meridian', his speech upon receiving the Büchner prize in 1960.[18] But dialogue – 'often it is a desperate dialogue'[19] – is not certain, it is never more than a precarious and vague possibility. It is the possibility of a relation, of approaching an Other, but nothing is certain or given, not the place from which to speak, not the words used to approach, not the establishment of the relation. Language that reaches out for openness and an opening to an Other offers no more than 'a possibility of relation and thus the possibility of a reality'.[20]

'Whenever we speak with things in this way, we are always broaching the question of their where-from and where-to: a question "remaining-open", coming-to-no-end, pointing toward the Open, the Empty, and the Free – We have ventured far out. The poem is, I think, also in search of this place', says Celan.[21] Language gives itself in its temporality and the openness it is longing for is the only possibility of poetry and of historical questioning. Celan reverses Adorno's dictum on the impossibility of poetry after Auschwitz in a way that affirms that, after what has happened, only poetry is possible because the place it is seeking is an open space, an emptiness which has not yet been designated, nor named, nor enclosed.[22] Only this endless writing 'coming-to-no-end' remains possible after this monstrosity, because the place it is 'pointing toward' is the non-place of a thinking and writing yet to come: 'la pensée à venir', as Blanchot says.

'This death continues. Hence the obligation of never dying again *only once*, without the *repetition* being able to familiarise us with the always inevitably fatal end', Blanchot says.[23] Celan writes himself from this event, this date, this unique date. He writes himself from this date, the rupture of conventional relations, the wreckage of meanings and this silence – I am not going to use the term 'trauma' – this silence which, as language passed through it, changed the latter, and 'enriched' it with time. Language and 'breathless stillness of muted silence in words'[24] show the – poetic – traces of this dating, an incision which marks its writing: 'Perhaps one may be allowed to say, that its own distinct 20th January remains inscribed in every poem? Perhaps this is what is novel about the poems that are written today, precisely this: that here is the most obvious attempt to commemorate such dates? But do we not, all of us, write ourselves, from such dates? And to which dates do we write ourselves?' Celan asks.[25] Celan's allusion to Büchner's Lenz fragment, to that particular Lenz who 'passed through the mountains on the 20th January', poses the question about that which appoints itself 'only once' a mark 'which at times is called date',[26] and which indicates unique, unrepeatable events. To this question Celan immediately adds a twofold 'but': 'But the poem does speak! It commemorates its date, but it speaks. For sure, it always speaks only in its own, very own behalf. But I think...that it has always been a hope of the poem...to speak on behalf of an Other's case in this way...'[27]

The date – understood not as the date itself but as the experience of a date in poetry – preserves the general and the specific, the unique, the unexchangeable, and the repetition, for the dating invokes a form of recurrence or return when it causes remembrance by the possibility of reading a repetition from it. In spite of its unrepeatable date, from which it writes itself, and to which it directs remembrance, in spite of 'its memory rooted in the uniqueness of an event',[28] the poem speaks, namely to an Other who does not share the experience or the knowledge of the unique so dated.

The secrecy and indecipherability of the unique and the unrepeatable are not enclosed within the poem, but the date breaks its unheard silence and enables a – possible – relation to an Other. 'The date, …by inscription of a reminder, a marker "for remembrance's sake" will have broken the silence of the pure uniqueness. However, to speak about the date, one has to erase it in order to make it readable, audible and perceptible beyond the pure uniqueness it is speaking about.'[29] This erasure, however, is not identical with the dissolution of the date into something general, but 'a cancellation in view of another date',[30] to which the date speaks, the date of an Other with whom 'in the secrecy of the encounter' it links up and overlaps.[31] Blanchot will understand this encounter as an infinite conversation ('*l'entretien infini*'), as an infinite dialogue, a dialogue made up of words which in the endlessness of infinite echoes, repetitions, inscriptions and cancellations pass across: dia-logos.[32]

This interior dating, these traces and incisions, which record and register the unique, and which the poem in its encoded silence embodies like a memory, has to de-mark itself. The date can mark and render readable something only if the dating, this recording of the unrepeatable, erases itself and contains within it the possibility of repetition – Celan speaks of 'annual rings [*Jahresringe*]'. The poem inscribes its date into the repeatability – but not as a repetition – of what cannot recur. 'This date will have designated and sealed the unique, the unrepeatable, but in order to be able to do so, it will itself be read in a sufficiently encoded, readable, decipherable form. And every time, on the same date, the memory is awakened of the date of what cannot return.'[33] Accordingly, the date contains a paradoxical but nonetheless inevitable duplication or reflection: it enshrines the remembered date and the date of remembrance which recites the unique through its mentioning and remembering and through a conventional performance of repeatable features and marks.[34] That which has to be remembered, which has at the same time to be gathered, assembled and repeated, is from that very moment on the destruction of the date, and this erasure of a mark, the loss of this unique meaning, leaves its trace in the poem. The poem then – this open and always uncertain possibility of a dialogical encounter with an other in the awareness of temporality and in the temporality of language which has passed through the uniqueness of this unspeakable death – has to be conceived as an overlapping of dates, a ghastly return of what is absent and cannot return, and thus at the same time a (necessary) erasure of a unique date by the date of its repetition. Yet this date has broken the silence and opens to a (possible) relation to an other.

'This is dying maybe, the merciless growth in the heart of dying, the witness without witness whom Celan has given a voice, uniting this voice with the voices soaked with night, voices where there are no more voices, only a belated murmuring, stranger to time, offered as a present to all thinking', as Blanchot says.[35]

Primo Levi

1919: born in Turin
1943: joins a group of partisans in the Valle d'Aosta
1944: deportation to Auschwitz
1987: on 11 April, commits suicide

Primo Levi has left us a nightmarish dream which kept recurring in Auschwitz and could not be shaken off – an ordeal of which he could not rid himself, which kept pursuing him and caused him to write. In this ordeal, there are:

> my sister, some of my friends and many other people. Everybody is listening while I am talking... I'm talking about our hunger, the lice checks, the Kapo who hit me on the nose and then sent me to wash since I was bleeding. It is an intense pleasure, physical and inexpressible, to be at home, with friends, and to tell everything: but I cannot ignore that my audience is not listening. What's more, they are totally disinterested: they talk among themselves about entirely different matters, just as if I did not exist. My sister looks at me, rises, and walks away without saying a word. At this moment, a desperate desolate pain wells up inside me, similar to that one remembers from childhood: a pain in its purest sense... Why does everyday pain always enter into our dreams, into this constantly recurring scene of talking and not being heard?[36]

'Conversation tends toward silence, and the one who listens is rather the one who is silent. It is from him that the one who speaks obtains meaning', comments Walter Benjamin on the character of dialogue.[37] But what if the one who listens, that is, the silent one who attributes significance and meaning to words and phrases, does not listen, refuses the words, turns and walks away? What if the 'you' Celan spoke about is not 'approachable' and what if the 'message-in-a-bottle' doesn't reach any destination? What, however, if the 'you'/'thou' of which Martin Buber and Paul Celan speak, does not listen and does not understand?[38] Nobody listens – this deprives things of their significance, deletes everything, renders it futile and surrenders events, one's own experience, one's own being to pain, desolation, the absolute void. All events repeat themselves in this refusal, but without ever having become a date able to speak to an Other.

To speak, but without a 'you' – only the silent inner voice, an unmediated word, but no response. What is lacking in this recurring scene is the repeating lack of response, there is no respons(e)ibility for the other,[39] as a possibility to step out of the fear. 'A desperate desolate pain wells up inside me, similar to that one remembers from childhood: a pain in its purest sense', says Levi – and Levinas: 'You sleep alone, and the adults continue life; the child perceives the silence of the bedroom as "noisy"… As if the void was full, as if silence was noise.'[40]

This was a collective dream, says Levi, the dream of nobody listening, of the absence of any response, common like the dream of eating.[41] 'This is how our nights drag on. The dream of Tantalus and the dream of my narration… One keeps forever waking up, cold with fear, and with all one's limbs trembling because one thinks one is hearing an order yelled by a furious voice in a language one does not understand.'[42] A nightmarish dream, enclosed in, and interrupted by, the delirium of words, by an unintelligible word magma of yelling voices, language that turns into a tormenting noise: 'Into the memory of all survivors, who were rarely polyglot, the first days at the camp are inscribed as a frenzied film, full of pounding noises, and rage, and without sense; a chaos of people without names, without faces, who are drowning in an incessant deafening background roar, from which no human word emerged. A greyish-black film, droning, but not talking.'[43] A word, deprived of its sense and meaning, is noise. 'Meaning is limited silence', says Blanchot.[44]

'These strange voices had imprinted themselves on our memories, as on empty, clean tapes; …they were fragments which had been torn out of the indistinguishable: the result of an absurd and unconscious effort to wrest sense from nonsense.'[45] Initiation into camp life meant faces without glances or language, a frenzied film and snatches of noise in an infernal noise, imprinted and incised into the memory as into a gramophone record as droning signs of absolute nonsense. Memory: a mechanical register of signs and traces, of single, disconnected snatches of words and sounds without meaning, which rise above the deafening drone, the hammering Babel of tongues. In this place, language has lost its unity and coherence, carries no significance and no sense. Here, it is infinite loss and endless separation.

'The chimney that rises from the center of the Buna works, and whose top can rarely be seen in the fog, we have built it. Its bricks were called Ziegel, briques, tegula, cegli, kamenny, téglak, and hatred cemented them; hatred and strife as in the Tower of Babel, which is why we call it: Babelturm,

Bobelturm...'[46] 'Babel, Tower of', as the *Encyclopaedia Britannica* (1968) puts it, is

> a structure built by the descendants of Noah. As related in the Book of Genesis, they journeyed westward after the Flood and settled in the plain of Shinar... There they began to build themselves a city with walls and a high tower, in order that they might make themselves a name and not be scattered abroad over the earth. The Lord came to these people, who spoke a single language, and confounded their speech so that they could not understand one another.

Here, an arrogant and fatal inversion and overturning of significance. Here, people speaking different languages build a tower, forced by those who aim at the annihilation of what was to be the Other. 'The Babel of tongues is a fundamental element of life down here; one is surrounded by an incessant Babel in which all orders and threats are bellowed in languages one has never heard before, and woe betide anyone who does not understand right away', says Levi.[47] The only language, the one language that has remained among the languages, knows only one single gesture, the gesture of violence, the gesture of destruction. 'All Kapos were beating...that was their language... the only language, incidentally, that was really understood by all in this unremitting Babel.'[48]

Language has created insurmountable and deadly boundaries and separations. How could anyone understand the orders which were 'loud and furious, then bellowed from the throat'? How to comprehend the incomprehensible, whose disjointed words became a condition for survival? To understand where to get spoons, shoes, an extra ration of soup: 'those who had not understood had left the stage', says Levi.[49] To understand in a place where even to understand the words would separate, mark a boundary, decide over life or death.

This violent disruption of unity, however, the loss of a common language which is not that of violence, also generates proximity, a special closeness to one's own language shared with one's fellow countrymen. 'Only one thing remained close and reachable amid all losses: Language. Yes, language. In spite of everything it remained unlost', says Celan. A closeness, though, encapsulated in the conditions of endless violence and subordination. In this disruption, this space between noise and closeness, in this system of absolute domination, words have been eclipsed and in the 'darknesses of murderous speech' the camp jargon has taken hold – this betrayed language: 'where human beings are violated, language is violated, too'.[50]

Nevertheless, to speak. In the disruption of language, in the scornful noises of the nonsensical, and in the falling silent of witnesses, to bear witness. To refuse consent. To live in order to speak, to report, to give an account. Passing through the event in order to save the lost language. The closeness of words: remembering and speaking as a thread of life; writing in order to survive: '...precisely because the camp is a big machine to turn us into animals, we must not become animals; and in this place, too, one can survive, and therefore one must want to survive, in order to tell, to bear witness'.[51]

Primo Levi did not regard himself a witness. For those who have touched the bottom, the utter witnesses, those who could give testimony, they disappeared, they submerged (*i sommersi*). In this falling silent one did not write, one did not write poems. Annihilation is the rule, survival the exception. The survivors, therefore, are obligated to report and analyse what goes beyond their own experience, the experience of the others, of the annihilated, even though this means speaking on behalf of and in the name of others without being authorised, a speech speaking without a mandate.

Thus it appears that nothing can be told, nothing can be written on these events, nothing but silence. But can silence be told, can it be written? 'From a temporal distance, one can say today that the history of the camps has been written almost without exception by those, including myself, who have not fathomed the bottom. Whoever has done that has not returned, or his powers of observation were paralyzed with pain and with not-being-able-to-understand.'[52] This silence cannot be written, but speech can unfold only amid such irreducible silence, an unending silence that carries language and haunts it, and against which words can and must emerge. Speech must rise against this falling silent, the paralysis – the 'suffocation' as Kofman will say. For 'silence, the absence of signs, is itself a sign', as Levi says. *This* silence fulfils the monstrous plan: 'Nobody with the sign incised in his flesh is allowed to get out of here, who might bring to the world the less-than-good tidings of what man has done to man in Auschwitz.'[53]

One has to remember against this plan and the 'murderers of remembrance', as Vidal-Naquet and Levi have pointed out,[54] to set remembrance against 'the refusal to remember in order to refuse an unbearable truth and create another'.[55] Against these silences, the silence of guilt, the silence of shame, the silence of the victims, the silence of terror, Levi must – one must – remember and give account.[56]

To speak about the crime, the massacre, against its 'secret', despite the wreckage of memory, despite its deformations in trauma, its instability and the interferences with competing memories, is an elementary need for Primo Levi.[57] It is a need for narration and encounter, an urgency of telling, but also a moral duty; the duty to give a voice to those who were silenced. To write, then, in the memory, in the thought of the silence of the voices before the words and between the words. A poem remains mindful of its dates; but its hopes include speaking 'on behalf of an Other's cause', says Celan. To give a voice to the annihilated, demands Levi, even if this speaking without a mandate 'in the name of others' is at the same time an attempt to rid oneself of the spectral haunt.[58]

And again, this recurring nightmare: to speak and not to be understood, to write oneself from a date and not to have a common date. Not to be able to say what one has to say, the overpowering impulse to write – to write again and against language. Writing in the pain of the rift in language. 'It was then that we became aware for the first time that our language lacks words to express this violation: the destruction of a human being'. [59] There are no words to express this scorn: 'to be an empty human being that consists only of pain and natural basic needs'.[60]

Sarah Kofman

1934: born in Paris
1942: father is deported to Auschwitz
1994: on 15 October, commits suicide

'What remained of him, is just his fountain pen... It has "left" me before I could make up my mind to abandon it. I still own it, it is lying on my desk in front of my eyes, and it forces me to write, to write, to write. Perhaps my numerous books were necessary detours to be able finally to narrate this.'[61] The fountain pen and the father who left her behind before she, the child, did so in order to grow up, and which she still owns, that forces her to write. That in which her murdered father is still present, can be seen, a writing tool with which this story can be recorded, must be recorded, by the gesture of writing, as a weight of endless repetition, as heritage and remembrance. (But she does not write with this particular fountain pen, not even the book that she had decided was to be her last.)

And again: to say what has to be said, although it cannot be said, finally to speak about this, for which her incessant writing has been a detour. To break the silence that has accompanied silence, to write across and extinguish the words that speak (of) silence. To remove and eliminate the substitute, the delegation, and finally to speak, to speak about this event.

And finally, she speaks, in a language which, in its nakedness, resembles that of Levi, finally she speaks – painfully reserved – about her childhood that is inextricably linked with these events. Finally she speaks, Celan's questions in view, without, however, the 'happiness of the narrating voice' to which Blanchot has referred[62] being able to expel her distress, without the 'joy that accompanies the invention of a new idiom' of which Lyotard has spoken,[63] that is, without the non-place that the poem searches for, according to Celan, in its/her being-on-the-way.

This death, her death too, a recurring death. For Celan, all knowledge about mortality is a heritage, a legacy from the time of the 'terrifying silence and murderous speech' – a time for which 'language gave no words', thus a time when death was without meaning. 'This death continues. Hence the obligation of never dying again only once, without the repetition being able to familiarize us with the always inevitably fatal end', Blanchot says.[64] It is this unique date Derrida speaks about, this unique date which marks itself only once without the repetition being able to domesticate it. It is of *this* death she speaks in 'suffocated words', this death that Blanchot commemorates, this kind of death that becomes the point of departure in her last book.

> Because he was a Jew, my father died in Auschwitz. How could one not speak about it? And how can one speak about it? How can one speak about something when, in confronting it, any possibility of speaking ceases?... To speak – it has to be spoken about – *without power*: without allowing the all-too-powerful, sovereign language to control the by all means aporetical situation, the absolute impotence and defenselessness, and confining it thereby in the brightness and happiness of the day? And how could one not speak about it, when it was the wish of all those who returned – but he did not return – to talk, talk endlessly, as if only an 'endless conversation' could do justice to the endless misery?[65]

To speak, but in what kind of language? Searching for a language which does not control and confine what it speaks about in its predominance and power, repeating thus domination and impotence, manifesting once again this relationship and, based on this complicity, helping it to rise once again to power and presence. To write, then, as '...writing, a writing without power, which can make us hear the silence of those who could not speak, a writing which can let us perceive the "true word" that is at one with the silent presence of an Other, of the Other who was prevented from speaking during the stay at the camp'.[66] It is only the powerlessness of this writing that allows one to hear the silence of those whose words were cut short and who can no longer speak. This representation which can never reach or catch up with the event/s, has to reassemble and link up its phrases differently, without allowing the sentences to master, to dominate the event/s (Lyotard), without including them in the law of writing, but rather like an endless encounter which Blanchot sees as a break with any form of totality since only this 'less' can match the voices and their endless narration. To listen to the silence of the voices, to give this silence a hearing and make this silence heard: language has to pass through silence, the falling silent and has to reach *through* – not above – events and time, demands Celan; becoming one with this word, demands Kofman. This dialogical writing, in which Celan, Blanchot, and Kofman encounter and evoke one another, can hardly be conclusive and come to a definite end. This writing must endlessly seek a new beginning and keep writing and re-writing itself ad infinitum.

And again: How, then, can one speak? How can one speak then, if the common rule of narration is not only based on the distinction between form and content, the separation between the spoken and the addressed, on the division and difference between signifier and signified, but based also on a presence of a narrating voice and its happiness? 'There is the undefinable speaking, the splendor of a "narrative voice" which makes itself clearly understood, without ever being eclipsed by the opaqueness or the enigma or the terrifying horror which communicate themselves.'[67] How can one narrate, if the one who could give an account of the catastrophe, the narrator, is absent?

It is maybe this absence of the narrator and its voice that made Adorno decide that there could be no narration-fiction on Auschwitz. It is in this unspeakable event itself that resides the impossibility of narration – which according to common definitions is characterised by a beginning, an intricacy and an end – and which strives for meaning and sense. It is in this event itself that resides the impossibility of a single, an all-encompassing and integrated discourse. How can one narrate, if the narrated is beyond any sense and when any meaning has been lost? 'On Auschwitz and after Auschwitz no narration is possible, if by narration one understands: to narrate a history of events which make/s sense', says Kofman.[68]

But this event whose sense cannot be determined or grasped – the *lack of answers* which, according to Celan, language had to pass through and which, with the force of the entire body being suffocated by it, marks the boundaries of explication and the cognitive regime – (this event) demands to speak, to say what has not (yet) been said. It demands speech, thereby referring to something 'unuttered, undefined', silent and approaching a silence. How can one understand at all this – suffocating – movement between silence and speaking which enforces silence before having even raised one's voice? Representation is a peculiar re-appropriation, retrieval of what is absent, of absence itself supposed to be delivered by words and brought about by speech, whereas there are only blank and empty spaces and silence, absence; 'The need to testify demands a testimony which, in its single uniqueness, only the impossible witnesses – the witnesses of the impossible' could bear.[69] A tremendous movement, trying to render present what is absent, whilst the silence of those absent has been confirmed and sealed long ago. 'Nobody bears witness for the witness', says

Celan.[70] Is this attempt not obscene and monstrous in itself? But nevertheless, this absence demands to speak; one cannot, must not be silent, fall into this other silence and forgetfulness – precisely because of this (nonsensical) destruction, these deaths which were worse than death.

> If no narration is possible after Auschwitz, the duty remains to speak, to speak incessantly, for those who were not able to speak because they wanted to preserve the true word to the last extreme, without giving it away, without betraying it. To speak in order to bear witness, but how?[71]

And again the question: how to speak? How to speak to bear witness, to testify to what happened, how to pass on knowledge about that which, in its immensity, cannot be grasped and passed on? How to write without relying on the literary devices which devaluate the single testimony and its truth, but not to have a choice except writing, that is, to choose from events and from meanings? And how to speak of the unimaginable without referring to imagination? How to write then, if this word itself already reveals the abyss between the one who experienced and the one who didn't pass through the unimaginable? How to write, if this lacuna cannot be filled by any word? The expression 'an unimaginable event' is 'certainly an expression too weak, too reassuring for what one cannot say, but what must still be said, according to an ethical demand that has to do with the demand for the most elevated writing that breaks with any form of idyllic language'.[72]

And does not this list, the list in which he, her father appears, escape the idyllic law (*'loi idyllique'*) of narration? He is entered onto this list, her father, his name, Berek Kofman, born 10 October 1900 in Sobin, together with the names of 1,000 more deportees. This list, testimony to and evidence of the crime, a 'voice without pathos' which withdraws itself from narration, from idyllic speech. This list, in which the particular communicates with the commonality without dissolving the individual into the general. It is on this list, then, that he appears, her father, on this list appears his name, Berek Kofman, born 10 October 1900 in Sobin. 'This voice renders speechless, makes you doubt human common sense, suffocates you in silence. "Silence like a scream without words, but endlessly screaming".'[73] And how to speak, if language has been betrayed by the 'murderous speech' (Celan) and contaminated by the 'darknesses of the words' (Levi); how to speak, if language has become an extinguished language whose words no longer signify any meanings, this language without sense – that noise at the edge of the abyss? There is nothing that has not been subjected to this violence, not even the language of the prisoners. These power relations also compromise language, they 'eclipse the words' (Levi), leaving nothing intact nor untouched. 'The prisoners could not escape this betrayal of the "true word", this "hell of language". There was in effect no language possible between the dominators, the SS men, the Kapos, their many mediators... between the all-powerful oppressors and the prisoners who were all but totally powerless', says Kofman.[74] There can be no unified discourse on the event, even though language, 'the linguistic identity, was this ultimate commonality',[75] and only one thing 'remained close amid all losses', which was language. The voices of the perpetrators and those of the victims are fundamentally heterogeneous, though, distinct and incommensurable (Lyotard). 'There is in effect no language possible between the oppressor...and the victims', as Kofman emphasises.[76] This unique event does not dissolve into one history which misses this difference and seeks to master the unbridgeable.

> How to narrate what cannot be 'communicated' without trickery? That for which there are too few – or too many – words, to say it, and not only because the 'borderline experience' of the utter need, like any other experiences, cannot be communicated? How to speak while having the frenetic and fervent wish to express the experience as such in words (an impossible task), to explain everything to an Other while being exposed to a delirium of words and at the same time finding it impossible to speak? Impossible without *suffocating*. As if the excessive retention, the keeping inside of the word which in this manner gets protected from any compromise with the language of power, provoked in the one who had lived constantly within the proximity of hell... at the moment of his liberation and victory, a strange *double bind*: an endless demand to speak, an infinite having-to-speak imposing itself with an irresistible force, and at the same time an almost physical impossibility of speaking: a *suffocation*; a word formed, called for, and forbidden because it was suppressed for too long, held back, and locked in the throat, and which makes you suffocate, lose your breath, asphyxiates you, deprives you of the possibility even to begin. To have to speak without power and not being heard, either, to have to suffocate, that is the ethical exigency...[77]

To speak, then. In endless questions, in spite of the lack of answers, but nevertheless, the attempt. To speak, in the emotion of words which, heaped on top of each other, break down in the throat before being formulated, or being ordered into a sentence, and which return to silence of which they cannot free themselves. To speak, driven by a greed for words, the nightmare not to be heard, to find no words amid the feeling at this moment of speech when something that has to be said cannot (yet) be said because phrases have to be linked in a different way, that is the (ethical) necessity. It is precisely to this unstable state that Lyotard refers,[78] this state of suffering, *le différend*, where something demands to be said and suffers from the fact that it has not yet been said or cannot be said

173

in the admitted idioms. It suffers and suffocates in this particular kind of silence and on the acknowledgement that that which can at present be said, exceeds what has to be said – Friedländer also refers to this excess.[79] It suffers and chokes on the fact that that which can be said are reassuring steps for that which has to be said.

How, then, can one write? How can one continue to write? It is in this intervening space between the impossibility of speaking and speaking, between presence and absence, distance and proximity, testimony and narration, discontinuity and continuity that resides the state that suffocates the words. In this interspace resides the silence that cuts short the words as a disruption and injury. To move in this in-between is – nevertheless – the task of writing, because it is in this site that these very differences can be activated and become a date.

How, then, can a writing think the enormity of this event in writing, and how can one continue to write? Can this monstrous rupture be carried over into the continuity of a narration and into the 'happiness of the narrating voice'? And is not this establishment of continuity precisely a monstrosity after the monstrosity – the establishment of a scornful continuity, life for life, day for day, word for word and text for text? 'The poem tends toward silence. It strives for its survival [*behauptet sich*] at the edges of itself; in order to survive, it calls itself endlessly back; it calls and fetches itself to be able to exist, persistently from its no-longer back into its further-still', says Celan.[80] Words carry the phantom or the echo of another word, and every word, because of its opening to silence, contains language. Words and silence then, enter into a precarious relation of uniqueness and repetition, too. What is at stake, however, is not the destruction of what strives towards language before it becomes language. At stake is writing itself and therewith keeping open the rift, the activation of differences and impossibilities within this writing. At stake is the writing in the interstices and between the borders that are set by the impossibility of representation in writing.

The monstrous occurrence cannot be thought, it withdraws and nevertheless it is a demand to which we are drawn and it calls for the uninterrupted thinking-of as a thinking-towards something that can never be reached or represented.[81] But is language, precisely because it constantly becomes language, not always already barely able to diminish the distance towards what had happened, or even to encounter the occurrence, as it is, as language, always already alien to it? Writing, nevertheless. Writing towards. This event demands a language that is conscious of the distance and keeps it open, because language was marked (and became specifically temporal) by the occurrence. What happened cannot be represented and has nevertheless to be addressed/written-towards and be made present. Writing thus cannot close and master the event in a conclusive and inclusive language. The event demands an endless writing 'coming-to-no-end' which is 'pointing toward' the non-place of a thinking and writing yet to come: '*la pensée à venir*' as Blanchot says, a thought 'that we are still not thinking'.[82] A writing, at the same time, which perennially revokes the written and a writing which speaks itself, hoping for an Other that it can never be certain of, a writing as responsibility, as answer to the endless silence of language.

To write, then, does not mean to write a history of silence, or to attempt to make speak those voices which in the speech of concepts and their sentences have been silenced, or to seize the thread of speech that has comfortably established itself within the noisy silence of forgetting. Writing, the work and the gestures of writing mean to move within this painful calamity, these places of differences, the thresholds of language, to bring these silences and voices 'into presence'.[83]

The question, therefore, is not speaking or being silent, but questioning language and a writing at the thresholds of language, a writing as an incessant re-writing, a writing not as a means of safe home-coming but a writing towards the edges of writing,[84] a writing as an infinite exile of writing. Writing, thus, as a difference, an inter-space (*Unter-Schied*), as a writing that maintains distance, measures and judges this distance and always remains mindful of it. Writing not as a joint for the rift, but as its incessant activation and exposure. Writing not as mourning and thus injunction of continuity, but as thinking-of, as in-between, separation and division, and thus as a perennial keeping open of this rift, this radical discontinuity (a keeping open of the dimension that measures and judges the separation, the towards and the away from each other.)

There can be no triumph of writing over the aporetic situation. Writing this event. Writing, thus, mindful of the silence of the voices before the words, in the words and between the words. Writing in the pain of the rift of language and writing. Writing, then.

Notes

1 Paul Celan, 'Ansprache anläßlich der Entgegennahme des Literaturpreises der Freien Hansestadt Bremen', in *Gesammelte Werke*, Vol.III [1958], Frankfurt: Suhrkamp, 1983, pp.185–86. A version of this chapter is to be published in *Theoretical Interpretations of the Holocaust*, ed. Dan Stone, Takoma Park: Rodopi, forthcoming. I would like to thank Detlef Hoffmann for having provided me with the opportunity to present these remarks at the conference on 'Representations of Auschwitz' held at Kraków in July 1995. I'm infinitely indebted to Christopher Fynsk to whom I owe the interpretation of Celan. If not indicated otherwise (+), translations are mine (+ = translation by Christopher Fynsk). See Christopher Fynsk, 'The Realities at Stake in a Poem. Celan's Bremen and Darmstadt Addresses', in Ans Fioretos (ed.), *Words, Traces*, Baltimore: Johns Hopkins University Press, 1994, pp.159–84, p.161.

2 Fynsk, 'Realities...', p.160.

3 Celan, 'Ansprache...', p.185+.

4 Fynsk, 'Realities...', p.181. On 'exiled' language, cf. Winfried Menninghaus, *Paul Celan: Magpie der Form*. Frankfurt: Suhrkamp, 1980, pp.33–34; on 'orphaned' language, cf. Werner Hamacher, 'Die Sekunde der Inversion: Bewegung einer Figur durch Celans Gedichte', in *Entferntes Verstehen*, Frankfurt: Suhrkamp, 1998, pp.324–77 (pp.361–64).

5 Theodor Adorno, 'Kulturkritik und Gesellschaft', in *Prismen: Kulturkritik und Gesellschaft* [1949], Frankfurt: Suhrkamp, 1976, pp.7–31, p.31. He did, however, qualify this remark later; see Theodor W. Adorno, *Negative Dialektik* [1966], Frankfurt: Suhrkamp, 1982, p.360. In 1938, Ernst Bloch noted the impotence of words to represent the monstrosity of the crime and remarked that because of unspeakability and the silencing of the word, language itself has become 'historical, historically laden', entrenched and marked by time without, however, being able to reach the event. See Ernst Bloch, 'Der Nazi und das Unsägliche' [1938], in *Werkausgabe*, Vol.XI, Frankfurt: Suhrkamp, 1985, pp.185–92 (p.186).

6 Jean Améry, *Jenseits von Schuld und Sühne. Bewältigungsversuche eines Überwältigten* [1966], Stuttgart: Klett-Cotta 1977 (ET *At the Mind's Limits: Contemplations by a Survivor on Auschwitz and its Realities*, Bloomington:Indiana University Press, 1980.

7 Saul Friedländer, 'Introduction', in *Probing the Limits of Representation: Nazism and the 'Final Solution'*, Cambridge: Harvard University Press, *idem* (ed.), pp.1–21.

8 Jean-François Lyotard, *Le différend*, Paris: Minuit, 1983.

9 Sarah Kofman, *Paroles suffoquées*, Paris: Galilée, 1987.

10 Maurice Blanchot, *Après coup. Précédé par le reassassement éternel*, Paris: Minuit, 1983, p.99.

11 Cf. Fynsk, 'Realities...', pp.161–62.

12 Maurice Blanchot, *Le dernier à parler*, Paris: Fata Morgana, 1984, p.45.

13 Edmond Jabès, *La mémoire des mots*, Paris: Fourbis, 1990, p.17.

14 Celan, 'Ansprache...', p.186+.

15 *Ibid.*

16 Paul Celan, 'Argumentum et Silentio', in *Gedichte*, Vol.II, Frankfurt: Suhrkamp, 1989, p.138. Cf. *Argumentum et Silentio. Internationales Paul Celan Symposium*, Berlin: Walter de Gruyter & Co., 1986.

17 Fynsk, 'Realities...', p.163.

18 Paul Celan, 'Der Meridian. Rede anläßlich der Verleihung des Georg-Büchner-Preises, Darmstadt', am 22. Oktober 1960, in *Gesammelte Werke*, Vol.III, Frankfurt: Suhrkamp, 1983, pp.187–202.

19 *Ibid.*

20 Fynsk, 'Realities...', p.164.

21 Celan, 'Der Meridian...', p.199; cf. Blanchot, *Le dernier...*, p.23.

22 Lyotard, *Le différend*, p.30.

23 Blanchot, *Après coup...*, p.99 (my emphasis).

24 Hans-Georg Gadamer, *Who Am I and Who Are You? And Other Essays*, trans. and ed. Richard Heinemann and Bruce Krajewski, New York: State University of New York Press, 1997, p.67 (orig., *Wer bin Ich und wer bist Du? Ein Kommentar zu Paul Celans Gedichtfolge 'Atemkristall'*, Frankfurt: Suhrkamp, 1973).

25 Celan, 'Der Meridian...', p.196.

26 Jacques Derrida, *Shibboleth. Pour Paul Celan*, Paris: Galilée, 1986, p.11.

27 Celan, 'Der Meridian...', p.196.

28 Derrida, *Shibboleth...*, p.21.

29 *Ibid.*, p.24.

30 *Ibid.*

31 Celan, 'Der Meridian...', p.198.

32 Maurice Blanchot, *L'entretien infini*, Paris: Gallimard, 1969. This encounter, however, is designed as a monologue which consists of the dialogic voices of thinking

which are separated, offering language the possibility of otherness. Infinity though is not conceived as a temporal category in a vulgar sense, but as the endlessness of infinite echoes, repetitions, inscriptions and cancellations.

33 Derrida, *Shibboleth...*, p.43.

34 *Ibid.*, p.101.

35 Blanchot, *Le dernier...*, pp.41–43.

36 Primo Levi, *Se questo è un uomo* [1958], Torino: Einaudi, 1989, pp.53–54. (ET *If This is a Man* [1979], London: Vintage, 1996).

37 Walter Benjamin, 'Das Gespräch', in *Gesammelte Schriften*, Vol.II, 1, Frankfurt: Suhrkamp, 1991, pp.89–96, p.91.

38 On Buber and Celan, cf. John Felstiner, *Paul Celan: Poet, Survivor, Jew*, New Haven/London: Yale University Press, 1995, pp.140–41.

39 Cf. Emmanuel Levinas, *Ethique et infini*, Paris: Fayard, 1982, p.51.

40 *Ibid.*, pp.45–46.

41 Levi, *Se questo...*, p.54; and Primo Levi, *I sommersi e i salvati*, Torino: Einaudi, 1986, p.4. ((ET *The Drowned and the Saved*, London: Joseph, 1988).

42 Levi, *Se questo...*, p.55.

43 Levi, *I sommersi...*, p.72.

44 Maurice Blanchot, *L'écriture du désastre*, Paris: Gallimard, 1980, p.87.

45 Levi, *I sommersi...*, p.73.

46 Levi, *Se questo...*, p.65.

47 *Ibid.*, p.33.

48 Levi, *I sommersi...*, p.56.

49 *Ibid.*, p.75.

50 *Ibid.*, p.76.

51 Levi, *Se questo...*, p.35.

52 Levi, *I sommersi...*, p.8.

53 Levi, *Se questo...*, p.49.

54 Pierre Vidal-Naquet, *Les assassins de la mémoire. 'Un Eichmann de papier' et autres essais sur le révisionisme*, Paris: La Découverte, 1987; Levi, *I sommersi...*, p.20.

55 Levi, *I sommersi...*, p.22.

56 Cf. Agner Heller, 'Scrivere dopo Auschwitz', in *Lettera internazionale*, Vol.11, Nos. 43/44, 1995, pp.46–48.

57 Levi, *I sommersi...*, p.129.

58 *Ibid.*, p.65.

59 Levi, *Se questo...*, p.23.

60 *Ibid.*; cf. Kofman, *Paroles suffoquées*, pp.72–73.

61 Sarah Kofman, *Rue Ordener, rue Labat*, Paris: Galilée, 1994, p.9.

62 Cf. Blanchot, *Après coup...*, p.97.

63 Lyotard, *Le différend*, p.30.

64 Blanchot, *Après coup...*, p.99.

65 Kofman, *Paroles suffoquées*, pp.15–16.

66 *Ibid.*, pp.47–48.

67 Blanchot, *Après coup...*, p.98.

68 Kofman, *Paroles suffoquées*, p.21.

69 Blanchot, *Après coup...*, p.98.

70 Paul Celan, 'Aschenglorie', in *Gedichte*, Vol.II, p.72.

71 Kofman, *Paroles suffoquées*, p.43.

72 *Ibid.*, p.39.

73 *Ibid.*, pp.16–17.

74 *Ibid.*, p.49.

75 *Ibid.*, pp.67–68.

76 *Ibid.*, p.57.
77 *Ibid.*, pp.45–46.
78 Lyotard, *Le différend*, pp.29–30.
79 Friedländer, 'Introduction', pp.19–20.
80 Celan, 'Der Meridian...', p.197.
81 On the relation between 'Andacht – Andenken – und Denken', cf. Martin Heidegger, 'Erläuterungen zu Hölderlins Dichtung' [1944], in *Gesamtausgabe*, Vol.IV, 1981, Frankfurt: Vittorio Klosterman, 1981, pp.79–151.
82 Martin Heidegger, *Was heißt Denken?*, Tübingen: Max Niemeyer, 1962, p.30.
83 Cf. Jean-Luc Nancy, *The Birth to Presence*, Stanford: Stanford University Press, 1993.
84 Cf. Edmond Jabès, *Le livre des marges*, Paris: Fata Morgana, 1984.

CHAPTER 9

Friends and Others:
Lessing's *Die Juden* and *Nathan der Weise*

ANDREW BENJAMIN

After the Shoah politics and political solidarity take on a different quality. The attribution of an identity and the affirmation of that identity have to be viewed as importantly different. It is no longer possible to define Jewish identity simply in terms of the object of persecution and oppression.[1] Such descriptions deny the possibility of that conception of identity that Jews would attribute to themselves. The politics of identity has to take the divide between attribution and affirmation as central to any understanding and evaluation of claims concerning identity. Within the investigations of solidarity friendship has emerged as a model whose resources have yet to be adequately explored. The project here is to investigate that model in relation to the problem of writing about the history of the figure of the Jew after the Shoah. Rather than pre-empt the analysis to come a beginning will be made with two questions: what can be made of friendship? What is it that marks out friendship? A concern with friendship opens the way as much to the political, understood as an account of a generalised belonging together, as it does to intimacy and thus to a form of particularity without generality.[2]

The matters that arise in the attempt to respond philosophically to the question of friendship concern, for the most part, the problem of the relationship between particular and universal.[3] For example, is friendship, understood as a relation, an instance of the self/other relation and thus explicable within the terms set by that relationship? Or is friendship such that it is not a particular of any universal? If this is so then this implies that friendship is a uniquely private affair, such that in being made public and being universalised, more than friendship would be involved. As a result, there could not be, for instance, a politics of friendship.

Once the public and the private are introduced they do not so much complicate friendship as allow for a more sustained examination of it. It would only be in the terms set by such a conception that it would then be possible to evaluate the claim that there is either an ethics or a politics linked to friendship. Part of that investigation involves situating friendship within the distinction between the public and the private. In other words, once it is allowed that there cannot be friendship *tout court* but that the term yields a set of relations that mark what is taken to be either a private or a public realm, then the place of friendship is integral to what could come to be sanctioned in its name. Therefore, not only is there a set of questions arising from the relationship between universal and particular. There are also those which stem from the recognition that for there to be friendship it must have a place; friendship must take (a) place.[4] What cannot be neglected in any attempt to pursue friendship philosophically is the place of friendship. The alternative is a metaphysics of friendship, or a mere typology of it.

Friendship: Literature/Philosophy

In order to pursue these questions we will examine the way friendship figures in two plays by Lessing. The first is an early work, *Die Juden* (written in 1749 and published in 1754); the second is the more famous work of 1779, *Nathan der Weise*.[5] It should be noted that elements of the former are reinscribed in the latter. While the earlier work predates Lessing's own friendship with Mendelssohn, Mendelssohn's own brief treatment of friendship in his essay 'Rhapsodie oder Zusätze zu den Briefen über die Empfindungen' serves to reiterate Lessing's formulation.[6] The difficulty confronted by both Lessing and Mendelssohn resides in a simple question: is it possible to have Jewish friends? It is this question that is to be addressed, if only *sotto voce*, in what follows.

A second question pertains to what could be described as the temporality of friendship. Blanchot's text *Pour l'amité*, for example, poses the question:

> But does one know when it starts? There is no thunderclap that begins a friendship, rather it takes place little by little, the slow work of time. We were friends and we did not know it.[7]

In this passage the problematic status of beginning a friendship opens up the space of a decision that confirms rather than inaugurates a friendship. The refusal of the temporality of a thunderclap means that what is also absent is the temporality of the decision. If there is a temporality of friendship, then, to utilise the implicit temporality within Blanchot's formulation – 'we were friends and we did not know it' – it is one that displaces the decision to be friends with another form of decision. It is in terms of this temporal structure that it becomes possible to return to the problem of particulars and universals. An investigation of these two plays by Lessing will allow for an investigation of the link between friendship and the decision.

While turning to Lessing's dramas may open up these problems, a question remains: why literature? Why, in other words, is recourse made to literature and not to the philosophical tradition from Aristotle to Levinas, in order to address friendship and the relationship between the universal and the particular? As will emerge, it is through a response that depends upon the very particularity of literature that friendship's philosophical dimension can be opened up.

The question 'why literature?' cannot be answered by invoking that conception of literature in which it is understood as no more than the interplay of characters, their differences and their relations, presenting differing world-views. Within such a view the literary text becomes a working out of moral exemplarity in which characters appear as symbols or concepts.[8] This element is not to be denied; however, were it to be pursued literature would be effaced in the name of the symbol or the concept. The answer to the question – why literature? – cannot be restricted to content. It must both acknowledge literature and yet dissolve that acknowledgement into a concentration on the generic specificity of the work. The question – why literature? – will be answered here by a recognition of the genre-specific work of theatre. Theatre demands an approach that incorporates the audience as integral to its activity. Both these plays in being staged would have the effect of uniting and dividing the audience. This will be the case with both present and future audiences, which take on the problematic status of the subject. Once it is no longer allowed that the audience is that which is automatically positioned and unified by a 'feeling for reconciliation', as in Hegel's *Aesthetics*, then the very differences that divide the characters and which remain divided in tragedy or which are allowed an eventual if only provisional reconciliation in other theatrical forms (e.g., Puck's closing soliloquy marking the end of *A Midsummer Night's Dream*) are reproduced within the audience. The 'feeling for reconciliation' is precisely that which is refused by the cosmopolitan audience. In the case of Hegel this feeling is linked to tragedy. In the *Aesthetics* it is present in the move from 'sympathy', through 'tragic suffering' to 'the feeling of reconciliation'.[9]

It is a feeling that arises due to tragedy's 'vision of eternal justice'. The reconciliation as taking place 'in us' yields a move from the particular to the universal insofar as the audience is the generalised particular and the particular is already a part of the universal.[10] Tragic suffering involves a response, felt by the audience as it is enacted on stage. Tragic suffering involves a collision of characters which evokes in the audience not despair but a 'feeling of reconciliation'. The audience becomes the site where that which cannot be resolved comes to be resolved. The audience is king.

And yet literature also brings with it a certain republicanism. To the extent that the audience remains divided, the theatrical text keeps positions open, though this need not be the text's design. What is possible is that the questions – reconciliation with whom? reconciled to what? – may cause the audience to divide precisely because the allegiances envisaged by the work, be they pragmatic or not, are those which are refused by the audience as a whole. The reality of an ineliminable alterity – not a generalised alterity but that which figures within such designations as ethnicity, race and gender – as definitional of the social, provides the possibility for the audience's refusal of the closure demanded by a particular theatrical text. This will be the case even at the moment of literal closure. For example, the final stage direction in *Nathan der Weise* is as follows: 'The curtain falls among the silent repetition of embraces.' The scene of reconciliation being staged is intended to elicit a similar response for what would have to have been an audience feeling as one. Indeed, it is possible to argue that the figure of friendship within Lessing's work is structured by a more generalised 'feeling as one'. It is precisely this set-up that has to be examined. It presupposes a certain symmetry of relations. What is staged in Blanchot's deferral of a founding decision and the inscription of a retroactive decision allowing form the formula 'we were friends but did not know it', is a retrospective awareness. It will be argued that it is the temporality proper to this form of awareness – the decision confirming the friendship – that introduces a structure of dissymmetry. Whether it leads to a politics of friendship in a sense other than the strictly metaphysical one is a different and separate question.

Lessing's *Die Juden* and *Nathan der Weise*

Taken together the plays stage the complex relations between Christian, Jew and Muslim. Within Lessing's own theological and philosophical writings each of these religions becomes a stage on the way to a more generalised and in the end secular Enlightenment. However, the religions themselves are, in part, defined in terms of exclusion and inclusion. For the Muslim Mohammed's description of Jews and Christians as *'Ahl al Kitab'* gives them special status. Their books are named within the tenets of Islamic law. More than that, the *Tawrat* (Torah), the *Zabur* (Psalter) and the *Indjil* (Gospels) are described as containing truths that were misrepresented and misunderstood. Inclusion and exclusion work together. The exclusion of the Jews by Christianity was in Pascal's terms 'the foundation of our belief'. They were included to be excluded. For Jews themselves, 'election' necessitated their radical divide from all others; an election presented within liturgy in, for example, the Benediction prior to the reading from the Torah. Election is maintained in the description of God as the one *asher bahar banu mikol ha'amim* ('who has chosen us from among all people'). It is then further refined by defining election in terms of the giving and the receiving of the Torah.

The question of election figures within *Nathan der Weise*. However, prior to turning to the plays themselves it is essential to note that these positions of exclusion and inclusion have to be understood as themselves involving singular and thus all-encompassing positions. They preclude conflict – conflict within, for example, Judaism over what is involved in Jewish being. Moreover they tend to imply that any one individual may be fully identified as Christian, Muslim or Jew, such that the only possibility of resisting that identification is denying it absolutely.

In order to delimit the analysis, one moment from each play will be taken. In the case of *Die Juden* it is Scene 21; the penultimate scene. In the case of *Nathan der Weise* it is Act II Scene V. *Die Juden* concerns an intentional confusion of identity. A traveller who is a Jew but who does not reveal himself as such until the end of the play is robbed by two men – one of them his own servant – who are themselves disguised as Jews. The setting for this scene is provided by the growing fondness between the Traveller and 'a young girl'. The latter's father – *Der Baron* – is integral both to the way the growing relation unfolds and the final staging in which the Traveller emerges as a Jew.

Having unmasked the robbers and thus, in revealing them not to be Jews, having undermined without needing to debunk the anti-semitism that surrounded the treatment and discussion of the robbers, the Traveller is offered, with her compliance, the Baron's daughter in marriage and by extension the Baron's wealth. The Traveller feels compelled to decline; a decline yielding consternation. To the question why? the Traveller replies, *'Ich bin ein Jude'* ('I am a Jew'); to which the Baron responds, *'Ein Jude? Grausamer Zufall!'* ('A Jew? Terrible accident').[11] The Traveller then suggests that his earlier silence over this matter was not because he felt 'shame' but

> *Ich sahe aber, dass Sie Neigung zu mir, und Abneigung gegen meine Nation hatten. Und die Freundschaft eines Menschens, er sei wer er wolle, ist mir allezeit unschatzbar gewesen.*[12]
>
> (I saw that you were fond of me but loathed my nation. And the friendship of a man, be he who he may, has always been priceless to me.)

Friendship has been given an almost transcendent quality in relation to the 'terrible accident' of being a Jew. Humanity would overcome the specific. This theme is reiterated both by the Traveller in regard to Christians and then by his servant in regard to Jews. In the words of the servant Christoph:

183

... es gibt doch wohl auch Juden, die keine Juden sind. Sie sind ein braver Mann.[13]
(...there are many Jews who are not Jews. You are a fine man.)

Being a man is contrasted with being a Jew. How is this contrast to be understood? The answer lies in the earlier passage in which the Traveller has distinguished between his personal identity and his 'Nation', and then in contrast to the value of his Nation describes the 'friendship of a man' as *'unschatzbar'*. A generalised humanity takes precedence over an identity defined in terms of what is here designated by the words *'meine Nation'*. The nature of that identity is yet to be established. Pursuing the structure of friendship here involves noting that it is presented in terms of an either/or yielding no exceptions. In this context even though the predominate concern is being a Jew the argument would also work for Christians. Read in the context of Lessing's *Die Erziehung des Menschengeschlechts*, for example, that has to be the case.

The conception of identity at work here entails either that one is delimited by being a Jew or that one belongs to the category of 'Man'. When Christoph responds to the Traveller, it is within that response that the negation of being a Jew allows for the claim that *'Sie sind ein braver Mann'* ('You are a fine man'). The counter to this claim is not that 'one' can be both – though on a strategic level that will be an important argument – but to recognise that the exclusion is the articulation of a specific philosophical position, one that defines the universal as refusing certain particulars. In this instance identity – the identity proper to the being of being human – is articulated in terms of an abstract conception of Humanity; the universalised subject of right.[14] While predicates are possible they cannot be allowed to intrude into the fundamental position which is the identification of the being of being human with abstracted Humanity. Participation within the world necessitates the refusal of particularity and thus the identification with that which necessitates that refusal. It is in these terms that the Traveller's claims about *'die Freundschaft eines Menschens'* (The friendship of a man) have to be understood. The structure of friendship here therefore has two defining characteristics. The first is that friendship concerns a relation between 'men' and secondly that it is nothing other than a more intense form of a general relationship that is possible between all men. Hence friendship would be the ideal condition for a generalised humanity.

A similar structure of friendship operates in *Nathan der Weise*. Emerging from that text is a further reiteration of the distinction between *Volk* and *Mensch*. The setting in this is that a Knight Templar has saved Nathan's daughter from a fire. It is possible that the fire was no accident. Fire threatening the home of Jews brings with it the real possibility of there having been a pogrom. The first significant moment in this scene is the Templar's surprise that a Jew should speak 'kind words' to him. In order to emphasise the dramatic quality of the text it is essential to note that this surprise is acted. It is in the acting out that there is a further instance of the draining away of the particularity. In other words the play's project cannot be separated, in this instance, from its own specificity; i.e., its presence as a specific literary form. Not only is there a faltering speech consisting almost of fragments, there is a significant inversion that occurs around the name; or to be more precise it occurs within the name's repetition.

> *Aber Jude – Ihr heisst Nathan? Aber Nathan – Ihr setzt Eure Worte sehr – sehr gut – sehr spitz...*[15]
>
> (But Jew – You are called Nathan? But Nathan – You have spoken to me such words – so good – so to the point –)

It is as though the first use of the name is linked to the opening words '*Aber Jude*' ('But Jew'). They repeat Nathan as a Jew. The second use follows the repetition of '*aber*' ('but') though the '*aber*' interrupts and with that interruption the Jewish content of the name is being drained away; a state of affairs reinforced by the implausibility of words from a Jew – the Jew Nathan – being describable as 'good', or 'to the point'. And once the audience is brought in then the question that would have to be addressed would concern what feeling 'as one' is envisaged by the reiteration of the name, as Nathan the Jew becomes Nathan der Weise? Even though it will be essential to return to these questions, it is none the less worth noting that the nature of the name is central. Once the true identity of those within the play is discovered and as one name is exchanged for another, what emerges is the irrelevance of the proper names. What will always be discovered beneath it is an abstract conception of humanity.

In the passage the lead away from particularity is begun by Nathan with the response of an identification of difference – hence particularity – coming from the Templar:

> Nathan: *Ich weiss, wie gute Menschen denken; weiss dass alle Länder gute Menschen tragen.*
>
> (I know how good men think; I know that all lands bear good men.)
>
> Tempelherr: *Mit Unterschied, doch hoffentlich?*[16]
>
> (With differences, hopefully?)

The difference is acknowledged and then, for Nathan, thought to be irrelevant. The counter by the Templar is to raise the question of Election.

> *Weisst Ihr, Nathan, welches Volk zuerst das auserwählte Volk sich nannte?*[17]
>
> (Do you know, Nathan, which people first called themselves the chosen people?)

Nathan is forced to speak the language of abstract humanity, to which the Templar responds not with a version of particularity that would allow for an affirmative conception of identity but with that version that leads inexorably to further isolation. Overcoming this counter does not take place simply in terms of claims about humanity but with the possibility of friendship. The details of Nathan's offer – an offer taken up by the Templar – become the denial of Election and thus the denial of that conception of particularity articulated within liturgy and thus within the daily life of Jews, even if the meaning and nature of Election is itself fiercely contested. Nathan's speech recalls that which has already been noted in *Die Juden*.

> *Wir müssen, müssen Freunde sein! – Verachtet Mein Volk sosehr Ihr wollt. Wir haben beide Uns unser Volk nicht auserlesen. Sind Wir unser Volk? Was heisst Volk? Sind Christ und Jude eher Christ und Jude, als Mensch? Ah! wenn ich einen mehr in Euch Gefunden hatte, dem es gnügt, ein Mensch zu heissen?*[18]
>
> (We must, must be friends! Despise my people if you will. We have not chosen our people. Are we our people? What does people mean? Are Christian and Jew Christian and Jew rather than men? Ah, had I found in you one more, of whom it is enough, to call a man?)

It is vital to note, before anything is made of this passage, that the answer to Nathan's final question is '*Ja, bei Gott, das habt Ihr, Nathan!*' ('Yes, by God, you have, Nathan!'). To this response the question 'who is this Nathan?' has to be posed.

Nathan's opening move is to demand friendship, and to repeat the demand, the 'must'.[19] Friendship is offered within and as part of the decision to be friends. A decision would inaugurate the friendship. Moreover it is a decision and thus an inauguration based on a generalised humanity. Indeed, it can be doubted whether the inaugurating decision could have been either offered or accepted without its having as its condition of possibility the naming of 'man'. Perhaps the question, announced by Nathan, that is the most striking in this context is: '*Sind Wir unser Volk?*' ('Are we our people?') The formulation of this question reiterates the either/or of identity. Either 'we' are our people, or 'we' are completely other and in being other than our people, 'we' become the Same. The latter, once again, becomes the only possible ground for friendship.

The language of obligation, will, and decision permeates the passage. Nathan allows for the Templar to 'despise his people'. This is only possible because of the divide between a 'people' construed as a synthetic unity and the individual construed as the particular of the universal; i.e., abstract humanity. The language of choice and thus election is turned about in this passage. In the earlier passage from the scene, the Templar uses the usual formulation '*das auserwählte*

Volk' ('The chosen people'). It is in response to the expression that Nathan uses the verb form – *auserlesen* ('to choose') – that once again reiterates the move to the individual: '*Wir haben beide Uns unser Volk nicht auserlesen*' ('Neither of us has chosen our people'). The insistence that there be a friendship and therefore that the friendship arise because of a founding decision, means that it depends upon an ineliminable symmetry. There are two interrelated consequences of this symmetry. The first pertains to the audience; the second concerns a commensurability between the relation to the friend and the relation to the other.

In regard to the second the significant point is that friendship, in this sense, has to lack any particularity. It becomes just a more intense version of the relations that could exist with anyone else. Everyone, including friends, is defined by a symmetry and thus a set of relations conditioned by the Same; here the Same is the framework of a generalised or abstract humanity. It is this framework that defines the expectations demanded of the audience by the theatrical presentation. The decision that inaugurates the friendship – and which allows it to go through and define the difficulties that such a friendship will encounter – demands a reciprocity within the audience. The audience must feel as one, in order that there be a registration of this friendship. As such the audience are invited to recognise that in the shared unity derived from the force of a generalised humanity there lies the potential for a reiteration of the founding decision of friendship. Friendship in this context depends upon the decision that inaugurates it. In contrast to '*unser Volk*' we can choose our friends.

In theatrical terms then the structure of friendship depends upon – thus it also demands – a unity within the audience which generates the audience as a unity. The symmetry that yields the audience is reproduced in the symmetry that marks out the structure of friendship itself. It is in these terms that the two consequences noted above – that which is demanded of the audience, and the commensurability between self and other or friend and friend – involve the same presuppositions and thus open themselves up to a similar form of interruption. Before pursuing the possibilities of such an interruption it is vital to stay with what has emerged thus far. In sum it involves the following: firstly, that friendship depends upon the overcoming of particularity in the name of a generalised humanity; secondly, that particularity stands in the way of friendship; thirdly, that friendship does not have a politics independent of or different from the politics proper to a generalised humanity; and finally that friendship is not qualitatively different from the generality of self/other relations, it is merely a more intense form.

A reworking of the relationship between public and private can arise from a disruption of the metaphysics of friendship. In other words, it would arise from a disruption of a relationship between friend and friend that was defined in terms of a generalised conception of humanity and thus defined by the relation of like and like. Moreover the interruption of this symmetry has to be in terms of a conception of dissymmetry where the latter is not defined by an either/or in which symmetry and dissymmetry are mere opposites. To the extent that friendship is not a relationship between like and like – a position that limits friendship in Lessing to that which resists friendship as a relation of difference – there must be a move away from a founding symmetry towards a founding dissymmetry. The problem remains, however, that even within an ethics determined by dissymmetry it still does not follow that friendship can be generalised or that friendship is a particular form of relations of dissymmetry. What has to be taken up is a relation of dissymmetry which would allow for friendship, while at the same time providing the basis for a reworking of the distinction between the public and the private. In order to pursue these possibilities it is essential to return to Lessing.

The Decision of Friendship

What emerged from *Nathan der Weise* was the interarticulation of friendship and the decision. How is this to be understood? In the first place its setting has to be noted. In the context of the play not only does it involve the effacing of particularity, it also demands that friendships differ only in terms of quantity from self/other relations. In the second place, the decision to be friends overcomes that positioning that the subject would not have chosen. Being friends will allow for the overcoming of the accident of being a Jew. It is not a question of an evaluation or even a critical distancing from tradition. Within the context of the play there is the possibility of founding friendship on the forgetting of tradition; forgetting as disavowal. After all has not Nathan conceded the presence of difference thus: '*An Farb, an Kleidung, an Gestalt verschieden.*' Once tradition is reduced to the repetition of appearance then there is little difficulty in arguing that behind the colour, beneath the clothing, present in the form, there is the continuity of the Same. What this means of course is that the recovery of this already present possibility involves a decision; a name for that decision – and note that it is only one name amongst a number – is friendship.

As has already been intimated what is at play here is an attempt to link and then disassociate friendship from that which has already been described as a metaphysics of friendship. This position does not take one form. It can be seen at work in the varying ways in which friendship emerges as a particular of the universal self/other relation. The reason for claiming that such a set-up retains the metaphysics of friendship is that it maintains differing forms of the particular/universal relation.

They are maintained in a manner that precludes criticism. There is another dimension to the connection between friendship and the decision. If, as the plays seem to indicate, a decision inaugurates a friendship, then there is a specific temporality at work with that decision. And yet, precisely because what has emerged from this treatment of friendship is the identification of friendship's complex articulation within the relationship between universal and particular, an interarticulation which obviates the possibility of posing the question of friendship's own propriety, the question has to be asked of whether or not a friendship is that which is even inaugurated by a decision? If it is not then the temporality of the decision would be that which refuses friendship. Moreover, the temporality of the founding moment would be incompatible with the temporality of friendship. It is, of course, precisely the possibility of the founding moment and the temporality of inauguration that are excluded by the temporality inherent in Blanchot's formulation: 'we were friends, and we did not know it'.

In Blanchot's text there are two significant references to the temporality of friendship. The first occurs in the line already cited while the second takes place in the closing passage of the text in which Blanchot invokes his friendship with Levinas. Within the terms set by the text – the distinction between friends and comrades, and hence the use of the distinction between *tu* and *vous* in maintaining that set-up, Blanchot writes the following concerning Levinas.

> ...le seul ami – ah ami lointain – que je tutoie et qui me tutoie, cela est arrivé, non parce que nous étions jeunes, mais par une décision délibérée, un pacte auquel j'espère ne jamais manquer.
> ...the sole friend – a distant friend – to whom I said 'tu' and who reciprocated, that happened, not because we were young, but by a *deliberate decision*, a pact I hope never to do without.[20]

How is this decision to be understood? In the first instance it is vital to be clear: it is not a decision that founds the friendship, nor moreover is it a decision that shifts, qualitatively, the register of the friendship. It is a decision – a 'deliberate decision' – that is taken within the friendship. As such, viewed from the outside it confirms the friendship – but the decision is itself irrelevant to the presence and thus the endurance of the friendship.

The decision confirms whatever it was that already existed. Existence here is the particularity of friendship; the particular friendship between Blanchot and Levinas. While this particularity has to be maintained it can, nonetheless, be given the setting of the epistemological and temporal structure already identified in the formula 'we were friends but did not know it'. Friendship sweeps over the participants such that being friends is a state of affairs whose reality comes to be recognised. What then would it be that was recognised? What within Blanchot's formulation was not known and then came to be known? On one level the answer is friendship. However, there is more since friendship names itself – the intimacy between two people – and yet it also names a state of affairs that occurs without having an inaugurating or founding moment. This is a set-up that is not explicable in generalised terms concerning the presence of the other. Rather, it is an already present relation in which its participants find themselves and therefore it is one where there is a dissolving and reconstituting of individuals as friends. It is the dissolving and reconstituting – themselves moments always bearing the trace of what they had been – that accounts for the fragility and the endurance of friendship.

Friendship has a foundation though it is not one given by a decision. Yet, of course, friendship is not arbitrary. The question is, can a politics be drawn from this conception of friendship? This question needs to be rewritten. If the political is linked to the public and thus to the site of deliberation and action – in sum the public as the site of judgement – then what place does friendship have within such a set-up? Actions that call for judgement are done by friends and yet responding to them cannot take place in terms of friendship. Nonetheless, that possibility is not completely precluded. What this means is that the actions of friends that call for judgement – public acts – strain and test friendships precisely because of the impossibility of the complete reincorporation of such actions back into the domain marked out by the friendship. Hence, there will always be a tension between relating to any one individual as friend and then as citizen. Both will be involved and yet one is not reducible to the other. How is this impossibility of the complete reduction of one to the other to be understood? We should remember, of course, that it was precisely this possibility that informs philosophical and literary treatments of friendship – for example those of Aristotle in the *Nichomachean Ethics*, Book VIII and Lessing in *Die Juden* and *Nathan der Weise*.

There are a number of different ways in which to respond to this question. Here three are central. The first is that it is in the very impossibility of a complete reduction that a distinction between the private and public can be said to figure. The distinction will have an ineliminable fluidity. The second is that the impossibility of a reduction allows for the introduction of a founding dissymmetry. The third is that, in its still being possible to hold friendship apart from the site of the generalised self/other relations, intimacy can be inscribed into the domain of the philosophical without having to be an instance of a generalised set of relations. In other words, it is through the possibility of there being a philosophical conception of friendship which is itself held apart from general oppositions – self/other, particular/universal – that intimacy is allowed a certain propriety. It is these three domains that have to be pursued. In so doing it becomes possible to draw together a number of the themes that have been advanced thus far; perhaps the most significant is the role of the audience as being constrained to respond to literature's work.

The public and private are, traditionally, given either as absolutely distinct domains, or merely in terms of a distinction of degree. In the case of the first the most serious consequence of holding to it is that it precludes, formally, any overlap of friendship and citizenship. In the case of the second it closes down the possibility of holding to that which is specific to friendship independently of self/other relations. In both instances there is the pervasive effect of a founding symmetry. In the case of the former symmetrical relations are maintained within the structure of friendship as well as outside. Rather than a dissymmetry there is a posited non-relation between the public and the private. Any detailed analysis of this non-relation would trace its collapse since what becomes important are the overlaps of citizen and friend such that part of maintaining a friendship would in fact be a continual negotiation with that overlap. A politics stemming from the presence of alterity would arise at the precise moment where alterity would not depend upon friendship for its recognition and reciprocally where the presence of alterity breaks with any necessity for the incorporation of friendship. What this means is that friendship is delimited by a type of reflexivity that does not open beyond itself – or at least not beyond itself in the name of friendship. Within such a set-up it becomes impossible to assert, other than as a pragmatic strategy, *'Wir müssen, müssen Freunde sein'* ('We must, must be friends'). The must names the necessity for solidarity or even a form of fraternity. Once freed from the prerequisite of friendship, this necessity becomes strategic. Even 'humanity' can be conceptualised in utilitarian terms, so that 'must' can imply 'you must protect me', 'I must protect you', where both appeals would presuppose 'even though we are not friends'.

In moving away from a conception of the audience as structured by the necessity to feel as one, there emerges the possibility that whatever unity could be given to the audience it had to allow for its being the belonging together of the different. As such the audience would have become a cosmopolitan site rather than one constructed by a theatrical practice which envisaged an audience as a synthetic unity. Here, there is the introduction of a founding dissymmetry as that which accounts for unity. The intrusion of dissymmetry changes the way in which self/other relations are understood. Rather than holding on to the possibility of the other being the same, or the other being absolutely other to the same – both positions are no more than the positive and negative instances of symmetry – the possibility of dissymmetry in this context becomes a version of the belonging together of the different. There is a coherence, but it is not a coherence that demands a synthetic unity. Belonging together is the already present coherence of original and thus ineliminable difference.[21] It is of course this state of affairs that is identified as a possibility within *Nathan der Weise* and then overcome in the name of friendship. Not friendship as such but that 'friendship' offered in the name of a generalised and thus homogeneous humanity. Writing friendship back into this series of complex relations cannot take place by arguing that friendship involves a more authentic or even more original sense of a founding relation of dissymmetry. In fact, it is possible to suggest that friendship, precisely because it involves a reflexivity that need not open beyond itself, may allow for dissymmetry but it would not be of a form that could be given greater generality in terms of the cosmopolitan. The point can be made simply: the cosmopolitan, understood as the belonging together of the different, need not be – and in fact is not – a society of friends.

The restriction of friendship has a twofold function. On the one hand it allows for a critical engagement with those positions that link friendship to a homogeneous conception of humanity. Developing such a critique indicates the impossibility of there being a politics of friendship because what occurs within such an argument is the effacing of the particularity of friendship through the link between the friend and a generalised humanity. On the other hand, this non-generalisable relation in defining a form of singularity – a singularity that can only be confirmed by the decision rather than inaugurated – allows for the incorporation into the philosophical of a conception of intimacy. Intimacy would be distinguished from emotion precisely because of its singularity. Emotion has to have a form of universality built into it in order to be communicable and thus to be understood. (Friendships can be inexplicable and yet understood by those participating in them.) In being singular yet not absolutely private friendship resists any incorporation into the political. As such, there cannot be a politics of friendship if it is to take place in the name of friendship. All that can be made of friendship is friendship itself. Friendship holds open intimacy. With intimacy the differences of race and gender figure, though they figure as sites of discovery and investigation. Intimacy demands continuity; perhaps, even a productive endlessness. The reality of what that entails will always be different because intimacy is descriptive of singular relations resisting universality. Within these relations Jewish friends abound.

Notes

1 This point is going to have a generality extending beyond the specific case of Jewish identity. In other words, it can be extended to deal with most claims for identity precisely because it involved that conception of generality that necessitates the ineliminability of specificity. What is of interest philosophically is the question of what conception of identity is at work here. Moreover, there is no attempt to deny the presence of the attribution of identity – and this can be positive in terms of seeing a necessary line between having an identity and being a victim and negative in the sense of accusations of racial or sexual inferiority. It is just that claims about identity can be defined in the terms that

attribution provides.

2 This paper needs to be read as part of an attempt to respond to Derrida's *The Politics of Friendship*, London: Verso, 1996. It does not pursue the detail of Derrida's text, but rather what is closed off by a politics of friendship; even a politics that is no longer delimited by fraternity.

3 The history of philosophy has continually taken up the theme of friendship. However, it does not follow from the presence of the theme that there has been a systematic investigation of that which is proper to friendship. For example, Aristotle in the *Nichomachean Ethics* links friendship and commonality (1159b 30–33). Commonality, if it is not the basis of friendship is at the very least fundamental, for Aristotle, to its actual existence. The difficulty with this formulation is that while it may be true of a given friendship it need not be true of others. More significantly, however, if it is taken as the paradigm for friendship then it would follow that wherever there was commonality there were possible friends and thus there is the potential for friendship within every relation defined by a shared sense of belonging. If that were the case then friendship is no more than a more intense form of a more generalised self/other relation where such relations are defined by commonality. Even if such a potential were false this, in this instance, does not matter. What is of greater significance is that such a formulation precludes any identification of friendship as anything in itself. In other words, traced to its extreme Aristotle's position – even though it will allow for a variety of friendships – fails to engage with that which is proper to friendship itself. That there is something proper to friendship and that friendship has a specific locus is part of what is under investigation in this paper. The treatment of the public and the private in this paper builds on an argument I have presented in greater detail in 'On Tolerance: Some Kantian Motifs', *European Journal of Social Theory* (forthcoming).

4 It would be significant in this regard to pursue the point made by Arendt – in a paper on Lessing – in which she argues that for the Greeks the move from friendship to 'humanness' was realised by discourse. Indeed in a general treatment of solidarity and thus of fraternity – whether it be strategic or generalised – unity as borne by language is fundamental. Unity will be a discursive activity. The question is whether solidarity and thus fraternity involves or indeed necessitates friendship. In fact it could be argued that there are times when solidarity, as Arendt seems to suggest, necessitates holding to particularity and not moving to a ground in a shared 'humanness'. Her work is far more strategic in orientation, linked as it is to her conception of the 'pariah', than the simple shift of quantity that allows Aristotle to move between friendship and citizenship. See H. Arendt, 'On Humanity in Dark Times: Thoughts about Lessing', in *Men in Dark Times*, New York: Harcourt Brace, 1968, pp.3–31.

5 All references to Lessing are to G.E. Lessing, *Werke* Vols.I–III, Munich: Artemis & Winkler Verlag, 1994. The two plays are in Vol.I. All translations are my own. In the case of *Die Juden* reference has been made to Ritchie Robertson's translation in R. Robertson (ed.), *The German-Jewish Dialogue. An Anthology of Literary Texts. 1749–1993*, Oxford: Oxford University Press, 1999. In relation to Lessing it is also essential to acknowledge Robertson's own study of the complex topic of German-Jewish relations, *The 'Jewish Question' in German Literature, 1749–1939*, Oxford: Oxford University Press, 1999. Robertson has a significant discussion of Lessing in this work. His most sustained treatment is in his earlier article, 'Dies hohe Lied der Duldung? The ambiguities of toleration in Lessing's *Die Juden* and *Nathan der Weise*', *Modern Language Review* 93, 1998, pp.105–20.

6 See M. Mendelssohn, *Ästhetische Schriften in Auswahl*, Darmstadt: Wissenschaftliche Buchgesellschaft, 1994, pp.148–49.

7 M. Blanchot, *Pour l'amité*, Paris: Fourbis, 1996 (my translation). The discussion of Blanchot is directed not only towards his text but also to Simon Critchley's treatment of

Blanchot's work as well as the general thematic of friendship. See S. Critchley, 'The Other's Decision in Me (What are the Politics of Friendship?)', in his *Ethics, Politics, Subjectivity*, London: Verso, 1999, pp.254–87. Critchley's is an important commentary on the issues arising from Derrida's *The Politics of Friendship*, London: Verso, 1997. Moreover it goes further than Derrida's text, by trying to think through some of its implications. The difficulty with Critchley's position is that while it allows for the existence of a metaphysics of friendship it does not address the question of what a philosophical thinking of friendship would be like once there was the affirmed abeyance of that metaphysics.

8 That certain novelists aspire to this end is evident from titles such as Jane Austen's *Sense and Sensibility*.

9 G.W.F. Hegel, *Aesthetics*, Oxford: Oxford University Press, 1988, Vol.I, p.234.

10 The generality of tragedy understood as the site of diremption is expressed by Hegel in summary form in a long footnote in the *Philosophy of Right*, trans. T.M. Knox, Oxford: Oxford University Press, 1981, p.102. Despite its familiarity and length the passage must be quoted, for its argumentative strategy, almost as much as its content, raises significant questions:

> The tragic destruction of figures whose ethical life is on the highest plane can interest and elevate us and on the scene in opposition to one another together with equally justified but different ethical powers which have come into collision through misfortune because the result is that then these figures acquire guilt through their opposition to an ethical law. Out of this situation there arises the right and wrong of both parties and therefore the true ethical idea, which, purified and in triumph over this one-sidedness, is thereby reconciled in us. Accordingly it is not the highest in us which perishes; we are elevated not by the destruction of the best but the triumph of the true. This it is which constitutes the true, purely ethical interests of ancient tragedy.

It is in terms of what Hegel identifies as 'in us' that it becomes possible to identify the centrality of the audience. The clash takes place for us to the extent that 'we' are the audience. As always what is central here is the implicit conceptions of identity and unity that are at work in the pronouns 'us' and 'we'.

11 There *is*, of course, something extremely significant about the description of being a Jew as a *'grausamer Zufall'*. The significance does not lie in the qualification of the occurrence as 'terrible', but in its being an accident or something that may have occurred by chance. This type of description reduces being a Jew to a mere predicate of being a human. Not only is it irrelevant to human being, its occurrence is calamitous. However, it is a calamity that can be remedied and thus overcome. The response by the Baron therefore prepares the way for what will come next. The audience having heard it are prepared. And yet there is another central question, one that inheres in the necessary retention of the audience as integral to any understanding of the presence of theatre as theatre. For what would an audience either made up of Jews or at least containing some Jews be prepared? Built into the structure of the text is the possibility of its own refusal. The structural presence is the demand of the audience. It is a demand that occurs once the particularity of theatre is held as central to any analysis of the play.

12 Lessing, *Werke*, Vol.I, p.290.

13 *Ibid.*, p.291.

14 The classic formulation of the position can be found in John Rawls' *A Theory of Justice*, Oxford: Oxford University Press, 1989. The key section is §85, 'The unity of the Self'. When distinguishing between 'right' and 'the good' Rawls notes that members of a society may disagree in terms of conceptions of the good and adds that 'this is not so for conceptions of right. In a well ordered society citizens hold the same principles of

right and they try to reach the same judgements in particular cases' (p.448).

There is an intriguing temporality at work in this passage, which pertains to what is clearly accented by Rawls, namely the 'antecedent unity of the self'. The priority of the self is temporal as well as existential, in that even though the 'essential unity of the self is provided by the conception of right', it is also presupposed by it. The unity is neither a production nor is it strategic. It is already there. In the same way 'unity being the same for all' means that the unity of the self is such that it, of necessity, pre-exists any one situation in which it finds itself and is thereby reproduced as itself – represented as being the same as itself – in any situation. The self in its presentation cannot alter in the re-presentation since such a possibility opens up the risk of conflict in which there would be an irreducible division between the presented and represented self. In sum, the priority of the self entails the elimination of the threat of difference that could cause either the subject to be itself the result of a production or the forms and institutions in which it participates to be sites of heterogeneity and thus sites of differential participation. The universalised subject of right precludes the cosmopolitan. What this generates is the need to rethink the subject of right within the structure of the cosmopolitan.

15 Lessing, *Werke*, Vol.I, p.753.

16 *Ibid.*

17 *Ibid.*

18 *Ibid.*, p.754.

19 Arendt comments on this doubling as does Peter Fenves; see 'Politics of Friendship – Once Again', in *Eighteenth-Century Studies*, Vol.32, No.2, 1998–99, 133–55. This is part of a larger treatment of friendship in the light of Derrida's *Politics of Friendship*.

20 Blanchot, *Pour l'amité*, p.35, my emphasis.

21 Any attempt to pursue this argument would need to start with Jean-Luc Nancy's important attempts to rework Heidegger's conception of *Mitsein* in order to think through such a conception of the social. See in particular *Etre singulier pluriel*, Paris: Galilée, 1996.

CHAPTER 10

The Visibility of the Holocaust: Franz Neumann and the Nuremburg Trials

MICHAEL SALTER

Although less well known to social theorists than that of other Frankfurt School members, the work of Franz Neumann has recently become the focus of renewed interest.[1] Within contemporary legal scholarship, that interest has centred largely upon how this 'junior' member of the Frankfurt School combined classic liberal constitutional values, particularly a belief in the rule of law, with a distinctive sociological analysis of law.[2] Several historians have studied the wartime record of Neumann, Kirchheimer and Marcuse,[3] but Neumann's wartime service with US military intelligence has received little attention from legal theorists, in spite of its clear relationship with his theoretical writings on war crimes and the rule of law.[4] The following study responds directly to both this omission of Neumann's war crimes contribution by legal theorists, and to the critique recently levelled by historians such as Shlomo Aronson and Richard Breitman, who accuse Neumann, Kirchheimer and Marcuse of a 'functionalist' analysis of anti-semitism which exerted an all-too-practical influence at the institutional level.[5] This critique refers to the period between 1943 and 1945 when Neumann, together with Otto Kirchheimer, a criminal law specialist, and Herbert Marcuse, worked as research analysts within the scholarly Research and Analysis (R&A) branch of the short-lived US Office of Strategic Services ('OSS'), a newly formed military intelligence organisation.[6] Here they co-wrote a series of detailed reports on war crimes, de-Nazification and post-war military government.[7] According to Neumann's critics, specific individuals within OSS, such as Allan Dulles[8] and Charles Irving Dwork,[9] were intent upon highlighting Nazi atrocities against Jews, and this organisation more generally participated in Jewish rescue missions. However, it is alleged that the legal culmination of such efforts at the Nuremberg trials was largely frustrated because the relevant

OSS team of research analysts responsible for the preparation and supervision of various prosecution briefs were heavily influenced by the functionalist 'spearhead theory' of anti-semitism which Neumann advanced. This theory will be discussed below.

Critics have maintained that Neumann's group of research analysts failed to discharge their specific official and moral responsibilities to the prosecution's preparation for the Nuremberg war crimes trials and that such neglect was partly responsible for the 'understated' place that the Holocaust occupied within the prosecution's case.[10] The present study highlights the difficulties facing this critique. It develops this project first by illustrating the continuing relevance of many of the issues that comprise this debate. Secondly, it analyses Neumann's spearhead theory of anti-semitism, and the main criticism levelled against its claims. The final section turns the tables upon Neumann's critics by highlighting the intellectually problematic and practically counter-productive nature of their assumptions.

Neumann's War Crimes Team and its Institutional Background[11]

In order to provide the important background context to recent criticisms of Neumann, it is important to review previously unacknowledged details about his team's institutional role within the OSS's contribution to the war crimes field. On publication in 1942, Neumann's classic analysis of National Socialism, *Behemoth*, was critically acclaimed.[12] Neumann soon became widely recognised as the leading authority on National Socialism both within and beyond the group of émigré scholars of the OSS's Central European sub-section of the R&A branch. Despite its neo-Marxist underpinnings, this work functioned as a major source and reference book for both the OSS's R&A branch and the Nuremberg prosecutors.[13] Between May and November 1945, during the frantic build-up to the Nuremberg trials, the OSS leadership selected Neumann to lead this 'top-flight' constituent of Justice Jackson's American prosecution office.[14] He was also included among the personnel who comprised Jackson's advance party to London and Paris who were largely responsible for negotiating with other Allied powers the 'London Agreement' of August 1945. The resulting 'charter', in effect a newly created international criminal statute with retrospective effect, purported to provide the legal basis for the Nuremberg trials that opened in November 1945.

Neumann's Spearhead Theory of Anti-Semitism

Although sensitivity to various institutional details is important to any adequate discussion of the recent critique of the impact of Neumann's spearhead theory of anti-semitism, it is vital to appreciate this theory's specific claims. Neumann's spearhead theory of anti-semitism consists of nine distinct but interrelated propositions:

1. Contrary to both Nazi and Allied propaganda, Nazi anti-semitism does not express the innate character of the German people. This is a counter-productive myth that led to Allied proposals for future mass sterilisation, which in turn were then re-deployed as internal propaganda by the Nazis.[15] Instead, it is a historically constructed, and hence contingent, political phenomenon integrally connected with the ideological legitimation of the interests of Germany's ruling power elite.[16]

2. The Nazi regime did not pursue anti-semitic persecution as an end in itself. Instead, it formed part of a wider programme of building, refining and extending the totalitarian machinery of social control, and of imposing a state of fear upon potential dissenters. Both of these were vital to the Nazis' grip upon power.[17]

3. The Nazi leadership implemented measures against Jewry in a strategic and calculating fashion. Thus they made exceptions, for instance, of German-Jewish war veterans, wherever any consistent application of their racist principles could have proved counter-productive for other competing interests of the regime, including the population's psychological preparation for war.[18]

4. Within the social hierarchy, propaganda against the Jews was directed downward from its indigenous historical source in Germany's ruling elites. This top-down imposition took place by means of an unprecedented mobilisation of the mass media and youth organisations. However, even after a decade of remorseless exposure to anti-semitic propaganda, such sentiments had not established deep roots amongst most ordinary working-class German people, from whom the gruesome details of the Holocaust, which mainly took place in remote rural areas of Poland, had to be hidden.[19]

5. The Nazis also designed anti-semitic measures to combat alternative socialist ideologies, which, through gaining majority support within parliament, threatened the interests of established power elites, including those of leading industrialists. The ideological need was to deflect pre-existing anti-capitalist sentiment away from its material source within the class divisions of an essentially antagonistic social structure, and towards the dehumanisation of a social group widely identified with commercial activities. The antagonistic nature of Germany's social structure meant that, at the level of ideology, the Nazis had to replace class-based forms of social integration, whose resolution

199

required the application of a redistributive socialist agenda, with racial and nationalist alternatives. Although dressed up for strategic reasons in a 'revolutionary' form of rhetoric, the nationalistic and racist sentiments of Nazi ideology deflected the challenge from below to the interests of Germany's leading industrialists[20] and allowed the 'petty bourgeoisie' to benefit from anti-semitic measures of 'Aryanisation' of property and businesses.[21]

6. Anti-semitic persecution was designed partly to misrepresent acts of domestic repression as an urgent form of national self-defence. This aimed to help legitimate the regime in the eyes of the remainder of the population, who could then be characterised in *Volkisch* terms as a racially based and homogeneous 'national community'.

7. The false and irrational character of the Nazis' racist principles required a distinctly ideological form of social integration based upon the mobilisation of fear, prejudice and the threat of violence for dissent.[22] The ideological projection of a racial 'enemy within', characterised by diametrically opposed qualities to those endorsed and promoted by the Nazis' own ideology, helped meet this social requirement.

8. The Nazi regime could not reproduce the conditions of its future existence without projecting itself as a stalwart defender of the national community from the mythical threat posed by an enemy of the people. Largely for strategic reasons, it selected the Jewish minority from amongst other groups of potential victims. Other possible victims, such as the Catholic Church or organised labour, were either too strongly supported or 'too weak' to be credibly (mis)represented as a 'supreme foe', who challenged the future of the 'national community'. Moreover, unlike religious persecution, only a specifically racist form of victimisation was consistent with the Nazis' master-race ideology.[23]

9. The much-needed 'supreme foe' had to be present both within and outside Germany's national borders in order to be (mis)represented as constituting a world-wide 'threat' to the global 'destiny' of the German nation. The Nazis could then appeal to the allegedly 'shared' interests of the entire 'national community' as a pretext for embarking upon a period of military expansionism.[24] The regime could justify this as both a strategy of vital self-defence, and in terms of securing adequate 'living space' for future generations.

In short, Neumann's spearhead theory rejected the idea of Nazi anti-semitism as an expression of the indigenous German (or 'Prussian') 'national character' pursued for its sake. Instead, such racism functioned as a strategically formulated and selectively applied ideology, which served the ulterior motives and specific political imperatives of Hitler's regime.

Recent Criticisms of the Spearhead Theory

The critics of the spearhead theory doubt whether it represents either an adequate account of the nature of anti-semitism or a viable basis for appropriate institutional analysis and political action. They accuse this theory of being excessively rationalistic, of failing to identify the singularity of the Holocaust and of exerting a deleterious impact upon the Nuremberg trials.

In his analysis of the historical role of OSS's R&A branch, for instance, Barry Katz treated Neumann's spearhead model as deficient at both theoretical and practical levels, although he has now qualified his earlier critique. For Katz, this model required 'explanation' in terms of Neumann's supposedly Marxist assumption that history was somehow pre-programmed to evolve in a rationally discernible trajectory.[25] Even in his most recent analysis, Katz continues to suggest that a 'prejudice' in favour of a rationalistic and teleological mode of analysis continued to distort the orientation of Neumann's team:

> Reading the war through the lenses of Marx, Nietzsche, and Max Weber, they were hindered in their appreciation of the singularity of the Holocaust by their need to locate it within some larger pragmatic design.[26]

During an otherwise sympathetic analysis, Petra Marquardt-Bigman also devoted considerable attention to the alleged limitations of Neumann's spearhead theory, and its impact upon a series of R&A reports. She argues that the OSS's analysis of Germany involved an excessive rationalisation of the 'irrational roots' of Nazi anti-semitism. This rationalisation led to an overly functional interpretation of anti-semitism as a deliberately chosen and consciously applied strategy. She suggests that the emphasis placed by the spearhead theory upon ideological imperatives lacked realism in the light of the disclosures of concrete acts of genocide between 1942 and 1944, which forced Neumann partially to revise his thesis in the second edition of *Behemoth*. However, this revision continued to show 'misjudgement of its irrational roots' and to impede appreciation of the *singular qualities* and particular dimensions of a genocidal policy 'rooted in the irrational':

> As soon as it was a question of the dimensions of the national socialist *Weltanschauung* and policy, rooted in the irrational, clear limits were set for the sustainability of the theoretical-methodical approaches of the Central Europe Section's analyses of Germany.[27]

This historian also maintains that, taken together, the powerful influence exerted by Neumann's *Behemoth* upon the CES's analysis of Nazi Germany generally, and its author's high reputation for unsurpassed expertise,[28] resulted in the relativisation of the Nazis' anti-semitic genocide as but one of many wartime atrocities. In particular, Neumann's alleged refusal to accept the real existence of working-class anti-semitism distorted his team's analysis of empirical events:

> This cool, functional interpretation which, in the end, reduced national socialist anti-Semitism to one of many forms of repression, may well have contributed to the fact that the Central Europe Section did not pay any particular attention to the fate of European Jews during the war, or even ignored it. Thus a report on concentration camps in Germany of October 1944 was limited to concentration camps within the German borders of 1937 and pointed out in plain terms that the inmates were predominantly political prisoners or criminals, since Jews had either already been executed or had been transferred to Polish camps. Admittedly it seems really strange that reports filed in R&A documents on Jewish refugees from Germany hardly go into anti-Jewish measures and are more suitable to confirm the conviction formulated in Neumann's *Behemoth* that 'the German people', although it may appear very paradoxical, is 'the least anti-semitic of all'.[29]

In similar vein, Barry Katz argues that the R&A reports on the Third Reich did not adequately connect the different manifestations of Nazi anti-semitism, such as mass deportations and imprisonment within concentration camps, as distinct but interrelated 'elements of a systematic policy of genocide'.[30] He recognises that, in some respects, the connection between aspects of the Holocaust did begin to crystallise during the CES's immediate post-war research for the Nuremberg prosecutors. But he argues that Neumann's 'narrowly instrumental analysis' of the mass extermination of Jews represents a departure from his general style of analysis and he asks whether this could be explained by 'a Marxist's lingering allegiance to the German working class'.[31] Katz's explanation of this apparent blind spot within Neumann's analysis is presented as though it accounts sufficiently for the notorious claim, in the second edition of *Behemoth*, that 'the German people are the least anti-Semitic of all'.[32]

Shlomo Aronson has argued that Neumann's spearhead theory and its author's personal orientation had a direct impact upon the neglect of the Holocaust during the OSS's provision of evidence for the Nuremberg trials. He focuses upon Irving Dwork's role within the OSS, a position 'created in 1943 for the purpose of gathering information on Jewish affairs, including evidence against Nazi war criminals'. Dwork's Washington-based unit was seeking to involve prominent representatives of the Jewish community in the pre-trial preparations. Allegedly, this aim was not realised partly because Dwork's office had built up considerable documentary resources but failed to employ them adequately, even in the high-powered preparatory international conference in

August 1945. This led directly to the failure by the Nuremberg trials to take the unique character of anti-semitic genocide seriously, a refusal to recognise adequately 'the tragic uniqueness of the Holocaust'.

Notwithstanding the fact that Neumann actively campaigned for the greater use of all OSS/R&A war crimes materials by Jackson's office, and personally arranged for their transportation to the prosecution team, Aronson sees the impact of Neumann's spearhead theory upon the OSS's analysis as one of the major contributing reasons for this institutional failure:

> OSS had very valuable documentation, but which did not reach its 'Jewish expert' Charles Dwork, on time, or rather was simply never used. But for the time being it was OSS's Franz Neumann who, having developed his own opinions about the Holocaust years before, seems to have played the major role in London, at least in preparation for the International Military Tribunal.[33]

Aronson seeks to explain the frustration of Dwork's project partly in terms of Neumann's 'major role' within Jackson's advance party, a point that is clear from his decision to devote an entire sub-section to his spearhead theory. Aronson states that this theory was important partly because of Neumann's institutional seniority:

> Within OSS, the prestigious political scientist-economist Franz Neumann carried far more weight than Dwork. Neumann's theory was that the Nazis' assault on the Jews, a hated, friendless, and defenceless group, was merely the 'spearhead' of an overall Nazi program for the terrorisation or annihilation of other peoples, creating the precedent and justification for their similar treatment. As a prosecutor at the Eichmann trial, Robinson later found traces of the theory in Hannah Arendt's *Eichmann in Jerusalem*. This was a development of the argument in Neumann's famous book *Behemoth*, first published in 1942, which offered a Marxist explanation of Nazi success where other radical right-wing groups in Weimar Germany had failed.[34]

Aronson's analysis has influenced other Holocaust specialists, such as Breitman, who suggests that Neumann's spearhead theory motivated the OSS team either to neglect or to underplay the 'reasonably accurate picture of the Final Solution' available by late 1942,[35] even when reporting specifically upon concentration camps. Breitman attributes this failing to Neumann's 'fundamentally inaccurate notions as to what was behind Nazi anti-semitism', which prevented his section of the OSS from 'understanding the obvious'.[36]

Difficulties Facing the Critique of the Spearhead Theory

There is little doubt that, when judged according to contemporary standards, the response to the Holocaust by even the best-intentioned and most liberal-minded sections of the OSS and other Allied agencies was inadequate, and represented a failure to face up to the evidence. There are, however, problems raised but not addressed explicitly by Neumann's critics, which require settling before these attacks can be accepted. Part of the hostility directed at Neumann derives from a misinterpretation of his statement in *Behemoth* that 'the German people are the least anti-Semitic of all'. The assumption that this statement expresses a nationalistic defence of his compatriots is questionable, particularly when taken in the context of his sociological opposition to the widespread view of the linkage between extreme nationalism, militarism and racism as an innate part of the German 'national character'. Neumann's statement draws attention to the prevalence of analogous levels of anti-semitism within other parts of Europe where Fascist parties failed to secure political power, and it insists upon the need for a sociological approach to the strategic exploitation of anti-semitism as an ideology. Breitman's accusation that Neumann's socialist orientation blinded him to the 'obvious' reality of Nazi genocide ignores the testimony of other émigré German-Jewish members of Neumann's war crimes team, such as Henry Kellermann, that the details of systematic extermination by gas chambers agreed at Wannsee Conference were not appreciated by the OSS until immediately after the war.[37] There are also empirical objections to Marquardt-Bigman's critique of Neumann's neglect of concentration camps. She does not address the two-part OSS report on Auschwitz, written on 10 and 12 August 1943, which was amongst the first to provide details of the use of gas chambers.[38] Nor does she acknowledge the OSS's role in monitoring the Treblinka[39] and Mauthausen[40] concentration camps. Aronson's two-line summary of the spearhead theory, cited above, unduly simplifies and misrepresents Neumann's specific claims, and does not place it in the context of the OSS's overall record on the monitoring of atrocities in its preparation for war crimes trials – something that would require close examination of the hundreds of pages of draft evidence it prepared.[41] More generally, the implication of Neumann's theory is that it was precisely because large sectors of the German population, who also defined themselves as Jewish, were fully integrated and assimilated into the life of German society, that the Nazi regime needed to devote considerable efforts to misrepresent this group as alien. Such ideological misrepresentation was directed at a nation, the majority of whose citizens never fully accepted the Nazis' virulent and genocidal brand of anti-semitism, even after a full decade of being subjected to a remorseless stream of official racist propaganda – a point made by the critics of the Goldhagen thesis. Aronson conflates the content of the National Socialists' ideological claims with Neumann's immanent critique of this ideology.[42]

Any interpretation of Neumann's position must take seriously its intellectual and political underpinnings. Against the charge of insensitivity to the singularity of the Holocaust, Neumann's position on Nazi war crimes was consistent with the left-Hegelian orientation of the Frankfurt School more generally. The latter emphasises the mediated, relational and complexly interwoven quality of every aspect of social reality. This dialectical approach to social theorising rejects the idea that any phenomenon could ever be understood as an utterly singular thing in itself. Neumann did not view his war crimes analysis as a separate topic in its own right. His analysis stemmed from an intellectual position maintaining that neither anti-semitic programmes nor war crimes trials can be understood when they are analysed in abstraction from how these phenomena contribute to and are mediated by the underlying principles of a complex and historically evolving social totality. Hence the practical implication of Neumann's left-Hegelian intellectual position was that holding war crimes trials for a relatively small group of leading figures within the Third Reich could never represent an end in itself. For Neumann, holding war crimes trials was a necessary but not sufficient response to Nazi atrocities. At most, these trials could represent one part of a wider project of post-war German de-Nazification and social reconstruction along democratic socialist lines.[43] During 1944 and early 1945, Neumann and Marcuse had already contributed many OSS/R&A and Civil Affairs reports on the challenges of democratic reconstruction and de-Nazification facing post-war military governance. Their wider project of giving a socialist or social democratic orientation to policies informed these reports. The idea that any type of criminal trial would in itself be a proportionate response to the Nazi regime would have been inconsistent with the thrust of Neumann's sociological approach to the nature of National Socialism. War crimes trials could form only a modest and largely symbolic part of the larger goal of realising a full-scale social and economic restructuring within post-war Germany. This project aimed at exposing and breaking those socio-economic connections that linked Germany's ruling power elites, monopoly capitalism and militaristic forms of nationalism.[44] From the start, there was always the danger that the Nuremberg trials could become a poor substitute for such thoroughgoing reconstruction of Germany's social structure. For Neumann's team, this legalistic substitution and displacement would fail to address the root structural causes of German militarism, which they located in the antagonistic social relations characteristic of monopoly capitalism, and would thereby endanger the prospects for future peace and democracy. In short, for both social theoretical and political reasons, Neumann's sociological analysis of Nazi anti-semitism as a functional 'spearhead' of wider policies of totalitarian control and economic exploitation within continental Europe necessarily rejected the purely legal condemnation of only thirty leading Nazis as a self-sufficient goal.[45]

These considerations may explain why Neumann was reportedly sceptical about the crusading fervour that had gripped Telford Taylor and other prosecutors.[46] Many prosecutors were insufficiently sensitive to the specifically social and economic dimensions of Nazism, not least the complicity of leading industrialists and business cartels in the profitable wartime exploitation of slave labour.[47] While endorsing the potential of anti-Fascist sectors of German society, particularly the suppressed trade unions and SPD, Neumann's team pressed for the unprecedented indictment of leading industrialists, particularly those who had both financially sponsored and then directly benefited from the militaristic policies of the Nazi regime.[48] In keeping with Neumann's analysis in *Behemoth* of the interaction of industrial, military and political power elites, his team's socialist interpretation of the economic case appeared to link Nazi war criminality with a distinctly capitalistic form of expansionism,[49] and suggested the need for a radical purge of the roots of German Fascism by eliminating the economic foundations of the anti-democratic policy of German big industry. Neither Jackson nor the British authorities were prepared to endorse the OSS's approach. Hence, for political reasons, Neumann's OSS team was sidelined from the economic case.

The marginalisation of the OSS not only caused internal tensions between the leadership of the OSS and Jackson, but also led to some embarrassing mistakes regarding the selection of defendants at Nuremberg. These 'had serious and continuing consequences', among them the fact that 'those whom we had listed first as "economic war criminals" were very quickly back in decisive positions of responsibility in the German economy'.[50]

No less important were other pragmatic legal factors that augmented Neumann's rejection, on analytical grounds, of the Holocaust as a genocidal programme pursued only for its own sake. From the outset of the prosecution's planning process, Jackson had entrusted Neumann's OSS team with the task of taking charge of the most difficult and innovative aspects of the prosecution strategy. Jackson's trial planning memorandum of May 1945, co-drafted with James Donovan, the OSS's General Counsel, made Neumann's team responsible for addressing the problem of how the prosecutors could employ previously untested charges of 'organisational liability' and 'criminal conspiracy' charges.[51] These innovative charges had to be refined to establish a clear and legally recognisable connection between domestic genocide of various minorities, the conspiracy to achieve 'world domination' and violations of previously established legal categories of international law. Hence, whilst there is merit in

Katz's critique that the systematic quality of the Holocaust was not initially recognised by Neumann's section, their work for the Nuremberg trials began to correct this deficiency.

Another difficulty within recent criticism lies in the untested assumption that the Frankfurt School's approach must necessarily be inappropriate to a phenomenon as irrational as anti-semitic genocide. This assumption conflates social scientific methodology with the substantive object of its analysis, and exaggerates – and thereby misrepresents – the nature of Neumann's rationalism. The latter insists only that social events, including the decline of Germany into an irrational social and political order, can become intelligible whenever researchers both uncover and account for the reasons behind them in a manner that accommodates all the available evidence. The critics' conflation of methodology and its object presupposes that Neumann's critics have themselves already fully established, by rational means and beyond reasonable doubt, that the Holocaust must necessarily be interpreted as a deeply irrational phenomenon. Yet the assumed truth-content of this interpretation presupposes the outcome of the application of a minimal core of rationalism to the analysis of the Holocaust as well as the applicability of those rationalistic assumptions that they otherwise deny.

Another relevant contextual factor concerns the unprecedented nature of the Nazi Holocaust and the understandable suspicion of wartime atrocity stories such as those which the Allies had manufactured during World War I for propaganda purposes. The very expression 'genocide' was only coined during the 1940s, by the OSS consultant Raphael Lemkin. Katz draws attention to the dangers of reconstructing the actions of Neumann, Marcuse and Kirchheimer in the light of contemporary insights and sensibilities, and rightly insists upon the need for Neumann's critics to acknowledge the implications of the prevailing climate in which the warped project of deploying the resources of modern technology systematically to eliminate an entire social group represented an unprecedented and inconceivable idea. As Katz notes:

> It must also be considered that the magnitude of the crime itself, a conspiracy to annihilate an entire population, was to many reasonable people literally unbelievable. Today we have absorbed the grim realities of Armenia, Auschwitz, Cambodia, Rwanda, and Bosnia; we have learned to live in a world in which civilians are not 'collateral damage' but are prime targets. We have, in short, lost whatever innocence we might once have claimed. In the early 1940s, however, the concept of genocide did not yet reside so securely in the conscience of the world and this may partially explain why so many people failed to grasp the larger meaning of the reports emanating from Hitler's Europe.[52]

Neumann's critics have also ignored the specific institutional constraints under which scholars working for the R&A branch of the OSS operated if their research was ever to exert any impact upon those who commissioned it. Those scholars committed to advancing an anti-Fascist and pro-socialist position upon policy questions, particularly regarding the future shape and direction of post-war Germany, were caught in a double bind. In order for their reports to be taken seriously, they had to be phrased in the objectivistic style of apparently value-free studies that renounced any specific political commitments.[53] They had to avoid appearing to trespass upon, pre-empt or otherwise usurp the specific policy-making jurisdiction of their ultimate superiors, not least the State Department, Department of War and Joint Chiefs of Staff.

Another precondition for Neumann's team to exert practical influence in the war crimes field, where it possessed undoubted analytical expertise, was the need to work in close co-operation with colleagues from other agencies. Katz emphasises that the direct interpersonal contact between Neumann's CES and Jackson's WCO represented a considerable improvement over the usually highly diffuse impact of their research reports:

> It may have been in this period that the German legal scholars – Neumann, Kirchheimer, and Henry Kellerman – finally learned that as confident as they were about their own practical expertise, if they wanted to have any serious advisory influence, they must direct their ideas in direct deliberate collaboration with their potential clients and not simply fire them off in the form of reports to be edited, distilled, excerpted, and ignored.[54]

This is an important point, indicating that it was precisely in the field of war crimes research that the CES exerted its most direct influence, and where their analysis could directly feed into the definition of the Nazi regime's nature, operation and chain of responsibility. Indeed, Carl Schorske, Neumann's immediate superior within the OSS/R&A, suggested to the present writer that 'war crimes research was as close to operations against the Nazis as R&A ever got'.[55]

It is a mistake, however, for present-day critics to evaluate any anonymous, collaboratively produced and heavily edited R&A report, even one commissioned by Justice Jackson, as if it were produced under the relatively liberal conditions of contemporary academia. This interpretation risks exaggerating the policy-making role of the OSS/R&A. Katz rightly concludes that the critics of the OSS's role in responding to the Holocaust have taken insufficient account of the empirical contingencies under which this agency operated. Consequently, they not only underestimate its significant, if necessarily limited, achievements in addressing the extermination of Jewish civilians, but also overstate this agency's capacity to affect high-level policy changes within the Allies' war priorities. It is important to acknowledge the implications of the fact that Neumann's CES represented merely one amongst many sub-sections within a single branch of the OSS.

It is important to recall that in *Behemoth* Neumann explicitly rejects not only the sentiments and genocidal practical implications of Nazi racism, but also the basis for constructing social scientific explanations around categories of racial identity, itself defined as an exclusive form of master identity of which all other features are merely derivative. The spearhead theory is consistent with Neumann's critique of the regressively pre-modern commitment of Fascism to a politics of identity based upon the selective exclusion of different classes of former citizens from citizenship entitlements. By contrast, certain of Aronson's criticisms of his spearhead model are premised, implicitly at least, upon a version of identity politics that Neumann himself rejected as inappropriate for any democratically inclined form of scholarship. More specifically, the accusation that Neumann failed to take into account the unique, singular and distinctive character of the anti-semitic dimension of Nazi genocide is problematic to the extent that it presupposes the validity of an approach that is incompatible with Neumann's wider critique of racial identity politics. This kind of criticism is perhaps unsurprising given the recent re-emergence of identity politics for which the affirmation of difference is taken, in itself, to represent a form of justice – even where the particular difference, affirmed in the name of respect for diversity, is itself exclusive and separatist in its motivation or impact. The alternative option, which Neumann is accused of failing to adopt, would have required him to differentiate between, and then grade on a percentage scale of suffering, the various categories of the victims of Fascism.

The implication of Aronson's critique that Neumann, an assimilated Jew, was unsympathetic to Jewish organisations is difficult to reconcile with, for instance, Neumann's reliance, as a primary source, upon materials and statistical analysis regarding the Holocaust supplied by the Institute of Jewish Affairs.[56] It is also worth recalling his collaborative work with the Research Institute of the American Jewish Committee.[57] In the evidence submitted to the Nuremberg prosecutors in the R&A report on 'the conspiracy against the Jews', Neumann's team insisted on including not only a report from this institute, but also another of its reports *co-written* with Neumann's CES. This represented an active institutional collaboration with one group of victims of the Nazi genocide that was not extended to any other group. Indeed, in one sense, it reflected an unstated commitment to give considerable recognition to the Holocaust, which was also a consistent feature of the OSS/R&A reports on war crimes where general points were often illustrated by specific reference to the extermination of Jews.[58] One member of Neumann's OSS war crimes team, Henry Kellermann, not only personally obtained details establishing the first documentary linkage between the Nazi party and the notorious *Kristallnacht* anti-semitic persecutions but also attended interrogations establishing the involvement of the German Army in civilian butchery in Eastern Europe and successfully sought out film evidence of the destruction of the Warsaw ghettos, later shown in the trial itself.[59]

The most serious problem with Aronson's critique of the spearhead theory and its institutional ramifications is that it is difficult to envisage how – given the existing state of international law – Neumann's team could have acted in ways which would not have left it open to critique. For example, Aronson's own analysis recognises that one of the central issues facing the Allied powers, including the United Nations War Crimes Commission, was that the Holocaust *fell outside existing legal definitions of war crimes*:

> The United Nations War Crimes Commission (UNWCC) was established in London in late 1943 on the initiative of nine governments-in-exile faced with the need to punish German war criminals... The challenge was to do so in a way that would allow for punishment of Holocaust perpetrators when no binding international norms yet existed with regard to such acts.[60]

Aronson is right to emphasise these legal difficulties, but he does not follow through their implications for his own critique of Neumann. In effect, Aronson's critique places Neumann in a catch-22 situation. Had Neumann decided to abandon his sociological analysis of Nazi anti-semitism by interpreting the Holocaust as an 'end in itself', independent of the ways in which Nazi military expansionism involved 'waging aggressive war' contrary to international law, then the Holocaust would have fallen under the heading of domestic persecution and murder. This, in turn, would have taken the question of ascertaining legal responsibilities for the Holocaust, including the pre-war persecutions and preparatory steps towards the ultimate genocide, outside the range of activities encompassed by even a broad interpretation of recognised 'war crimes'. On the other hand, Aronson is also critical of the manner in which the Holocaust was not allowed to emerge as a separate heading at Nuremberg, but was submerged as a mediated and partial element in the Nazis' assorted 'crimes against humanity'.[61]

My own view is that, had Neumann's spearhead theory exerted no influence over leading figures within the US prosecution team, it might have jeopardised the prospects of making any significant reference to the Holocaust during these trials. This would have represented the opposite of the recognition of its 'centrality and uniqueness' that Aronson asserts should have occurred. My point here is a pragmatic one. Whatever the possible strengths and weaknesses of the spearhead theory at a general sociological level, something very similar to it was what the prevailing state of international law required from the OSS strategists within the US prosecution team. Such law dictated that, in order for the Holocaust to be introduced at all at the Nuremberg trials, it was *first necessary to conceptualise it in broadly functionalist terms* as one constituent and mediated part of a wider context of other criminal policies of domestic repression, i.e., in a way akin to Neumann's spearhead theory. It was only this functionalist interpretation that was able to supply the otherwise missing piece of the jigsaw necessary for the prosecution to establish an internal connection between the Holocaust and related acts of military aggression that did fall clearly within recognised categories of war crimes. In short, Neumann's spearhead theory was appropriate to the legal requirement for a broadly functionalist model of Nazi anti-semitism linked to both the 'conspiracy' and 'criminal organisation' charges that Jackson's trial plan had specifically entrusted to Neumann's team at the OSS.[62]

Aronson's critique is further weakened by its reliance upon a spurious dichotomy between the 'legal experts' and 'European social scientists-turned-intelligence men, above all Frankfurt School associates such as Franz Neumann, Herbert Marcuse and Otto Kirchheimer', whom Jackson apparently dispensed with. This dichotomy fails to acknowledge the legal contribution of Neumann's section, nor does it credit it with helping to supply the strategic thinking that informed those innovative charges whose remit was sufficiently wide to encompass the domestic murder of the Jews and other groups, including pre-war acts of persecution. Katz's exemplary summary of the overall thrust of the CES's analysis of Nazi war crimes in effect testifies against Aronson's later critique of the spearhead theory:

> The structure of their case against the Nazi *Behemoth* grew out of Neumann's claim that it was a tightly integrated system, a corporate state managed by an interlocking directorate of political, military and economic leaders. The tactics of the 1920s were only the first act of a tragic drama that closed with total war; Party ideology and party practice were mutually adjusting elements of a single mechanism; domestic terror and foreign aggression issued from the same mandate. In effect, the émigré socialists treated National Socialism as the negative realisation of the Marxist eschatology that had permeated their pre-war theoretical work: a social totality that transcends the alienation of inner and outer, public and private, civil society and the state.[63]

In other words, in their analysis of the Third Reich for Jackson's prosecution office, the CES applied the general framework of *Behemoth* to suggest that the

Nuremberg prosecutors should treat the military aspect of Nazism as one element of a wider mandate. Since 1933, this mandate had included committing acts of internal state terrorism and genocide as preparatory steps orientated from the outset towards a policy of systematic genocide.

Conclusion

In their preparation for the Nuremberg trials and for German de-Nazification more generally, Neumann, together with Marcuse and Kirchheimer, exemplified the nearest that the Frankfurt School came to participation within the institutional practicalities of historically significant events. They left a continuing legacy, allowing pragmatism to endanger neither the socialist implications of their theoretical positions nor the integrity of their political activities.[64] Few, if any, of the criticisms levelled recently against Neumann's group present an unanswerable case. It is fair to conclude that the record of Neumann's team remains impressive, particularly when set against the record of other government agencies.

Their wartime record is also valuable as an instructive case study of the difficulties that face attempts to fulfil, from the side of practice, the interaction between social theory and concrete institutional practice. It offers a case study of how a distinct social theory of the ideological exploitation of racism was applied, and in some measure frustrated, as part of a wider anti-Fascist politics in the most challenging of institutional contexts. When assessing the Frankfurt School's contributions to a viable theory of anti-semitism, formulated with critical and practical intent, an essential question arises: which of this School's various contributions was better engaged with the practicalities of highlighting the evils of racism, and then devising contextually appropriate ways of translating any resulting insights into practical effect?

The practical attribution of political, moral and legal responsibility is certainly required. It is needed to ensure that critical social theory's own ambitions to escape the illusions of semi-detached theoreticism are realised in the world beyond the university seminar room. The partial success of Neumann's team in re-connecting social theory to the empirical exigencies of anti-Fascist politics compares favourably with the retreat into melancholic resignation and political hibernation characteristic of the more philosophically sophisticated post-war works of Adorno and Horkheimer. The latter's response to the immediate threat of a Fascist-controlled Europe was to escape to the sunshine of California finally to write *Dialectic of Enlightenment*. Unsurprisingly, this is a profoundly self-contradictory work, whose difficulties embody the disengagement with concrete political and institutional realities that underpinned its own mode of production.[65] Given the wartime contribution of Neumann, Kirchheimer and Marcuse, immersed as they were within the often frustrating practicalities of seeking to translate aspects of critical theory into institutional practice, the greater attention paid by contemporary social theorists to the legacy of Adorno and Horkheimer is regrettable. It tends to reproduce in contemporary theoretical practice these writers' own undialectical relationship between social theory and institutional practice, that is, a self-cancelling, and hence ultimately futile, form of theoretical sophistication. One lesson taught by this reconstruction of Neumann's activism on the war crimes and de-Nazification issues is that the object of social theory is not just other theories or theories about theories, but the ongoing and contingent praxis that shapes, actively or by default, concrete events, underlying material processes and relationships, together with their intended and unintended consequences.

Notes

1 See Franz Neumann, *Behemoth*, London: Gollancz, 1942; *The Democratic and Authoritarian State*, New York: Free Press, 1957; *The Rule of Law*, Leamington Spa: Berg, 1986; Martin Jay, *The Dialectical Imagination*, Berkeley: University of California Press, 1996, p.xv.

2 Keith Tribe, 'Introduction to Neumann, Law and Socialist Political Theory', *Economy and Society*, Vol.10, 1981, p.316; *Strategies of Economic Order*, Cambridge: Cambridge University Press; William Scheuerman, *Between the Norms and the Exception: The Frankfurt School and the Rule Of Law*, Cambridge, Mass.: MIT Press, 1994; *idem.* (ed.), *The Rule of Law Under Siege: Selected Essays of Franz L. Neumann and Otto Kirchheimer*, Berkeley: University of California Press, 1996.

3 Barry M. Katz, *Foreign Intelligence: Research and Analysis in the Office of Strategic Services, 1941–1945*, Cambridge: Harvard University Press, 1989; 'The Holocaust and American Intelligence', in *The Jewish Legacy and the German Conscience: Essays in Memory of Rabbi Joseph Asher*, ed. Moses Rischtin and Raphael Asher, Berkeley: Judah L. Magnes Museum, 1991, pp.297–307; 'OSS and the Jewish Question: An Ambiguous Record', conference paper presented to the International Conference on World War II, the Holocaust, and the Rise of the State of Israel, 14–16 December, 1998 at Jerusalem and Tel Aviv (I quote from my personal copy of this important but hitherto unpublished study); Petra Marquardt-Bigman, 'Amerikanische Geheimdienstanalysen über Deutschland 1942–1949', *Studien zur Zeitgeschichte*, No.45, 1995; 'Amerikanische Geheimdienstanalysen des Nationalsozialistischen Deutschlands', *Tel-Aviver Jahrbuch für Deutsche Geschichte*, 325–44; '*Behemoth* Revisited: The Research and Analysis Branch of the Office of Strategic Services in the Debate of U.S. Policies towards Germany, 1943–46', *Intelligence and National Security* 12, No.2, 1997, pp.91–100.

4 On the interaction between war crimes scholarship and government practice, see Kirchheimer's *Political Justice*, 1961, pp.323–38, 423, and his OSS/CES colleague John Herz's 'Denazification and Related Policies', in *Between Dictatorship and Democracy*, New York: Greenwood Press, 1982, pp.19ff.

5 See Shlomo Aronson, 'Preparations for the Nuremberg Trial: The O.S.S., Charles Dwork, and the Holocaust', *Holocaust and Genocide Studies*, Vol.12, No.2 (Fall 1998), pp.257–81; Richard Breitman, *Official Secrets*, London: Penguin-Viking, 1988. Martin

Jay has a remarkable discussion of how this school's predominantly Jewish senior membership were predisposed vehemently to deny any ethnic/religious element behind their views, association, inner bonds and judgements, even to the point of giving the impression of some kind of distorted 'repression'.

6 The OSS was established by Presidential military order on 13 June 1942, and served under the Joint Chiefs of Staff (JCS). Its role was to conduct overt and covert intelligence procurement activities in the war against the Axis Powers, including clandestine operations in support of planned military operations, to analyse 'raw' intelligence and disseminate finished intelligence reports to appropriate government agencies. Its predecessor agency was the Office of the Co-ordinator of Information (OCOI, 1941–42). The OSS was abolished by EO 9621, 20 September 1945 (Effective 1 October 1945). The creation of the CIA in 1947 re-invented certain aspects of the OSS's role, albeit without the OSS's anti-Fascist commitments. For additional studies on the OSS see: Robert Hayden Alcorn, *No Bugles for Spies: Tales of the OSS*, London: Jarrolds, 1963; *No Banners, No Bands: More Tales of the OSS*, New York: David McKay, 1965; Stewart Alsop and Thomas Braden, *Sub Rosa: The OSS and American Espionage*, New York: Reynal & Hitchcock, 1946; Richard B. Beal Jnr, 'Sifting Through History's Records Brings the OSS into the Daylight', *Army*, 1996, Jan.14; Katherine Breaks, 'Ladies of the OSS: The Apron Strings of Intelligence in World War II', *American Intelligence Journal* 13, No.3 (Summer 1992), pp.91–96; George C. Chalou (ed.), *The Secrets War: The Office of Strategic Services in World War II*, Washington, DC: National Archives, 1992; Betty Abrahamsen Dessants, 'Ambivalent Allies: OSS' USSR Division, the State Department, and the Bureaucracy of Intelligence Analysis, 1941–1945', *Intelligence and National Security* 11, No.4, Oct. 1996, pp.722–53; Lawrence H. McDonald, 'The OSS: America's First National Intelligence Agency', *Prologue*, Spring 1992, pp.7–22; Gerald Schwab, *OSS Agents in Hitler's Heartland: Destination Innsbruck*, Westport: Praeger, 1996; T.F. Troy, '"George": OSS's FBI Secret', in *In the Name of Intelligence: Essays in Honor of Walter Pforzheimer*, ed. Hayden B. Peake and Samuel Halpern, Washington, DC: NIBC Press, pp.479–98; *Wild Bill and Intrepid: Bill Donovan, Bill Stephenson, and the Origin of CIA*, New Haven: Yale University Press, 1996.

7 See A. Soellner (ed.), *Zur Archaeologie der Demokratie in Deutschland*, 2 volumes, Frankfurt: Europäischer Verlagsanstalt, 1981/86; Security-Classified 'Civil Affairs Guides' and 'Correspondence Relating to Conditions and Institutions in Germany and German-Occupied Countries 1944–1945', US National Archive, Record Group (hereafter abbreviated to NA, RG) 226, E. (hereafter abbreviated to E.) 44, B. (hereafter abbreviated to B), location: 190/5/4/05; particularly those on Germany, i.e., Guides to the Elimination of Nazis and Pro-Nazis From Positions of Power (7 folders); Guides to the Elimination of Nazi Political, Cultural and Quasi-Governmental Institutions; Economic Planning Guides; Guides to Ownership and Control of Property (6 folders), location: 190/5/4/03; Guides to Trade and Financial Institutions (8 folders), location: 190/5/4/03.

8 On Dulles' pre-CIA period as a senior OSS official see Allan Dulles, *Germany's Underground*, New York: Macmillan, 1947; 'William J. Donovan and National Security: Speech to the Erie Bar Association, Buffalo, New York, May 4, 1959', *Congressional Record* 105 (14 May 1959), pp.8103–8105; *The Secret Surrender*, New York: Harper & Row, 1966; Peter Grose, *Gentleman Spy: The Life of Allan Dulles*, Boston: Houghton Mifflin, 1994.

9 See US NA Gift Collections RG 200 Abraham G. Duker/Irving Dwork Papers (OSS R&A Branch, Jewish Desk – World War II). The documents in the Duker/Dwork Papers, the majority of which are OSS war crimes records addressing primarily the persecution of Jews during World War II, were compiled by Dr Charles Irving Dwork. These papers were transferred to Abraham G. Duker, who had been employed in the OSS's Foreign

Nationalities Branch. This collection includes documents the OSS received from other agencies, including the State Department and the Assistant Secretary of War. Their analysis needs to be supplemented by consideration of the Records Relating to the R&A Branch Jewish Desk NARG 226, E. 191, including the following folders located at 190/10/5/05: B. 1: Folder 1: Concentration Camps, Germany; Folder 4: Jews in Hungary, Research and Analysis Branch Report #2027 19 October 1944; Folder 6: Buchenwald 1945; Folder 8: Axis Concentration Camps and Detention Centers in Europe – Basic Handbook; Folder 12: Conspiracy Against the Jewish People–Poland 1945; Folder 14: Hungary, Jews 1944; Folder 15: Hungarian Jews 1944; Folder 16: War Crimes–from Bern October 1944; Folder 17: Budapest, Jews in, October 1944; B. 2, Folder 18: Central Europe; Folder 19: Allied Military Government and the Jewish Problem–Civil Affairs Guide, 29 April 1944; B. 2 Folder 20: Anti-Jewish Measures 15 October 1943; B. 2 Folder 22: The Gestapo, 6 August 1945; B. 2 Folder 23: Anti Semitic Propaganda of the Nazis in Latin America; B. 2 Folder 24: Conspiracy Against the Jewish People, Germany, 1933–44; B. 3 Folder 25: OSS Report on Rescue Work [for Jewish refugees] 25 October 1944.

10 Aronson, 'Preparations...', p.269.

11 Neumann's role within the Nuremberg trials as 'First Chief of Research' for the US prosecution office developed from his earlier responsibilities as head of a specially created war crimes unit. This unit included at its core a remarkable group of interdisciplinary research analysts drawn from the OSS, including Otto Kirchheimer and Herbert Marcuse (Katz, *Foreign Intelligence...*, pp.29–35). Whilst attached to Justice Robert Jackson's US prosecution team, this OSS unit prepared a series of lengthy draft prosecution briefs and strategy documents, including the *legally most innovative* parts of the war crimes prosecution strategy: the charges against Nazi organisations as such and the application of all-encompassing 'conspiracy' charges to pre-war domestic persecution. Prior to his leadership of the OSS war crimes unit, Neumann had been a senior OSS analyst and intellectual leader of a small 'Central European Section' ('CES') of this agency's interdisciplinary R&A branch. During 1943–44, this R&A sub-section composed a series of other reports on various legal, political and institutional difficulties facing any successful prosecution of Nazi war criminals. It also wrote studies addressing the question of the implications for psychological warfare of the attribution of war criminality

12 See *Times Literary Supplement*'s list of the hundred most influential books published since World War II, cited in the editorial to *The Antioch Review*, 1 Jan. 1996; also Peter Intellman, *Franz L. Neumann: Chancen und Dilemma des Politischen Reformismus*, Baden-Baden: Nomos Verlagsgesellschaft, 1996.

13 See Marquardt-Bigman, '*Behemoth* Revisited...'.

14 NA, RG 226, E. 37, B. 6: War Crimes Program; NA, RG 226, E. 1, B 2: War Crimes: Correspondence May–July 1945; NA, RG 226, E. 42, B. 1, R&A/Europe-Africa Division progress report, May 1945.

15 See also Neumann's OSS report 'German Morale after Tunisia', R&A 933, 25 June 1943, p.2.

16 Neumann, *Behemoth*, p.xiii.

17 *Ibid.*, pp.550–51.

18 *Ibid.*, p.550.

19 *Ibid.*, p.551.

20 On the strategic deployment of anti-semitism as a rhetoric designed to have 'revolutionary anti-capitalist appeal', see 'German Morale after Tunisia', pp.3–4.

21 See 'The Significance of Prussian Militarism for Nazi Imperialism', R&A 1281, 20 October 1943, NA, RG 153, E. 135, B. 6; introduction to 'Sixty-Five Leading German Businessmen', R&A 3020, 28 June 1945, NA, RG153, E. 135, B. 14.

22 See also Neumann's OSS report 'German Morale after Tunisia', pp.2–3, which analyses anti-semitism in line with the spearhead theory as a strategy of generalised repressive control through the mobilisation of fear.

23 Neumann, *Behemoth*, p.551.

24 See 'The Significance of Prussian Militarism for Nazi Imperialism'.

25 Katz, *Foreign Intelligence…*, pp.56–57.

26 Katz, 'OSS and the Jewish Question…'.

27 Marquardt-Bigman, 'Amerikanische Geheimdienstanalysen…', p.335.

28 For an appreciation of Neumann as 'the uncontested intellectual leader of OSS/CES', see Henry Kellermann, 'Settling Accounts – The Nuremberg Trial', *Leo Baeck Yearbook*, Vol.XLII, 1997, pp.337–55.

29 Marquardt-Bigman, 'Amerikanische Geheimdienstanalysen…', p.334.

30 Katz, *Foreign Intelligence…*, p.55.

31 *Ibid.*, p.57.

32 Neumann, *Behemoth*, 2nd edn, p.551.

33 Aronson, 'Preparations…', p.269.

34 *Ibid.*, p.269.

35 On Breitman's account the main sources of specific evidence of the Holocaust available to the OSS should be Spring 1944, not 1942 (*Official Secrets*, p.120).

36 Breitman, *Official Secrets*, p.308.

37 Kellermann, 'Settling Accounts…', p.339 n.3.

38 Re-published in John Mendelsohn (ed.), *The Holocaust: Selected Documents in Eighteen Volumes*, Vol.11: 'The Wannsee Protocol and a 1944 Report on Auschwitz by the OSS', New York: Garland, 1982, pp.18–32. This, the first detailed report to reach the West, was received by the London field office of the OSS in April 1944. It was based upon information gathered by the Polish underground in Auschwitz, and provides details about the number of inmates at Auschwitz; the names of core Nazi staff in charge of extermination; figures relating to the number of Jews and gypsies gassed up to September 1942; and the numbers of Jews arriving from various countries between September 1942 and June 1943. The report noted that only two per cent of these arrivals was still alive. The report also discusses conditions in the camp and medical experimentation on internees, as well as providing descriptions of both the gassing and cremation procedures.

39 See the detailed statement by David Milgrom in Bratislava, 30 August 1943, enclosed by US Vice-Consul Melbourne (Instanbul) to Secretary of State, 13 January 1944, NA, RG 226/OSS58603.

40 In autumn 1941 a gas chamber was constructed in the concentration camp at Mauthausen. OSS records include a photograph of the device used to introduce poison gas into the gassing chamber at this camp, which was taken by in May 1945 by the American troops who liberated its inmates, amongst whom was an OSS official, see Dupont Mission, photo US signal corps, RG 226, E. 110, B. 4, folder 86.

41 Further reports of war criminality are contained in NA, RG 226, 3935: 'Italy and Germany – Domestic Situation', 6.9.1941; NA, RG 226, 76527: German War Criminals in Occupied Yugoslavia, 12.1.1944; NA, RG 226, 58852: 'Sachsenhausen Concentration Camp' [1944]; NA, RG 226, 102832: 'German Execution of Jews in Occupied Russia', 23.8.1944. The draft briefs included the following reports NA, RG 238, E. 52f, B. 28 R&A 3113.3, 'Legislative Agencies Involved in War Crimes' (draft for the War Crimes Staff), 28.8. 1945; NA, RG 238, E. 52f, B. 28, R&A 3113.6, 'The Gestapo' (draft for use of War Crimes Staff), 6.8.1945; NA, RG 59, R&A 3113.7, 'The Nazi Party, Parts I and II' (draft for the use of the War Crimes Staff), 24.7.1945.

42 See G. Pearson and M. Salter, 'Putting Public Law in a Critical Condition', *Social and Legal Studies*, Vol.8, No.4, 1999, pp.483–508; M. Salter and J. Shaw, 'Towards a Critical Theory of Constitutional Law: Hegel's Contribution', *Journal of Law and Society*,

Vol.21, 1994, pp.464–86; Michael Salter, 'Dialectical Lessons from the Failure of Marxism', *Social and Legal Studies*, Vol.7, No.3, 1996, pp.437–42.

43 A. Soellner, 'Franz Neumann', *Telos*, Winter 1981–82, p.171; *idem.* (ed.) *Zur Archaeologie der Demokratie in Deutschland*; 'Leftist Students of the Conservative Revolution: Neumann, Kirchheimer and Marcuse', *Telos*, Vol.61, 1994, p.55; Henry Pachter, 'On Being an Exile', *Salmagundi*, 10/11, 1969/70, Fall/Winter, p.36.

44 See Marcuse's preface to Neumann's *The Democratic and Authoritarian State*, p.viii; and 'The Significance of Prussian Militarism for Nazi Imperialism'. This is a view supported by my telephone interview with John Herz 18 August 1998.

45 This was recently confirmed in a telephone interview with H. Stuart Hughes, who was Neumann's immediate superior in the R&A branch, and a close personal friend (22 January 1999). Sympathetic scholars, such as Soellner, analyse Neumann's CES work on war crimes as one partial aspect of his wider analysis of the proposed post-war reconstruction of German democracy. Soellner's important study analyses two CES / R&A reports on the 'Leadership Principle' and the most important Nazi organisations, alongside two other civil affairs and R&A reports on post-war German reconstruction more generally. See note 39.

46 I owe this point to correspondence with Alfons Soellner 13 May 1998 who informs us that: 'In my opinion, Neumann was not so critical of the legal shortcomings of the Nuremberg trials as for example Kirchheimer in his *Political Justice*. I remember however Marcuse saying that Neumann's first spontaneous reaction was: "Shoot the Nazi criminals without any trial". This was certainly only in a private context.'

47 Telephone interview with John Herz, 18 August 1998.

48 H. Marcuse, 'Theory and Politics: A Discussion with Herbert Marcuse, Jürgen Habermas, Heinz Lubasz and Tilman Spengler', *Telos*, 38, Winter 1977–78, pp.130–31.

49 See 'The Significance of Prussian Militarism for Nazi Imperialism'.

50 Marcuse, 'Theory and Politics...', p.131.

51 See 'Memorandum on Trial Preparation', 17 May 1945, in James Donovan's files, Hoover Institute Archives, B. 34, Folder 6.

52 Katz, 'OSS and the Jewish Question...'.

53 See 'Functions of the Research and Analysis Branch', 30 October 1942, NA, RG 226, E. 45, B.2, Folder 45; and 'Draft of Proposed Guide to Preparation of Political Reports', RG 226, E. 37, B. 5, Folder: Projects Committee Correspondence.

54 Katz, *Foreign Intelligence...*, p.51.

55 Author's telephone interview with Carl Schorske, 1 July 1998.

56 Others studying the anti-Fascist contribution of German-Jewish exiles in the OSS have not discerned any lack of sympathy within Neumann's section of the OSS; see G. Stern, 'In the Service of American Intelligence: German-Jewish Exiles in the War Against Hitler', *Leo Baeck Institute Yearbook*, Vol.XXXVII, 1992, p.461.

57 See *Behemoth*, p.550.

58 An example is found in the OSS/R&A report of July 1945 on the 'leadership principle', where Neumann's team specifically cited the genocide of the Jews as a field where the practical relevance of this principle could be turned back upon the Nuremberg defendants to bypass various legalistic defences, such as following 'superior orders', of claims of lack of proof of any subjective knowledge of specific atrocities:

> For example: If a general policy adopted on the highest level of leadership has been to the effect to 'eliminate all Jews from European life once and for all', and if in pursuance of such policy a large part of the Jewish population under Nazi rule has actually been exterminated, the acts of physical extermination may be attributed to all leaders and sub-leaders who, under the highest leadership, had functional and regional jurisdiction in connection with the implementation of the Jewish policies of the Nazi regime. All of them can be presumed to have known the Nazi

217

program and the Nazi policies in this respect, all of them have used their positions to implement them, and all of them have known that in the execution of policy directives no legal restrictions would be observed. Whether or not under such conditions, they have been aware of the particular details of execution in specific cases, appears immaterial. ('Leadership Principle and Criminal Responsibility', R&A 3110, pp.14–15, 18 July 1945, NA, RG 238, E. 52 B. 28.)

59 Kellermann, 'Settling Accounts…', pp.346–48.

60 Aronson, 'Preparations…', pp.259–60.

61 *Ibid.*, pp.275–76.

62 See 'Memorandum on Trial Preparation', 17 May 1945, in James Donovan's files, Hoover Institute Archives, B. 34, Folder 6.

63 Katz, *Foreign Intelligence…*, p.54.

64 Douglas Kellner, *Herbert Marcuse: On Technology, War and Fascism*, London: Routledge, 1998, pp.36–38.

65 For an instructive critique of these contradictions, see Jürgen Habermas, *The Philosophical Discourse of Modernity*, Cambridge: Polity, 1989, Ch.5.

CHAPTER 11

Holocaust Testimony and the Challenge to the Philosophy of History

DAN STONE

One does not need to be a prophet to predict that Holocaust research will provide an impetus for history as a whole, strong enough to throw overboard a whole string of its paradigmatic fortifications...The century of ideologies is coming to an end – even in the explanatory patterns of historiography.

Ulrich Raulff[1]

In her testimony written in the immediate aftermath of the war, Suzanne Birnbaum, stunned by the pace at which the Jews of Hungary had been decimated at Auschwitz, wrote that 600,000 were murdered in July and August of 1944. The reality was somewhat less – we know now that the number of Hungarian Jews killed in this period was around 435,000. Nevertheless, Annette Wieviorka, in her study of testimonies of the immediate post-war period – of which there are a surprisingly large number – notes in response to this error that it 'makes no difference to the insane scale of the massacre'.[2]

But discrepancies of this sort do exercise historians, and rightly so, since they aim to compile the most accurate body of information possible. A well-known example of this sort of error is recorded by Dori Laub. At a conference on Holocaust education, a survivor's testimony was shown during which the narrator described how, during the *Sonderkommando* uprising at Auschwitz, she had seen the four chimneys of the crematoria blown up. The historians objected:

Historically, only one chimney was blown up, not all four. Since the memory of the testifying woman turned out to be, in this way, fallible, one could not accept – nor give credence to – her whole account of the events. It was utterly important to remain accurate, lest the revisionists in history discredit everything.[3]

But as Jean-François Lyotard has shown, it is precisely because the factual record will remain incomplete, a result of the nature of the events themselves as well as the loss of documents, that Holocaust negationists are able to ply their trade. When historians argue over the number of people killed in death camps, for example, the negationists claim that nothing relating to the Holocaust can be ascertained. Turning the assumptions of historians on their heads, Lyotard argues that 'the "perfect crime" does not consist in killing the victim or the witnesses...but rather in obtaining the silence of the witnesses, the deafness of the judges, and the inconsistency (insanity) of the testimony'.[4]

In other words, it is the attempt to gain cognitive control over the events of the Holocaust, to master them by fitting them into existing narrative frameworks, what Lawrence Langer calls 'the totalitarian impulse of a historicism that believes it can account for everything',[5] that really constitutes a 'wrong' (*tort*) to the victims. In attempting to counter this wrong, Lyotard puts forward the notion of the Holocaust as a sublime event, a 'sign of history' which must be 'felt' rather than known because the magnitude of the event has rendered the usual instruments of measurement obsolete: the name Auschwitz 'marks the confines wherein historical knowledge sees its competence impugned'.[6]

For philosophers, then, it is not really the problem of factual inaccuracy that is the main source of discomfort in these examples. But historians who reflect on these matters think otherwise. Even before the war, for example, one British book on the Nazi persecution of the Jews was praised in the foreword for being 'the first book that has been written which gives a systematic survey of the anti-Jewish policy in Nazi Germany based not on disconnected stories nor on personal narratives, but on facts published by the Nazis themselves'.[7] This bias, a reflection of readers' attitudes as well as those of writers, continued after the war. For example, Robert Wolfe, US national archivist of captured German records, writes that

> Memoirs, oral history, courtroom testimony, and sworn affidavits are indirect and unavoidably subjective. None of these is immediate, contemporaneous, objective, or unaffected by hindsight... In short, the most reliable sources are *primary textual* sources, contemporaneous in fact and purpose, provided they are authentic.[8]

Lucy Dawidowicz concurred. Whilst she saw the importance of survivor testimonies, Dawidowicz did not regard them particularly highly since, for her, the role of the historian was a far more subtle and demanding art in the service of fulfilling Lord Acton's dictum of 'discerning truth from falsehood and certainty from doubt'. Historians, unlike survivors, have the ability, according to Dawidowicz, to take the necessary distance from the events they describe to be able to produce a balanced picture of the past. Survivors, by contrast, 'caught up in the whirlwind of history, were so buffeted by its winds that they could not chart the storm's course, measure its velocity, assess the damage it wrought'. They were unable to implement the 'imposition of discipline over self' so vital to what Dawidowicz sees as the more important task of writing neutral history.[9] Dawidowicz's stance is echoed in Raul Hilberg's assertion that all Holocaust testimonies are basically the same and that only exceptionally does one find out anything about the 'the "before" and "after" enclosing the Holocaust years'.[10] And Hilberg's and Dawidowicz's claims about the relationship of testimonies to 'real history' are reminiscent of Georges Perec's claim from 1963 that testimonies from the concentration camps (which in France at that time did not deal with the extermination of the Jews) were regarded as useful, necessary, and precious, indispensable for understanding the period and its 'ambience', 'but it is clear that one carefully distinguishes these books from "true" literature'.[11] Perhaps the historians and Perec's satirised literary critics are looking for the wrong thing in these testimonies.

Even Pierre Vidal-Naquet, who is more theoretically inclined than most Holocaust historians, and is sensitive to questions of memory and historical construction – 'it is obviously pointless to oppose "facts" to "interpretations". The chronicle the most stripped of commentary is itself an interpretation'[12] – says that 'As it becomes possible to check on what we have remembered, the dated, written document always carries more weight than a subjective recollection.'[13]

The fact is, however, that historians have, since Ranke, been just as wary of written documents as they have of oral testimony. Even the partial exception to this claim of documents written contemporaneously with the events they describe – such as the Oneg Shabbes archive in the Warsaw ghetto, or the 'Scrolls of Auschwitz' written by members of the *Sonderkommando* and buried in the ground next to the gas chambers – is tempered by the fact that Jewish documents are often avoided (usually not explicitly) in favour of the less emotional, hence more 'objective' Nazi documents. This is a curious state of affairs when one considers the etymological origins of the word 'history':

> Like the word indicating the act of knowledge [*eidénai*], so too the word *historia* derives from the root *id-*, which means to see. *Histor* is in origin the eyewitness, the one who has seen... The determination of authenticity as 'present before the look' rules out an experience of history as what is already there without ever appearing before our eyes as such.[14]

In what follows I argue that although it is necessary for historians to be wary of factual errors, it is not primarily for fear of these that most choose not to make extensive use of Holocaust testimonies. After all, it is the case that as well as errors, there are also many instances to be found in testimonies of things being described for which there are no other records. Furthermore, the errors themselves, as James Young has recently pointed out, are themselves valuable evidence of what people *saw*, as opposed to what actually happened; and, 'in the final analysis, no document can be more historically authentic than that embodying the victims' grasp of events at the time'.[15] Historians choose not to make use of testimonies for a reason that is not made explicit, mainly because historians rarely reflect on questions of philosophy of history: it is that in Holocaust testimonies one is confronted with a temporality which renders them – and hence the Holocaust itself – inimical to the conventional apparatus of historiography. This is the time of trauma.

*

In order to back up these claims I shall look at two very different recent books – one the work of an author who supposedly spent his childhood in Majdanek, the other a travel-story-cum-testimony of a London man fascinated by the devastation of the *shtetl* that his parents left before World War I. They are the by now familiar *Fragments: Memories of a Childhood, 1939–1948* by Binjamin Wilkomirski, and *Konin: A Quest*, by Theo Richmond.[16] Differentiated as much by approach as by the utterly incommensurate life-experiences of their respective authors of almost exactly the same age, these two books nevertheless illustrate the fact that the Holocaust – as it is revealed in testimony especially – resists assimilation by the philosophy of history commonly held by professional historians. They both offer us entries into the 'death world' – a term favoured by Edith Wyschogrod and Alan Milchman among others – whose temporality, unlike conventional notions of historical time, exceeds the boundaries of the books themselves.

What then does this philosophy consist of? Historiography is of course not a homogeneous discipline – there are many different methods which historians employ, from traditional narrative history to structural or sociological history, to the feminist, anthropological, and 'new cultural history' approaches that have developed since the 1970s.[17] In Holocaust historiography, however, it is a curious fact that conventional paradigms reign supreme. This dominance of the traditional approach – as exemplified by the major monographs of Raul Hilberg, Lucy Dawidowicz, Martin Gilbert, Leni Yahil, and, most recently, Saul Friedländer – means that innovative methodologies are felt to be somehow inappropriate to represent the Jewish tragedy; as Friedländer himself said a few years before producing his major history of the Holocaust, *Nazi Germany and the Jews*, 'there is a sense of self-restraint about the available interpretive repertoire'.[18]

Irrespective of the many differences that exist between these histories, they are bound by a broad philosophical framework. This framework is one that emplots the events of the Holocaust into a sequence which lends them a sense of inevitability which was surely lacking as they unfolded in real time, a teleological approach which deprives the past of its radical otherness. It is one which stresses linearity (even when the narrative focuses on different protagonists, as does Friedländer's), hence robbing contingent moments of time of their power to shock. And, most importantly, they are narratives which conform to the classical theological device of soteriology: catastrophe and redemption, whether this comes in the shape of the liberation of the camps, the founding of the state of Israel, or settling in America. All of these approaches indicate a certain philosophy of history at work. I shall call this philosophy historism because it implies a process in history even though this process is not – *pace* traditional historicism – one which is divine or ongoing irrespective of the actions of humans. In other words, what one philosopher of history identifies as a lingering desire for *Universalgeschichte* in historiography.[19]

Now all of the above textual attributes may be found in the testimonies of survivors, especially the feeling of redemption, which is common. What the debate about the representation of the Holocaust concerns, however, is the sense that there is something that eludes discourse, and it is in testimony that this excess most forcefully breaks the bounds of the discourse imposed upon it by the speaker. It is in such moments – when the Holocaust literally escapes history – that the radical challenge of the Holocaust to historiography lies.

Talking to Theo Richmond in Omaha, Miriam Grossman, a survivor – like all his interviewees – of the town of Konin, says of her experiences in the Lodz ghetto and then in Auschwitz:

> Every time we go to the synagogue and they say the Kaddish, I see in front of my eyes a heap of bones and I say the Kaddish for the heap of bones, because I know that so many have no one to say Kaddish for them, and many of my close relatives were among the bones. It doesn't go out of my mind. I am living a normal life and yet I am not. And as for my husband [Ignac, a Czech survivor], not one day goes by that he will not speak about the losses, the horrors and the cruelties, and he is outwardly such a cheerful man with a smiling face and his passion in his work. Every day he speaks about it. We live a double life, because we cannot stop living and we should not stop remembering.[20]

The context of the last sentence here belies the notion that remembering is simply an ethical imperative. Miriam Grossman remembers not because of the biblical injunction, *Zakhor!*, but because she has no choice. Her call for anamnesis is not made on theoretical grounds, but because it is what she does anyway. Daily she is back, temporarily, in the camps, and no longer existing in linear time. Living a double life does not mean simply being in America as a survivor of Auschwitz; it means being in Auschwitz even when one is in America.

There are many examples of such 'double lives' throughout Richmond's book. The son of one survivor, a successful Texas businessman, for example, says of his father:

> It seems trite to say this, but he could never remember the names of friends in Texas. It's to do with not being there, a sign of not living in the here-and-now. I think the Holocaust greatly influences the way he lives his day-to-day life – whether consciously on his part or not, I don't know. But it's there. It's like a low-level hum.[21]

Once again we see that the experience of the Holocaust has not been subdued by time. Instead, the experience is revisited every day in a way which renders it very real indeed. What does it mean to a historian that, as yet another survivor, a former partisan, says of her husband, 'The Holocaust is with him day and night'?[22] How can this sort of personal experience be made to conform to the rules of historiography, rules which insist on the essential 'pastness' of the past, and the ongoing inevitability of the 'river of time'?[23]

The answer is that it cannot. Since historians often seem more determined to maintain their procedural and methodological norms than to adjust them in the light of events that cannot be incorporated by them, testimonies of trauma such as the Holocaust are regularly bypassed. It is interesting to note that where they are used, for example in Martin Gilbert's *The Holocaust: The Jewish Tragedy*, the most ambitious attempt in historiography to present the voices of the victims, they are situated firmly within the context of a compensatory framework: after the barrage of testimony, Gilbert ends by celebrating the triumph of the human spirit, and the return to normality in history.

Recent work on the nature of trauma helps us understand why it contravenes the laws of historism. Freud understood that under the strain of overwhelming events, the response is repression as a means of keeping the danger at bay. But this does not eliminate the experience; instead it returns as a symptom, distorted and misunderstood. As Eduardo Cadava writes, bridging the writing of Freud and Benjamin on this issue,

> what characterises experience in general – experience understood in its strict sense as the traversal of a danger, the passage through a peril – is that it retains no trace of itself: experience experiences itself as the vertigo of memory, as an experience whereby what is experienced is not experienced. For both Freud and Benjamin, consciousness emerges as memory begins to withdraw.[24]

Historiography is ill-equipped to deal with this notion of the 'posthumous shock' because it demands that the past *be* past, that the river of time leave the debris of past horrors behind. Benjamin writes that 'only what has not been experienced explicitly and consciously, what has not happened to the subject as an experience [*Erlebnis*], can become a component of the *mémoire involontaire*'.[25] Only this sort of experience that is not experienced explicitly, an experience that continues to occur *even after the event*, is what characterises the Holocaust. And involuntary memory, trauma, cannot be the subject of historism. Or rather, it can, but only by denying the trauma, domesticating it, rendering it subject to a sense of finality: a failure to respond to what is truly fearsome about trauma. Put simply, the trauma found in Holocaust testimonies conforms to a different concept of historicity than that ordinarily employed in historiography. This is signalled most clearly in Cathy Caruth's comment that turning trauma into text necessitates a loss of precision and force, but that, more importantly, 'beyond the loss of precision there is another, more profound disappearance: the loss, precisely, of the event's essential incomprehensibility, the force of its *affront to understanding*'.[26]

Nowhere is the mutual exclusivity of trauma and historism more in evidence than in Binjamin Wilkomirski's *Fragments*. In this little book, more is revealed than the childhood memories of its author, though these alone make difficult reading. One reason why the book is so important is that it breaks away from conceptions of testimony which see the necessity of ending with some sort of formal resolution, the sort which historism finds obligatory. The reader finishes the book, but there is no sense that the events that it describes, despite having happened fifty years ago, are *past*.

The scenes of the book – written in sparse language – are embodiments of Benjamin's *Jetztzeit*, 'the time of the now', since they do not presuppose a concept of linear time, of time as an endlessly flowing river. Some philosophers of history have pointed out that the notion of the river of time employed by historians is already a self-subverting one, since the concept presumes that history is written by a historian who at any moment can extricate him- or herself from that river and, in Louis Mink's metaphor, survey it from the hilltops.[27] But Wilkomirski's book makes this theoretical point clear in the simplest of terms: each of the moments of time which he describes are moments of shock, 'shards of memory with knife-sharp edges',[28] both for him and for the reader, photographic in intensity (though unlike with photographs, Wilkomirski does not enjoy the luxury of deciding when to view the 'snapshots'). The sense of contingency is one which is alien to works of history, given as they are, thanks to the nature of historical narrative, to lending the past a sense of determinism, construing temporality as an immutable sequence of moments, each containing the same degree of intensity.[29] Wilkomirski's book, although chronological, is not linear. It does not give the same weight to different moments of the past, but emphasises only those which are, for him, not past at all, but which return in the now. As Wilkomirski has explained in a recent interview,

> Without interpretation, the pictures remain fixed in your head. People go on about 'recovered memory', but that's not the problem. Child survivors haven't lost their memories but they can't speak about them because they come from the non-verbal period of their lives – we have no words.[30]

Wilkomirski was able to write down these memories only after years of therapy, and *Fragments* is the way in which he has mastered them to some extent. But in the post-war years, being told to forget what it was impossible to forget compares to the operation of historism, in which the possibility of 'therapy' is also denied.

It is almost pointless to cite from the book, since each of its pages is an illustration of the time of trauma. In fact, the theoretical points being derived from it here bear no relation to the impact that reading the book makes. But if one has to isolate one element of testimony in general and Wilkomirski's in particular which contribute to its resistance to historism, the role of violence stands out. It is the violence in testimonies which escapes the discourse on it, and it is violence which presents difficulties to those trying to understand the events of the Holocaust. The emphasis in the literature on 'industrial killing' – the perverse fascination with 'modernity' equated with 'emotionless technology' – ignores the fact that in every testimony from those days there are so many acts of extreme violence that they cannot all be dismissed as isolated incidents of sadism. Instead, the evidence is overwhelming that brutality was a fact of everyday life, and that factory-line genocide was only a part of what constitutes the Holocaust. This is the 'useless violence' of which Primo Levi spoke, but which he could not get to grips with since, although he recognised that the perpetrators were not 'made of a perverse human substance', he ascribed their becoming violent to the fact that 'for a few years they had been subjected to a school in which current morality was turned upside-down'.[31]

Contrary to Amgaben's claim that history is only meaningful as the site of human happiness, it seems, from reading Richmond and Wilkomirski, that the interruption of historicist time can result from pain as much as from pleasure. Amgaben writes:

> For history is not, as the dominant ideology would have it, man's servitude to continuous linear time, but man's liberation from it: the time of history and the *cairos* in which man, by his initiative, grasps favourable opportunity and chooses his own freedom in the moment. Just as the full, discontinuous

time of pleasure must be set against the empty, continuous and infinite time of vulgar historicism, so the chronological time of pseudo-history [i.e., historism] must be opposed by the cairological time of authentic history.[32]

This passage is interesting; it criticises the chronological time of historiography in a way which accords with my reading of Holocaust testimonies. But in another respect there is a major omission in Agamben's writing just as in the texts that he criticises: the notion of trauma. Why is it that for Agamben only pleasure can interrupt a historist temporality? Once again, the recurring experiences of victims of trauma, in this case Holocaust victims, are expunged, or at least domesticated.

Now it is not the case that the generations that came after the survivors are afflicted by trauma in the same way as their parents and grandparents. But it is true that the memory of the Holocaust has had an impact far beyond the circle of survivors, to encompass virtually every thinking person in Europe, Israel, North America, and even beyond. Saul Friedländer believes that 'The memory of these victims is more present than ever in our historical consciousness', but this was written in a Jewish context.[33] It is probably true to say that, more widely, 'the more the years pass by, the more memory seems to be present'.[34] It seems, then, that the time of extreme pain, the time of the Holocaust, is so uncomfortable for historians to deal with because, like Agamben's time of liberating pleasure (though of course altogether different from it), it too cannot be bound by the 'empty, continuous and infinite time of vulgar historicism'.

★

Are there ways then in which writing the Holocaust can take these considerations into account? Some examples will prove that it is possible to make the reader aware of the nature of testimony, its ability to escape a historist temporality.

Wilkomirski's *Fragments* is probably the supreme example of the challenge of testimony to philosophy of history. Other works by survivors which challenge linear chronology include Ruth Klüger's *Weiter leben* (1992) and Saul Friedländer's *When Memory Comes* (1978). Interestingly, all three of these books (Wilkomirski's, Klüger's, and Friedländer's) were written by child survivors, Wilkomirski and Klüger survivors of Majdanek and Auschwitz respectively, and Friedländer a survivor thanks to being hidden in a French convent for the duration of the war.

Klüger's book constructs a narrative of the camps not just by describing her experiences – which she does – but by continually interrupting those descriptions with scenes from her current life as a professor of German at the University of

California, Irvine, and other events in her life since the war. In these she recounts discussions she has had about the concentration camps, and other people's interpretations of the camps which they have presumed to impose upon her. But most importantly, she reflects on the impossibility of her task.

For example, talking of a trip to Dachau she once made 'because American friends wanted to go', Klüger can only describe the camp as it is now: a museum:

> Everything was clean and orderly there, and one already needed more imagination than most people have got in order to picture what occurred there [*gespielt wurde*] forty years before... What comes into one's mind there one perhaps associates more with a holiday camp than with a tortured life [*gefoltertes Leben*].[35]

This is why she claims that what people find in the camps is essentially what they have brought with them, 'in their baggage', for what could be further removed from the camps' old constellation of 'camp' (*Gefängnis*) and 'prisoner' (*Häftling*) than the new one of memorial site (*Gedenkstätte*) and visitor (*Besucher*)?[36] For Klüger 'it is senseless to want to represent the camps three-dimensionally', just as it is senseless to try and do so in words, 'as though nothing lay between us and the time when it still existed'.[37]

For Friedländer writing his testimony was an altogether different undertaking. He is not a survivor in the sense that we have come to expect from most accounts of ghettoisation and life in the camps, but he is certainly a survivor in the sense that had his hiding place been discovered he would have suffered the same fate as his parents, deportation to Auschwitz. And his book is no ordinary account. Instead the narrative is split, his account of the war years juxtaposed with a diary written in 1977, containing reflections on Israel after the Yom Kippur War. The result is a disturbing interaction between the two texts which leaves the reader wondering where exactly 'history' ends and 'personal reminiscence' begins.[38]

A similar strategy is to be found in Georges Perec's 'autobiography', *W, Or the Memory of Childhood* (1975). Like Friedländer, Perec, who later became famous as the author of the novel *Life: A User's Guide*, was the son of Eastern European (this time Polish) immigrants who was hidden in a remote part of southern France during the war. But, as befits a novelist obsessed by dissimulation and absences, Perec's book is far more oblique than Friedländer's.[39]

Again, there are two texts running side by side. The first is a supposed account of Perec's childhood which, as his biographer has pointed out, is almost entirely factually incorrect; the second, a narrative describing an unknown island in the South American archipelago of Tierra del Fuego whose society is based entirely on the harsh rules of sport. As in Friedländer's book, the interaction between the two narratives is profoundly disturbing, but Perec's disturbs all the more since the connection between the two accounts is neither explicit nor even easy to discern. It is obvious that the island of W is a thinly-veiled metaphor for the camps, but the reader leaves the book as much confused as enlightened. But this, on reflection, is exactly the impact that thinking about the Holocaust, especially in the context of testimony, ought to have.

These short summaries are insufficient really to get a feel for the books, but they show that the temporality of the philosophy of history can be explicitly challenged. When Perec begins *W*, for example, by claiming to remember nothing of his childhood, we should be warned that this will be no ordinary account of memory. Other books, not by survivors in the strict sense, which also serve to illustrate this point, include Sarah Kofman's *Paroles suffoquées* (1987), a book which talks about the impossibility of talking about the death of her father in Auschwitz, thereby finding a way of talking about it, in her words, 'without power', and Edmond Jabès' *The Book of Questions* (1963–73), the multi-volume work of an Egyptian Jew who left for France in 1956, in which the sayings of imagined rabbis are intermingled with the just-followable story of Sara and Yukel, a young couple whose lives are destroyed in the Holocaust.

★

I have argued that testimonies make more clear than other evidence why the excess of the Holocaust breaks the bounds of 'normal' philosophy of history, of historism. And I have argued that this is the primary reason why historians tend to shy away from testimonies, or else envelop them in a framework which offers some kind of compensation (be it intellectual, emotional, political) that cannot be derived from the events themselves (unless one takes a Nazi's view of history). In doing so I hope that I have not homogenised the experience of survivors or rendered their narratives indistinguishable. Most of all, by suggesting that the historiography of the Holocaust is bound by a philosophical framework which transcends methodological differences, and by equally suggesting that testimonies illustrate the time of trauma irrespective of *their* differences, I have run the risk of drawing an absolute barrier between the two genres. Of course, the boundaries are blurred, testimony should not simply replace historiography as a privileged category; but I hope that I have shown that testimony escapes the laws of historism, which are therefore shown to be not as 'natural' as it is supposed: as Hannah Arendt noted, time only became conceived of as a linear sequence with the modern understanding of history.[40]

Ultimately, it seems that trauma cannot be written *as trauma*, not without something essential to trauma being overlooked. But there are texts which can help one understand this point better than others. What they reveal is not something that can be shared by the ordinary reader; it is what the protagonist of Alan Resnais' film *Hiroshima mon amour* calls 'neither a time for living nor a time for dying.' In other words, a time which cannot be confined to linear chronology.

Afterword

Since I wrote this paper in the autumn of 1997, Binjamin Wilkomirski's book *Fragments* has been exposed as a fake. The Swiss journalist Daniel Ganzfried claims, after research in the Swiss public records, that Wilkomirski was born not in Riga, but near Bern, that his mother Yvonne Grosjean named him Bruno and shortly afterwards gave him to an orphanage, from where he was adopted by a couple named Doesseker. Ganzfried has uncovered photographs of Wilkomirski as a child, and spoken to childhood contemporaries who confirm his suspicions.[41] It is clear that Ganzfried's investigations are correct; Wilkomirski's German publishers have withdrawn the book, and he himself has remained stubbornly silent on the matter. The unearthed documents seem to be incontrovertible – as Ganzfried said of Switzerland, 'This is a country where record-keeping is taken seriously. All the documents were there to be found. It was simply that no one had bothered to look for them' – but the denouement of this particular episode has yet to be reached.

A few comments on this are certainly necessary, since the majority of Holocaust scholars – myself included – and very many lay readers have been deeply moved by what they believed to be a true account. What is different if the book was made up? Firstly, and most importantly, it should be noted that if this book is a figment of Wilkomirski's vivid imagination, it is an insult to the survivors of the Holocaust. They have suffered enough without having the memory of their suffering impugned by faked testimonies. Nor does it help wage the war against Holocaust deniers.

But this condemnation still leaves difficult questions unanswered, questions about the construction of collective memory, about recovered personal memory, about the difference between fact and fiction, and about the role of testimony in memory and history. The uncomfortable fact remains that we are dealing with an extremely powerful and important book; whether it is 'true' or not, there is a truth in it to which many have responded. There is not the space here to develop all of these ideas, but some comments about Wilkomirski's claims seems pertinent.

In a recent article about Holocaust testimonies, post-traumatic stress disorder, the recovery of repressed memory, and false memory syndrome, Pamela Ballinger makes several important comments. She notes on the one hand that Holocaust survivors have typically suffered from the opposite problem to those patients undergoing therapy to release repressed memories after sexual or satanic ritual abuse: 'In many cases, then, the problem appears not an inability to remember – as in the case of abuse survivors – but an inability to forget.' She goes on to argue that claims to de-repressed memories need to be viewed with suspicion, not just because of Western culture's current obsession with memory in general and with the memories of victimisation in particular, but because 'Many de-repression cases…involve claims of wholesale recovery of completely novel memories, a feature that does not generally characterise the other survivors' memories [examined in the article].'[42] And in one of the articles in the British press about the 'Wilkomirski affair', the possibility is raised, based on comments made by Ganzfried, that the book, though a work of fiction, was written by a man obsessed by the facts of the Holocaust, obsessed to the point of believing in his own participation, and hence not written in bad faith. Indeed the journalists, taking the work of their Swiss colleague as conclusive, ponder the question, 'how did he make the leap from studying the Holocaust to proclaiming himself a part of it?'[43]

Now the details of Wilkomirski's therapy are naturally not all open to scrutiny. Nevertheless, it seems clear that he employed some sort of recovered memory treatment in order to grapple with his memories. Questions therefore need to be asked about how these memories have been 'recovered' and about his claims mentioned in my article above (which could now be construed as convenient) that his memories stem from his pre-verbal childhood and that therefore he had no means of giving voice to them before undergoing extensive treatment.

I do not wish to indulge in speculation as to whether Wilkomirski has lied or not, or whether the intriguing suggestion that he is simply obsessed with the Holocaust to an unhealthy degree is correct or not. After all, the matter has not yet been cleared up, and may not be for some time, whilst Wilkomirski's lawyers attempt to kill the discussion. Just as interesting as the question of whether or not the book is a fake is the question of how it can be taken seriously that a man could become so obsessed with the Holocaust to have ended up believing that he was one of its victims. That this suggestion needs to be taken seriously is itself an indictment of what Ballinger calls the 'culture of survivors', in which societal approval is conferred on those in the position of victim. If this is the case – if Wilkomirski is not a Holocaust survivor but did not consciously write a work of fiction – then it might be time not just to reassess the way in which historians treat testimonies, as I have suggested above, but also to consider the way in which testimonies themselves need to be opened up to a whole separate set of questions.

231

Such questions would centre on how testimonies are shaped by each other, how historiography and collective memories influence survivors' decisions about narrative strategy, and how different ideas about the nature of the Holocaust lead to survivors constructing different testimonial narratives. All of these are sensitive areas which need to be treated with extreme caution, and which can only be suggested here. It is a field of enquiry which requires some courage to enter into, and one which must not be undertaken lightly, for it is tinkering with the memories of survivors of the event which has defined the failures of this century, even (as Raulff proposes) its thought-processes. But if an impetus were needed to begin this work, then the controversy over Wilkomirski and his astonishing book *Fragments* must be it.[39]

Notes

1 Ulrich Raulff, 'Die letzte Quelle: Der Holocaust im Licht des Fin de siècle', *Frankfurter Allgemeine Zeitung*, 4 April 1997, p.38.

2 Suzanne Birnbaum, *Une française juive est revenue* (Paris: Éditions du livre français, n.d.), cited in Annette Wieviorka, 'Indicible ou inaudible? La déportation: premiers récits (1944–1947)', *Pardès*, 9–10 (1989), p.35.

3 Dori Laub, 'Bearing Witness or the Vicissitudes of Listening', in Shoshana Felman and Dori Laub, *Testimony: Crises of Witnessing in Literature, Psychoanalysis, and History*, New York: Routledge, 1992, pp.59–60. For another reading of this passage see Ravit Reichman, 'The Myth of Old Forms: On the Unknowable and Representation', in *Theoretical Interpretations of the Holocaust*, ed. Dan Stone, Amsterdam and Atlanta: Rodopi, forthcoming.

4 Jean-François Lyotard, *The Differend: Phrases in Dispute*, trans. Georges van den Abbeele, Manchester: Manchester University Press, 1988, §9 p.8.

5 Lawrence L. Langer, *Holocaust Testimonies: The Ruins of Memory*, New Haven: Yale University Press, 1991, p.174.

6 Lyotard, *The Differend*, §93, p.58.

7 Neville Laski, 'Foreword' to G. Warburg, *Six Years of Terror: The Jews under the Nazi Regime*, London: George Allen and Unwin, 1939, p.7.

8 Robert Wolfe, 'Nazi Paperwork for the Final Solution', in *Perspectives on the Holocaust: Essays in Honor of Raul Hilberg*, ed. James S. Pacy and Alan P. Wertheimer, Boulder: Westview Press, 1995, pp.5, 6.

9 Lucy Dawidowicz, *The Holocaust and the Historians*, Cambridge, Mass.: Harvard University Press, 1981, pp.129 and 130.

10 Raul Hilberg, 'I Was Not There', in *Writing and the Holocaust*, ed. Berel Lang, New York: Holmes and Meier, 1988, p.19.

11 Georges Perec, 'Robert Antelme ou la vérité de la littérature', *Partisans*, 8, January–February 1963, pp.121–34. Reprinted in Georges Perec, *L.G. Une aventure des années soixantes*, Paris: Éditions du Seuil, 1992, pp.87–114, here at p.88. On this essay see my 'Perec's Antelme', *French Cultural Studies*, Vol.10, No.2 1999, pp.161–72.

12 Pierre Vidal-Naquet, 'L'Épreuve de l'historien: réflexions d'un généraliste', in *Au sujet de Shoah: le film de Claude Lanzmann*, Paris: Belin, 1990, p.201.

13 Pierre Vidal-Naquet, 'Memory and History', *Common Knowledge*, Vol.5, No.2, 1996, p.14.

14 Giorgio Agamben, *Infancy and History: Essays on the Destruction of Experience*, trans.

Liz Heron, London: Verso, 1993, p.94.

15 James E. Young, 'Between History and Memory: The Uncanny Voices of Historian and Survivor', *History & Memory*, Vol.9, Nos.1–2, 1997, pp.54 and 56.

16 Binjamin Wilkomirski, *Fragments: Memories of a Childhood, 1939–1948*, trans. Carol Brown Janeway, London: Picador, 1996; Theo Richmond, *Konin: A Quest*, London: Vintage, 1996.

17 See, for example, Georg G. Iggers, *Geschichtswissenschaft im 20. Jahrhundert: Ein kritischer Überblick im internationalen Zusammenhang*, Göttingen: Vandenhoeck & Ruprecht, 1993; Lynn Hunt (ed.), *The New Cultural History*, Berkeley: University of California Press, 1989.

18 Saul Friedländer, 'The "Final Solution": On the Unease in Historical Interpretation', in *Lessons and Legacies: The Meaning of the Holocaust in a Changing World*, ed. Peter Hayes, Evanston: Northwestern University Press, 1991, p.32.

19 Alan Megill, '"Grand Narrative" and the Discipline of History', in *A New Philosophy of History*, eds Frank Ankersmit and Hans Kellner, London: Reaktion, 1995.

20 Richmond, *Konin*, pp.267–68.

21 *Ibid.*, p.301.

22 *Ibid.*, p.321.

23 On the 'river of time' see Louis Mink, *Historical Understanding*, ed. Brian Fay, Eugene O. Golob and Richard T. Vann, Ithaca: Cornell University Press, 1987, pp.56–57, and F.R. Ankersmit, *History and Tropology: The Rise and Fall of Metaphor*, Berkeley: University of California Press, 1994, pp.216–23.

24 Eduardo Cadava, *Words of Light: Theses on the Photography of History*, Princeton: Princeton University Press, 1997, p.103.

25 Walter Benjamin, *Illuminations*, London: Fontana, 1992, p.157; cited in Cadava, *Words of Light*, p.104.

26 Cathy Caruth, 'Introduction' to Part II of *idem* (ed.) *Trauma*, Baltimore: Johns Hopkins University Press, 1995, pp.153 and 154.

27 See Ankersmit, *History and Tropology*, p.217: 'The spatial metaphor thus suggests a "deconstruction" of time through space, in the sense that temporal succession is nullified thanks to the point of view that is located in a space outside the river of time itself.'

28 Wilcomirski, *Fragments*, p.4.

29 I have discussed the nature of narrative in 'Paul Ricoeur, Hayden White, and Holocaust Historiography' in *Metageschichte: Hayden White und Paul Ricoeur*, ed. Jörn Stückrath and Jürg Zbinden, Baden-Baden: Nomos Verlagsgesellschaft, 1997, pp.254–74.

30 Anne Karpf, 'Child of the Shoah', *The Guardian*, 11 February 1998, G2, p.6.

31 Primo Levi, *The Drowned and the Saved*, London: Abacus, 1989, p.97.

32 Agamben, *Infancy and History*, pp.104–05.

33 Saul Friedländer, 'The Shoah Between Memory and History', *Jewish Quarterly*, 37, 1990, p.11.

34 Nicolas Weill and Annette Wieviorka, 'La construction de la mémoire de la Shoah: les cas français et israéliens', in *Les cahiers de la Shoah*, ed. André Kaspi, Paris: Liana Levi, 1994, p.164.

35 Ruth Klüger, *Weiter leben: Eine Jugend*, Munich: Deutscher Taschenbuch Verlag, 1995, p.77.

36 *Ibid.*, p.75.

37 *Ibid.*, p.78.

38 Saul Friedländer, *When Memory Comes*, trans. Helen R. Lane, New York: The Noonday Press, 1991.

39 Georges Perec, *W, or the Memory of Childhood*, trans. David Bellos, London: The

Harvill Press, 1996.

40 See Hannah Arendt, 'The Concept of History' in *Between Past and Future*, Harmondsworth, Penguin, 1977, pp.41–90. See also Jean-Luc Nancy, 'Finite History', in *The Birth to Presence*, Stanford: Stanford University Press, 1993, p.146; and especially *idem*, 'Un Souffle', in *Shoah: Formen der Erinnerung. Geschichte, Philosophie, Literatur, Kunst*, eds Nicolas Berg, Jens Joachimsen and Bernd Stiegler, Munich: Wilhelm Fink Verlag, 1996, pp.122–29, for the idea that the Holocaust resists historical time.

41 Daniel Ganzfried. 'Die geliehene Holocaust-Biographie – The Purloined Holocaust Biography', *Die Weltwoche*, 27 August 1998. Available online at http://www.stoppedtherapy.com.

42 Pamela Ballinger, 'The Culture of Survivors: Post-Traumatic Stress Disorder and Traumatic Memory', *History & Memory*, Vol.10, No.1, 1998, pp.117 and 122. See also Mark Prendergast, 'Recovered Memories and the Holocaust', http://www.stoppedtherapy.com.

43 William Langley and Nick Fielding, 'The Victim Who Never Was', *The Mail on Sunday*, 18 October 1998, pp.30–31. The Ganzfried quotation also comes from this article. See also now Elena Lappin, 'The Man with Two Heads', *Granta*, 66, Summer 1999, pp.8–65, and Philip Gourevitch, 'The Memory Thief', *The New Yorker*, LXXV, 15, 14 June 1999, pp.48–68.

44 Zoë Waxman of St Antony's College, Oxford, is currently undertaking work along these lines.

CHAPTER 12

Open Behind: Myth and Politics

CHARLES TURNER

... every culture that has lost myth has lost, by the same token, its natural, healthy creativity. Only a horizon ringed about by myths can unify a culture. The forces of imagination and of Appollonian dream are saved only by myth from indiscriminate rambling. Nor does the commonwealth know any more potent unwritten law than the mythic foundation which guarantees its union with religion and its basis in mythic conceptions. Over against this, let us consider abstract man stripped of myth, abstract education, abstract mores, abstract law, abstract government; the random vagaries of the artistic imagination unchanneled by myth; a culture without any fixed or consecrated origin, condemned to exhaust all possibilities and feed miserably and parasitically on every culture under the sun. Here we have our present age, the result of Socratism bent on the extermination of myth. Man today, stripped of myth, stands famished among all his pasts and must dig frantically for roots, be it among the most remote antiquities. Let us ask ourselves whether our feverish and frightening agitation is anything but the greedy grasping for food of a hungry man. And who would care to offer further nourishment to a culture which, no matter how much it consumes, remains insatiable and which converts the strongest and most wholesome food into 'history' and 'criticism'. *Friedrich Nietzsche*[1]

The ego of antiquity and its consciousness of itself were different from our own, less exclusive, less sharply defined. It was, as it were, open behind; it received much from the past and by repeating it gave it presentness again. The Spanish scholar Ortega y Gasset puts it that the man of antiquity, before he did anything, took a step backwards, like the bullfighter who leaps back to deliver the mortal thrust. He searched the past for a pattern into which he might slip as into a diving-bell, and being thus at once disguised and protected might rush upon his present problem.   *Thomas Mann*[2]

Introduction

However heroically they seek to escape them, social theorists are inevitably burdened by the concerns of the present. The expressions 'after the Holocaust' or 'after Auschwitz' make such a pragmatic context plain, implying that a single historical event might be of sufficient magnitude to define the terms of whatever social theory follows it. They suggest that the Holocaust not only cost millions of lives but may have put paid to some of the basic elements of the self-under-standing of modern man. Be that as it may, there is little agreement over whether the Holocaust can be seen as a definitive break, and if it was, over what ways of thinking are now no longer possible or desirable. The principal disagreement here is one between those who perceive in the Holocaust the realisation of mod-ernity's ownmost bureaucratic possibilities, culminating in the classification and sub-classification of populations, meticulously organised timetables of the transports, and ethical displacment;[3] and those for whom it is the product of a pre-modern irrationalism secreted with the political culture of early twentieth-century Europe, a corrosive but eliminable residue.[4] The social philosophies of post-modernism and modernism are two broadly conceived responses to these diagnoses, the one advocating forms of non-contractual ethics or resolutely anti-bureaucratic forms of life, the other maintaining a faith in forms of institutional and ethical life whose contours were defined before World War II and whose consolidation after it will prevent the repetition of Holocaust-like events in the future.[5] Rather than enter into the debate about whether the Holocaust was the culmination of or an aberration within 'modernity', here I consider one possible response to the idea that we inhabit a post-Holocaust universe.

The expression 'post-Holocaust universe' refers less to a world in which the Holocaust's shadow is cast uniformly over subsequent theorising, than to one in which the Holocaust is part of a field of problems to which it bears a family resemblance, a resemblance which allows it to resonate with current ethical and political concerns. Contemporary humanity is faced with a set of problems which confer upon the Holocaust a broader significance than that of being the most extreme instance of human cruelty, or the unavoidable background reference in searches for universal ethical principles. I call the most important of these 'the problem of the destruction of humanity in a post-historical age'. This expression refers to three related claims: firstly, that the Holocaust destroyed 'humanity' as an ethical ideal; secondly, that modern societies have provided themselves with the means of making life on earth unsustainable, not merely through nuclear weapons but in the persistent and daily harm done to the conditions of human existence; thirdly, that 'history', as something to be made by human beings or as something whose direction and purpose might be fathomed, has become largely irrelevant to the conduct of political affairs in the Western democracies.

'Humanity' refers here not to a Kantian standard of universal ethical obligation but to a Herderian conception of humanity as consisting of the various peoples of the earth. In these terms, the Holocaust was a crime against humanity because it sought to deprive one of humanity's constitutent groups of the right ever to inabit the earth in the future. Today, the possibility of an unsustainable earth has become a danger common to all, has removed from all human groups the right to expect that future generations will exist, and turned the existence of those future generations into our current responsibility. Finally, when such circumstance is taken seriously there can be no place for a philosophy of history premised upon the promise of future fulfilment, and only limited space for the milder versions of social hope and notions of human happiness suggested by contemporary pragmatism. When the idea of a post-Holocaust universe is taken seriously, then, the problem of securing human existence in the face of its potential annihilation can take precedence over the provision of arrangements for more desirable types of society. When this precedence is granted, the anthropological problematic of *man and world* becomes as pressing a problem for social theory as that of *man and society*.

It is for these reasons that the following essay considers the relationship between mythic modes of world orientation and political culture. At first blush this appears a bold, not to say rash move, one not readily endorsed even by the most convinced anti-Enlightenment thinkers.[6] Indeed, the scope for an active promotion of mythic modes of world orientation within modern democratic/ rationalised societies and polities is limited by the suspicion that it expresses a nostalgic yearning for a lost cultural unity or the aggressive assertion of particularistic loyalties. When myth is discussed at all in relation to politics, it is as part of the study of ancient pantheons or primitive conceptions of sovereignty.[7]

To the modern mind the dangers of myth are obvious: it is easily mobilised by nationalist political parties; it implies a conception of time and space which is at odds with that which governs modern politics and history; and the mythic construal of political events and processes reifies them. Moreover, the 'scope' of myth and that of politics are discrepant. Myth is a mode of world-perception and world-orientation; politics is a way of acting or existing within a determinate domain with a distinct regional ontology. On this basis there is a distinction between a properly political conception of 'real' politics and various extraneous (culturalist) conceptions of which 'mythic' interpretations are an example.[8] The modern age is one of absolutist politics in which politics has carved out its own domain,[9] so that 'politics' means constitutional devices, policy regimes, security services and welfare institutions, and the conflicts which arise over their direction and control. If Ernst Cassirer is correct that after Machiavelli, 'the political world stands alone – in an empty space',[10] then to construe it in terms of Nietzsche's unwritten, meaning-generating laws is an attempt to re-enchant it. While it is true that the theorisation of sovereignty has been larded with mythical images, not least that of the biblical sea monster Leviathan, in the modern state the idea of meaning generation lives on only as the problem of legitimacy, a legitimacy which is a question of contingent claim and counter-claim, not prescription. To be sure, the abstract man whose emergence Nietzsche lamented lacks the resources to construe the world's meaning from within his own breast, and so looks for answers outside himself. But there, where mythic symbolism once was, he will find a thriving market for secular gods and demons, competing for the title of the only point of view from which the world could be justified and explained. Or as Weber put it, referring ironically to a world in which myth was once comprehensible: 'If one begins with experience, one ends not with one god but with polytheism'.[11]

Because in the modern world of distinct value spheres the referent of mythical modes of addressing the world is both broader and narrower than that of politics – questions of meaning generation are dealt with 'subsystemically' yet imply claims of general validity – this basic discrepancy produces explosive effects when the attempt is made to bring them into conjunction. This appears only too readily confirmed by the use which National Socialism made of myth. Myth becomes the myth of a community or people, a particularist foundation for politics in an age in which modern states strive to embody universalist principles. Moreover, the community which opens itself to myth is always tempted to close itself to a culture of interpretation which would produce an extended argument about what the community's highest values were.[12] A polity grounded in myth will tell a story of its origins detailed enough to encourage a modicum of historical research but not so detailed that it might lead to extensive scholarly debate or discussion. It will seek to avoid the danger of interpretative variation and public argument through the institutionalisation of repetitious and celebratory rituals.

Our reluctance to countenance a mythic understanding of politics, then, results largely from what we know about myth's relationship to time and space and about the abuses which have followed its popular embrace. Myth is unapologetically particularistic and communitarian; it lives and dies with its appeal to a past golden age, and with the denial or abolition of historical time through repetitious practices which make present an originating act. Not even the most committed communitarian would buttress a disdain for liberal rationalist universalism with a theory of myth.

Myth and the Human Future

Despite these well-known fears, three reasons might be suggested for a tentative affirmation of the mythic sensibility and of the mythico-poetic rendering of political events and processes, not least because of the number of broadly 'liberal' twentieth-century thinkers who have endorsed them. Firstly, as Hans Jonas has put it, we live in an age of untrammelled Baconianism, which threatens either an unsustainable earth or unprecedented experiments with the human-nonhuman threshold. In such circumstances, 'the starry-eyed ethics of perfectibility has to give way to the sterner one of repsonsibility'.[13] In accordance with such an ethics, a philosophical anthropology based on human *vulnerability* may be more adequate to our times than one based on the immodesty and presumption of hope, even the pared-down versions of hope sponsored by writers such as Rorty. The category of 'fear' which would have to be mobilised here would be different from the Hobbesian fear of immediate aggression from others or of the more sophisticated forms of 'cruelty' of which Rorty has written.[14] It would be future-oriented and require cultivation. As Jonas has it:

> The fear in question... cannot be, as in Hobbes, of the 'pathological' sort, ... but rather a spiritual sort of fear which is, in a sense, the work of our own deliberate attitude. Such an attitude must be cultivated; we must educate our soul to a willingness to let itself be affected by the mere thought of possible fortunes and calamities of future generations...[15]

Secondly, since nation states are loosening their claims on their members' sense of obligation, and as the idea of politics as a bounded domain or empty space or autonomous subsystem appears increasingly implausible, a theory of politics must increasingly seek to address the more deterritorialised and hybrid forms of awareness which these institutional changes bring about. In a Europe, moreover, whose political institutions are grounded in none of the political traditions of the European nation states, it might be appropriate to ask whether such modes of awareness might provide the resources through which the future citizens of Europe might see themselves belonging to a community which is more than a free trade or low inflation zone, and make sense of the need to be on the move between shifting, uncertain, and transformable identities.

Thirdly, the idea that mythic renderings of major political processes reifies them now belongs to a bygone age of ideology critique. There are ways in which myth and the pursuit of truth are not antithetical but allies. Both, for instance,

239

may be contrasted with the gnostic claim to know better which has informed this century's totalitarian movements.[16] Both the mythic imagination and critical rationality may contribute to the strength of liberal political cultures at the end of the twentieth century, myth through its openness to reinterpretation, the pursuit of truth through the institutionalised provisionality of scientific knowledge.[17]

The attempt to grasp the modern predicament through recourse to myth is not new. In the years immediately after World War II a range of thinkers accounted for the collapse of European civilisation either in mythic terms or in terms of myth's misappropriation.[18] Despite their differences, these authors shared a disdain for what Karl Löwith identified as the secularised eschatology which grounded modern ideologies of progress. Each assumed that the relationship of mutual entailment between rationality, freedom, and the making of history had come to an end, not least because of the bleak truth about the Soviet Union. Each sought to explore forms of consciousness and awareness, and modes of social and political comportment, which were not based upon the assumption of such entailment. Some sought to define the contours of a post-historical world and post-historical way of living, one in which making history will no longer be the most elevated thing a human being could do. Others confronted more explicitly the nature of non-historical, mythic consciousness, and in particular its time-defying or time-arresting quality. Still others explored the unexpected ways in which the claims to rationality made on behalf of the modern world and modern politics are haunted, through a dialectical reversal, by mythic residues or survivals.

These European intellectuals came to believe that the only vision which Europe was capable of bearing without tearing itself and the rest of the world apart was one which renounced the question of a desirable or better future for humanity, and which accordingly renounced attempts to shape that future in accordance with the idea of a certain type of human being. A Europe with a future would be one whose citizens would be attracted neither by the prospect of making history nor by explanations of its direction and destiny. Three years after the end of World War II Mircea Eliade could write that:

> ... it is not inadmissible to think of an epoch, and an epoch not too far distant, when humanity, to ensure its survival, will find itself reduced to desisting from any further making of history...will confine itself to repeating prescribed archetypal gestures, and will strive to forget, as meaningless and dangerous, any spontaneous gesture which might entail 'historical' consequences.[19]

As post-war Europe settled down to three decades or more of growth, welfare and full employment, this pared-down vision of a human future appeared to be more a form of counter-Enlightenment cultural despair than a serious confrontation with reality. The cold war, moreover, pitted against one another competing versions of the good society, different visions of a viable human future which were to be realised by forms of action having historical consequences. While the threat of nuclear annihilation hung over them, neither party assumed that the other had no right to inhabit the earth, so that such annihilation was merely a contingent possibility in a struggle whose logic was one of ways of living under conditions which were assumed to be sustainable. Both sides sought to harness the capacities of their members for action which would result in the greater happiness, welfare and comfort of future generations. The contest, in short, was one between a civilisation which purported to have solved the riddle of history and one which continued to take the riddle seriously. Any talk of 'post-history' was part of an aristocratic-conservative mantra. Today, however, in the post-cold war world, the idea has gained a new audience.[20]

The thrust of this chapter is to suggest that once 'history' as a process with a meaning or as a product which can be 'made' is abandoned, once the elements of the neologism 'world history' are separated,[21] post-historical human beings are confronted more directly with the problem which the philosophy of history avoided: how to sustain a position in the world. 'Making history' and harnessing it to human purposes, is a late, contingent achievement of modern man.[22] It is not negligible, but in the face of the possibility that there will be no future generations to benefit from our current history-shaping activity, it must now make space for a conception of man and world which addresses the basic achievement of overcoming a defining insecurity. If the question which hung over Max Weber's future was 'not will human beings be happy but how will they be?',[23] one of the questions which hangs over our future is 'will there be human beings?'[24]

One form which social theorising based upon fear might take is not only the provision of strategies for avoiding ecological catastrophe or theorisation of the risk society, but the integration within social theory of mythic modes of imagining the human-world relation, and a concomitant rethinking of the nature of political culture in a world in which the problem of 'security' is not that of the territorially conceived state in its relationship with its enemies, or an original danger giving rise to an original contract, but that of the annihilation of future generations as a result of present folly. In these circumstances, the central question for social theorising would be that of the devices through which human beings give themselves a world which is habitable. The question of how such devices work is a question of political culture because it is a question of the self-assertion and ultimately constitution of man, the product of the human effort to make an *environment* out of a *world*. This does not and cannot imply a seismic shift from an age dominated by 'history' and 'progress' to one in which cosmological orientation is once again possible, from human striving and shaping to a passive retreat into archetypal forms of identification. The legacy of historical modes of awareness is too powerful for that, the label 'progressive' still a badge of honour, and even as resolutely an anti-historicist thinker as Nietzsche was never able to produce convincing evidence in favour of his 'innocent cosmic child'.[25] What is more plausible, and accords with the dilemmas confronting Western societies, is, as Jonas has shown, a form of social theory which implies a distinctive temporal reorientation, in which the future is conceived of not as the fulfilment of current demands or possibilities but in terms of the potential disappearance of the possibility of possibility, while the past is seen less as the necessary labours on a road to fulfilment than as a repository of already-existing achievement. These distinctions have been theorised by Leszek Kolakowski in terms of a primary distinction between *the consciousness of a creditor* and the *consciousness of indebtedness*. While the former may give rise to conceptions of a future which is expected to fulfil present claims and meet as-yet-unsatisfied demands, the latter may create 'a reciprocal bond of actual assistance among participants in the debt'.[26] Such a reciprocal bond between participants in indebtedness – not guilt! – is the basis of mythic awareness as Kolakowski defines it. It seems to me that a social theory appropriate to a post-Holocaust universe would be one whose conception of historical time fostered such consciousness, for it would then be equipped to avoid the contempt for the past which is shared by all philosophies of history premised upon ultimate fulfilment. The hope for a better world, any better world than the present, moreover, forfeits its claim to universality in the very act of being expressed, an observation which applies to Rortyan pragmatism as much as to messianic versions of Marxism. For the upshot of all theories of progress is that the lives and deeds of our predecessors were provisional, a preparation for something else. That this implies that we too are the accidental beneficiaries of what happens to have been achieved up to now does not prevent us from believing that we confront past and future as creditors, and that we are able to demand of the future that it be an improvement on the present. By contrast, a mythical consciousness fosters a reciprocal bond among participants in indebtedness, the reciprocity extending across generations as well as across contemporaries.[27] Such reciprocity is the foundation of a community of the living, the dead, and the not yet born.

Human Insecurity and the Work of Myth

To this point I have used the terms 'vulnerability' and 'fear' as though they were a contingent feature of our current predicament, and implied that the grounds for optimism which might once have been an appropriate ingredient of social theory have been removed by events of which the Holocaust is the starkest example. In such a scenario, the consciousness of creditors would then 'yield' to that of debtors. But it is important to be clear that the grounds for such consciousness have been theorised in terms in which questions of historical appropriateness were irrelevant. Such grounds were formulated in the 1920s and 1930s by Helmuth Plessner and Arnold Gehlen, for whom the uniqueness of the human being consists in its eccentricity, in the risk and insecurity which follows from having no natural environment. The human being is unique in being not established in the world, in lacking a biologically given environment. It is destined to be 'world-open': '*Der Mensch hat eine Welt, aber keine Umwelt*' [Man has a world but no environment]. It occupies a field of surprises while lacking the instinctual apparatus with which other beings respond to such surprises. This establishes the basic anthropological problematic, the intrinsic vulnerability of the human being, the questionable character of our capacity for existence, the attendant burden of world-openness, and the primary human task of relieving that burden. Out of the insecurity of world-openness the human being creates the higher functions which enable him to create a *distance* towards an otherwise importunate world, and to relieve himself of the otherwise overwhelming burden of decision. In the 1950s Gehlen theorised the function and meaning of *social institutions* in these terms – the raison d'être of all institutional life is relief from the burden of decision-making which their eccentricity imposes on human beings. In a modern society of growing complexity, which threatens to throw the burden of decision-making back on individuals, the relief provided by institutions was to be more highly valued than the freedom for discontinuous acts of self-creation or self-transformation.

In Gehlen's hands, the conceptual apparatus of philosophical anthropology – eccentricity, biological insecurity, world-openness, absence of environment – was mobilised in support of a conservative theory of institutions, particularly after World War II in his account of cultural crystallisation. The problem of man and world with which this body of work set out resolved itself into a theory of man and society founded upon the rejection of utopian hopes and most forms of social engineering. Its principles helped ground Jonas' philosophy of the future in *The Principle of Responsibility*. But I refer to it here because in 1979, alongside the work of Freud,[28] it formed the basis for Hans Blumenberg's *Work on Myth*.

Rather than addressing a set of institutional organisations or arrangements, as Gehlen had done, Blumenberg fastens on myth. Just as institutions for Gehlen are complexity-reducing devices which relieve us of the burden of decision-making, so myth is formulated as that which performs a distance-creating function for a being who needs to overcome an importunate, immediate reality. Whatever the origin or content of myth might be, it meets a basic anthropological need – it relieves human beings of a burden described simply as 'the absolutism of reality' which, were it allowed to triumph, would impose upon human beings an intolerable decision-making burden: 'What it means is that man came close to not having control of the conditions of his existence and, what is more important, believed that he simply lacked control of them.'[29]

It is this, beyond any mythical content, which confers upon myth the status of something more than a pre-conceptual, image-based form of world orientation destined to give way to or develop into *Logos*. What ensures that myth will survive all demythologisations, and explains what Blumenberg takes to be the persistence of myth as a form of orientation even for those who took modernity to be an emancipatory project in which human beings might shape their own future, is its rootedness in a fundamental human experience of vulnerability. Moreover, myth is not an explanation of this vulnerability or an answer to a question which might be placed on the same level as the questions asked by science, which the enlightenment critique of myth insists that it must be. The 'grotesque effort at rationalisation'[30] which was Lévi-Strauss' account of myth as primitive logic misses the point that myth is not an explanation of the world but an opening towards it which at the same time contributes to the overcoming of the danger which such opening presents.

What Blumenberg calls the work of myth transforms the unnameable into the named, raises that which generates anxiety into the realm of the familiar, and through its form-shaping power produces, by means of narration, stories. These stories in turn generate and sustain a distinction between the significant and the insignificant. Growing out of a fear of power, this creation of significance is an overcoming of the world's indifference and a taming of power, in the case of classical myth the taming of power by the naming of individual powers and playing them off against one another – a case not so much of divide and rule as divide and avoid being overwhelmed by the power of a single God. In this way, the uncanniness of the world is diffused by being distributed.

> [In] the interpretation of the institutions, practices, and rituals [themselves the result of the earlier practice of naming, which made it possible to be addressed] the power that they are directed at becomes entangled in a story, which naturally is the story of the greater possibility, at least occasionally, of getting along with it. *Every story gives an Achilles heel to sheer power.*[31]

Stories are told in order to kill something, says Blumenberg, and while for Eliade or Lévi-Strauss or even Kolakowski they exist in order to kill time – which is the source of our hesitation, our fear of reification whenever we seek to render the political world and political events through mythic speech – they also kill fear.

> Terror [*Entsetzen*], for which there are few equivalents in other languages, becomes 'nameless' at the highest level of fright. So the earliest and not the least reliable form of familiarity with the world is to find names for what is undefined.[32]

What Blumenberg reminds us of is the fact that myth, rather than being something to be overcome by *Logos*, is 'already an overcoming, the gaining of a distance, a moderation of bitter earnestness'.[33] Though this moderation is never definitively achieved, the myths and narratives which have been handed down to us have survived, and the reason for this survival is not our persistent self-imposed immaturity or a permanent receptiveness to archetypes, but the fact that 'they convince us again and again that they are useful material for grasping *how matters stand with human existence*'.[34] Thus, for instance, when seeking to conceptualise the problem of environmental destruction or biotechnology, or current threats to the human/nonhuman threshold, anyone seeking to grasp the relationship between man and world has available to them a set of non-conceptual images contained, for instance, in the Prometheus and Faust stories and their numerous subsequent variations. Indeed, the last three hundred pages of *Work on Myth* are given over to an account of the variations and uses to which the Prometheus myth has been put, particularly in the nineteenth century, a century which, according to Blumenberg's exaggerated formulation, 'understood itself in terms of the Titan'. How could one, he implies, in any discussion of, say, the current capacity to manipulate the human-nonhuman threshold, or the future of energy sources, avoid referring to those images of secondary intra-human creation made available in the Prometheus material or in the section on the homunculus in *Faust* Part II? Why should Mary Shelley bother to subtitle *Frankenstein* 'The Modern Prometheus'? Why indeed should Marx have identified himself so closely with Prometheus?[35] The answer is that the myths of the European tradition are inexhaustible, open to reworking, even as they draw upon a basic original material, and are so not because of their content or because they are edifying or entertaining or decorative, but because they bear the memory of a response to a basic, ineliminable anthropological need, the need for security-through-distance-creation. This is why Roberto Calasso writes that 'every notion of progress is refuted by the existence of *The Iliad*'.[36]

But why concern ourselves with this today, in the context, moreover, of 'social theory after the Holocaust'? There are, I think, two reasons. Firstly, the

Holocaust, and the camps through which many who perished were processed, present us with a spectacle not of total institutionalisation, but of total institutional failure.[37] Alongside all the details of suffering and human cruelty which historians continue to document, the Holocaust, seen as a process whose roots may be interpreted if not explained, placed its victims, or intended victims, in a situation in which the reality in which they moved was as absolute and importunate as is imaginable, in which whatever devices they had available for putting that reality at a distance – what Paul Ricoeur has called simply 'primary symbolism'[38] – were taken away from them, and they were left to fend for themselves, to make decisions which it is the task and achievement of social institutions to enable us to avoid.[39] Secondly, after the three decades or more of institutional consolidation which followed World War II, it has become a staple element in the theorising of post-modernity to argue that contemporary social reality increasingly throws down the gauntlet of immediacy and challenges us to find new, non-institutional ways of putting the world at a distance. In such circumstances, the need for security, the overcoming of human vulnerability, calls for more creative and individualised solutions than those which provided the backdrop to most mainstream sociology of the post-war period.

It is the conviction of this author at least that there might be worse things for post-Enlightenment culture to do than to remind itself that myth, rightly understood, makes available a repertoire of narratives which remain part of the collective identity of European societies, and which may become more relevant to their self-understanding as the populations of those societies experience an increasing need to negotiate their way between identities which offer them only provisional and elusive sources of attachment.[40] I say 'rightly understood' because by myth we refer to a set of narrative or symbolic or interpretative devices shorn of their ties to cultic and ritual performance, and thus more – and less – than the verbal envelope for repetitious, imitative gesture.[41] Myth here is a story told rather than a reality lived.[42] Hence the continuing possibility of formulating the problems which confront contemporary human beings in their relationship with technology, bio-technology or genetically modified food in terms of the fundamental images of human presumption, triumph and failure set down in the stories of Faust or Prometheus.[43] Of the latter, Eric Voegelin once wrote that:

> the Promethean symbols of Shaftesbury or Goethe, of Shelley and Marx, belong to the age of enlightened, human self-reliance, of the titanism of the artist, and of the defiant revolutionary who will take the destiny of mankind into his own hands. All that has nothing to do with Aeschylus, but it has become an additional obstacle to understanding him in our time.[44]

This may be true. The point, however, is that the basic configuration of the Titan's relationship to the gods and to the world served such writers – who shaped the modern European mind – in their efforts to grasp the human condition in their time. In this sense, the story of Prometheus, or rather, the variations on it, is a European art myth which confirms the existence of a reservoir of pre-conceptual images from which conceptuality can continue to draw sustenance. It may be that myth today is merely a story told rather than a reality lived, but such stories as myth provides remain an indispensable resource in an age in which institutions are less and less able to perform the task of distantiation which writers like Gehlen once attributed to them, in which individuals are increasingly confronted with and reminded of the proximity of the human situation in their everyday lives.

Myth, Knowledge and Politics

Yet even if this is so, if myth is already, as Blumenberg puts it, 'a piece of high-carat *Logos*',[45] should it be grafted onto an understanding of mainstream political processes? Does the theorisation of basic man–world orientations have a bearing on man–society relationships? In the sense in which myth is intended here, it is tangential, say, to questions of whether a given polity is democratic or non-democratic. One way around this is to say that myth addresses 'the political' rather than politics, the self-constitution of man as a fundamental achievement. As Sheldon Wolin has it:

> The mythic understanding teaches that the establishment of the political brings protection and security that enables human practices to take hold and nurture life; from these practices...powers are generated that become the object of strategies of appropriation: politics is born.[46]

But the problem remains that in an age of territorial, Machiavellian, secular politics the problem of security became a matter of balances of powers between already existing entities, while the problem of the origin of polities became one of rational foundation. In an age in which politics is an empty space, and in which no purpose can be ascribed to the modern state,[47] 'myth' is an invasion of that space and the forced attribution of purpose, to the detriment of both myth and politics.

The problem of where to place myth in relation to politics is compounded by the absence of consensus on the broader relationship between knowledge, political power and society. How should myth be characterised as a 'style of thinking', in Karl Mannheim's terms? And once it is so characterised, how should it be assessed for its appropriateness to political processes? Not only is there no agreement on this question, the same style of thinking may be interpreted as both mythical and anti-mythical. Take Mannheim's essays of the 1920s on morphological and analytical thinking and their relationship with democracy, which remain one of the more sustained and badly neglected efforts to address this theme.

> Conservative thought is 'morphological'. It explains the world in terms of unanalysed and unanalysable given wholes in their unique Gestalt. As against this, liberal and progressive thought is analytical; it decomposes the seemingly monolithic entities of the traditional world view into functional elements... A social entity like a group or institution will appear to me as a static whole, a Gestalt, only if I am far enough removed from it, that is, from a distance. If I am part of the group myself, I can see from within both its internal divisions and the mechanism that makes it run... democratisation entails a shift from the morphological to the analytical outlook.[48]

In an increasingly complex and differentiated society, in which radically different collective actors found themselves side by side on the political stage, there could be no place for the morphological outlook, which would entail both a blindness to the diversity of styles of thinking to which only the analytic mind was able to do justice, and an attempt to restrict the range of stories a society might tell itself about itself. The terms Mannheim used to describe the conservative and radical morphologies were, of course, 'ideology' and 'utopia'. Any attempt to mobilise a morphological style of thought within the political sphere, and with it 'political myth', was either ideological or utopian.

However, this association of morphological thinking and myth did not prevent Mannheim himself being accused by Adorno of effectively mythifying social and political relations. Mannheim's sociology of knowledge, in its purported sensitivity to the dangers of political myth, was a prime example of a *classificatory* approach to the social world, in which social, political and intellectual phenomena were categorised and pigeon-holed in such a way that social thought became akin to natural history, 'an evening out of the contradictions of the whole'.[49] For Adorno, the classification and subclassification of the social world renders that world in static categories; such classification is an index of how far the Enlightenment promise of emancipatory rationality has congealed into the positivist mastery of nature; and because this mastery expresses nothing more than self-preservation, 'positivism is mythic fear turned radical'. In other words, for Adorno, a mythic orientation to the world is consistent with an epistemology in which the social world is divided into classes and subclasses and any emancipatory human promise denied. The perversion of political culture and social passivity which results is exemplified by a culture industry which creates identities through an increasingly refined classification of consumers – 'something is provided for everyone so that none may escape'.[50] In similar vein Roland Barthes would later write that 'the world enters language as a dialectical relation between activities...; it comes out of myth as a harmonious display of essences'.[51]

One cannot help concluding, however, that Adorno and Horkheimer's account of enlightenment and myth was a conscious attempt to deny that myth, and in particular mythic narration, might represent a way of construing the world which, far from being a shorthand way of characterising classificatory logic, called it into question. The reason for this wilful neglect is no doubt that myth's challenge to classificatory logic, or analytic thought, is more radical and exuberant than dialectics could ever achieve. Here, for instance, is Ernst Cassirer, a neo-Kantian ultimately hostile to anti-classificatory rhetoric, on the epistemological status of myth:

Life is not divided into classes and sub-classes. It is felt as an unbroken continuous whole which does not admit of any clean-cut and trenchant distinctions. The limits between the different spheres are not insurmountable barriers; they are fluent and fluctuating. There is no specific difference between the various realms of life... By a sudden metamorphosis everything can be turned into everything. If there is any characteristic and outstanding feature of the mythical world, any law by which it is governed – it is this law of metamorphosis.[52]

For classical scholars and anthropologists alike Cassirer was clearly wrong, the attribution of the law of metamorphosis to myth part of the *'Mythos* to *Logos'* story which vitiated the initial claims of *The Philosophy of Symbolic Forms*. And yet, as the final section will recall, literary critics have little hesitation in using the term 'mythopoeia' to describe the work of modernist 'anti-fascist' writers whose narrative techniques subscribe with relish to the law of metamorphosis.

Europe and the Nation State

I said above that the relationship between myth and politics under modern conditions is a discrepant one between a mode of world-perception and a mode of action, and that attempts to construe the latter in terms of the former risk aestheticising political life and fostering particularistic loyalties. In a Europe in which the claims of loyalty made upon citizens by nation states are weakening, the individual's involvements in democratic states based upon universal principles are threatened by alternative identities and the cultural entrepeneurs who promote them.[53] In this situation, one pressing question is that of whether 'Europe' can attain to the status of a community capable of eliciting obligations from its members, and if so, whether the grounds of that community meet universalist criteria.

A discussion of the relationship between mythical, monotheistic/Christian, and formal-rational groundings of community in modern European polities is beyond the scope of this paper, save to note that 'the modern European mind' is less a mind subject to Foucauldian epistemic mutations or Kuhnian paradigm shifts than the result of classical, Judeo-Christian, and rational-scientific influences and pressures.

> The modern mind is not single-minded: it eliminates from its progressive outlook the Christian implication of creation and consummation, while it assimilates from the ancient world view the circular idea of an endless structure. The modern mind has not made up its mind whether it should be Christian or pagan.[54]

Even Löwith's statement here – the 'Jerusalem or Athens?' problematic[55] – is a simplification of the truth, as readers of Max Weber's research programme at the end of *The Protestant Ethic* will recall.[56] Be that as it may, it is notable how today's theorisation of a 'European community' brings with it a neglect of this complexity, and a concomitant search for *symbols of order*. Löwith himself invoked renaissance humanism as 'the one spirit of European humanity'.[57] Anti-modern writers from Novalis to Max Scheler and T.S. Eliot theorised 'Europe' as a Christian community which would contest the bankrupt modern spirit.[58] And Jürgen Habermas has adapted his discourse ethics to the cause of a European constitution.

Scheler's invocation of universal solidarity based on Christian love, in particular, appears to meet the kind of demands laid down by Jonas' anti-Baconian principle of responsibility adumbrated above, and to offer a vision of a community which is not married to determinate political or administrative organs yet which is capable of generating binding symbols of order. The responsibility of members of a Christian European community would be *co-responsibility in guilt*, and they would subscribe to 'the closely associated principle that every individual and subdivision of society shall within a given circle be as much an independent and legitimate authority in its own original right, as it is a free servant of the wider community'.[59]

But this vision, accepted substantially by many Catholic politicians in the European union, is clearly inadequate to the tasks implied by the definition of a post-Holocaust universe sketched above. Firstly, it cannot conceive of the existence of substantial non-Christian communities within the community it defines. Secondly, it provides for the pluralism of what would otherwise be a homogeneous if expanded cultural vision by reference to the principle of subsidiarity in which non-state groups are conceived of as formal organisations, regions and the like. While the Catholic-Christian vision of Europe recognises, in a way in which Habermasian/Protestant appeals to European constitutional arrangements cannot, the need for a *symbolic referent for European identity formation*, it fails to address two problems at the heart of current European cultural identity – the advance of bio-technologies to the limit of the human-non-human threshold and the damage to the environment to the point of its possible destruction and with it the destruction of the human species; and the development of European societies themselves to the point where the institutional forms of belonging upon which the principle of subsidiarity rests are increasingly intersected by forms of identification and group belonging which are at once more and less stable, more and less permanent, than those for which formal organisations and local authorities can provide.

While Scheler's vision of Christian love plus subsidiarity acknowledges the need for a symbolic referent for European identity but finds it in a particularist criterion, Habermas's vision of a European constitution neglects the need for any such symbolic referent.[60] Each sees local particularity as a matter of interest and organisation rather than identity and network. Yet given the inevitable need for the articulation of a European consciousness, and the need to address cultural plurality, not to say hybridity, the exploration of the mythic sensibility might not be the worst way of grounding European identity. By this I do not mean that Europe needs a defining myth in the way in which it might need a constitution, but that in searching for the grounds of a common European identity, an identity which, moreover, might be open to the cultural plurality and diversity in which modern/post-modern human beings have to get about, one might do worse than draw upon the mythic resources which have sustained European literature. These continue to manifest themselves in the modern novel, which since Rabelais and Cervantes has sustained European consciousness as much as contract law, double-entry bookkeeping, human rights or modern science. Indeed, Milan Kundera has recently argued that the 'culture of excess' which now permeates much of the non-European 'novel of the south' is an extension of the European novel and a return to its early modern Rabelaisian exuberance.[61] It is in the European novel which exhibits the narrative freedom to apply the law of metamorphosis that contemporary Europeans might see reflected some of their own need to live in a world of plural identities, overlapping loyalties, diverse forms of authority and transformations of identity. The European novel in its late medieval-cum-new Southern form enacts the kind of epistemological, political and private freedoms which the champions of particularistic loyalties, ethnic belonging and religious orthodoxy would seek to suppress.

It should be obvious that there is no more reason to associate mythic modes of awareness with territorially defined states or with particular ethnic groups than with looser, more flexible forms of belonging. Many commentators, however, are fond of referring to a nation's 'founding myths', as the irrational sources of national self-assertion. As was said above, modern theories of sovereignty have made use of mythological material, while writers as different as Lévi-Strauss and Sheldon Wolin have referred to the founding myths of modern republicanism.[62] The 'sovereignty' of ancient states was inseparable from mythical stories about founding acts, original dramas of creation in which God and King were one.[63]

Yet in the case of both the founding myths of modern ethnic nationalism and those of modern republicanism, we deal with stories which belong to a *historical*, rather than a genuinely mythological, universe of discourse. The founding acts which defined modern France or the United States are historically locatable, and the claims made for the older events which define the parameters of ethnic belonging are themselves pieces of contentious history, no less open to historical research and argument than any other. Moreover, in the case of ethnic nationalism, the narration of the national story often takes the form of poetry, a national epic. Such epics, with their linguistic specificity and restricted range of cultural reference, can be contrasted with the scope and intention of the mythical material which makes up the European tradition. As Paul Ricoeur, himself an advocate of the critical appropriation of myth, writes:

> The horizon of any genuine myth always exceeds the political and geographical boundaries of a specific national or tribal community. Even if we may say that mythical structures founded political institutions, they always go beyond the territorial limitations imposed by politics. Nothing travels more extensively and effectively than myth.[64]

What is true here of myth is still true of the European novel.

Myth and the Representation of Political Reality

Finally, and here we return to the theme of social theory after the Holocaust, if myth places an importunate reality at a distance, and obeys the law of metamorphosis rather than classification, would it be the worst way in which to render, to transform, the most terrifying political events of the century? What, after all, has come closer to total institutional failure, to an absolutised reality, to unrelenting immediacy, than the death camps? Admittedly, the mythicisation of the Holocaust is a move few are willing to endorse, and the whiff of 'bitter earnestness' is never far from discussions of how to represent it. A mythical representation, with a few superhuman creatures thrown in, a few reversals of time, speedings up and slowings down, impossible happenings, fabulous creatures, and jokes, to many may seem inappropriate, tasteless, a tampering with the boundaries of things. Yet for all the respect granted Primo Levi's accounts, for all the unsurpassable realism of Borowski, in 1989 the Holocaust did finally receive its mythical treatment, did find its Günter Grass, its Marquez, its Salman Rushdie. Following Martin Amis' brave and convincing experiment with temporal reversal in *Time's Arrow*, which itself employed Promethean motifs to suggest a world in which the SS's task is to fashion human beings out of mud, slime and ashes,[65] David Grossman's *See Under: Love* appeared as an even more audacious piece of mythologisation.[66] In fact, it is a mythologisation of the mythic function, its longest chapter being devoted to the relationship between the concentration camp commandant Neigel, and Anshel Wasserman, the Warsaw writer who before the war published children's stories, stories which the commandant had himself read and loved in his youth. Wasserman's plight is presented by Grossman not as that of one damned by the selections, but as that of one who wishes to be selected, who cannot bear continuing to live and having to witness day in day out the slaughter of his people. He thus persuades the commandant to shoot him. Yet when the commandant fires, the execution fails, the bullet passing clean through Wasserman's head. He demands that the commandant try again, and the commandant agrees, but only on one condition: that Wasserman tell him more stories of the sort he loved as a boy. And so begins a relationship which, founded on the exchange of stories for the possibility of death, draws upon and inverts the story of Scheherezade and *The Thousand and One Nights*, with the twist that however hard he tries, however fantastic the tales he tells, however often the commandant fires the revolver as his 'reward', the bullet continues to pass through Wasserman's body and shatter the window behind him. The stories grow more fantastic, more impossible, the location shifts suddenly from a mine in the Ukraine to Warsaw Zoo, and a struggle ensues as Neigel's sense of classificatory and sub-classificatory logic confronts the force of Wasserman's imagination, with its proliferation of images, and suddenly emerging, disappearing, and metamorphosed characters. Grossman's novel is not merely a triumph of storytelling, but a staged confrontation between the possibilities of narration and power's Achilles heel, between a mode of world-perception based upon the instability and fluidity of forms and one based upon the division of the world into rigid classes and subclasses. Between, in short, the synthetic/non-conceptual and the analytic-conceptual.

Conclusion

The interpretation and re-interpretation of mythical narratives are among the devices by which a culture perpetually varies its relationship to an achievement which each interpretation acknowledges – the putting at a distance of absolute reality, the diminishing of sheer power, what Faulkner liked to call the capacity to endure.[67] If, despite what has been said above about the possible annihilation of humanity in an unsustainable environment, there is a triumphant character to European modernity, then it consists not only in the scientific breakthroughs of the seventeenth century or the link between criticism and the growth of knowledge, but in the institutionalisation of cultures of interpretation. To the extent that the major European myths continue to be the object of such interpretation, and survive not through being scripture but through being worked on, then mythic modes of narration, though they be stories told rather than realities lived, are participants in that triumph because they sustain the very culture which supports them. The triumph of European modernity would then be a triumph not over myth but over gnosticism, over those visions of the future which at once claim acquaintance with history's *Logos*, and which suppress the endless human search for significance in the name of a final vocabulary for the articulation of history's meaning. Among its victories would be neither that of Christianity over Islam, nor of science over superstition, but that of the licence to tell, of Salman Rushdie over the Ayatollahs, of Kundera over his censors. To tell stories about any event, even the most appalling political event, in any way. The politicians have after all only changed the world in various ways. The point however is to interpret that world in the name of a world which will continue to need interpreting in order for its inhabitants to survive.

Notes

1 Friedrich Nietzsche, *The Birth of Tragedy*, New York: Doubleday, pp.136–37.

2 Thomas Mann, *Essays of Three Decades*, London: Secker and Warburg, 1947, p.480.

3 See Z. Bauman, *Modernity and the Holocaust*, Cambridge: Polity, 1989; T. Adorno and M. Horkheimer, *Dialectic of Enlightenment* [1944], London: Verso, 1979.

4 See for instance T. Parsons, 'The Problem of Controled Institutional Change', in *Politics and Social Structure*, New York: Free Press, 1969.

5 Despite his claims to have developed a 'post-traditional ethics', much of Habermas' work is a refinement of traditional liberal intuitions. For his latest foray, see *The Inclusion of the Other*, Frankfurt: Suhrkamp, 1996, esp. Ch.1.

6 Rortyan pragmatism, deconstruction, post-modern theology, and neo-Aristotelian or Foucauldian philosophies of praxis are only the most notable examples.

7 See G. Dumezil, *Mitra-Varuna*, New York: Zone, 1988.

8 On the explicit appeal to myth by National Socialist theoreticians see M. Frank, *Gott im Exil*, Frankfurt: Suhrkamp, 1991.

9 See A. Pizzorno, 'Politics Unbound', in C. Maier, *Changing Boundaries of the*

Political, Cambridge: Cambridge University Press, 1987.

10 E. Cassirer, *The Myth of the State*, New Haven: Yale University Press, 1946.

11 M. Weber, *Political Writings*, Cambridge: Cambridge University Press, 1994, p.480.

12 On traditions as extended arguments, see A. MacIntyre, *After Virtue*, Aldershot: Duckworth, 1981, Ch.15.

13 H. Jonas, *The Imperative of Responsibility*, Chicago: University of Chicago Press, 1984, p.102.

14 On this see his *Contingency, Irony and Solidarity*, Cambridge: Cambridge University Press, 1991.

15 Jonas, *The Imperative...*, p.28.

16 On modern politics as gnosticism see E. Voegelin, *The New Science of Politics*, Chicago: University of Chicago Press, 1952, Ch.6; *Science, Politics and Gnosticism*, Washington: Regnery, 1968.

17 On this see of course Weber's classic account of 'wanting to be surpassed', in I. Velody and P. Lassman, *Max Weber's Science as a Vocation*, London: Unwin Hyman, 1989.

18 See, for example, Albert Camus, *The Myth of Sisyphus*, London: Penguin, 1955; Thomas Mann, *Doctor Faustus*, London: Everyman, 1944; Adorno and Horkheimer, *Dialectic of Enlightenment*; Cassirer, *The Myth of the State*); Mircea Eliade, *The Myth of the Eternal Return*, Princeton: Princeton University Press, 1954; Alexandre Kojeve, *Introduction to the Reading of Hegel*, New York: Basic Books, 1957; T.S. Eliot, *Notes Towards a Definition of Culture*, London: Faber & Faber, 1948.

19 Eliade, *Myth...*, pp.153–54.

20 See G. Vattimo, *The End of Modernity*, Cambridge: Polity, 1988; F. Fukuyama, *The End of History*, London: Penguin, 1992; L. Niethammer, *Posthistoire*, London: Verso, 1992; P. Anderson, 'The Ends of History', in *A Zone of Engagement*, London: Verso, 1992.

21 Goethe once described world history as 'a tissue of nonsense for the higher thinker'. See K. Löwith, *From Hegel to Nietzsche* [1939], New York: Columbia University Press, 1964, p.227.

22 See H. Arendt, 'The Concept of History', in *Between Past and Future*, London: Penguin, 1954; R. Koselleck, 'Über die Verfügbarkeit der Geschichte', in *Vergangene Zukunft*, Frankfurt: Suhrkamp, 1979.

23 Weber, *Political Writings*, p.15.

24 In terms of such a philosophical anthropological perspective, Richard Rorty's increasing use of terms such as 'hope' and 'happiness', and now 'we leftists', places him alongside, rather than opposed to, the Marxism he otherwise rejects. The following remark from Hannah Arendt might have been written with Rorty in mind: 'today the Kantian and Hegelian way of becoming reconciled to reality through understanding the innermost meaning of the entire historical process seems to be quite as much refuted by our experience as the simultaneous attempt of pragmatism and utilitarianism to "make history"...', in *Between Past and Future*, p.86. On hope and happiness in Rorty, see now *Achieving Our Country*, London: Harvard University Press, 1998; and *Philosophy and Social Hope*, London: Penguin, 1999.

25 See K. Löwith 'The Eternal Return in Nietzsche', in *Martin Heidegger and European Nihilism*, New York: Columbia University Press, 1995.

26 Leszek Kołakowski, *The Presence of Myth* [1967], Chicago: University of Chicago Press, 1989, p.95.

27 It is worth noting that such a conception of intergenerational reciprocity is quite distinct from that suggested by Walter Benjamin's famous angel of history image. In Benjamin's conception of history, the community of the living and the dead is sustained

by a consciousness of victimhood which in turn becomes the basis for messianic hopes. The image I am suggesting here is one in which the future is the object of stewardship in the face of annihilation, while the past is remembered not for history's victims but as a record of human achievement. With respect to the Holocaust, there are signs of a popular shift in this direction. For instance, the re-creation and celebration of *shtetl* communities and pre-war Jewish cultural achievements generally, or post-1989 events such as the annual Festival of Jewish Culture in Kraków, have become more than an imperative act of mourning or redemptive criticism. See Theo Richmond, *Konin*, London: Vintage, 1994; Ewa Hoffman, *Shtetl*, London: Vintage, 1997.

28 See especially 'Beyond the Pleasure Principle', in *The Penguin Freud Library*, Vol.11.

29 H. Blumenberg, *Work on Myth*, Cambridge, Mass.: MIT Press, 1985, p 4.

30 Kolakowski, *The Presence of Myth*, p.6.

31 Blumenberg, *Myth*, p.16, my emphasis.

32 *Ibid.*, p.35.

33 *Ibid.*, p.16.

34 *Ibid.*, p.151.

35 See *Ibid.*, pp.584–94.

36 R. Calasso, *The Marriage of Cadmus and Harmony*, London: Vintage, 1994, p.103.

37 See S. Buckler, 'Historical Narrative, Identity and the Holocaust', *History of the Human Sciences*, Vol.9, No.4, 1996, pp.1–20.

38 See P. Ricoeur, *The Symbolism of Evil*, Boston: Beacon Press, 1967, pp.161–70.

39 Though it is beyond the remit of this essay, there is perhaps scope for an interpretation of Bauman's work which would show that he provides evidence that bureaucracy under National Socialism was a travesty of itself and introduced the individual bureaucrat to a range of decisions and inventive problem-solving far greater than that expected of officialdom in liberal democracies.

40 This theme, of the development of a do-it-yourself culture in an age of weakening organisational and institutional ties, is by now a familiar one. See for example Z. Bauman, *Intimations of Postmodernity*, London: Routledge, 1991, and his essay in this volume; A. Giddens, *Modernity and Self-Identity*, Cambridge: Polity, 1991; R. Sennett, *The Corrosion of Character*, London: Norton, 1998.

41 It is worth noting that Blumenberg, for example, has nothing to say on the British 'myth and ritual' school around Jane Harrison, which argued that myth grew out of ritual. See Jane Harrison, *Themis*, London: Merlin, 1963.

42 For the opposite view see B. Malinowski, 'Myth as a Dramatic Development of Dogma', in *Sex, Culture and Myth*, London: Hart-Davis, 1963.

43 See the excellent essay by Herminio Martins, 'Technology, Modernity, Politics', in I. Velody and J. Good (eds), *The Politics of Postmodernity*, London: Sage, 1998.

44 Eric Voegelin, *Order and History*, Vol.3, Baton Rouge: Louisiana State University Press, 1957, p.254.

45 Blumenberg, *Myth*, p.12.

46 Sheldon Wolin, 'Postmodern Politics and the Absence of Myth', *Social Research*, Vol.52, 1985, p.230.

47 For a classic statement, see M. Weber, *Economy and Society*, California: University of California Press, 1978, p.55. For a rejection of the very idea that the modern state should have a purpose, see Michael Oakeshott, *On Human Conduct*, Oxford: Clarendon Press, Ch.3.

48 Karl Mannheim, 'The Problem of Democratisation', in *Essays in the Sociology of Knowledge*, London: Routledge and Kegan Paul, 1956, p.314.

49 Theodor Adorno, 'The Sociology of Knowledge and its Consciousness', in *Prisms*, London: Spearman, 1967, p.38.

50 Adorno and Horkheimer, *Dialectic of Enlightenment*, p.123.

51 Roland Barthes, 'Myth Today', in *Mythologies*, London: Paladin, p.142. It is also worth recalling here that Barthes' definition of myth as depoliticised speech entails a conception of politics as the activity of producing the world and history. And since revolution is the ulimate productive-political-historical act, revolution is defined by 'the absence of myth'. The asserted affinity between myth and classification is also found in a tradition stretching from Durkheim and Mauss to Lévi-Strauss and Mary Douglas, though here classification is a collective intellectual *accomplishment* which is a foundation of order in traditional societies and a necessary component of order in modern societies. 'Myth' is an ineliminable and somewhat innocent component of coherent and stable systems of belief. Hence for instance Durkheim's refusal to accept a sharp distinction between myth and religion. See Emile Durkheim, *The Elementary Forms of Religious Life*, New York: Free Press, 1994, pp.76–81.

52 E. Cassirer, *An Essay on Man*, New York: Anchor, 1956, p.108.

53 J.G.A. Pocock, 'Deconstructing Europe', in Perry Anderson and Peter Gowan (eds), *The Question of Europe*, London: Verso, 1996.

54 Karl Löwith, *Meaning in History*, London: University of Chicago Press, 1953, p.207.

55 For a recent version see Gillian Rose, 'Jerusalem or Athens?', in *Mourning Becomes the Law*, Cambridge: Cambridge University Press, 1996.

56 Max Weber, *The Protestant Ethic and the Spirit of Capitalism*, London: Allen and Unwin, 1930, p.183.

57 Löwith, *Martin Heidegger*, p.175.

58 See Novalis, 'Christianity or Europe', in Frederick C. Beiser (ed.), *The Early Political Writings of the German Romantics*, Cambridge: Cambridge University Press, 1996; Eliot, *Notes Towards a Definition of Culture*; Max Scheler, *On The Eternal in Man*, London: SCM Press, 1960.

59 Scheler, *On the Eternal...*, p.382.

60 Both Scheler and Habermas explicitly state that the decentralised *German* polity – whether it be the decentralised empire of 1917 or the decentralised federal republic of 1991 – is a good model for a future European polity based on the principle of subsidiarity! See Scheler, *On the Eternal...*, p.448; Jürgen Habermas, 'Does Europe need a Constitution?', in Gowan and Anderson (eds), *Question...*, p.264.

61 Milan Kundera, *Testaments Betrayed*, London: Faber & Faber, 1993, p.31.

62 Claude Lévi-Strauss, *Structural Anthropology*, Harmondsworth: Penguin, 1963, p.209; Wolin, 'Postmodern Politics...'.

63 Ricoeur, *Symbolism...*, pp.191–97.

64 M. Valdes (ed.), *A Ricoeur Reader*, London: Harvester, 1991, p.488.

65 Martin Amis, *Time's Arrow*, London: Vintage, pp.132, 154.

66 David Grossman, *See Under: Love*, London: Picador, 1991.

67 See especially 'Absalom, Absalom', in *The Collected Works of William Faulkner*, London: Chatto and Windus, 1969.

Notes on Contributors

Jeremy Adler is Professor of German at King's College, London. He specialises in interdisciplinary studies such as the relations between literature and science, painting and anthropology. He has published a commentary on Goethe's *Elective Affinities* and a book on visual poetry as well as editions of August Stramm, two books by H.G. Adler, and Hölderlin's *Selected Poems*. His most recent publications include F.B. Steiner's *Selected Writings* and a collected edition of Steiner's poetry.

Zygmunt Bauman is Emeritus Professor of Sociology at the University of Leeds. Among his numerous publications are *Modernity and the Holocaust*, *Postmodern Ethics*, and *Modernity and Ambivalence*. His most recent book is *Globalisation*.

Andrew Benjamin is Professor of Philosophy and Director of the Centre for Research in Philosophy and Literature at the University of Warwick. His publications include *The Plural Event* (Routledge 1993), *Present Hope* (Routledge 1997), *Philosophy's Literature* (Climamen Press 2000) and *Architectural Philosophy* (Athlone Press 2000).

J.M. Bernstein, after nearly a quarter of a century at the University of Essex, is now W. Alton Jones Professor of Philosophy at Vanderbilt University. At present he is completing a book on Adorno's ethical thought (CUP) and putting together a collection of his essays on aesthetic modernism and modernist art, provisionally entitled *Against Voluptuous Bodies: And Other Essays for a Late Modernism*.

Robert Fine is Reader in Sociology and is Director of the Social Theory Centre at the University of Warwick. He has written widely in the sociology of law, on political thought, on nationalism and on the South African labour movement. He is author of *Democracy and the Rule of Law* (Pluto 1985), *Beyond Apartheid: Labour and Liberation in South Africa* (Pluto 1991), and *Being Stalked* (Chatto and Windus 1998). He is co-editor of *Civil Society: Democratic Perspectives* (Frank Cass 1997) and *People, Nation and State* (IB Tauris 1999). He has recently completed a book to be published by Routledge (2001) on *The Politics of Hegel, Marx and Arendt.*

Heidrun Friese received her PhD from the University of Amsterdam. She held Fellowships at the Maison des Sciences de l'Homme, Paris; the Institute for Interdisciplinary Studies (ZiF), Bielefeld; the Centre of International and Area Studies, University of California at Berkeley; the Centre for Studies in Higher Education, University of California at Berkeley; Kulturwissenschaftliches Institut, Essen; and at the École des Hautes Études en Sciences Sociales, Paris. She has published widely on social constructions of time and history, the anthropology of the sciences and on social imagination. Her book publications include *Der Raum des Gelehrten. Eine Topographie akademischer Praxis* (with Peter Wagner, 1993); *Lampedusa. Historische Anthropologie einer Insel* (1996); *Identitäten* (with Aleida Assmann, 1998). *The Moment* (edited), *Identities* (edited) as well as *Praktische Philosophie des Glücks* are scheduled for 2000.

Anthony Gorman lectures in philosophy at Staffordshire University, where he specialises in the philosophy of Hegel, philosophy of religion, political philosophy and ethics. He is currently working on a full-length study of the work of Gillian Rose.

Michael Salter is Professor of Law at the University of Central Lancashire. He has published in the fields of legal discourse and property theory and legal responses to child abuse and debt. His current research is on Hegel's legal theory, critical theory and international criminal law at Nuremburg. His publications include 'Laws of Language in Hegel's Semiology' (*International Journal for the Semiotics of Law* 1992), 'Toward a Critical Theory of Constitutional Law: Hegel's Contribution' (*Journal of Law and Society* 1994, with J. Shaw), and 'Dialectical Lessons from the Failure of Marxism' (*Social and Legal Studies* 1998).

Victor J. Seidler is Professor of Social Theory in the Department of Sociology at Goldsmith's College, University of London. His main interests are in ethics and gender. His publications include *Recovering the Self* and *Unreasonable Men* (Routledge 1993). His most recent book is *Shadows of the Shoah* (New York University Press 2000).

David Seymour is Lecturer in Law at the University of Lancaster. His recent research has been on *Critical Theories of Antisemitism* (PhD 1999 University of Warwick) and his current work concerns legal issues that have arisen in connection with the Holocaust. He has published an article on Shylock and anti-semitism called 'Letter from Venice' in *Law and Critique* (1997).

Dan Stone is Lecturer in Twentieth-Century European History at Royal Holloway, University of London. His main areas of research are the historiography of the Holocaust, modern intellectual history, eugenics and the extreme right in Britain.

Charles Turner lectures in sociology at the University of Warwick. His main interests are social theory, conceptions of history and collective memory. His publications include *Modernity and Politics in the Work of Max Weber* (Routledge 1992). He is currently working on the politics of commemorative practices.

Name Index

Name Index

Subject Index